Affectionate Communicatio

C000137361

Few communication behaviors are more consequential to the development and maintenance of close relationships than the expression of affection. Indeed, people often use affectionate gestures to initiate or accelerate relationship development. In contrast, the absence of affection in established relationships frequently coincides with relational deterioration. This text explores the scientific research on affection exchange that has emerged from the disciplines of communication, social and clinical psychology, family studies, psychophysiology, sociology, nursing, and behavioral health. Specific points of focus include the individual and relational benefits – including health benefits – of affectionate behavior, the significant detriments associated with lacking sufficient affection, and the risks of expressing affection. It also discusses the primary social and cultural influences on affection exchange, critiques principal theories and measurement models, and offers suggestions for future empirical research.

KORY FLOYD is Professor of Communication at the University of Arizona, USA. His research focuses on the communication of affection in close relationships and its effects on stress and physiological functioning. He has written fifteen books and more than a hundred scientific papers and book chapters on the topics of affection, emotion, family communication, nonverbal behavior, and health. A former editor of *Communication Monographs* and the *Journal of Family Communication*, Floyd has won the Early Career Achievement award from the International Association for Relationship Research and the Charles H. Woolbert Award and the Bernard J. Brommel Award from the National Communication Association.

Affectionate Communication in Close Relationships

Kory Floyd

University of Arizona

CAMBRIDGE
UNIVERSITY PRESS

University Printing House, Cambridge CB2 8BS, United Kingdom

One Liberty Plaza, 20th Floor, New York, NY 10006, USA

477 Williamstown Road, Port Melbourne, VIC 3207, Australia

314-321, 3rd Floor, Plot 3, Splendor Forum, Jasola District Centre, New Delhi - 110025, India

79 Anson Road, #06-04/06, Singapore 079906

Cambridge University Press is part of the University of Cambridge.

It furthers the University's mission by disseminating knowledge in the pursuit of education, learning and research at the highest international levels of excellence.

www.cambridge.org
Information on this title: www.cambridge.org/9781108456210
DOI: 10.1017/9781108653510

© Kory Floyd 2019

This publication is in copyright. Subject to statutory exception and to the provisions of relevant collective licensing agreements, no reproduction of any part may take place without the written permission of Cambridge University Press.

First published 2019
First paperback edition 2020

A catalogue record for this publication is available from the British Library

ISBN 978-1-108-47058-2 Hardback
ISBN 978-1-108-45621-0 Paperback

Cambridge University Press has no responsibility for the persistence or accuracy of URLs for external or third-party internet websites referred to in this publication, and does not guarantee that any content on such websites is, or will remain, accurate or appropriate.

Contents

Tables

Preface

I started studying the communication of affection around the age of twelve. Having been raised by parents who both valued and practiced the expression of affection, I assumed – like many people do – that what was true in my family was true in *every* family. It was therefore utterly perplexing to me when, as an adolescent, I made the discovery that not everyone enjoys affectionate behavior.

Being a highly affectionate person myself, I found that incomprehensible. In my mind, communicating affection was one of the absolute best parts of having close relationships, so I failed to understand why anyone might react negatively to a hug, a pat on the back, or an *I love you*. Many years later, when I began graduate school and realized I was going to need a question to research, I saw my opportunity to unravel that mystery.

Although my empirical work on affectionate communication began with a focus on its risks, I quickly discovered that there was much about affectionate behavior that was intriguing. Why do we express affection in the first place? How do we do so? Which people and relationships are more affectionate than others, and why? When is affection good for us, and under what circumstances is it bad for us? Who suffers from affection deprivation, and how do they cope? These and other questions have fueled my scholarly curiosity for more than two decades now, and despite dozens of studies with thousands of participants, I believe there is still much more to be learned.

In 2006, I published *Communicating Affection: Interpersonal Behavior and Social Context* (Cambridge University Press). That was the first text that attempted a somewhat comprehensive review of the affectionate communication literature, and it was also the formal delineation of my theory, affection exchange theory. One rhetorical device I employed in that book was to pose research questions that were provocative but as yet unaddressed. I did so at the time to highlight the fact that there was much left to learn about affectionate behavior. Since the publication of that book, many of those questions – and many others not even envisioned at the time – have been answered. The affectionate communication literature has advanced substantially in the last twelve years – indeed, of the published empirical studies on affectionate communication cited in this book, more than half were published after 2006 – which made me realize the time was ripe for a new and even more comprehensive text.

This book is my own product, but the research that made it possible belongs to many people. First and foremost, I am extremely grateful for a long and productive collaboration with Mark Morman. Mark and I began studying affectionate communication in the late 1990s when we were both finishing our doctoral programs, and many of the foundational components of the literature – including the Affectionate Communication Index and the Tripartite Model of Affectionate Behavior – emerged from our work together. He has been a true partner in this endeavor and I will always be thankful for his contributions and his friendship.

In addition, I have been blessed to work with many wonderful co-authors to illuminate the intricacies of affectionate communication, and I am extremely grateful for their insights and contributions: Tamara Afifi, Justin Boren, Judee Burgoon, Lou Clark, Kristen Davis, Doug Deiss, Amanda Denes, Mark Di Corcia, Dana Dinsmore, Jen Eden, Larry Erbert, Lisa Farinelli, Mark Generous, Kelby Halone, Annegret Hannawa, Mark Haynes, Jon Hess, Colin Hesse, Jeff Judd, Angela La Valley, Daniel Mansson, Bree McEwan, Ian McLeod, Lisa Miczo, Alan Mikkelson, Mary Claire Morr Serewicz, Malcolm Parks, Perry Pauley, Corey Pavlich, Colter Ray, George Ray, Sarah Riforgiate, James Roberts, Jack Sargent, Albert Simon, Jordan Soliz, James Stein, Melissa Tafoya, Kyle Tusing, Lisa van Raalte, Alice Veksler, Mike Voloudakis, Jason Wilson, Nathan Woo, and Michael Wu. I am certainly also grateful for the many other scholars – some whom I know and most whom I do not – whose research has produced important discoveries about affectionate behavior in human relationships.

This book would not have been possible without the valuable assistance of Janka Romero, Abigail Walkington, and Emily Watton at Cambridge University Press, as well as the scholars who were kind enough to serve as reviewers of the proposal and manuscript. I am also indebted to clinical psychologist A. Jordan Wright and physician Jeff Erickson for advising me on the mental and physical health details appearing in Chapters 7 and 8.

My final and most profound thanks belong to my partner, Brian, and our three canine companions, Cruise, Buster, and Champ. Together, they serve as a constant reminder to me of why affection is so valuable.

1 An Introduction to Affectionate Communication

Few communicative behaviors are more consequential to human survival and flourishing than the exchange of affection. If that claim sounds hyperbolic, one need consider only a few important truths about the human condition to appreciate its accuracy.

Chief among these is the observation that humans are born in a state of considerable immaturity. A newborn giraffe (*Giraffa camelopardalis*) will walk and run behind its mother within its first few hours of life. Mountain lion cubs (*Puma concolor*) learn to hunt within six months, and giant tortoises (*Aldabrachelys gigantea*) fend for themselves from the moment they are born. In sharp contrast, humans lack the physical and cognitive capacity at birth to meet even their most basic needs and typically do not achieve self-sufficiency until the second or third decade of their lives.

Humans therefore rely nearly entirely on others to meet all of their needs – food, shelter, clothing, security, medical care, education – for their first several years. A child who cannot elicit significant continual investments in its care is a child who will not survive infancy. Child-rearing, however, is a costly endeavor (US Department of Agriculture, 2017). Raising even a single child to adulthood requires substantial sacrifices with respect to money, time, space, privacy, freedom, and career opportunity. It is often a considerable marital stressor, as well (Belsky & Pensky, 1988), particularly when a family contains multiple children (Heaton, 1990).

To make such a significant investment – and willingly so, as most humans do – requires an equally significant motivator. Codified laws (Levesque, 2011) and culturally defined expectations (Keller, Vöelker, & Yovsi, 2005) certainly prompt parental caregiving, at least in modern times, but a more primal and more ubiquitous motivator for investing in offspring exists among humans in the form of the emotional experience known as *love* (Kanazawa, 2001).

Evolutionary psychologists such as Buss (2015), Freese, Li, and Wade (2003), and Kanazawa (2004) explain that humans – like all living organisms – have evolved phenotypic characteristics that promote at least

1

two superordinate goals: *viability* (individual survival) and *fertility* (replication of individual genetic material). Some such characteristics manifest physically, such as immunocompetence for recovery from illness or beauty for mate attraction, but psychological characteristics such as intelligence and social competence have also evolved to contribute to survival and reproductive success.

Among the most potent psychological characteristics to serve human evolutionary goals are emotions, which can powerfully motivate behaviors critical for survival and reproduction (Niedenthal & Ric, 2017). Fear, for instance, motivates caution when interacting with potentially harmful elements (Öhman & Mineka, 2001). Jealousy prompts increased surveillance of potential threats to a significant pair bond (Wiedermana & Kendalla, 1999). Even disgust contributes to safety by promoting expulsion and avoidance of pathogenic contamination (Oaten, Stevenson, & Case, 2009). Similarly, as articulated by Buss (2006), love serves multiple functions related to reproductive success. These include attracting mates and solidifying romantic partnerships, displaying relational commitment and sexual fidelity, and facilitating sexual access.

Importantly, the evolutionary functions of love also include motivating investments in the wellness of offspring. Apart from legal, cultural, ethical, or religious obligations to do so, humans routinely invest resources in raising and caring for their children out of a profound sense of love for those children. By motivating parents to sacrifice their own resources for the health and welfare of their offspring, parental love contributes not only to the parents' reproductive success but also, and even more crucially, to the children's survival.[1]

Considered in these terms, it is perhaps not an exaggeration to call love a matter of life or death.

The internal experience of love is insufficient for producing these outcomes, however. Rather, the *manifestation* of that emotional experience – the expression and exchange of affection – is required. The subsequent sections define and clarify the concepts of the experience and expression of affection and detail how social scientists came to understand their importance for well-being.

Affection and Affectionate Communication

To understand how humans experience and express affection – and, more importantly, *why* they do so – it is necessary to clarify the conceptual definitions of these terms. That is particularly useful for a phenomenon such as affection, both to sort through the multiple ways in which researchers have defined it and to make clear the distinction between affection and the behaviors through which it is expressed. This section begins by defining the *experience* of affection and then addresses the *communication* of affection, which is the principal focus of this text.

The Experience of Affection

The term *affection* derives from the Latin term *affectio*, and its earliest appearances (c. AD 1230) were in reference to "an emotion of the mind" or a "permanent state of feeling." During the late 1300s, its connotative meaning evolved from a mere "disposition" to a "good disposition toward" something, such as a person or an idea. Later, writers such as Descartes, Spinoza, and most of the early British ethical writers used *affection* to index a positive emotional disposition toward others that bore a resemblance to *passion* but was relatively free of its sensuous elements and volatile nature, such as parents' affection for their children as opposed to their passion for each other.

Theoretic and empirical work on affection in the late twentieth and early twenty-first centuries has largely ignored this conceptual distinction from passion, but it has continued to reflect the focus on a positive, externally directed emotional disposition. In their paper on the psychometrics of affectionate communication, for instance, Floyd and Morman (1998) conceptually defined affection as an emotional state of fondness and intense positive regard that is directed at a living or once-living target. The target of an individual's affection is often another human, of course, and in this conceptual definition, feelings of affection can arise in a range of human bonds, including those between romantic partners, parents and children, siblings and other relatives, friends, neighbors, and co-workers (e.g., Bartels & Zeki, 2000; Lawton, Silverstein, & Bengtson, 1994). People typically feel different magnitudes of affection in various relationship types, and often express their affection differently in different relationships (see, e.g., Floyd, Sargent, & Di Corcia, 2004), but genuine feelings of affection can develop in virtually any positive interpersonal bond. Genuine affection can also characterize people's relationships with public figures, such as celebrities (Leets, De Becker, & Giles, 1995), even when those relationships are merely parasocial rather than interpersonal (see, e.g., Bond & Calvert, 2014).

People most certainly also experience affection toward animals, especially those kept as pets. Several studies attest to humans' feelings of attachment and love for their pets (Julius, Beetz, Kotrschal, Turner, & Uvnäs-Moberg, 2013; Smolkovic, Fajfar, & Mlinaric, 2012) and the ability of pet keeping to attenuate loneliness (Marinšek & Tušak, 2007). Pet keepers report significant attachment to pets – especially dogs

(Zasloff, 1996) – and experience both support (McConnell, Brown, Shoda, Stayton, & Martin, 2011) and stress reduction (Miller et al., 2009) in interactions with their animal companions. Perhaps unsurprisingly, people grieve the death of a pet (Podrazik, Shackford, Becker, & Heckert, 2000), although not typically with the same magnitude as the death of a close human companion (Rajaram, Garrity, Stallones, & Marx, 1993).

From the perspective of evolutionary psychology, keeping and feeling affection for an animal is a somewhat puzzling behavior, given that it entails virtually no benefit for viability or fertility, at least beyond the animal's value to protect its owners from attack.[2] Archer (1997) argued persuasively, however, that pets engage adaptive human responses that evolved to facilitate human bonds (particularly parental bonds). Consequently, humans can feel intense levels of affection for their pets and derive great satisfaction from those relationships, perhaps even more so than with other humans.

Several distinctions are worth noting about the emotional experience of affection. First, unlike some emotions, affection is not typically evoked by a simple stimulus. Whereas a discrete event can elicit surprise, fear, disgust, or anger, feelings of affection usually develop longitudinally as a collective response to multiple stimuli from the same target. Although Fredrickson (2013) has proposed a redefinition of love as existing in micro-momentary interactions between people, several studies using a prototype approach have found that people inherently conceptualize love and affection as more stable and long-term experiences of intimacy, commitment, and trust (see Aron & Westbay, 1996; Fehr & Russell, 1991; Regan, Kocan, & Whitlock, 1998).

Second, whereas humans have an innate capacity to experience and express affection (a point that will receive more focused attention in the next chapter), the application of affection to a particular recipient is conditioned and target-specific. For instance, most people feel more affection toward their own children than toward the children of others (see Floyd & Morman, 2001).[3] Similarly, one may feel affection toward a co-worker or neighbor whom no one else appears to like. Moreover, people can develop affection for others whom they themselves previously disliked; first impressions, although powerful, are not necessarily irrevocable.

Finally, like many emotions, affection should be distinguished from the behaviors through which it is communicated. This distinction is sometimes not drawn in empirical research; scholars may purport, for instance, to study *affection* when in fact they are studying *affectionate behavior*. It is imperative to draw this distinction, however, for the simple reason that affectionate feelings and affectionate behaviors do not necessarily coincide. As this text will discuss in detail, most communicators have the capacity to feel affection without expressing it, and to express affection without feeling it. Thus, to truly understand affectionate communication, it is necessary to separate it from its underlying emotional experience.

The Communication of Affection

The primary focus of this text is on the communication of affection, or the behaviors through which the experience of affection is presented. The term *presented* is used deliberately here, to acknowledge that one need not actually be experiencing affection in order to express it. Consequently, affectionate communication is defined herein as encompassing those behaviors that portray or present the internal experience of affection, whether accurately or not.

The goal of presenting or portraying affectionate feelings is therefore dependent on the enactment of behaviors that either denote or connote such feelings to the recipient. Whereas some affectionate behaviors are minimally equivocal (e.g., kissing, saying "I love you"), many others are far more indirect, and some, such as idiomatic expressions, connote affectionate feelings only for a specific target who will interpret them in that manner. Communicators have many possible reasons for conveying affection equivocally, and this text discusses the strategic use of indirect affectionate gestures and the important relational purposes they can serve.

The experience and the expression of affection are inextricably linked, but for many possible reasons, they do not *necessarily* co-occur. As empirical research has indicated, it is not uncommon for feelings of affection not to be communicated or for expressions of affection to be insincere or even deceptive (see Gillen & Horan, 2013). Some incongruencies between experience and behavior are strategic; for example, one might fail to express felt affection to avoid appearing overly eager for relational escalation (Owen, 1987), or one might express unfelt affection to gain sexual access or other favors (Floyd, Erbert, Davis, & Haynes, 2005). Other incongruencies between experience and behavior may be purely unintentional. For instance, one might intend to say, "I love you" to one's spouse before leaving for work but get sidetracked and leave the expression unsaid.

Understanding what affection and affectionate communication are is necessary, but it is not sufficient for supporting the claim that they matter. As the next section details, such a claim has been widely accepted only for a relatively short period of time.

Understanding the Value of Affectionate Communication

It may seem axiomatic that healthy relationships – particularly romantic and parental bonds – are affectionate relationships. In marriage, a lack of spousal affection is one of the two most-cited reasons for seeking marital therapy (Doss, Simpson, & Christensen, 2004) and is among the most commonly identified bases for seeking divorce (Amato & Previti, 2003). In parent–child pairs, multiple studies attest to the long-term psychological and even physical damage that can be done to children who grow up lacking parental affection (e.g., Carroll et al., 2013; Michiels, Grietens, Onghena, & Kuppens, 2010). Indeed, the suggestion that any intimate relationship can thrive without affection may seem fundamentally untenable.

The importance of affection was neither presumed nor accepted as obvious prior to the mid-twentieth century, however. Before that time, medical authorities warned parents against showing affection to their children. Psychologists argued that expressing affection to children would make them needy and demanding, and physicians cautioned that it would promote the spread of infectious disease (Blum, 2002). Those views went largely unchallenged until the pioneering work of Harry Harlow.

In seminal experiments (Harlow, 1958; see also Harlow & Zimmermann, 1958), Harlow separated infant rhesus macaques (*Macaca mulatta*) from their mothers and situated them in his primate laboratory to be reared by two types of mechanical surrogate "mothers." One surrogate was covered with heavy mesh wire; the other, although also crafted from wire, was covered with thick, soft terrycloth. Harlow divided the macaques into two groups, one in which the wire surrogate dispensed food and the terrycloth surrogate did not, and one in which the opposite was true.

Regardless of the experimental condition, Harlow observed the same pattern of behavior: the macaques clung to the terrycloth surrogate whether it provided food or not and visited the wire surrogate only to receive food. In his later studies, Harlow exposed the macaques to stressful stimuli, such as a noise-making teddy bear, and he found that, virtually without exception, the macaques would cling to the terrycloth surrogate for comfort. When he denied them that opportunity by removing the cloth-covered surrogates from their environments, the macaques quickly demonstrated signs of physical and psychological distress, such as disengaging, curling up in a ball, and sucking their thumbs.

Although they strained the limits of what would today be considered ethical animal research, Harlow's studies were nonetheless groundbreaking in their demonstration of both the need for attachment and the consequences of denying that need. Humans share approximately 95 percent of their DNA with rhesus macaques, elevating the likelihood that the two species share various central nervous system structures that make attachment behaviors – including comforting and the sharing of affection – similarly rewarding and beneficial. In the latter half of the twentieth century and the early part of the twenty-first century, behavioral science has taken on the mantle of extending Harlow's insights by exploring the benefits of attachment and affection to humans and human relationships.

Among humans, many questions about affection and affectionate communication have attracted empirical attention:

- Which verbal and nonverbal behaviors do people use to express affection to others? How is the encoding of affection influenced by age, sex, type of relationship, or situational context?
- Under what conditions are people most likely to communicate affection to others, and for what reasons do they do so?
- Why might people express affection when they do not feel it? Why might they fail to express affection when they do feel it?
- Do people have a "trait" level of affectionate behavior? Do highly affectionate people, as a group, differ from less affectionate people?
- When are people most likely to reciprocate affectionate expressions? What happens when they do not?
- What are the mental and physical health benefits associated with receiving affection? When people lack an adequate degree of affection, what mental and physical consequences correspond with that deprivation?

A large and diverse body of research has addressed many of these questions, and many other questions remain to be answered. The purpose of this text is therefore twofold: to summarize and critique the existing body of theoretic and empirical work on affectionate communication, and to acknowledge some of the questions about affection and affectionate behavior that have yet to be addressed. A more detailed preview of the text appears subsequently.

A Preview of the Chapters

Before reviewing the empirical research on affectionate communication, it is helpful to revisit the major theoretic paradigms that have framed such research. Chapter 2 undertakes this task by differentiating socio-cultural and bio-evolutionary paradigms and identifying several specific theories within each that either have been empirically tested or propose principles that are relevant to the experience or expression of affection. Although many of the theories discussed in that chapter have been profitable for the advancement of knowledge related to affectionate communication, most were not developed with the specific purpose of explaining affectionate behavior, which necessarily limits their explanatory and predictive power for understanding the expression of affection. Chapter 2 therefore ends with a review of affection exchange theory, which was developed specifically to remedy those limitations.

The subsequent eight chapters are devoted to detailing the empirical research on affectionate communication and to summarizing both what is known and what is yet to be learned. Chapter 3 addresses both conceptual and operational definitions of affectionate communication, introducing a commonly used tripartite model for affectionate expression and critiquing frequently used measurement models and manipulation strategies. Chapter 4 describes research that accounts for individual variation in the propensity to express affection. Genetic and environmental antecedents are identified and distinguished. This chapter also discusses the effects of individual, contextual, and relational characteristics that influence how affectionate people are and what forms of encoding affection are considered appropriate for a given situation. Conversely, Chapter 5 focuses on studies of decoding and response. This chapter examines the behaviors that carry affectionate meaning for receivers and observers, and the manner in which people react to expressions of affection cognitively and behaviorally.

In Chapter 6, research that compares and contrasts relationship types is reviewed. This chapter offers theoretic arguments for why romantic, familial, and platonic relationships should differ in their affectionate behavior, and then summarizes empirical findings regarding how relationships vary in both their form and frequency of affectionate expressions. In addition, this chapter describes how affectionate communication is associated with indices of relational quality, such as satisfaction, closeness, liking, and love.

Some of the most provocative research on affectionate communication has explored its associations with health and wellness. Chapter 7 details the strong and varied associations between affectionate communication and mental health outcomes, including anxiety, depression, loneliness, self-esteem, and autism spectrum disorders. The focus on wellness is extended in Chapter 8 into the realm of physical health, where connections to cardiovascular, metabolic, endocrine, and immune function, as well as susceptibility to illness and pain, are described.

Despite their many benefits, affectionate exchanges often also expose senders and receivers to multiple risks and opportunities for abuse. Chapter 9 details the "dark side" of affectionate communication by explicating its most potent risks and problems and by describing ways in which affectionate behavior can be used for deceptive and even manipulative purposes. This chapter also addresses the correlates and consequences of being deprived of adequate affection (including mental health impairments and deficits in sleep function and pain management) and explores the counterintuitive idea that receiving too much affection is associated with drawbacks for individuals and their relationships.

The purpose of the final chapter is to be both retrospective and prospective. Chapter 10 begins by looking back at some of the broad claims that the affectionate communication literature supports, including critiques of existing theory. It then looks to the future of affectionate communication research by posing provocative and fruitful questions, such as whether the propensity for affection is heritable, how technology and social media can serve people's affection needs, and the extent to which affectionate behavior is a promising clinical intervention for physical or mental ailments.

The study of affectionate communication presents social scientists, and consumers of their work, with a true challenge. It is imperative to physical and mental wellness that humans give and receive affectionate expressions, yet those expressions can evoke uncertainty, discomfort, and even physical distress if presented in unexpected or unwelcomed ways. Affectionate behavior is critical to the formation and maintenance of personal relationships, yet it can also be the demise of those relationships. It is a paradoxical human phenomenon and therefore fertile ground for scientific inquiry.

2 Thinking about Affection
The Theories

To fully appreciate the implications of social scientific research, it is useful to apply both a working knowledge and a critical assessment of the theory informing that research. The literature on affectionate communication has been a theoretically eclectic one, for at least two reasons. First, researchers studying affectionate communication have directed their attention toward a diversity of questions, so theories that are useful in one area have not necessarily been useful in others. Second, and perhaps more important, the first comprehensive theory about affectionate communication emerged only in the early 2000s, being formally published in 2006 (Floyd, 2006a). The lack of such a theory necessarily limited the growth of that area of research previously.

This chapter begins with an overview of the two theoretic paradigms within which research on affectionate communication (and indeed, much of human communication) has been conducted. These are labeled the *socio-cultural* and *bio-evolutionary* paradigms. Each approach is described in terms of its focus and paradigmatic assumptions, and then several specific theories representing each paradigm are detailed. Some of these theories have guided research on affectionate communication, and others are included for their ability to illuminate aspects of affectionate behavior in ways that competing theories cannot.[1]

Although most of these theories have provided clarity to scholars studying affectionate communication, none has come close to illuminating the phenomenon with a notable degree of completeness. Indeed, even as some of these theories have answered questions about affection exchange, they also made evident the need for a more comprehensive theoretic treatment, one that could explicate the fundamental nature and functions of affectionate behavior. A candidate for such a theory – titled *affection exchange theory* – was published in 2006 and is detailed in the latter half of this chapter.

Socio-Cultural Paradigm

In behavioral research, the socio-cultural paradigm focuses on the ways in which the meanings of behaviors are prescribed at social or cultural levels and the means by which those meanings are learned and taught. The descriptor "socio-cultural" is used broadly, so that this paradigm is inclusive of social learning approaches (e.g., Bandura, 1971) and traditions focused on the social construction of meaning (e.g., Burgoon & Newton's 1991 social meaning model).

A fundamental assumption of theories in the socio-cultural paradigm is that a given behavior (e.g., a kiss) conveys a specified meaning (e.g., an expression of affection) because, and only because, that meaning has been prescribed to it by the social or cultural group in which it is observed. This assumption implies that a behavior or behavioral repertoire encodes particular meanings, and is decoded as having those meanings, only within the social or cultural group that has prescribed those meanings to it. The socio-cultural paradigm does not necessarily assume consistency in how expressions are encoded or decoded *between* social or cultural groups, but only *within* such groups.

At the heart of this paradigmatic approach is the idea that most communicative behavior is learned, either through observation or direct instruction, or both. For example, people learn what are considered to be appropriate ways of expressing affection within the culture or even the family in which they are raised. If the rules of appropriateness differ – as they often do from culture to culture (Ekman & Friesen, 1969) and family to family (Halberstadt, 1986) – then observed patterns of behavior would likewise be expected to differ. The means through which people acquire the knowledge necessary to guide their behavior are, therefore, of paramount interest to researchers working with this paradigm.

Some Specific Theories in the Socio-Cultural Paradigm

Gendered Closeness Perspective

One example from the affectionate communication literature is a perspective that has been referred to, alternatively, as the *gendered closeness perspective* (Floyd, 1996b; Morman & Floyd, 1999), the *male deficit model* (Doherty, 1991), and the *covert intimacy perspective* (Swain, 1989). This perspective aims to explain the common perception that women's relationships are closer, more intimate, and more affectionate than men's, based on a concept of affectionate communication as a type of relational currency (see Wilkinson, 2000). The claim is that men's relationships are *not* inherently less affectionate or intimate than women's, but that men express their affection for each other using different relational currencies than women use. Whereas affection between women might be expressed primarily through verbal statements (e.g., saying "I care about you") or through direct nonverbal gestures (e.g., hugging), affection between men is expressed primarily through the provision of instrumental support, such as helping with a project or lending the use of a car.

The reason offered for this difference is that men are socialized to value gestures of instrumental support more than gestures of emotional support, and that using such behaviors as forms of expressing affection allows the affectionate message to be conveyed without drawing undue attention from others. Swain (1989) referred to these behaviors as "covert" because they may not be interpreted by observers as affectionate expressions, thereby mitigating the potential ridicule that more direct expressions might invite (for further reviews, see Parks, 1995; Wood & Inman, 1993). This perspective predicts that men, particularly when communicating with other men, use instrumental gestures of support more often than direct verbal or nonverbal statements as means of expressing affection, and that they use instrumental gestures of support to express affection more often than women do.

Social Exchange Theory

Social exchange theory (SET, which has also been called the theory of interdependence; Thibaut & Kelley, 1959) is founded on an economic model of human social interaction. It assumes that humans are continually driven to maximize rewards and minimize costs. More specifically, SET provides that humans assess the costs and rewards of their personal relationships when making decisions about maintaining them. Two types of comparisons are of primary importance. The first is one's *comparison level* (CL), which represents one's abstract standard for a relationship, or one's idea of how costly and how rewarding a given relationship ought to be. For instance, one might expect romantic relationships to be highly rewarding, so if one's own romantic relationship is not so rewarding, this creates a low CL. The second comparison is the *comparison level for alternatives* (CL_{alt}), which represents the lowest ratio of rewards to costs that a person is willing to accept in a relationship, given what the alternatives (such as being in a different relationship or being alone) are. One would be willing to endure an unsatisfying marriage, for example, when doing so is preferable to being alone and when no preferred suitors are available.

If one conceives of affectionate expressions as a contributor to relational satisfaction, then SET can offer hypotheses about the exchange of affectionate expressions. Comparison levels and comparison levels for alternatives could be measured with respect to the form or amount of affectionate communication characterizing a given relationship. People who desire a great deal of affection would consider relationships in which they receive few affectionate messages to have a low CL. Similarly, those who desire very little affection would consider relationships with highly affectionate people to have a low CL. In both cases, CL_{alt} may be influenced by the other types of rewards people perceive in such relationships, as well as by their own desired levels of affectionate behavior.

Interaction Adaptation Theory

Interaction adaptation theory (IAT; Burgoon, Dillman, & Stern, 1993; Burgoon, Stern, & Dillman, 1995) places people's desires, needs, and their expectations in central explanatory roles. It supposes that people enter any given interaction with a mix of *requirements* (what they need from the interaction), *expectations* (what they anticipate from the interaction), and *desires* (what they want from the interaction). These elements combine to form an *interaction position*, which is then compared with the actual behavior enacted by others. According to IAT, when one encounters behaviors that match one's interaction position, or behaviors that are more positive than those initially required, expected, or desired, one is apt to reciprocate those behaviors by behaving in a similar manner. Conversely, when one encounters behaviors that are more negative than those initially required, expected, or desired, one is likely to compensate for those behaviors by acting in an opposing manner. This reasoning can be used to identify the specific circumstances under which expressions of affection may be unreciprocated.

Expectancy Violations Theory

Expectancy violations theory (EVT; Burgoon, 1978; Burgoon & Hale, 1988; Burgoon & Le Poire, 1993; Burgoon & Walther, 1990; Burgoon, Walther, & Baesler, 1992) proposes that humans have expectations about their own and others' behaviors. When people behave in ways that deviate noticeably from these expectancies, EVT proposes that these expectancy violations heighten the arousal of the recipient or observer and initiate a series of cognitive appraisals to assess the meaning of the behavior and the reward value of the violator. At question is the overall valence of the violation, whether positive or negative. Some behaviors have a consensually shared meaning that dictates their valence, such as an obscene gesture. When the meaning of the behavior is ambiguous, however, attention is turned to the violator. Some people, because of their attractiveness, credibility, fame, wealth, familiarity, or power, are considered to be high-reward communicators; others who do not bear such characteristics are considered to be low-reward communicators. EVT provides that when the meaning of a behavior is ambiguous, people judge it positively when enacted by a high-reward communicator and negatively when enacted by a low-reward communicator. This explanation provides a basis for understanding not only why a recipient of an affectionate expression might judge it positively, but also why he or she might judge it negatively.

Social Meaning Model

The social meaning model (SMM; Burgoon & Newton, 1991) deals specifically with the evaluation and interpretation of nonverbal messages. The model predicts that, within a given speech community, there are consensually recognized relational meanings for some nonverbal behaviors. That is, nonverbal behaviors "comprise a socially shared vocabulary of relational communication" (Burgoon & Newton, 1991, p. 96; see also Burgoon, Coker, & Coker, 1986; Burgoon, Manusov, Mineo, & Hale, 1985). To that end, all observers of a given behavior should make similar interpretations of its relational meaning. According to Burgoon and Newton, support for the SMM requires attention to at least three issues. First, the range of meanings attributable to a given nonverbal behavior should be identified. Second, there must be evidence that encoders and decoders converge in their interpretations of a given behavior. Finally, the congruence between the perspectives of participants and third-party, nonparticipant observers must be identified. This reasoning can be used to examine congruence in people's interpretations of nonverbal affection behavior.

Politeness Theory

Politeness theory (PT; Brown & Levinson, 1987) espouses that all individuals have, and are concerned with maintaining, *face*. As first articulated by Goffman (1959, 1967), face refers to a person's desired public image. Politeness theory identifies two types of face needs to which individuals are posited to attend. *Positive face* refers to one's desire for acceptance and approval from others, whereas *negative face* refers to one's desire for autonomy and freedom from imposition or constraint. Behaviors that run contrary to people's face needs are called face-threatening acts (FTAs). For instance, insults or criticisms can threaten people's positive face because they imply disapproval, whereas requests for favors can threaten people's negative face by constraining their behaviors and imposing on their autonomy. Although affectionate messages might be expected to support positive face through their implication of acceptance and approval, they could simultaneously threaten negative face by implying that the sender wishes to modify the status of the relationship with the receiver (e.g., a platonic friend wanting to become a romantic partner) and/or by making the receiver feel manipulated (i.e., that the sender was using the expression as a form of persuasion or manipulation).

Bio-Evolutionary Paradigm

At its heart, the bio-evolutionary paradigm suggests that tendencies for particular behaviors are rooted in the adaptive advantages those behaviors conferred on our premodern ancestors and in how such advantages are currently manifested in human physiological systems. For instance, to explain why people are more affectionate with their biological children than with their stepchildren (Floyd & Morman, 2001), the bio-evolutionary approach focuses on the survival or reproductive benefits of receiving affectionate expressions and on the adaptive nature of benefiting one's genetic relatives (biological children) more than nongenetic others (stepchildren). Similarly, to explain why highly affectionate people have more-differentiated twenty-four-hour cortisol rhythms than nonaffectionate people (Floyd, 2006b), this paradigm focuses on the adaptive advantages of *giving* affectionate expressions and on the ways in which they manifest themselves in the physiological stress response.

This paradigm is referred to as "bio-evolutionary" to imply that it is inclusive both of theories rooted in psychophysiology and of those grounded in principles of natural or sexual selection. Theories of neither type necessarily reference the principles important to the other, but all theories in this paradigm can be distinguished from those in the sociocultural paradigm by their relative emphasis on adaptive motivations and/or physiological processes rather than socially or culturally constructed explanations for behavior. Bio-evolutionary theories by no means dismiss the influences of social context or culturally engrained motivations for behavior, but instead emphasize how propensities for behavior can be linked to the ability to survive and/or to procreate.

Central to the bio-evolutionary paradigm is the Darwinian concept of natural selection. In their efforts to understand how species changed over time in apparent response to environmental challenges (e.g., extreme temperatures, access to food, predatory threats), scientists have proposed various theoretic explanations, the most ubiquitous of which is Darwin's (1859) theory of evolution by means of natural selection. The underlying premise of Darwin's theory is that some organisms (e.g., some fish, some birds, some humans) are better adapted than others to the demands of their environments and are, therefore, more likely than others to survive and reproduce. To the extent that these organisms' advantageous characteristics are passed on to their offspring genetically, those characteristics should occur with increasing frequency in each succeeding generation. In Darwinian terminology, these advantageous characteristics – which might include the ability of fish to camouflage themselves to evade predators or the ability of highly attractive people to entice high-quality reproductive partners – are *selected for*, because the survival or procreative advantages they confer will ensure that they are passed on to new generations at a greater frequency than less-advantageous characteristics.[2]

Two observations related to this theory are particularly relevant to the bio-evolutionary paradigm. The first is that advantageous characteristics need not be physical (e.g., strength, attractiveness, height), but may also be cognitive or psychological (e.g., intelligence, empathic ability). This is the premise behind the subdiscipline of evolutionary psychology (Buss, 2015; Workman & Reader, 2014), which focuses both on the adaptive advantages and the heritability (the extent to which characteristics are transmitted genetically) of various psychological abilities or attributes. The second observation is that emotional and psychological activities (whether adaptive or not) often coincide with physiological processes. For instance, weak psychological attachment tends to covary with poor immunocompetence (Coe & Lubach, 2001), whereas the experience of positive, loving emotion often prompts the release of analgesic hormones such as oxytocin (Uvnäs-Moberg, 1998). These associations are the purview of the subdiscipline of psychophysiology (Andreassi, 2006; Cacioppo, Tassinary, & Berntson, 2017). As noted above, the principles of both evolutionary psychology and psychophysiology, along with those of classical Darwinian thought, are enveloped in the bio-evolutionary paradigm.

Some Specific Theories in the Bio-Evolutionary Paradigm

Darwin's Theory of Emotion Expression

In his seminal work on the expression of emotion, Darwin (1872/1965) proposed three general principles regarding forms of emotional communication. The first two of these have particular relevance for the study of affectionate expressions. The first, known as the *principle of serviceable associated habits*, suggests in essence that humans perform certain physical actions to meet particular needs or desires (e.g., plugging one's nose in the presence of a foul odor to block that odor from the nasal passages) and that when humans experience states of mind similar to those they experience when they have these needs or desires, "there is a tendency through the force of habit and association for the same movements to be performed, though they may not then be of the least use" (p. 28). For example, when confronted with an offensive person or a particularly bad idea, one might plug his or her nose to express contempt because one's state of mind in such a situation is similar to that experienced in the presence of an offensive odor, causing one to plug his or her nose out of habit or association. The action is functional in the primary situation (protecting oneself from an offensive odor), but it is merely symbolic in the associated situations, conveying the message that "you (or your ideas) stink." The second principle, known as the *principle of antithesis*, builds on the first by suggesting that when we experience states of mind that are opposite to those that lead to functional behaviors, we tend to perform the opposite behaviors (e.g., taking a long, deep breath in instead of plugging one's nose).

Inherent in these principles is the idea that emotional states approximate mental states associated with physical needs. The need for protection from physical threats mentally approximates the emotional desire to protect oneself from offensive or distasteful ideas, interactions, or social situations, according to these principles, and therefore the behaviors associated with each are similar. There are three important implications of this paradigm. The first is that one can identify a repertoire of behaviors associated with particular emotional states by identifying states of mind analogous to those emotions and considering the behaviors that functionally serve those states. Two other important implications of this approach are that the repertoire for each particular emotional state ought to be relatively stable across individuals and cultures and that there ought to be relative consensus across individuals and cultures in recognizing the behaviors that convey each emotion. Darwin devoted much of his 1872 book to detailing the repertoire of behaviors associated with each major emotional state, and he posited a great deal of similarity across races and cultures in both the encoding and decoding of such emotions, a proposition that garnered support in the 1970s with cross-cultural comparisons conducted by Eibl-Eibesfeldt (1972), Ekman, Friesen, and Ellsworth (1972), Izard (1971), and others.

Darwin did not go into great detail about the repertoire of behaviors associated with expressing affection specifically, although he did offer an explicitly associative argument:

No doubt, as affection is a pleasurable sensation, it generally causes a gentle smile and some brightening of the eyes. A strong desire to touch the beloved person is commonly felt; and love is expressed by this means more plainly than by any other. Hence we long to clasp in our arms those whom we tenderly love. We probably owe this desire to inherited habit, in association with the nursing and tending of our children. (p. 213)

Tend and Befriend Theory

Developed in response to the fight-or-flight model of stress management, tend and befriend theory (TBT; Taylor et al., 2000) challenges the primacy of fighting and fleeing as the most adaptive responses to environmental threats. Whereas men may have benefited evolutionarily from either fighting or fleeing from potential challenges, TBT argues that neither response would have been as adaptive for women, due to the peril to which either approach would subject the women's offspring. Specifically, if a mother is expending her energies and attention fighting a threat or fleeing from it, her children are likely to be left unprotected in the process. Consequently, the theory predicts, these tendencies on the part of women will eventually be selected against.

As alternatives, TBT proposes that the complexity of protecting and caring for offspring (particularly under threatening circumstances) has made it adaptive for women to adopt two related strategies for responding to stress. The first, *tending*, involves "quieting and caring for offspring and blending into the environment" (Taylor et al., 2000, p. 412) and is thought to be adaptive particularly insofar as it reduces the offspring's own stress response, maximizing its capacity to survive to reproductive age. The second strategy, *befriending*, refers specifically to creating and maintaining social relationships that can provide resources and protection for the mother and her children, particularly under stressful circumstances. For example, women may have benefited from forming intimate social bonds with female relatives and female friends who were physically proximal and could therefore be a source of emotional and instrumental support.

Befriending is the strategy of the two that more directly implicates affectionate communication. Given that befriending involves forming and maintaining positive, intimate social bonds – and given that affectionate behavior is one of the principal communicative means of relational development and maintenance – it is logical to predict on the basis of TBT an inverse relationship between expressing affection and experiencing stress, particularly for women.

The Need to Belong

Perhaps the most succinct theoretic statement relevant to the importance of affection appears in Baumeister and Leary's (1995) explication of the *need to belong* as a fundamental human motivation. These authors offered that humans are innately prepared to seek, form, maintain, and protect strong interpersonal relationships and that this drive is fundamental to the human condition. In their essay, Baumeister and Leary presented evidence from a wide range of literatures that humans habitually seek

significant interpersonal bonds, that they suffer from relational deprivation, and that both the emotional experience and the behavioral expression of those bonds are necessary. On this latter point, the authors argued
that the need to belong is so fundamental that it cannot be truly satisfied
either by love without interaction (as in the case of long-distance
romance or the military deployment or incarceration of one's relational
partner) or by interaction without love (as in the case of loveless marriages or anonymous sexual encounters). One could deduce from this
proposition that people have a need to *express* and *exchange* feelings of
love with those for whom they have them. That is, because people
experience distress at the deprivation of interaction opportunities with
significant others, one could argue that this partially reflects a need not
only to *be loved* but to tell others they are loved and to be told one is loved
in return.

Somatosensory Affectional Deprivation Theory

Somatosensory affectional deprivation theory (SADT; Prescott, 1970,
1975, 1976a, b, 1980; Prescott & Wallace, 1978) is founded on the
premise that physically and psychosocially healthy infant development
requires sufficient stimulation of at least three sensory modalities: (1) the
vestibular-cerebellar system, involving postnatal continuation of constant
movement; (2) the somesthetic system, involving frequent tactile stimulation; and (3) the olfactory system, involving smell and the ability to
identify primary caregivers by smell. Prescott (1976a) noted that there is
considerable evidence from animal and human studies (including cross-
cultural studies) to support the principle that insufficient stimulation of
these sensory modalities inhibits infant development. Working from this
premise, SADT posits that these sensory modalities mediate experiences
of somatosensory pleasure in infants' initial caregiving relationships,
which are typically with their mothers, and that these pleasure experiences are necessary to the development of a primary affectional bond
with the mother or mother surrogate. SADT further proposes that sensory deprivation (in any or all of these modalities) experienced by infants
in their initial caregiving relationships prevents the formation of a primary affectional bond with the mother and that failure to develop a
primary affectional bond during infancy has two detrimental effects later
in life. First, it impairs the ability to form secondary affectional bonds,
particularly sexual bonds, in adulthood. Second, it inhibits the ability to
provide sufficient sensory stimulation to one's own offspring, resulting in
the intergenerational transmission of affectional deprivation.

SADT has been used to explain a variety of behavioral outcomes, such
as the pervasiveness of human violence (Prescott, 1979), the tendency

toward drug and alcohol use and abuse (Prescott, 1980), and even sexual behavior among the blind (Prescott, 1973). For instance, Prescott has shown that the average degree of physical affection between mother and infant (holding, touching, carrying) characterizing a primitive culture predicts with nearly perfect accuracy the propensity toward violence in that culture (Prescott, 1976a, 1979). Similarly, he has theorized that the reduced ability to enjoy adult sexual pleasure (resulting from impaired somatosensory development) predicts the use of alcohol and other drugs and has presented data that support (although do not conclusively prove) this assertion (Prescott, 1980). SADT explains both behavioral patterns as the consequence of depriving the body of the affectional behavior it requires to fulfill its engrained needs for somatosensory stimulation.

Importantly, Prescott's theory gives primacy to physical manifestations of affectionate interaction: touch, smell, and motion. As such, it proposes that infant development is arrested not by a lack of love or emotional attachment on the part of the parent but by a lack of intimate physical contact that stimulates the sensory modalities (behaviors such as rocking a baby, touching the baby's skin, or holding the baby close to one's chest). As noted in the previous chapter, although behaviors of these sorts frequently derive from strong emotional experiences of love and commitment (i.e., experiences and expressions of affection often covary), there is no *necessary* relationship between the emotions and the behaviors. Whereas perspectives such as the need to belong give primacy to emotional experiences – indeed, Baumeister and Leary (1995, p. 513) explicitly provide that relational behavior in the absence of an emotional bond only partially satisfies people's affiliative motivations – SADT is unique among bio-evolutionary theories in its focus on the behaviors themselves as causal agents.

In support of SADT's assertions is the robust literature on the therapeutic effects of touch among humans. Much of the scientific research in this area has been conducted by the Touch Research Institute at the University of Miami School of Medicine, which has demonstrated the beneficial effects of tactile contact on a broad range of physical conditions, including anorexia (Hart et al., 2001), asthma (Field et al., 1998), dermatitis (Schachner, Field, Hernandez-Reif, Duarte, & Krasnegor, 1998), diabetes (Field et al., 1997), HIV (Diego et al., 2001), hypertension (Hernandez-Reif et al., 2000), leukemia (Field et al., 2001), nicotine addiction (Hernandez-Reif, Field, & Hart, 1999), Parkinson's disease (Hernandez-Reif et al., 2002), and sleep disorders (Field & Hernandez-Reif, 2001). In each case, the observed physiological, psychological, and behavioral benefits of touch were unattributable to the emotional connection between the source and the recipient of the touch. Importantly, although Prescott's theory makes no dismissal of the assertion that somatosensory stimulation is often accompanied by intimate emotional bonds, the emotional bonds are neither necessary nor sufficient precursors to the outcomes SADT predicts. Rather, it is the behaviors themselves that are theorized to affect outcomes such as delayed physical development, propensity toward violence, and propensity toward drug and alcohol abuse.

Affection Exchange Theory: A More Comprehensive Approach

Each of the perspectives and theories previously reviewed provides something important in the way of explaining an aspect of affectionate communication. This section reviews areas in which previous theories have been profitable, as well as questions they have left unresolved, before detailing affection exchange theory as a more comprehensive approach.

Strengths of Previous Theories

Theories in the socio-cultural and bio-evolutionary paradigms have been fruitful for examining many aspects of affectionate behavior, including questions of encoding and decoding, of interpretation, and of reciprocity.

Questions of Encoding and Decoding

The social meaning model has helped illuminate issues such as encoder–decoder agreement on affectionate behavior (Ray & Floyd, 2006), and means of expressing affection within given relationships. Several studies, for instance, have found that the means of conveying affection within personal relationships are often strongly influenced by the nature of the relationship (whether romantic, platonic, or familial; e.g., Floyd, 1999; Floyd & Morman, 1997, 2003; Floyd & Morr, 2003). Expectancy violations theory has also been useful at identifying the individual, relational, or contextual factors that most strongly influence how affection is encoded and decoded. Research has shown, for instance, that people expect romantic partners to express affection in more intimate ways than relatives, who, in turn, should express affection more intimately than platonic friends, and that these relational distinctions are particularly salient for male–male interaction (e.g., Floyd, 1997b; Floyd & Morman, 1997). Thus, a given behavior (e.g., a bear hug) that represents an expectancy confirmation in one type of relationship (e.g., between brothers) may qualify as an expectancy violation in a different relationship type (e.g., between male friends; see Morman & Floyd, 1998).

Questions of Interpretation

Closely related to issues of encoding and decoding are those of interpretation, which include making evaluations and attributions for behaviors observed between others. One prediction derivable from expectancy violations theory is that unexpected behavior is more likely than expected behavior to provoke evaluations and attributions, and Floyd and Voloudakis (1999b) demonstrated that this was the case with nonverbal affection behavior. Another prediction derivable from expectancy violations theory and the social meaning model is that observers should evaluate affectionate behavior positively, and make favorable attributions for it, in the absence of a reason not to do so. That is, positive evaluations and attributions should be the "default," given the generally positive nature of affectionate behavior. Such a prediction could also be derived from Baumeister and Leary's (1995) proposal of the need to belong, given the role of affectionate behavior in establishing and maintaining social bonds. Several studies have demonstrated this general pattern, including those by Floyd (1999), Floyd and Morman (2000b), Harrison-Speake and Willis (1995), and Rane and Draper (1995).

Other research has used politeness theory to consider the face-supporting or face-threatening nature of some affectionate behaviors. Recognizing that some affectionate behaviors are unwelcome even if they are not considered inappropriate for a given relationship or social context, Erbert and Floyd (2004) surmised that the behaviors may be interpreted negatively because they carry implicit threats to the receiver's positive or negative face needs. Indeed, their study suggested that receivers do perceive face threats in some affectionate behaviors that would seem, on their surface, to be both appropriate and largely positive.

Questions of Reciprocity

Finally, several studies have focused on the questions of when people are the most likely to reciprocate affectionate expressions and what consequences ensue when they do not. As a general principle, social exchange theory would provide that if affectionate communication within a given relationship is perceived as a resource, then relational partners should perceive pressure to maintain a reasonably equitable exchange of affectionate behavior. This suggests, for instance, that relationships in which one partner feels under-benefited with respect to affection (i.e., feels that he or she gives more affection than is received in return) should be less stable than those in which greater equity is maintained. Although it was not conducted explicitly to test social exchange theory, research by

Lawson (1988) reports that married women's most commonly cited reason for engaging in extramarital affairs was their husbands' failure to meet their affection needs, making the women feel under-benefited with respect to affection.

The reciprocity conceived of by social exchange theory is relatively broad, however, occurring over the duration of a relationship. What predicts reciprocity of a given behavior *at the time it is enacted* is a more specific issue, and the existing theory that has proven the most useful in addressing this question is interaction adaptation theory. This theory provides that communicators enter interactions with their desires, expectations, and desires operational. Communicators are theorized to evaluate behavior they receive from others against the sum of what they need, expect, and want; behaviors that conform to or exceed these are predicted to be reciprocated, whereas behaviors that fall short of these are predicted to be compensated for. Interaction adaptation theory has informed investigations of reciprocity and compensation of affectionate behavior, including those by Floyd and Burgoon (1999) and Floyd and Ray (2000).

On the issues of encoding/decoding, interpretation, and reciprocity, then, previous theories have been able to contribute in meaningful ways to the understanding of affectionate communication. Two important limitations are troublesome, however, the first being that none of these previous theories is able to account for all of these issues (encoding, decoding, interpretation, and reciprocity). That is, none offers an explanatory framework broad enough to encompass all of these questions. Indeed, none of these theories was designed with that purpose in mind, so this is not a limitation of these theories, per se. However, the lack of a broad explanatory framework leads to a theoretically piecemeal approach to studying affectionate communication, such that each theory is able to explain only particular elements of the phenomenon (although it may explain them well).

Second, previous theories have been less profitable in addressing other, often conceptually broader, issues. Of course, theories vary with respect to their levels of abstraction, so it is untenable to expect them to be equally adept at addressing questions that are conceptually expansive (e.g., why are people affectionate?) and conceptually narrow (e.g., what are the immunological correlates of nonverbal affection among newlyweds?). Previous theories have proven more proficient at answering precise, focused questions than at explaining broader issues relevant to the importance and utility of affectionate communication. Some of these conceptually broader questions are delineated below.

Limitations of Previous Theories

At least three theoretic issues regarding affectionate communication have been insufficiently addressed by previous theories. These relate to the dually social and physiological nature of affectionate behavior, the benefits of giving affection as opposed to receiving it, and the fact that affectionate communication sometimes precedes negative, rather than positive, outcomes.

Questions of Dual Physiological and Social Influence

Theories in the bio-evolutionary and socio-cultural paradigms differ from each other primarily in the relative emphases they place on evolutionary/physiological and social/cultural explanatory mechanisms. If one considers the question of why people hug, for instance, one can easily formulate socio-cultural explanations on the basis of extant theory (e.g., hugging is culturally interpreted as conveying love or respect; hugging symbolizes the socially constructed role of women as caregivers and thus reflects social patriarchy). Bio-evolutionary explanations are also easily derived (e.g., hugging evolved from adaptive parental protective instincts; hugging provides somatosensory stimulation necessary for neurological development).

For a question such as this, there is little difficulty in formulating theoretically grounded answers within each paradigm; deriving an explanation that considers *both* socio-cultural *and* bio-evolutionary influences is considerably more challenging, however. Although few theories in either paradigm explicitly exclude the explanatory mechanisms offered in the other paradigm, some theories do implicitly preclude alternative mechanisms through their assumptions or higher-order propositions. If a theory in the socio-cultural paradigm assumes (either explicitly or implicitly) that all social behavior is fundamentally motivated by, for example, the quest for power or status, then although that theory's propositions may not explicitly preclude the possibility of hormonal influences on behavior, that possibility is effectively excluded by the theory's underlying assumptions. Conversely, if a theory in the bio-evolutionary paradigm assumes that individual behavior reflects only genetic predispositions, then there is likewise little room to account for variance on the basis of cultural norms.

Certainly, few theories make such exclusionary assumptions explicitly, yet their implicit assumptions can nonetheless strongly preclude the alternative explanations offered by a different theoretic paradigm. This has two deleterious effects, the more obvious of which is that, because almost no social phenomenon (including affectionate communication) can reasonably be said to be influenced only by *either* socio-cultural *or* bio-evolutionary mechanisms, many theoretic accounts are necessarily incomplete. Indeed, as the research in this text explains, affectionate behavior varies both as a function of social and cultural norms (e.g., more intimate affectionate behavior is sanctioned in emotionally charged social contexts than in emotionally neutral ones) and as a function of physiological traits (e.g., people with differentiated diurnal cortisol rhythms are more affectionate than people with undifferentiated rhythms). The point that social behavior is influenced by both socio-cultural and bio-evolutionary forces may seem so self-evident that it fails to warrant explicit mention, yet communication theories often strongly favor one form of explanation to the relative exclusion of the other, which can lead to programs of research that may be severely narrow and limited in their focus.

A second, and perhaps less evident, problem brought on by this type of theoretic myopia is that empirical tests of the theories may not be designed in such a way that the relative influences of "competing" explanations can be parceled out. For instance, the prediction that *US fathers show more affection to biological sons than to stepsons* is derivable from at least two competing explanations: (1) in US culture, biological nuclear family relationships are privileged over nonbiological ones; therefore, men feel closer to their biological sons than to their stepsons and they communicate their affection accordingly; and (2) affectionate communication is a resource with implications for health and survival, and it is evolutionarily adaptive to prefer genetic relatives over others in the provision of resources; therefore, men are more affectionate with biological sons than with stepsons.

In principle, one need only compare affectionate behavior in biological and step relationships to test this prediction, and if one's theory even implicitly precludes the possibility of competing influences, then the motivation to attend to that possibility would be low. The problem with such an approach is that, if the hypothesis is supported (i.e., if men show more affection to their biological sons), both explanations are, by implication, *equally* supported unless the design of the study allows one explanation to be tested while the other is controlled. In the present example, for instance, Floyd and Morman (2001) showed that fathers were more affectionate with biological sons than stepsons even when the emotional closeness of the father–son relationships was controlled for. Importantly, the point of such an approach was not to *rule out* closeness as an influence on paternal affection behavior – indeed, closeness was significantly correlated with men's affectionate communication with their sons – but to test the potential influence of the genetic relationship (biological vs. nonbiological) net of the influence of closeness.

Questions of Giving Versus Receiving Affection

Particularly with respect to the benefits of affectionate behavior, much existing research has focused on the receipt of affectionate communication as opposed to its provision. Most, if not all, of the socio-cultural theories reviewed in this chapter would adopt such a focus; for example, both expectancy violations theory and interaction adaptation theory would focus on reacting to received affection, whereas the social meaning model would focus on assigning meaning to affectionate behavior one has received or observed. Some theories in the bio-evolutionary paradigm likewise adopt a receiver focus; somatosensory affectional deprivation theory focuses on the benefits of receiving affectionate behavior and the detrimental effects of not receiving it, whereas the need to belong would lead one (at least, implicitly) to focus on received behaviors that indicate social inclusion, such as the receipt of affection. Of the bio-evolutionary theories described in this chapter, only tend and befriend theory focuses on the effects of *conveying* affection, and then only for women who are experiencing stress (Darwin's theory of emotion expression addresses only the behavioral means by which affectionate messages are encoded).

Aside from the fact that receiving and expressing affection are strongly reciprocal, there is merit in considering the effects of conveying affection, apart from those of receiving it, for which no previous theory provides an adequate account. Chief among the reasons for studying expressed affection is that it covaries with a host of mental and physical health benefits that are separable from those associated with received affection, as this book will detail. Importantly, these benefits do not appear to be confined to women – or even to be more characteristic of women than men – as tend and befriend theory would imply, nor do they appear to be operative only when people are in distress. Rather, the benefits are diverse and robust for both sexes, yet no previous theory provides a sufficient account as to why. Baumeister and Leary's (1995) need to belong could, in principle, be used to explain the mental health benefits of providing affection – at least to the extent that providing affection to others helps to reinforce one's social inclusion – yet the theory would provide no adequate account for its physical health benefits. Conversely, somatosensory affectional deprivation theory could account for the physical health benefits of expressing affection, but only as a function of the affectionate behavior received in return (i.e., one benefits from being affectionate because one receives affection in return, which is beneficial). Given the empirical evidence that expressed affection covaries with benefits that are independent of those associated with received affection, a more adequate theoretic account is warranted.

Questions of Positive Versus Negative Outcomes

Perhaps the most counterintuitive aspect of affectionate communication is its potential to elicit negative, rather than positive, outcomes. Affectionate behavior conveyed in particular ways or in particular contexts can cause cognitive, emotional, and even physical distress on the part of the recipient that has the potential to lead not only to compensatory behavior but also to confusion over the status of the relationship and perhaps even to relational de-escalation. Whereas only bio-evolutionary theories offer partial explanations for the benefits of conveying (as opposed to receiving) affection, only socio-cultural theories currently provide any measure of explanation for why affectionate behavior can produce either positive or negative outcomes.

Specifically, expectancy violations theory and interaction adaptation theory both provide for the possibility that even a behavior as inherently positive as an affectionate expression could be reacted to negatively. (Social exchange theory would certainly provide that if one's affection is not reciprocated, the resulting inequity would be aversive; however, it does not provide the explanatory means for predicting when nonreciprocity is likely to occur in the first place.) The causal element in both theories' explanations is a *violation*: the affectionate expression violated the receiver's expectations, cultural norms, desires, perceived needs, or some other property.

To the extent that one's affectionate expression is met with negative emotion or behavior, therefore, these theories would explain such an outcome as following from a violation of the receiver's expectations, values, needs, or other characteristics. Indeed, it is not difficult to conceive of affectionate behaviors that would negatively violate, for instance, one's expectations or social norms. For instance, an intimate hug or kiss from a stranger would, under many circumstances, be considered abnormal and cause a measure of distress for the recipient. The fundamental question is not why the gesture would be unexpected, but why it would be aversive. Although EVT and IAT do provide that the valence of a violation depends on a receiver's assessment of the sender (whether the sender is rewarding or not) and of the behavior itself (whether it is inherently positive or negative), both theories are broad in their explication of which aspects of the sender or behavior exert the most influence on the valence.

This breadth is probably a necessary feature of these theories, given the range of interpersonal behaviors each is intended to explain, and so this is not a criticism of these theories so much as it is a limitation of their application to affectionate communication. The consequence of this limitation is the lack of a singular explanatory mechanism to account for the sometimes-negative effects of affectionate behaviors. The preference for a singular mechanism does not imply that individual, social, cultural, or contextual variation should be (or even can be) disregarded. Rather, it reflects the advantage, in terms of accounting for variance, of referencing behavioral motivations that are not socially or contextually variant, as the theory detailed herein attempts to do.

As described here, previous theories have been fruitful in guiding exploration of several aspects of affectionate communication, and it is a strength of several of these theories that they have done so despite not having been constructed for that specific purpose. Other aspects of affectionate communication remain insufficiently explained, however, limiting the ability of researchers to explicate and understand these issues. In an attempt to provide a more comprehensive account of human affectionate behavior, this chapter describes a newer theory that is grounded in the Darwinian concept of natural selection yet takes account of variance in social and contextual norms.

Affection Exchange Theory

Affection exchange theory (AET) treats affectionate communication as an adaptive behavior that both directly and indirectly contributes to human survival and reproductive success. It is not intended to be an extension or modification of the theory of natural selection or any other associated theory. Rather, it treats affectionate communication as a class of behaviors that serves both superordinate evolutionary goals (survival and procreation) and that is, as such, influenced by human motivations to meet these goals.

Full explication of the theory, including the arguments supportive of each postulate, appears in Floyd (2006a). A condensed explication appears in this section, and subsequent chapters will make specific reference to AET when discussing relevant findings.

Axioms

Three principles fundamental to Darwinian thought are axiomatic to AET. The first is that survival and reproduction are the two superordinate human motivations. This assumption focuses theoretic attention on the advantages that a prospective adaptation has for survival, procreative success, or both. Second, behaviors need not serve a superordinate evolutionary goal in a proximal sense – that is, in the moment – in order to serve it in a longer-term, ultimate sense. Forming a friendship, for instance, may not aid one's survival immediately, but because social inclusion is a strong predictor of health (House, Landis, & Umberson, 1988), having that friendship may aid one's survival in the long term. The final axiom is that individuals need not be consciously aware of the evolutionary goals being served by their behaviors. That is, a behavior such as expressing affection can contribute to one's survival and/or reproductive success even outside one's awareness.

Postulates

Affection exchange theory comprises five postulates, some of which include subpostulates that provide empirical generalizations and applications. Readers are referred to Floyd (2006a, chapter 7) for a more in-depth discussion and development of each postulate.

Postulate 1: The need and capacity for affection are inborn.

As a higher-order postulate, AET offers that humans have both a fundamental need and a fundamental ability to love and receive love from others. This proposition refers to the internal experience of affection rather than to its behavioral manifestations, and it positions the need and capacity for affection among humans' innate experiences (see also Miller et al., 1999; Miller, Pasta, MacMurray, Muhleman, & Comings, 2000; Miller & Rodgers, 2001).[3] Research on affection in infants and young children adds support to this proposition (see, e.g., Banham, 1950; Gerhardt, 2006; Günindi, 2015; Moore et al., 2017; Zanolli, Saudargas, & Twardosz, 1990).

To call the need and capacity for affection *inborn* is not to deny that they are also subject to environmental conditioning. This postulate proposes only that humans are endowed with the need and ability to love and be loved, although the magnitude and effects of these needs and capacities can differ across groups, across individuals, and even within individuals over time.

Postulate 2: Affectionate feelings and affectionate expressions are distinct experiences that often, but need not, covary.

This point was introduced in Chapter 1 and it is an important higher-order postulate in AET. Although people can express feelings (including affectionate feelings) with no attempt to censor their emotion displays, they can also elect to downplay or hide expressions of genuine affection, as well as simulate expressions of unfelt affection (see Ekman & Friesen, 1975).

That the experience and expression of affection can be conceived of as distinct constructs is important because it raises a number of provocative research questions, such as why communicators elect to hide affectionate feelings when they have them or when they are likely to express affection that they do not actually feel. Both instances have implications for the development and maintenance of personal relationships; the former because it can leave relational partners' needs for affectionate behavior unfulfilled, and the latter because it can initiate or accelerate relational development under false pretenses. (For more extended discussion on the dissociation of emotional experience and emotional expression, consult Gross, John, & Richards, 2000.)

> *Postulate 3*: Affectionate communication is adaptive with respect to human viability and fertility.

The third, and perhaps most important, higher-order postulate offers that the exchange of affectionate behavior benefits both senders and receivers by serving their superordinate motivations for survival and procreation and is, in this sense, an evolutionarily adaptive behavior. Various subpostulates explicate both ultimate (long-term) and proximal (short-term) pathways through which affection exchange can influence viability and fertility.

> *Subpostulate 3a*: Affectionate communication serves the super-ordinate motivation for viability by promoting the establishment and maintenance of significant human pair bonds.

Unlike many other mammals, humans routinely form pair bonds, and MacDonald (1992) argued that pair bonding and its associated affection in intimate relationships are human adaptations evolved for the purpose of protecting the young. In a purely evolutionary sense, effort and resources expended in the service of producing offspring are wasted with respect to reproductive success if those offspring fail to survive to sexual maturity; thus, providing for and protecting the young are critical for reproductive success. Such provisions and protection are more efficiently disbursed when a child's parents compose a bonded, cooperative pair, because they each have an evolutionary stake in that child's well-being that is not necessarily shared by guardians who have no biological bond with the child (see Lamb, Pleck, Charnov, & Levine, 1987).

Hamilton (1964) made clear that although individual reproduction is not *required* for reproductive success (given that one also achieves such success via the reproduction of genetic relatives), it is certainly *sufficient* for reproductive success if offspring survive to sexual maturity. There-fore, to the extent that affectionate behavior increases the likelihood of individual reproductive potential, it consequently contributes to repro-ductive success. AET proposes that expressing affection increases repro-ductive opportunity by portraying the communicator as having high parental fitness, as shown in the next subpostulate.

Subpostulate 3b: Affectionate communication serves the super-ordinate motivation for fertility by representing to potential mating partners that the communicator is a viable partner and a fit potential parent.

Reproductive success is never guaranteed when humans interact sexually, partly because not all individuals are willing or able to undertake the long-term responsibility of rearing offspring. Therefore, included among the traits that contribute to reproductive success must be the ability to discriminate between fit and unfit partners, or what is referred to here as *potential parental fitness*. Sorokowski et al. (2017) offered evidence that the experience of affection is significantly associated with reproductive success (measured solely as the number of offspring produced). According to this subpostulate, however, the expression of affection contributes to reproductive success specifically because it portrays, whether accurately or not, a high degree of potential parental fitness to recipients who are potential reproductive partners.

Trivers (1972) observed that the assessment of fitness (in its various forms) for a potential reproductive partner is not equally consequential for women and men (nor for females and males of many species); rather, he noted that a poor mating choice is far more detrimental to women, in terms of resource depletion, than to men. Trivers proposed that this was due to *differential parental investment*, or the minimum investment of resources required to rear a healthy child. His theory predicted that, in any species, whichever sex has the greater minimum parental investment will exercise greater selectivity in choosing sexual partners of the opposite sex. For humans and many other species, therefore, Trivers's theory explains why males generally compete for sexual access to females, rather than the other way around.

The implication of Trivers's theory for affectionate communication is that, compared with men, women should be more motivated than men to attend (at least subconsciously) to their reproductive partners' potential to be fit parents and good providers for themselves and their children. Several studies have demonstrated just such a propensity in patterns of human mate selection (e.g., Feingold, 1992; Kenrick, Groth, Trost, & Sadalla, 1993; Kenrick, Sadalla, Broth, & Trost, 1990). Therefore, if affectionate communication connotes a tendency to be a committed partner and a fit parent, this should be more consequential to women's mate choices than to men's. This idea is formalized in a third subpostulate.

Subpostulate 3c: The relationship between affectionate communication and reproductive opportunity is stronger for women's mate selections than for men's.

Accompanying these ultimate explanations for the influence of affectionate communication on well-being is the proximal explanation that sharing affection covaries with important regulatory physiological functions. Rather than being a competing explanation for why affectionate communication contributes to viability and fertility, the focus on proximal psychophysiological processes explains the manners in which affectionate behavior can serve relational maintenance and convey parental fitness at a localized level.

Subpostulate 3d: The experiences of feeling, communicating, and receiving affection covary with immunocompetence and regulatory physiological pathways for stress and reward.

As a partial explanatory mechanism not only for diversity in the valence of responses to affectionate behavior but also for discrepancies in the relative effects of affectionate behavior and its underlying emotion, AET acknowledges individual variation in the inborn need and capacity for affection.

Postulate 4: Humans vary in their optimal tolerances for affection and affectionate behavior.

Proposed here is that individuals vary in their needs and abilities to experience affectionate emotions and in their trait-like tendencies to communicate affection or receive affectionate expressions. Initial research on trait-like tendencies for expressing and receiving expressions of affection was conducted by Floyd (2002), who found considerable variation in scores on both trait affection given and trait affection received. On seven-point scales, both measures produced scores ranging from a low of 2.00 to a high of 7.00, indicating substantial individual variation in trait-like tendencies to express and receive affectionate behaviors. Later research by Floyd, Hess, et al. (2005) found similar individual variation.

Importantly, however, AET does not simply recognize variation in the need, capacity, and tendency toward affection and affectionate behavior, but posits that individuals have a range of optimal tolerance for affection and affectionate behavior. The range of optimal tolerance is bounded on the lower end by *need*, or how much affectionate emotion or behavior are required, and on the upper end by *desire*, or how much affectionate emotion or behavior are wanted. Thus, the optimal tolerance for affection and affectionate behavior represents a range spanning the lowest sufficient amount to the highest desired amount, and existing research demonstrates the pitfalls of receiving both too little (Floyd, 2016) and too much (Hesse, Mikkelson, & Saracco, 2017; van Raalte, Kloeber, Veluscek, & Floyd, 2016) affection. According to the postulate, both the width of the range and the absolute values for the minimum and maximum thresholds can vary from person to person.

The concept of a range of optimal tolerance has two direct implications for the third postulate, which provides that affection and affectionate communication are adaptive. The first implication qualifies subpostulate 3d, in particular, and is presented here as a new subpostulate.

> *Subpostulate 4a*: The experience, expression, and receipt of affection contribute to immunocompetence and regulatory pathways for reward and stress management when they occur within an individual's range of optimal tolerance.

This qualifies subpostulate 3d by specifying that when the experience or expression of affection occurs within the range of optimal tolerance, it does not merely covary with immunocompetence or regulatory functions but *enhances* them. Van Raalte et al. (2016), for instance, offered evidence that affection received outside one's desired range is associated with detriments such as somatic anxiety and stress. The second implication is that if receiving affectionate behavior that falls within one's range of optimal tolerance makes positive contributions to physiological well-being, then parents can fortify their children's health by communicating affection to them, thereby indirectly contributing to the parents' own reproductive success. This can be formalized as a second subpostulate.

> *Subpostulate 4b*: Affectionate communication to one's biological offspring enhances reproductive success by contributing to the health and viability of the offspring, so long as the affectionate behavior falls within the receivers' range of optimal tolerance.

This subpostulate rests on the logical assumption that healthier individuals have more opportunity than unhealthy individuals to reproduce successfully, ceteris paribus, and several studies have supported this prediction (e.g., Gangestad & Simpson, 2000; Gangestad, Thornhill, & Yeo, 1994; Mealy, Bridgestock, & Townsend, 1999; Thornhill & Gangestad, 1994).[4]

What, then, of affectionate behaviors that violate the range of optimal tolerance? As noted above, AET predicts that they will engender unfavorable consequences. In this way, AET shares conceptual space with expectancy violations theory (Burgoon, 1978), which postulates a range of expected behavior, outside of which a behavior is considered to be an expectancy violation. Like EVT, AET proposes that violating behaviors are noticed and that they initiate cognitive appraisals on the part of the recipient. However, AET further proposes that behavioral violations initiate sympathetic nervous system arousal that becomes the primary focus of the recipient's cognitive appraisals (wherein the violating behavior and the characteristics of the sender are the primary foci of cognitive appraisals in EVT). This can be stated as a formal postulate.

> *Postulate 5*: Conveying or receiving affectionate behaviors that violate one's range of optimal tolerance initiates noticeable sympathetic nervous system arousal and further initiates a cognitive appraisal of the same.

Although EVT provides for both positive and negative violations from a range of expected behavior, AET proposes that all violations of the range of optimal tolerance for affection produce negative outcomes. However, violations of the minimum and maximum thresholds are posited to be negative in different ways, specifically as shown in the following subpostulate.

> *Subpostulate 5a*: A violation of the minimum threshold in the range of optimal tolerance constitutes a threat to viability.

In the range of optimal tolerance, the minimum threshold represents the minimum amount of affection that a person needs to give or receive. As Chapter 9 details, deprivation of affectionate interaction is associated with pronounced physical detriments, such as chronic pain and sleep disorders. These and similar detriments constitute threats, in varying degrees, to a person's viability. Anecdotal accounts notwithstanding of people dying of a broken heart or perishing for lack of love, physical detriments can threaten viability and long- and short-term well-being. As clearly suggested by the pioneering research of Harlow (1958) with macaques, and Prescott (1970, 1975, 1980) with humans, a threshold exists for the minimum amount of affection an organism must receive in order to sustain normal development, and substantial physical and mental deficits often accompany the failure to receive the necessary level of affectionate behavior. AET extends this research by positing a corollary minimum threshold for the *expression* of affection, such that humans need not only to receive a minimum amount of affection from others but also to give a minimum amount to others.

Giving or receiving affectionate communication that violates the maximum threshold in the range of optimal tolerance is a qualitatively different experience. Whereas the minimum threshold represents the minimal amount of affectionate behavior that a person can give or receive before experiencing the detrimental physical and mental effects of deprivation, the maximum threshold reflects the greatest amount of affectionate communication that an individual desires to give or receive. Giving or receiving affectionate behavior that violates the maximum threshold does not necessarily lead to the physical and mental problems that accompany violations of the minimum threshold, according to AET. Rather, this theory proposes that it initiates an immediate stress response due to the possibility that it may represent interference with an individual's ability to successfully achieve his or her procreation goals, which can be stated as a second subpostulate.

> *Subpostulate 5b*: A violation of the maximum threshold in the range of optimal tolerance initially initiates a physiological stress response that covaries in intensity with the probability that the violating behavior represents a threat to one's procreation success.

Whether genuine or not, affectionate behaviors that are more intense or intimate than one desires convey, at least potentially, a relational *interest* that is more intense or intimate than one desires (see Floyd, 2000b). In other words, a person who receives an affectionate expression that violates his or her maximum threshold is forced to confront the possibility that such an expression signals a desire for more relational intimacy, emotional closeness, and/or sexual involvement than he or she is comfortable with. Such a desire can constitute a legitimate threat to an individual's chances for reproducing with a healthy and wisely chosen partner. The subpostulate also provides that the stress response will covary in intensity with the probability that the event threatens procreative success.

Collectively, the fifth postulate and its two subpostulates can account for a range of situations in which giving or receiving affectionate communication are, counterintuitively, distressing. For instance, people sometimes receive expressions of affection from others that are more intense than they are comfortable with. Politeness norms may even dictate that they must reciprocate those expressions in kind, further compounding their discomfort. At the other end of the continuum, relational partners (perhaps especially those in newly developing relationships) may come to their relationship with different affection needs, and if one partner has a particularly high need for affection, he or she may experience fairly frequent distress if that need is not fulfilled.

This chapter has reviewed the strengths and liabilities of existing socio-cultural and bio-evolutionary theories for explaining patterns of human affection exchange and has explicated a newer theory offering a more comprehensive account of affectionate behavior. Several empirical investigations have already supported hypotheses derived from AET, and these are described and critiqued in subsequent chapters.

3 Encoding and Measuring Affectionate Messages

One might imagine that expressing affection in close relationships is such a natural human function that questions about *how* that task is accomplished are superfluous. In actuality, people use a wide variety of both verbal and nonverbal behaviors to convey messages of affection. This chapter reviews research on affection encoding via verbal messages, direct nonverbal gestures, socially supportive behaviors, and idiosyncratic acts. It then describes and critiques the principal methods by which affectionate communication is measured in social scientific research and ends with a discussion of how experimental studies have manipulated affectionate behavior to ascertain its effects.

Encoding Messages of Affection

Via which behaviors do people convey messages of interpersonal affection? As Pendell (2002) pointed out, a wide variety of behaviors can "count" as affectionate expressions, from touching and cuddling to mutual gaze, facial pleasantness, vocal warmth, self-disclosure, and even empathic listening (see Floyd, 2014a). In an effort to categorize forms of affectionate expression – both theoretically and for the sake of measurement – Floyd and Morman (1998) proposed a tripartite model that includes affectionate behaviors enacted verbally, in direct nonverbal ways, and in socially supportive ways. This section reviews Floyd and Morman's model in detail and also acknowledges that idiomatic expressions of affection – although they defy categorization – are frequently observed in close relationships.

Floyd and Morman's Tripartite Model

Early work on the encoding of affectionate communication adopted, at least implicitly, a two-dimensional model, wherein affectionate messages were encoded either verbally (e.g., by saying "I love you" or "I care about you") or nonverbally (e.g., by hugging, kissing, or holding hands). Some early measurement models even assessed verbal and nonverbal expressions without making an a priori distinction between them. For instance, Noller (1978) examined videotaped interactions of eighty-seven parent–child dyads and coded "the number of instances of interactive behavior that would normally be regarded as affectionate," including kissing, cuddling, or saying "I love you" (p. 317). Other measurement models placed specific emphasis on nonverbal expressions of affection, such as kissing or hugging (see Acker, Acker, & Pearson, 1973; Acker & Marton, 1984; Lovaas, Schaeffer, & Simmons, 1965). Floyd (1997a, b; Floyd & Morman, 1997) retained the two-dimensional model in the development of a self-report measure used to ascertain affectionate behavior, as did Huston and Vangelisti (1991) in the development of their self-report measure of marital affection.

These two categories (verbal and nonverbal) are mutually exclusive and logically exhaustive, and it would appear at first that they ought to capture fully the range of potentially observable affectionate messages. Largely unaccounted for in this two-dimensional model, however, is the notion that, within particular relationships, individuals may express affection through the provision of social and instrumental support, such as doing favors for each other, helping with projects, or lending the use of resources. Although these behaviors *may* accompany other, more direct expressions of affection within these relationships, they often do not. Regardless, the critical point is that individuals in particular relationships both *use supportive behaviors to express affection* to each other and *decode these behaviors as such.*

A more extensive examination of each category in the tripartite model follows.

Verbal Statements

The verbal category includes expressions of one's affectionate feelings for another that are spoken aloud, written, or otherwise transmitted in linguistic form (including being texted or conveyed via sign language). Some such statements convey the nature of a sender's feelings for the receiver, such as "I love you" and "I care about you." Others establish or reinforce the status of the relationship between sender and receiver, such as "You're important to me" and "You're one of my best friends." Still others project hopes or dreams for a future relationship, including "I want us to be together forever" and "I can't wait to be married to you." Finally, some verbal statements convey the value of the relationship by noting how the sender would feel without it, such as "I can't stand the thought of losing you" or "My life would be empty if I hadn't met you."

The characteristic most clearly distinguishing verbal statements from the other two forms of communication in this model is their use of words, which makes verbal statements unique in their specificity relative to other forms of expression. When people wish to be unambiguous about their feelings for one another, they may opt to put those feelings into words, rather than convey them through nonverbal channels, so as to diminish opportunities for misinterpretation. They may do so either to convey intense affection for each other (e.g., "I'm in love with you; let's get married") or to be clear that the affection is less intense (e.g., "I like you; let's be friends"). There is a substantial qualitative difference between saying "I like you" and "I'm in love with you," a distinction that may not be conveyed as accurately through nonverbal behaviors.

This is not to suggest that verbal statements are unambiguous in an absolute sense, however. If one says "I love you" to another, he or she can intend to convey many different types of love, and the intention may not be evident at first. Indeed, as addressed in Chapter 9, misinterpretation of affectionate expressions (even verbal expressions) is one of their most potent risks – and although verbal statements are usually less ambiguous in their meaning than are direct nonverbal gestures or social support behaviors, the potential for misunderstanding can still be great, especially in less-established relationships.

Language is both spoken and written, of course, and this first category includes both forms. Researchers may question which factors influence people's decisions to convey affection via one form or the other. One might speculate that senders prefer to express their affectionate feelings in writing (instead of by speaking) when they are more certain of those feelings, insofar as the written word seems more "permanent" than the spoken word. That is, because recall of the spoken word (if unrecorded) relies on memory, spoken expressions of affection may be easier than written statements for senders to deny later if their feelings change. That speculation assumes that the written medium can be saved or archived in some fashion, so it may be truer for a card, an e-mail message, or text message than for a medium such as Snapchat, in which messages appear only for a short time before becoming inaccessible. At least for young adults, Chang (2017) found that seeking and providing affection was not a principal task for Snapchat use, although Ohadi, Brown, Trub, and Rosenthal (2018) documented that similarity in the use of text messaging (including for conveying affection) is positively associated with relationship satisfaction for young adults.

Another speculation is that senders prefer spoken to written statements when their goal is to be as unambiguous as possible. A written message of "I love you," for instance, could be interpreted as conveying either romantic or nonromantic forms of love. To reduce ambiguity, a sender may choose to speak the words, so that the cues as to their intended meaning can be conveyed through the sender's facial expressions, body language, or tone of voice (see, e.g., Burgoon & Newton, 1991).

Direct Nonverbal Gestures

The second category of affectionate behaviors in the tripartite model is direct nonverbal gestures. Here, the meaning of the term "gestures" is not exclusive to gesticulation (i.e., the use of hand and arm movements in an emblematic or illustrative fashion). Rather, the term is used in a broader sense that simply denotes a nonverbal social behavior (in the way that one might compliment another by saying "What you did for that person was a nice gesture").

Calling the gestures in this category "direct" implies that they are limited to nonverbal behaviors that are readily decoded as affectionate within the speech community in which they are observed. These behaviors sometimes vary from culture to culture and sometimes do not. In US culture, for instance, hugging, kissing, smiling, sharing prolonged mutual gaze, winking, holding hands, putting one's arm around another, and sharing physical proximity are examples of behaviors that are commonly used to encode affectionate messages and are commonly decoded as such, at least by others in the same cultures.

Although these gestures are referred to as "direct," their meaning is often more ambiguous than that of verbal statements. That is due partly to the relative specificity of language, as noted above, and partly to the fact that many direct nonverbal gestures of affection can be performed in multiple ways, each of which may carry a somewhat different meaning. The kiss is illustrative (Landau, 1989). Kisses can range in intensity from a perfunctory peck on the cheek to a prolonged, open-mouth-to-open-mouth encounter. Several aspects of a kiss might vary as a function of its intended meaning. Longer kisses may connote affection of a romantic nature, whereas shorter ones connote familial or platonic affection. A kiss on the mouth is often more intimate than a kiss on the cheek, and an open-mouth kiss is more intimate than a closed-mouth kiss. A "dry" kiss (with no tongue contact) might be used when nonromantic affection is conveyed, whereas romantic or sexual affection might call for a "wet" kiss (see, e.g., von Sadovszky, Keller, & McKinney, 2002).

Another example is the embrace (Floyd, 1999), which can also vary on multiple dimensions. One such dimension is duration; longer hugs are often used to convey more intense affection than shorter hugs. Another dimension is intensity, which is a function of both the pressure and the proportion of body contact. Intimates may engage in intense, full-body-contact embraces, whereas casual friends might prefer lighter hugs that are restricted to upper-body contact (see Gurevitch, 1990). Finally, hugs vary in their form, which is primarily a function of relative arm placement. Floyd (1999) referenced three forms of hugging: (1) the "criss-cross hug," in which each person has one arm above and one arm below the other's; (2) the "neck–waist hug," in which one person's arms wrap around the other's neck and the other person's arms wrap around the person's waist; and (3) the "engulfing hug," in which one person's arms are held together on his or her chest and the other's arms are wrapped entirely around this person. (See also van Raalte's 2017 explication of cuddling as a nonverbal affectionate behavior.)

Behaviors in this category are not limited to touch, however. People also convey affection through the use of distinctive vocal patterns. For instance, several studies have documented that in affectionate interactions with romantic partners, humans often adopt a vocalic pattern known as *baby talk* or *parentese* (Golinkoff, Can, Soderstrom, & Hirsh-Pasek, 2015), a form of speaking that mimics verbal interaction with infants. Baby talk has been observed in multiple cultures in North America, Asia, Europe, and Africa and is practiced both by men and women (regardless of whether they are parents) and by children (Fernald & Simon, 1984; Toda, Fogal, & Kawai, 1990). Apart from its linguistic features – which include the use of idioms and "pet" names, simplified sentence structure, and word repetition – baby talk is characterized by increased vocal pitch and pitch variance, exaggerated intonation, and a decrease in amplitude (Fernald & Simon, 1984; Zebrowitz, Brownlow, & Olson, 1992). Importantly, several studies have indicated that it is the acoustic properties of baby talk, rather than its linguistic features, that most strongly elicit positive affect from the receiver (Fernald, 1989, 1993; Werker & McLeod, 1989).

Farley, Hughes, and LaFayette (2013) demonstrated that some of these acoustic properties are evident in romantic partners' shared vocalic patterns even when the partners are not engaged in baby talk. These authors recruited adults to record five-minute conversational-style telephone calls with their romantic partner as well as with a close same-sex friend. Calls were not scripted, but participants were asked to pose the questions "How are you?" and "What are you doing?" at some point during their conversations. These phrases were analyzed for pitch, to test the prediction that men speak in a higher-pitched voice to their romantic partners than to their friends, whereas the opposite is true for women.

Acoustic analysis demonstrated that both sexes modulated their pitch in the manner hypothesized for the phrase "How are you?" Specifically, men spoke this phrase in a higher-pitched voice when addressing their romantic partners as opposed to their same-sex friends, whereas women spoke in a lower-pitched voice to romantic partners than to friends. Farley et al. (2013) also reported that third-party listeners could identify at a greater-than-chance level whether callers were saying "How are you?" to their romantic partners or to their friends. Moreover, independent raters perceived the vocal samples directed at romantic partners to reflect greater romantic interest than those directed at friends.

In a similar study, Floyd and Ray (2003) asked strangers to engage in a "get to know you" conversation. One participant in each dyad (a participant confederate) was instructed to act as though he or she either liked or disliked the partner. The acoustic properties of the confederate's voice during the conversation were analyzed with reference to the partner's assessment of how affectionate the confederate was. Contrary to the findings of Farley et al. (2013), Floyd and Ray found that greater affection was denoted by higher pitch for women and lower pitch for men – although it should be reiterated that Farley et al.'s participants were speaking to romantic partners, whereas Floyd and Ray's participants were speaking to same-sex strangers. Floyd and Ray also reported that greater variation in pitch encoded greater affection for both women and men.

Nonverbal behaviors are provocative, in part, *because* their meaning is often more ambiguous than that of verbal statements. The verbal content of the message "I love you" is consistent, always comprising those three words in that exact order. Its consistency does not imply that its meaning is always unambiguous (as noted above), but it does suggest that variation in its meaning cannot be attributed to variation in its verbal form, because no such variation exists. The same cannot be said for most direct nonverbal gestures of affection, raising the question of how variation in the form of a direct nonverbal gesture is associated with variation in its intended meaning and/or its interpreted meaning. Studies such as that of Floyd (1999) have begun to address this question, but there is much left to learn on this point.

Socially Supportive Behaviors

The final category in the model includes behaviors that are provisions of social or instrumental support. Such behaviors convey affection indirectly (and often discreetly), through acts of assistance, rather than via gestures that directly denote affectionate feelings. Some uses of these behaviors involve the provision of psychological or emotional support. For instance, relatives might show their affection to a newly widowed young mother by providing a sympathetic ear, making themselves available to her at all hours, empathizing with her plight, and telling her that she is going to "make it through." This type of support is closest to what social scientists typically consider "social support" (Goldsmith, 2008); however, the model also recognizes the provision of more instrumental types of support. For example, the relatives of the young mother might also show their affection by offering to babysit, bringing her meals, taking care of her yard work, and sending her money to help with her financial needs.

None of the support behaviors mentioned here encodes an affectionate message directly, in the manner that behaviors such as kissing or saying "I love you" do. Indeed, one can easily identify situations in which many of these behaviors would have no affectionate connotations whatsoever (a therapist lending a sympathetic ear or a social service agency sending money, for instance). When these behaviors are enacted *for the purpose of conveying affection*, however, they may do so in a more profound way than verbal statements or direct nonverbal gestures do.

The provision of a resource, whether money, time and effort, a material resource (such as the use of a car), or merely attention, is often significant both denotatively and connotatively to the recipient of such support. While denoting that "I wish to meet the need you are experiencing," such provisions also connote that "You are so important to me that I am willing to use my own resources to meet your need."

These types of social support behaviors seem to be outside the realm of traditional affectionate behaviors; if they were not, they would have been included among those behaviors already being measured in two-dimensional models. This observation alone might lead researchers not to include such behaviors in an operational definition of affectionate communication. If, however, the behaviors are used (at least in some types of relationships) for the purpose of expressing affection, and are decoded as such within these relationships, then the decision to exclude such behaviors from one's operational definition necessarily entails the risk of failing to capture the construct at any level beyond its most overt. Certainly, one need not incorporate every idiosyncratic form of expressing affection that is used within individual relationships; such a practice would, by definition, preclude generalizability. However, if a behavior or set of behaviors is used by groups of people or relationships for the purpose of encoding affectionate messages and is decoded as such by those people or in those relationships, then it inhibits the scientist's understanding of that construct to ignore such behaviors.

Social support behaviors are distinguished from verbal and direct nonverbal forms of affectionate communication by the relative indirectness with which they encode affectionate messages, which is consequential for at least three reasons. First, it makes them more likely to be overlooked by recipients. A hypothetical example concerns a husband who, advised by a marital therapist to show more affection to his wife, goes home and washes her car. He is later astonished that neither his wife nor their therapist recognized this instrumental behavior as an expression of affection, because to him, it clearly was. If he had instead kissed his wife and said he loved her, no such misunderstanding would have ensued.

Second, the relative indirectness of support behaviors as affectionate messages makes them more likely to be overlooked by third-party observers. This may, in fact, be one of their primary advantages over verbal and direct nonverbal gestures, because it allows people to express affection "covertly" if they choose, in ways that may not be evident to onlookers. Swain (1989) suggested that men may prefer to express affection for male friends through instrumental support behaviors, such as helping with a project, rather than more overtly. He proposed that using covert forms of affection protects men from possible ridicule or negative attributions from others, who may evaluate more overt expressions of affection as unmanly or feminine (see also Morman & Floyd, 1998, 1999; Parks & Floyd, 1996; Wood & Inman, 1993).

Finally, the relative indirectness of supportive behaviors as affectionate expressions is significant because researchers may overlook them. This is certainly not problematic if a researcher's goal is to study only overt expressions. For scholars who seek a broader understanding of affectionate communication within human relationships, however, a more inclusive conceptual definition is clearly warranted. It was for this reason, more than any other, that Floyd and Morman (1998) included support behaviors in their tripartite model.

A Note on Idiomatic Expressions

The tripartite model of affectionate communication was designed to include behaviors that are commonly used to encode affectionate messages and are typically decoded by recipients as such. Its companion operational definition, the Affectionate Communication Index (described later), captures specific behaviors within each of the three categories, but the list of behaviors is representative, not exhaustive. Of course, this is true of many operational definitions used in the social sciences, and the researcher aims, through careful selection of items and rigorous validity and reliability testing, to compile a list of referents for the variable being measured that will truly represent the variance to be captured. Science works to account for what is true of most people most of the time.

By focusing on the broad picture, however, social science inevitably misses idiosyncrasies that characterize people's behaviors in specific relationships.

There are several reasons why individuals may devise ways of expressing affection that are idiosyncratic to particular relationships. Perhaps people develop idioms that will allow them to express their affection to each other secretly. In the 1997 film *Bent*, two prisoners in a Nazi POW camp discover feelings of affection for each other but are too afraid of repercussions from the guards to express their feelings openly. Instead, they developed a code system whereby one would scratch his eyebrow and both would recognize it as an expression of affection. These types of idioms allow relational partners to communicate their affection openly in public contexts without concern for how others in the same context might respond.

Idioms of this nature may also allow people to express affection in situations when it simply might not be appropriate to express it more overtly (for instance, during a business meeting or a church service). Moreover, as Oring (1984) suggested, individuals can use idioms to underscore the intimacy of their relationships, because their use indicates that the users "know one another in ways unknown and unknowable to others" (p. 21). Finally, physical distance or other constraints may restrict relational partners' means of expressing affection. Consequently, relational partners may elect to establish means of conveying affection that circumvent these constraints, such as through the use of computer-mediated communication.

Although idioms defy generalization by definition, social scientists can still study patterns and purposes in their use. Bell, Buerkel-Rothfuss, and Gore (1987) examined idiom use in heterosexual romantic couples and reported that expressing affection was among the most common functions of personal idioms. They found that idioms for affection were more likely to be verbal than nonverbal and more likely to be used in public contexts than in private. They also discovered that it was usually the man in the relationship who invented idioms for affection. Moreover, for both men and women, the number of idioms for expressing affection was linearly related to reported levels of love, closeness, and commitment in the relationship (see also Hopper, Knapp, & Scott, 1981).

Identifying the variety of ways in which affection can be encoded is useful not only because it adds conceptual clarity to the concept of affectionate communication but, more pragmatically, because it can guide efforts to operationalize and measure the behavior. Scholars have developed a variety of operational approaches to studying affectionate communication, and the most common measures are described and critiqued subsequently.

Measuring Affectionate Communication

Research on affectionate communication has employed a diverse range of operational definitions, which is both a benefit and a shortcoming of this literature. Because people express affection in a wide variety of ways, the diversity of operational definitions has likely helped to capture that breadth of experience in a way that relying on only one or two measures may not. Conversely, it necessitates caution when comparing results identified with one measurement strategy and those identified with another.

By and large, affectionate behavior can be assessed through only two strategies: self-report and direct observation. Self-report measures are often maligned in social scientific research, and deservedly so, in many cases. Specifically, they can be susceptible to a number of limitations, including social desirability bias (van de Mortel, 2008), acquiescence response sets (Bernstein & Nunnally, 1994), response-shift bias (Howard & Dailey, 1979), inflation bias (Floyd, Generous, Clark, Simon, & McLeod, 2015), faulty memory and honesty (Subar et al., 2015), and questionable cross-cultural applicability (Beaton, Bombardier, Guillemin, & Ferraz, 2000). Self-reports of behavior are also frequently found to be faulty when compared with more objective measures (e.g., Garber, Nau, Erickson, Aikens, & Lawrence, 2004; but see Okura, Urban, Mahoney, Jacobsen, & Rodeheffer, 2004). These concerns – along with the unverified psychometric adequacy of many scales – have fueled long-standing criticisms of self-report measures except as indices of self-perception (e.g., McCroskey & McCroskey, 1988).

These are valid concerns, yet for the task of measuring affectionate communication, they must be weighed against the value and feasibility of the other operational alternative, direct observation. At least two issues make observation a suspect methodology for studying affectionate communication, except under very specific circumstances. First, affectionate behavior is often shared privately (Vaquera & Kao, 2005), in contexts that are inaccessible to observation. Second, affectionate behavior may occur too infrequently within a given relationship to be enumerated reliably by observation. Of course, observational methods in general are subject to their own limitations, including the Hawthorne effect (McCambridge, Witton, & Elbourne, 2014) and problematic interrater reliability (Tinsley & Weiss, 1975).

The sum of these observations is that, despite their well-articulated limitations, self-report measures serve an instrumental role in the study of affectionate communication. In the following sections, two general self-report measures that are common in the affectionate behavior research will be assessed: the Affectionate Communication Index and the Trait Affection Scale. These scales are widely used not only because of their psychometric adequacy but also because of their versatility in being unbound to any particular social context or type of relationship. Nonetheless, additional self-report and observational methods have been developed to index affectionate behavior within specified relationships (such as between grandparents and grandchildren) or within particular contexts (such as in schools or hospitals), and these measures are addressed subsequently.

The Affectionate Communication Index

Floyd and Morman (1998) pursued a measurement strategy for their tripartite model of affectionate behavior with the publication of the Affectionate Communication Index (ACI), one of the two most widely used operational definitions of affectionate communication in the scholarly literature (see also Floyd & van Raalte, in press). This section reviews the scale's development, psychometric adequacy, and dimensionality, and then comments on its limitations.

Scale Development

This measure was designed with the explicit goal of capturing native referents – those behaviors through which people report expressing affection in their close relationships – rather than imposing a set of behaviors identified a priori. Such an approach admittedly concedes some conceptual control at the outset, and some empiricists may find that a problematic concession. At the time of the measure's development, however, no comprehensive theory of affection exchange existed to inform a priori selection of behaviors to measure. The lack of existing theory, in addition to the observation that affectionate messages may intentionally be conveyed covertly, in ways not apparent to scholars, led Floyd and Morman to initiate scale development inductively by asking groups of individuals to indicate how they communicated affection in their most affectionate relationships. That strategy mirrored the approach advocated by Berscheid, Snyder, and Omoto (1989) in the development of their widely used measure of relational closeness, which is to investigate a construct within the context of the relationships in which it is most salient. Working with the initial list of participants' responses, Floyd and Morman eliminated items mentioned by less than 10 percent of the sample. This strategy narrowed their initial list to thirty-four items, which comprised a working version of the scale.

Table 3.1 *Representative items from the Affectionate Communication Index (Floyd & Morman, 1998)*

Dimension	Representative Items
Verbal	Say "I love you"
	Say "I care about you"
	Say he or she is one of your best friends
Nonverbal	Kiss on lips
	Kiss on cheek
	Hug him or her
	Put your arm around him or her
Social Support	Help him or her with problems
	Share private information
	Praise his or her accomplishments

Floyd and Morman presented the thirty-four items to a subsequent sample of participants who were asked to think of their most affectionate same- or opposite-sex relationship and to indicate, on a seven-point scale, how often they engaged in each of the behaviors *as a way to express affection in these relationships*. The original thirty-four items were subjected to principal components analyses using nonorthogonal (oblique) rotation, and Cattell's scree test indicated the utility of a three-component solution comprising verbal expressions, direct nonverbal gestures, and socially supportive behaviors. This factor structure was supported when independent data were submitted to confirmatory factor analyses.

The final version of the ACI contains eighteen items, with eight items assessing nonverbal affection, five items assessing verbal affection, and five items assessing socially supportive affection. Some representative items included in the ACI from each dimension appear in Table 3.1.

Psychometric Adequacy

Unlike other self-report measures of affectionate behavior (many of which are reviewed in Floyd & Morman, 1998), the ACI has successfully demonstrated multiple forms of psychometric adequacy (see, e.g., Floyd & Mikkelson, 2005). With respect to reliability, Floyd and Morman (1998) reported Cronbach's alpha coefficients of .91, .80, and .77 for nonverbal, verbal, and supportive subscales, respectively, and alpha coefficients were all $\geq$ .70 in supplemental studies reported by Floyd and Morman. Average internal reliability estimates have been higher in subsequent studies. For instance, Schrodt, Ledbetter, and Ohrt (2007) reported alpha coefficients of .87 for nonverbal affection, .80 for verbal affection, and .84 for supportive affection, whereas a later study by Park, Vo, and Tsong (2009) reported reliability estimates of .89 for nonverbal affection, .89 for verbal affection, and .89 for supportive affection (in both studies, coefficients were averaged between mothers and fathers). Similarly, in a study of adult sibling relationships, Myers, Byrnes, Frisby, and Mansson (2011) reported average reliability coefficients of .79 for verbal affection, .86 for nonverbal affection, and .80 for supportive affection (see also Rittenour, Myers, & Brann, 2007).

In the original publication of the scale, Floyd and Morman (1998) also subjected the ACI to test-retest reliability over a fourteen-day period. Scores were significantly correlated from time 1 to time 2 ($r = .87$ for verbal expressions, .89 for nonverbal expressions, and .83 for socially supportive expressions). Moreover, none of the subscale scores changed significantly during that two-week test. Both findings attest to the scale's stability.

With respect to validity, face validity was supported by the inductive nature of item generation. By asking respondents to generate referents of their own affectionate communication, rather than imposing items a priori, Floyd and Morman helped to ensure that the resulting scale would be a prima facie reflection of how individuals actually convey affection in their close relationships. In demonstrations of construct validity, the ACI was correlated with multiple scales with specific theorized outcomes, such as relational closeness ($r = .25$), psychological distance ($r = -.22$), and psychological affection ($r = .58$), and was uncorrelated with social desirability (.05; see Floyd & Morman, 1998). Discriminant validity was demonstrated when ACI scores differentiated between relationships known in advance to be highly affectionate or nonaffectionate (Floyd & Morman, 1998), and between biological and nonbiological family relationships (Floyd & Morman, 2003).

Dimensionality

Multiple studies have used the ACI in its dimensional form, often to compare forms of affection with each other or across relationship types (e.g., Floyd & Morman, 2001). As addressed previously, all three subscales show adequate internal reliability; however, the nonverbal subscale usually (although not always) demonstrates the highest internal consistency due to its larger number of items (compared with the verbal and socially supportive subscales).

For the sake of parsimony, and when there is no theoretic or exploratory reason to differentiate between verbal, nonverbal, and socially supportive forms of affectionate behavior, some studies use the ACI unidimensionally, as an overall assessment of the level of affectionate communication in a given relationship. This is a viable use of the instrument, and it tends also to produce adequate reliability estimates. For instance, Morman and Floyd (2001) reported an overall alpha coefficient of .89 for fathers in their study, and the same for sons.

Limitations

Despite its psychometric adequacy and its widespread use in affectionate communication research, the ACI is limited in some important ways. First, the items reflect behaviors that emerged as indicators of affection in data collected primarily from Caucasian, middle-class American adults. As such, it may not include behaviors that are instrumental for the expression of affection in other cultural and socioeconomic groups (see, e.g., Mansson & Sigurðardóttir, 2017; Mansson et al., 2016). Similarly, it was not designed to account for idiosyncratic expressions of affection, which can be potent in personal relationships (Bell & Healey, 1992).

An additional limitation is that the ACI measures the frequency of various affectionate behaviors without accounting for potential variation in their intensity. Some behaviors, such as kissing on the lips, have more intimate connotations than others, such as helping with a task (Floyd, 1997b). The ACI does not weight items differently depending on their perceived intensity, however, thereby failing to account for such differences.

Finally, completing the ACI requires participants to report on one particular relationship. That is, it can assess an individual's level of affectionate behavior within a single, specified relationship (whether a dyadic relationship, such as a marriage, or a small-group relationship, such as a nuclear family). This is not a limitation of the measure, per se, as the ACI was designed specifically for this purpose. However, it does pose a limitation to the measure's utility, insofar as the ACI does not assess an individual's typical or trait-like level of affectionate behavior, independent of a particular relationship. To remedy this limitation, Floyd (2002) developed the Trait Affection Scale.

Trait Affection Scale

Most people behave more affectionately in some relationships and some circumstances than in others. Nonetheless, individuals also evidence a typical level or trait-like tendency, wherein some people are simply more affectionate than others, irrespective of the relationship or context. Particularly as researchers began pursuing questions surrounding the mental and physical wellness implications of being highly affectionate (as a trait), it became clear that a relationally bound measure of affectionate behavior would be inadequate. This observation sparked the construction of the Trait Affection Scale (TAS; see Floyd & Generous, in press). This section reviews the scale's development, psychometric adequacy, dimensionality, and limitations.

Scale Development

The TAS assesses an individual's typical or trait-like level of affectionate communication. The instrument asks participants to indicate how much they agree or disagree with each of sixteen statements as descriptions of themselves. Ten statements comprise the Trait Affection Scale – Given (TAS-G), which measures a person's general tendency to give or express affection to others. Five items are positively worded (e.g., "I consider myself to be a very affectionate person") and five are negatively worded (e.g., "I'm not a very affectionate person"). Six statements comprise the Trait Affection Scale – Received (TAS-R), which assesses the individual's tendency to receive expressions of affection from others. Four items are positively worded (e.g., "People are always telling me that they like me, love me, or care about me") and two are negatively worded (e.g., "Most of the people I know don't express affection to me very often"). Both measures first appeared in Floyd (2002). TAS-G and TAS-R are usually administered using a seven-point scale (1 = strongly disagree; 7 = strongly agree), although some studies have employed a five-point scale (e.g., Lewis, Heisel, Reinhart, & Tian, 2011).

The TAS-G was originally developed not as a stand-alone measure, but instead for use as a manipulation check. Floyd (2002) recruited known-divergent samples of highly affectionate and less-affectionate adults and created the TAS-G to confirm that the two groups differed in their trait-level tendencies to express affection. Unlike with the ACI, the items for TAS-G were constructed a priori to assess whether individuals have a tendency to be highly affectionate. In Floyd's (2002) manipulation check, 92 percent of the variance in the TAS-G score was accounted for by group membership (i.e., whether the individuals were in the high- or low-affection condition).

In the Floyd (2002) study, TAS-R served as a dependent variable, having been constructed to index how much affection an individual typically receives from others. The groups composed of highly affectionate and less-affectionate adults differed significantly in their tendency to receive affectionate expressions from others, with 49 percent of the variance in TAS-R accounted for by group membership.

Psychometric Adequacy

In published research, Cronbach alpha coefficients have been .79 or higher for TAS-G (see Floyd et al., 2005) and .84 or higher for TAS-R (Floyd, Hesse, & Haynes, 2007). These values indicate that both the TAS-G and TAS-R are internally consistent measures. As mentioned below, some researchers have also averaged the scores from the TAS-R and TAS-G to create a composite trait affection score, and that procedure has produced alpha coefficients of .93 or higher (see Floyd, Pauley, & Hesse, 2010; Hesse & Floyd, 2008; Pauley, Hesse, & Mikkelson, 2014).

Several studies support the construct validity of the TAS, whether used as individual subscales or averaged to form one composite score. For example, Floyd, Hess, et al. (2005) reported that TAS-G scores were positively correlated with social activity ($r = .38$), relationship satisfaction ($r = .36$), and the likelihood of being in a romantic relationship ($r = .25$). TAS-G scores were negatively correlated with markers of insecure attachment, such as discomfort with closeness ($r = -.67$), fear of intimacy ($r = -.53$), and the perception that relationships are unimportant ($r = -.50$). Hesse and Trask (2014) also reported that secure attachment was directly related to both TAS-G ($\beta = .49$) and TAS-R ($\beta = .24$) and that fearful attachment was inversely related to TAS-G ($\beta = -.51$) and TAS-R ($\beta = -.11$), whereas dismissive attachment was associated with TAS-G ($\beta = -.43$) but not TAS-R.

Hesse and Floyd (2008) used a composite trait affection score representing the mean of TAS-G and TAS-R and reported an inverse association with alexithymia, an inability to encode and interpret displays of emotion ($r = -.56$). With respect to personality traits, Floyd, Hess, et al. (2005, study one) reported that TAS-G was positively related to extraversion ($r = .61$) and negatively related to psychoticism ($r = -.56$) and neuroticism ($r = -.22$). Notably, all three correlations remained significant even after controlling for the effect of received affection (TAS-R scores). The third study in Floyd, Hess, et al. also reported that TAS-G scores predicted liking ($r = .49$), love ($r = .50$), and relationship satisfaction ($r = .59$) in participants' close relationships. Lewis et al. (2011) even found that a composite trait affection score predicted relative electrical activity in the left anterior cortex of the brain versus the right anterior cortex.

Dimensionality

Scores for TAS-G and TAS-R usually represent the means of the items for each respective subscale. Some studies, including Floyd (2002) and Floyd, Hesse, Boren, and Veksler (2014), have examined the effects of the two subscales separately. Other studies have kept the two subscales separate but have assessed the influence of TAS-G while controlling for the effects of TAS-R (see Floyd, Hess, et al., 2005; Floyd, Hesse, et al., 2007).

Depending on the purpose and predictions of a given study, however, there may be no reason to separate the amount of affection one typically expresses from the amount he or she typically receives. In such instances, as mentioned above, scores from the two subscales can be combined to provide one holistic measure of trait affectionate communication, as in studies by Floyd, Pauley, et al. (2010), Hesse and Floyd (2008), and Pauley et al. (2014).

Recently, Hesse (personal communication, November 7, 2017) performed a confirmatory factor analysis on data using the TAS, structuring the analysis with two correlated latent variables representing TAS-G and TAS-R. Model fit was strong, with the comparative fit index exceeding .95 and the root mean square error of approximation below .075.

Limitations

Despite its utility, the TAS suffers certain limitations. For instance, some items in the scale are double-barreled, such as "I love giving people hugs or putting my arms around them" and "People are always telling me that they like me, love me, or care about me." Using double-barreled items has been identified as problematic in scale construction by other interpersonal communication scholars (see Stafford, 2010, for a discussion of this issue with the Relational Maintenance Strategies Measure). Moreover, no published evidence yet addresses the test–retest reliability of the TAS, which would be expected to be high if both scales index a trait.

Context-Specific Measures

The ACI and TAS are both largely context-nonspecific assessments, with the former measuring the amount of affection characterizing a specific relationship (regardless of context) and the latter measuring an individual's trait levels of affection expressed and received (regardless of context or relationship). Because they are untied to any particular contexts, both measures are relatively versatile, as their common use in affectionate communication research attests. Their generalized nature may make them less sensitive to the nuances of specific contexts in which affection exchange occurs, however. Over the years, several other measures have been developed to assess levels of affectionate behavior in particular communication platforms, with particular relationships or constituencies, and/or in particular social situations, and the most common of these are reviewed subsequently.

Affectionate Communication on Facebook

For a study of college students' expressions of affection to platonic friends via the social media platform Facebook, Mansson and Myers (2011) developed a two-part self-report measure assessing the *amount* of affection communicated via Facebook and the *appropriateness* of affection expressed in this manner. To create an initial set of items, the authors asked 47 undergraduate students to "identify the ways in which they communicated affection, based on Floyd's definition of affectionate communication, to their close friends through Facebook" (p. 160). This procedure generated 51 potential items, which were then rated for face validity by a separate sample of 56 undergraduate students. A total of 29 items remained after the second step. Many of these items are genuinely unique to the social media platform, such as "add as friends," "tag them in pictures," and "comment on their wall." Others are more general, applicable to both online and offline interaction, such as "send them a gift," "offer support when friends are going through a lot," and "congratulate them on accomplishments" (Mansson & Myers, 2011, p. 162).

Finally, 214 research participants were presented with the 29 items and asked to indicate both the extent to which they used each behavior as a way to express affection to their platonic friends on Facebook and the extent to which they believed each behavior was appropriate as a means of expressing affection. Both assessments were collected using seven-point Likert scales.

Principal components factor analyses initially suggested a multifactor structure for both subscales (amount of affection and appropriateness of affection). In both cases, however, multiple items cross-loaded on two or more factors, and the first factor accounted for a substantial proportion of the total variance, leading Mansson and Myers to treat both subscales as unidimensional. Floyd's TAS-G was significantly correlated with both the amount of affection subscale ($r = .37$) and the appropriateness of affection subscale ($r = .38$).

Affection Received from Grandparents

Much of Mansson's research program has been directed at identifying the correlates of affectionate communication that grandchildren receive from their grandparents. Rather than using the relationship-nonspecific ACI, Mansson has systematically developed and tested the Grandchildren's Received Affection Scale (GRAS; Mansson, 2013c, d, e). Like the ACI, the GRAS was initiated inductively, in this case by asking young adults to identify behaviors that their grandparents used to communicate affection to them. A list of 64 unique items was then pilot tested with additional samples of young adults, and a 48-item version of the scale was subsequently tested for reliability, validity, and factor structure.

A series of principal components analyses eventually yielded a 17-item scale comprising four factors: (1) love and esteem (e.g., "Tells me s/he loves me"), (2) caring (e.g., "Asks me how things are going"), (3) memories and humor (e.g., "Tells me jokes"), and (4) celebratory affection (e.g., "Sends cards for my birthday and holidays"). Mansson (2013e) reported internal reliability estimates of .91 for love and esteem, .91 for caring, .78 for memories and humor, and .73 for celebratory affection, whereas Bernhold and Giles (2017) reported reliabilities of .92, .92, .83, and .70, respectively. All four subscales demonstrate significant correlations with important relational qualities in the grandparent–grandchild relationship, including liking, relational satisfaction, and communication satisfaction (Mansson, 2013e). A separate study (Mansson, 2013c) established that the GRAS subscales are significantly correlated with the TAS-R and the verbal, nonverbal, and support subscales of the ACI, and uncorrelated with a measure of social desirability. Supporting the scale's uniqueness, Mansson (2013c) also demonstrated that grandchildren's GRAS scores loaded on separate factors than their TAS-R scores when subjected to exploratory factor analysis.

Scales for Emotionally Impaired Children

Sofronoff and colleagues (e.g., Sofronoff, Eloff, Sheffield, & Attwood, 2011; Sofronoff, Lee, Sheffield, & Attwood, 2014; see also Andrews, Attwood, & Sofronoff, 2013) have developed a program of research to study the communication of affection in children with functional impairments, such as Asperger syndrome, high-functioning autism, and pervasive developmental disorder. As part of this program, they have developed three self-report measures to assess parents' perceptions of their children's experiences of affectionate communication.

General Affection Questionnaire

The General Affection Questionnaire (GAQ) consists of twelve items assessing (1) parents' perceptions of a child's level of affection (e.g., "He/she shows a lack of affection"), (2) the child's knowledge of affection (e.g., "I have had to spend time teaching him/her about affection"), (3) the appropriateness of a child's affection (e.g., "He/she uses inappropriate expressions of affection"), and (4) the detrimental effects of a child's discomfort with affection (e.g., "He/she has difficulties with affection that cause problems with his/her siblings"). Sofronoff et al. (2011) reported an average internal reliability coefficient of .81.

Affection for You Questionnaire

The nineteen-item Affection for You Questionnaire (AYQ) measures parents' reports of how much their children communicate affection to them. Despite its title's focus on a child's expressed affection, the scale comprises five subscales assessing a mix of expressed and received messages: (1) giving verbal affection to you, (2) giving physical affection to you, (3) receiving verbal affection from you, (4) receiving physical affection from you, and (5) communicating empathy to you. Sofronoff et al. (2011) reported internal reliability scores for the five subscales ranging from .90 to .95.

Affection for Others Questionnaire

Finally, the twenty-item Affection for Others Questionnaire (AOQ) uses the same five subscales from the AYQ to assess parents' perceptions of how much affection their children express to and receive from others besides the parents themselves. For this scale, Sofronoff et al. (2011) reported internal reliability scores for the five subscales ranging from .85 to .94.

Positive Verbal Parenting

Polcari and Teicher (2007) created a Verbal Affection Questionnaire (VAQ), a twelve-item instrument measuring the frequency of positive verbal expressions from parents. Items include the parent saying he or she loves the child, "offering praise, providing verbal comfort, expressing affection through stories or singing for younger children, and engaging in meaningful conversations for an older child" (Polcari, Rabi, Bolger, & Teicher, 2014, p. 95). Based on confirmatory principal components analysis, Polcari and Teicher (2007) identified a two-factor solution for mothers, consisting of one factor assessing verbal love and praise from infancy through childhood, and a second factor assessing praise, verbal comfort, and meaningful conversation during adolescence. The paternal version of the scale yielded a single-factor solution. Polcari and Teicher reported internal consistencies of .95 for mothers and .97 for fathers.

Teacher Affection

Botkin and Twardosz (1988) modified a previously developed coding scheme (Twardosz, Schwartz, Fox, & Cunningham, 1979; see also Twardosz et al., 1987) for assessing preschool teachers' expressions of affection toward students. The specific categories coded were (1) smiling, which included smiles and laughs except those done to ridicule others; (2) affectionate words; (3) active affectionate physical contact, including hugging, playful wrestling, and tickling; and (4) passive affectionate physical contact, including hand-holding and holding another on one's lap. According to the coding scheme, passive affectionate physical contact behaviors had to occur for a minimum of five consecutive seconds to be coded, whereas any duration was sufficient for the other categories. Teacher behavior was coded in ten-second intervals.

Interrater reliabilities were unreported by Botkin and Twardosz (1988). The coding scheme was validated by comparing the scores of trained observers with those of third-party community volunteers. Correlations between observers' and volunteers' ratings ranged from .57 to .69, indicating relatively high agreement.

Maternal Affection with NICU Infants

Christopher, Bauman, and Veness-Meehan (1999) developed the Affectionate Behavior Assessment (ABA) for coding mothers' affectionate behaviors toward their infants in neonatal intensive care units (NICUs). The ABA was based on a coding protocol previously developed by Minde and colleagues (Minde, Marton, Manning, & Hines, 1980; Minde et al., 1978). The coding scheme included five behaviors: (1) noninstrumental touch, or touch from the mother that was unrelated to routine care; (2) smiling at baby; (3) looking at baby; (4) looking specifically at the baby's face; and (5) vocalizing to the infant. Christopher et al. trained NICU nurses to conduct APA coding of mothers during fifteen-minute intervals. Intraclass correlations used to assess interrater reliabilities were .54 for noninstrumental touch, .68 for smiling, .33 for looking at baby, .65 for looking at baby's face, and .80 for vocalizing. The scale produced an overall Cronbach's alpha coefficient of .85 based on 107 total observations.

Assessing Affectionate Communication Measurement

As noted above, the diversity in operational approaches to affectionate communication has been a strength in terms of capturing the diversity of the construct but a limitation in terms of facilitating comparisons across studies. Although much research has used either the ACI or the TAS, a substantial proportion of the literature has not, so other operational definitions certainly cannot be overlooked. Overall, then, what is the adequacy of affectionate communication measurement? At least two issues are pertinent to that question: how well operational definitions represent the construct, and how generalizable their findings are.

The issue of representation refers not only to whether a measure assesses what it is intended to measure – affectionate communication, in this case – which is, at heart, a question of validity. It also refers to whether the measure is assessing the diversity of that construct adequately. Whether intentionally or not, many existing measures of affectionate communication conform to Floyd and Morman's (1998) tripartite model, in which affection is expressed through verbal state-ments, nonverbal gestures, or socially supportive behaviors. For instance, Mansson and Myers's (2011) measure of affection expressed on Face-book includes items that represent verbal ("comment on their wall"), nonverbal ("tag them in pictures"), and supportive ("offer support when friends are going through a lot") modes of expression, even though it does not divide into discrete subscales for these separate modalities. The same is true of Mansson's (2013c) GRAS; although it divides into sub-scales for love and esteem, caring, memories and humor, and celebratory affection, its items represent verbal ("tells me s/he loves me"), nonverbal ("listens to what I have to say"), and supportive ("sends cards for birthday") forms of expression. Sofronoff et al.'s (2011) GAQ is not composed of items measuring the frequency of specific forms of affec-tionate behavior, but their AOQ and AYQ scales also index verbal ("give 'I love you'"), nonverbal ("give a pat on the back"), and supportive ("shows interest") behaviors. Nonverbal behavior is understandably absent from Polcari and Teicher's (2007) VAQ, whereas supportive behavior is absent from Botkin and Twardosz's (1988) teacher affection coding scheme and from Christopher et al.'s (1999) ABA, but on bal-ance, all three forms are well represented in existing operational definitions.

The key question is whether the construct of affectionate communi-cation is adequately assessed by measuring its verbal, nonverbal, and socially supportive forms. Empirical evidence to this effect comes from Floyd and Morman's (1998) original articulation of the tripartite model and the ACI, which (as described earlier) took an inductive approach to indexing the types of behaviors people use to communicate affection in their close relationships. As noted, the populations sampled in that process were relatively homogenous in their ethnic and cultural back-grounds, and that raises the distinct possibility that *specific items* used to measure affection – such as kissing on the lips or saying "I love you" – may be less relevant in some cultural contexts than in others (although see Jankowiak, Volsche, & Garcia, 2015). Putting variation in specific items aside, however, we may ask: Are the *categories* of verbal, nonverbal, and supportive behaviors adequate for capturing affectionate behavior?

Given that the categories of "verbal" and "nonverbal" are effectively both mutually exclusive and exhaustive, one might be inclined to say that those two categories, on their own, are by definition adequate to capture the diversity of affectionate behavior. That is not an inaccurate statement, especially insofar as behaviors labeled as supportive – and even behaviors labeled as idiomatic – are still either verbal or nonverbal in nature. In Floyd and Morman's tripartite model and ACI, the inclusion of the category of supportive behaviors is not meant to suggest a type of behavior that is neither verbal nor nonverbal but of some other variety entirely; rather, it is to distinguish between behaviors that are readily interpreted as affectionate and those that often encode their affectionate meaning more covertly, through the provision of an emotional or instrumental resource. Given that individuals in some relationships identify socially supportive behaviors as not only the most frequent but also the most valued means of conveying affection (see, e.g., Morman & Floyd, 1999), it seems important for the sake of representing the diversity of affectionate forms to include supportive behaviors alongside more direct verbal and nonverbal actions when operationally defining affectionate communication.

The second important evaluation point is the extent to which a measure produces findings that are generalizable. This, of course, is related to how well the measure represents the construct, but a more consequential characteristic is how bound a measure is to a specific type of relationship, social context, or channel of communicating. Specificity as to the relationship, context, or channel being examined in a measure is a dual-edged sword for research. A measure that is bound to a particular relationship, for instance, can perhaps illuminate interactions in that relationship better than a measure that is not relationally bound. Similarly, social contexts and communication channels have unique nuances that are better adjudicated by measures that address them than by measures that do not. Conversely, however, the more relationally, contextually, or channel-bound a measure is, the less generalizable its findings will be to other relationships, contexts, and channels, and the less comparable its results will be to those of other studies.

On this point, existing operational definitions of affectionate behavior can be said to run the gamut from those that are not bound to any particular relationship type, social context, or communication channel to those that are highly specific. Floyd and Morman's (1998) ACI, although intended to index affectionate communication within a specified relationship, is not bound to the *type* of relationship being examined. That is, it is no more relevant for marriages or romantic partnerships than for friendships or family relationships. Similarly, it is not bound to any particular social context – for example, it does not index affectionate communication exchanged only at home or in school – and it represents a variety of prospective communication channels.

At the other end of the spectrum are scales designed specifically for particular relationships, such as Polcari and Teicher's (2007) VAQ (measuring affectionate behavior between parents and children) and Mansson's (2013c) GRAS (measuring affectionate communication between grandparents and grandchildren). Some measures are also bound to specific social contexts, including Botkin and Twardosz's (1988) coding scheme for teacher–student affection in preschool and Christopher et al.'s (1999) ABA (measuring mother–infant affection in the NICU). Finally, some measures, such as Mansson and Myers's (2011) assessment of affectionate communication on Facebook, are intentionally designed for a specific communication channel.

To be certain, there is utility in both broad and specific measurement strategies. If a given relationship, context, or channel is different enough from others that a broad measure fails to capture its unique characteristics, then researchers may choose to sacrifice generalizability for the sake of specificity. For example, Sofronoff et al.'s (2011) measures of affectionate communication with emotionally impaired children likely illuminate that behavior in a way that a broader measure, such as the ACI, would not. Similarly, expressing affection to infants in the NICU may be sufficiently different from expressing affection to infants in other contexts as to warrant a context-specific measure.

It is useful to point out, however, that many items on relationship-, context-, or channel-specific scales are *relevant* for their particular focus, but are not *unique* to that focus. As noted above, for instance, Mansson and Myers's (2011) measure of affection on Facebook includes several items that are unique to that context, such as "add as friend" and "comment on their wall," but also items that are not unique to Facebook or even to social media in general, such as "send them a gift" or "congratulate them on accomplishments." This is an important consideration when choosing between a general or more specific instrument, because to the extent an instrument includes items that are not unique to (or, at least, highly characteristic of) the relationship, context, or channel on which it focuses, that instrument loses some of its advantages over a broader, more generalizable operational approach.

Although the majority of affectionate communication research has *measured* the phenomenon, affectionate behavior is often instead *manipulated* in experimental studies. A brief summary of manipulation strategies appears subsequently.

Manipulating Affectionate Communication

When a researcher's objective is to examine how affectionate behavior *influences* – rather than simply covaries with – some type of outcome, experimental design dictates manipulating rather than measuring it. Fewer studies have taken this approach, but those that do have at least three general manipulation strategies. These can be categorized as face-to-face manipulations, written manipulations, and visual manipulations.

Face-to-Face Manipulations

Some studies have aimed to ascertain how engaging in affectionate interaction with a partner affects the actor, the partner, or both in some way. One method for doing so is to fashion a dyadic interaction wherein partners are induced to interact in an affectionate manner, usually for a specified duration. For instance, Grewen, Girdler, Amico, and Light (2005) sought to determine how a period of "warm contact" would affect romantic partners' blood pressure and stress hormone levels. In this experimental condition, couples were seated on a loveseat and instructed to sit close together, to hold hands if that felt natural, and to talk about a time when they felt close as a couple. Physiological outcomes were measured from participants during this condition and compared with pre- and post-contact resting conditions to determine the effects of affectionate contact (see also Grewen, Anderson, Girdler, & Light, 2003). This strategy provides a minimally invasive set of instructions to participants, allowing them to enact those instructions as they choose and hopefully to create a genuinely affectionate interaction. Pauley, Floyd, and Hesse (2015) adopted a similar manipulation strategy in a later experiment involving both romantic partners and platonic friends.

A second face-to-face strategy is to instruct experimental participants to enact a specific affectionate behavior. To determine the effects of kissing on allergic reactions, for instance, Kimata (2003, 2006) induced participants to kiss their spouses or romantic partners for thirty minutes while alone in a room listening to soft music. This strategy has also been employed in field experiments; Floyd et al. (2009) instructed participants to kiss their romantic partners more frequently than usual for a six-week period, and van Raalte (2017) instructed romantic couples to cuddle more than usual for a similar period.

Finally, some face-to-face studies employ the use of a confederate to enact affectionate behavior, usually for the purpose of determining how the recipient responds. Both Floyd and Voloudakis (1999a) and Ray and Floyd (2006) utilized a participant confederate. Participants were recruited in those experiments to take part in a conversation, and one participant in each dyad was randomly selected to receive specific instructions about how to act during the conversation (becoming the participant confederate). For instance, participant confederates in the high-affection condition of the Floyd and Voloudakis study were instructed to "increase the extent to which they communicated a sense of closeness, liking, affection, and appreciation toward the naïve participant" in the second of two experimental conversations (p. 350). Ray and Floyd instructed participant confederates in their high-affection condition simply to "act like you really like your partner" (p. 53).

Using participant confederates is advantageous in that it allows this role to be enacted by a relational partner, such as one's spouse, relative, or friend. Thus, it is optimal for experiments examining the effects of manipulated affectionate behavior in existing close relationships. Because they are simply instructed in their role – rather than trained – however, participant confederates often evidence substantial variation in how they portray affectionate behavior, which hampers consistency in the behaviors to which their partners are responding. An alternate strategy is to use trained confederates, who are in the employ of the researcher. To examine the conditions under which people reciprocate affectionate expressions, for example, Floyd and Burgoon (1999) trained two male and two female confederates to modify specific behaviors during a "get to know each other" conversation with strangers. Confederates received extensive individual and group training in behaviors such as eye contact, smiling, touch, proximity, forward lean, and postural mirroring, and were consequently able to enact those behaviors in a manner that was highly consistent across confederates and conversations. Besides being more costly and labor-intensive than using participant confederates, however, the use of trained confederates is largely limited to experiments examining interaction between strangers.

Written Manipulations

Among studies manipulating the enactment of affectionate behavior, an altogether different approach has been to induce participants to express affection to a target in writing. In two experiments, Floyd, Mikkelson, Tafoya, et al. (2007a) and Floyd, Mikkelson, Hesse, and Pauley (2007) instructed participants to write a love letter to the person with whom they had the closest, most affectionate relationship. In both instances, participants were asked to describe, in writing, why they loved and cared for the other person so much.

This strategy has two advantages over face-to-face manipulations, the first being that the target of one's affectionate message need not be present at the time of the experiment. Researchers can therefore recruit individuals rather than dyads, which is usually faster and simpler. Second, having a written product allows researchers, if they choose, to analyze the writing for its linguistic features, as Pennebaker has done in several investigations (Pennebaker & King, 1999; Tausczik & Pennebaker, 2009).

Some research has instead used written depictions to gauge individuals' cognitive reactions to affectionate behavior. In an experiment by Floyd and Morman (2000b), for example, participants read a transcript of a conversation, ostensibly between either two men or two women, in which one communicator says "I love you" to the other. Participants were asked to read the transcript, make evaluative judgments about the conversation, and indicate the type of relationship they believed the communicators shared with each other. Similarly, Floyd and Morman (1997) asked young adults to report on their relationship with either a same- or opposite-sex friend or sibling, and then to imagine themselves in one of four scenarios. The scenarios were manipulated for their level of contextual privacy (public vs. private setting) and emotional intensity (emotionally intense vs. emotionally neutral). After reading each scenario, participants indicated how appropriate they would consider it to receive each of thirteen different verbal and nonverbal forms of affectionate behavior from their target sibling or friend.

Visual Manipulations

Whereas some experiments have focused on inducing the enactment of affectionate communication, others have instead examined how people react to affectionate behaviors that they observe visually among others. Studies in this vein have used a variety of stimuli to present participants with representations of affectionate behavior and to measure their evaluation of the same. To determine how participants' homophobia influenced their perception of an observed same-sex embrace, Floyd (2000a) showed participants a series of three photographs depicting two actors walking toward each other, hugging, and then walking away from each other. Similarly, to see how the form and duration of an embrace affected observers' perceptions of its appropriateness, Floyd (1999) created video segments of two actors alternating three different forms of an embrace for three different durations, and each experimental participant saw and evaluated one such video.

Compared with measures, manipulations offer the advantage of serving as a cause in a cause-and-effect relationship, thereby supporting causal inferences. To examine whether sharing affection decreases stress or increases feelings of intimacy, for instance, it is insufficient simply to measure affectionate behavior and determine its correlation to those outcomes; the affectionate behavior must be manipulated in some fashion to answer that question.

Regardless of the form or purpose of a manipulation, however, experimental design demands that the success of the manipulation be evaluated separately from its effects. This is the idea behind a manipulation check, and it serves to ensure that the manipulation functioned as intended, regardless of whether it produced the hypothesized outcome. In a study predicting that hugging lowers blood pressure, for example, participants may be instructed to hug for twenty minutes while their cardiovascular activity is monitored. If participants experience a decrease in blood pressure in the wake of hugging, that may at first glance seem sufficient to conclude that the manipulation "worked." In reality, although it worked in the sense of producing a predicted outcome, that in itself is not a guarantee that the manipulation was actually enacted as designed. In this instance, the researcher must have some way of verifying that participants did, in fact, hug for twenty minutes, such as by videotaping and coding their behavior or by asking them to verify that they followed instructions. Without independently verifying that the manipulation operated as intended, one cannot claim experimental success even if the hypothesized outcome – lowered blood pressure, in this example – was observed.

4   Predicting Affectionate Behavior

Even anecdotal observations support the contention that some people are more affectionate than others. That is true at a trait level, such that some individuals are highly affectionate and others less so, regardless of the relationships or circumstances in which they are communicating. It is also true at a state level, such that one person is more affectionate than another in the same specific relationships or circumstances. This variation begs explanation, and research has begun to illuminate how both innate and environmental factors influence the tendency to be affectionate.

This chapter begins by reviewing individual differences, including the effects of genetics, neurological activity, hormone levels, sex, gender, age, and attachment style. Next, research on the effects of culture and familial environment is described, followed by research on the influence of contextual characteristics. A brief discussion of the interplay between innate and environmental factors concludes the chapter.

Individual Differences in Affectionate Behavior

When it comes to predicting how affectionate individuals are, researchers have generally taken one of two approaches. One goal has been to account for variance in people's trait affection levels – that is, their general levels of affectionate behavior, irrespective of the relationships in which they share it. A second, and more common, goal has been to predict people's levels of affectionate communication within specific relationships, such as marriages, friendships, and familial bonds. Operationally, this difference mirrors that between the measurement strategies of the Trait Affection Scale (trait-level measurement) and the Affectionate Communication Index (relational-level measurement), which were detailed in Chapter 3.

Besides varying in what, specifically, they are attempting to predict, these two approaches have also differed in the types of antecedents they have tended to examine. As described below, research to predict trait affection levels has focused principally on innate influences, such as differences at the genetic, neurological, and hormonal levels. On the contrary, research to predict relationship-specific affection levels has prioritized environmental influences such as learning, culture, and social expectations related to sex and gender. This difference is not absolute, insofar as research predicting relational affection has also considered the influence of personality, which is highly heritable (Vukasović & Bratko, 2015). On balance, however, more is currently known about innate predictors of trait affection levels and environmental predictors of relational affection levels than vice versa.

This section reviews research on multiple individual differences accounting for variance in trait or relational affection levels. Innate influences – such as genetic effects, neurological activity, hormone levels, and biological sex – are reviewed first, followed by other individual differences and familial and environmental effects. Relationship-type differences in affectionate behavior (as opposed to individual differences) are addressed in Chapter 6.

Genetic Effects

As Chapter 3 described, affectionate communication is often measured as a behavioral trait rather than as a discrete behavior. People can certainly vary from occasion to occasion in how affectionate they choose to be, as their goals or the demands of the situation dictate. Nonetheless, multiple studies – beginning with Floyd (2002) – have shown that individuals also have a trait-like set point for giving and receiving affectionate behavior. Situational variation aside, some people have the trait of being highly affectionate, whereas others are moderate and others are low on this trait. This manner of thinking about affectionate communication has an analogy in personality psychology. If the situation calls for it, most anyone can behave in an outgoing manner, yet at the trait level, individuals vary along a continuum between introversion and extraversion (Larsen & Buss, 2017). Humans similarly vary along a continuum between highly affectionate and nonaffectionate, and some research suggests that differences in genetics, neurological function, and baseline hormone levels account for portions of that variance.

Although still very much in its infancy, research has identified some specific genetic differences that account for variance in individuals' levels of trait affection and similar behavioral tendencies. Most of this research has focused on single-nucleotide polymorphisms on the human oxytocin receptor gene.

Oxytocin is a peptide hormone produced by the hypothalamus and released by the pituitary gland (Uvnäs-Moberg, Arn, & Magnusson, 2005).

As with all hormones, oxytocin is active only on cells containing a receptor, a molecular protein that fulfills the hormone's instructions to affect a cell's metabolism. The receptor for oxytocin is encoded by the oxytocin receptor gene (*OXTR*), which appears in humans on the third chromosome. Some genes, including *OXTR*, evidence single-nucleotide polymorphisms (SNPs, pronounced "snips"). These are variations in one of four single nucleotides – adenine (A), thymine (T), cytosine (C), or guanine (G) – that occur at a specific position in the genome for at least 1 percent of the population.

Researchers have known for some time that people with different genotypes on specific single-nucleotide polymorphisms on *OXTR* differ from each other in their levels of various prosocial behaviors. The most common focus thus far has been on empathy. For instance, Rodrigues, Saslow, Garcia, John, and Keltner (2009) examined a specific SNP on *OXTR*, called rs53576. This SNP comes in three genotypes, or pairs of nucleotides: AA, AG, and GG. Rodrigues and colleagues recruited 192 young adults who varied – as confirmed by a salivary DNA test – in which rs53576 genotype they carried. These participants completed the "Reading the Mind in the Eyes" test, a task in which they are shown thirty-six black-and-white photographs of different individuals' eyes and are asked to identify each individual's affective state by choosing from among four options (e.g., "jealous," "panicked," "arrogant," "hateful"; see Baron-Cohen, Wheelwright, Hill, Raste, & Plumb, 2001). The researchers predicted that genotypic variation in rs53576 would manifest in different levels of accuracy on this test of empathic ability. Specifically, they hypothesized that participants with the GG genotype would show higher empathic accuracy than would those with one or two copies of the A allele (AA and AG genotypes). The hypothesis was confirmed for both women and men. Women and men with the GG genotype also had higher levels of trait empathy than their counterparts. Research has demonstrated that the GG genotype on rs53576 is also associated with other prosocial behaviors, including a prosocial temperament (Tost et al., 2010) and sympathy for others in distress (Smith, Porges, Norman, Connelly, & Decety, 2014). These studies suggest that, for rs53576, G is a beneficial allele when it comes to prosociality, whereas A is a "risk allele," lowering the odds of prosocial behavior. Similar research has identified risk alleles for other *OXTR* SNPs for empathy (Wu, Li, & Su, 2012) and other forms of prosociality, including face recognition memory (Skuse et al., 2014), social reciprocity (Feldman, Gordon, Influs, Gutbir, & Epstein, 2013), affiliation (Kogan et al., 2011), and communication in romantic relationships (e.g., Schneiderman, Kanot-Maymon, Ebstein, & Feldman, 2013).

To be sure, empathy and reciprocity are not the same as affectionate communication. To the extent that other prosocial behaviors and dispositions are encoded genetically, however, Floyd and Denes (2015) argued that it is only a minor inferential leap to the prediction that an affectionate disposition shows a similar genetic basis. Indeed, Floyd's affection exchange theory provides that the tendency to behave affectionately is an adaptation that has been selected for, due to its contributions to viability and fertility, and that argument presumes a nontrivial level of heritability for the affectionate disposition.

Using that theoretic argument and previous research identifying *OXTR* as a candidate gene influencing conceptually similar prosocial behaviors, Floyd and Denes proposed that carriers of the GG genotype on rs53576 would evidence higher trait affection levels than would those with AA or AG genotypes. As other studies have demonstrated, however, genotype on rs53576 sometimes interacts with other characteristics to influence prosociality. Weisman et al. (2015), for example, showed that performance on the Reading the Mind in the Eyes test was predicted by an interaction between genotype and 2D:4D, the ratio of the length of the hand's second and fourth digits, which is a phenotypic marker of prenatal testosterone exposure (see further discussion of 2D:4D later). With respect to trait affectionate communication, Floyd and Denes theorized that a psychological characteristic – one's level of attachment security – would interact with the rs53576 genotype to predict trait affection levels. As first studied by Ainsworth (see, e.g., Ainsworth, Blehar, Waters, & Wall, 2015), attachment security is the extent to which people perceive they can trust and count on their significant relational partners. Individuals with strong attachment security think of their close relationships as dependable and they tend not to fear abandonment, whereas those with weak attachment security believe their close relational bonds cannot be counted on.

Floyd and Denes hypothesized that the rs53576 genotype has a greater influence on affectionate behavior for those with weak attachment security than strong attachment security. Their reasoning was that affectionate communication can function to compensate for the relatively deficient social connections that characterize weak attachment security, whereas it would not have the same purpose when attachment security is already strong. Importantly, the authors did not predict that weakly attached individuals are more affectionate than strongly attached individuals – indeed, as described later in this chapter, just the opposite is true – but simply that genetic effects on trait affectionate communication are greater when attachment security is not already strong.

Using a sample of 164 young adults who were genotyped for rs53576, Floyd and Denes found that scores on the Trait Affection Scale were not subject to a main effect of genotype. Although carriers of the GG genotype had higher trait affection scores than carriers of the AG or AA genotypes, as predicted, the main effect was not statistically significant. However, as hypothesized, the *OXTR* genotype interacted with attachment security to influence trait affectionate communication. In line with the hypothesis, the genotype had a stronger effect on the trait affectionate behavior of those with weak attachment security than of those with strong attachment security. The beta weight for the interaction was .64, indicating that the interaction of rs53576 genotype and attachment security accounted for a substantial proportion of the variance in Trait Affection Scale scores.

Two important caveats are worth mentioning with respect to a potential genetic basis for affectionate communication. First, the results of Floyd and Denes do not imply that genes – either alone or in interaction with attachment security – *cause* affectionate behavior. Any genetic variation could most likely be expected only to predispose individuals toward greater or lesser levels of affectionate communication or other prosocial behaviors, but the inference cannot be drawn that the genotype is causing those behaviors; it is only accounting for variance in their tendencies.

Second, rs53576 is only one SNP on *OXTR*. Several other SNPs on the oxytocin receptor gene also show associations with prosociality, including rs1042778, rs13316193, and rs2268490. That observation led Schneiderman et al. (2013) to propose a "cumulative risk" methodology in which, instead of genotyping participants on a single SNP and doing mean comparisons between different genotypic groups, researchers genotype participants on multiple SNPs and identify the number of SNPs on which participants carry the genotype associated with the lowest level of prosociality (e.g., AA on rs53576). This produces a continuous score ranging theoretically from 0 to the number of SNPs genotyped, and Schneiderman et al. demonstrated that this approach is superior to the typical approach of comparing genotypic groups for predicting relational communication. Using six SNPs from the oxytocin receptor gene, Floyd, Generous, et al. (2017) also demonstrated a significant association between empathic communication and cumulative genetic risk for a group of physician assistant students.

To date, Floyd and Denes (2015) is the only study to demonstrate a genetic association with trait affectionate communication. Additional SNPs, both on *OXTR* and other receptor genes, await investigation, but the findings of Floyd and Denes do suggest that variance in trait affection scores has at least some genetic basis.

Neurological Effects

Preliminary evidence suggests that differences in the trait-level tendency to communicate affection are related to differential patterns of neurological activity. Working from AET's claim that affectionate tendencies have a biological basis, Lewis et al. (2011) speculated that the neurological mechanisms that mediate those tendencies may overlap with those responsible for personality. Gray (1994) argued that the major dimensions of personality emerge from variation in two fundamental systems: the approach system and the avoidance system. The former underlies positive affect, reward, and goal-oriented behavior, whereas the latter underlies punishment, anxiety, and sensitivity to negativity. Davidson (1995, 1998) observed that the brain's left and right prefrontal cortices (PFCs) mediate approach and avoidance, respectively (see also Coan & Allen, 2003). On that basis, Lewis and colleagues reasoned that the tendency to express affection – which can be characterized as an approach behavior – is associated with left PFC dominance, amplifying the motivational response to the potential reward of exchanging affectionate messages.

Lewis and colleagues had 290 young adults complete Floyd's TAS and then subjected thirty-two of those participants to electroencephalography, which measures the brain's electrical activity via electrodes situated along the scalp. Only half of the EEG sessions yielded usable data, resulting in a final sample size of sixteen. The researchers looked specifically for asymmetries between the left and right PFCs, which were operationally defined as the difference in the alpha band of baseline recordings between two specific electrodes: the F7 electrode over the left PFC and the F8 electrode over the right (see Minnix & Kline, 2004). The hypothesis was that asymmetry evidencing greater dominance in the left PFC (which mediates the approach system) is positively associated with trait affectionate communication. As predicted, the researchers found a strong positive association ($r = .74$), indicating that higher trait affection scores correlated with stronger left PFC dominance.

This was the first study to demonstrate that variance in trait affectionate communication is attributable to differences in neurological activity, specifically EEG asymmetry, which is at least partially heritable (see Coan, Allen, Malone, & Iacono, 2003) and which underlies a fundamental difference in temperament and personality (the division between approach and avoidance). No research to date has replicated these findings or explored other neurological features as antecedents of affectionate behavior, so these results must be considered preliminary.

Hormonal Effects

It may seem counterintuitive to include hormonal effects on a list of innate influences, given that the levels of many hormones are constantly responsive to environmental factors. The adrenal hormone cortisol, for instance, is elevated in reaction to environmental stressors, including interpersonal stressors (Walter et al., 2008). The pituitary hormone prolactin is decreased when individuals engage in conflict (Malarkey, Kiecolt-Glaser, Pearl, & Glaser, 1994), and a second pituitary hormone, oxytocin, is increased when people receive interpersonal touch (Holt-Lunstad, Birmingham, & Light, 2008). Even prolonged exposure to environmental influences – such as the stress of facing chronic unemployment (Ockenfels et al., 1995), enduring sexual abuse (Trickett, Noll, Susman, Shenk, & Putnam, 2010), or being forced to conceal one's sexual orientation (Juster, Smith, Ouellet, Sindi, & Lupien, 2013) – can alter hormonal function and responsiveness.

Their reactivity to environmental stimuli aside, however, hormones have baseline levels – also known as *basal* or *tonic* levels – that vary from person to person. There are approximately ninety different hormones in the human body, but most serve purely physiological functions, such as producing blood platelets (thrombopoietin), causing dilation of the blood vessels (prostaglandins), and regulating electrolyte and water transport (guanylin). Others, however, are also implicated in experiences of emotion and social interaction. Basal prolactin, for instance, is associated with self-perceived anxiety (Jeffcoate, Lincoln, Selby, & Herbert, 1986). The peptide hormone vasopressin is implicated in pair bonding, especially for men (Goodson & Bass, 2001). And experiencing social closeness with new acquaintances is associated with basal levels of the steroid hormone progesterone (Brown et al., 2009). To date, the two hormones that have been directly explored for their relationship to trait affectionate communication are testosterone and cortisol, each explicated subsequently.

Testosterone

Of all the hormones studied for their association to social behavior, perhaps the most commonly measured is testosterone. Testosterone is a steroid hormone secreted by the male testes and, to a much lesser extent, the female ovaries. Researchers have known for decades that testosterone levels are positively related to aggressive emotions and behaviors in both women (Harris, Rushton, Hampson, & Jackson, 1996) and men (Ehrenkranz, Bliss, & Sheard, 1974). Dabbs and colleagues have shown that testosterone predicts criminal violence – again, for both men (Dabbs, Frady, Carr, & Besch, 1987) and women (Dabbs, Ruback, Frady, Hopper, & Sgoutas, 1988). Other research documents that testosterone is responsive to more socially approved forms of aggression, such as athletic competition; winning an athletic contest increases testosterone not only for athletes (Booth, Shelley, Mazur, Tharp, & Kittok, 1989) but also for their fans (Bernhardt, Dabbs, Fielden, & Lutter, 1998).

To the extent that testosterone is positively associated with the tendency to be aggressive – as a formidable empirical literature has verified – it stands to reason that it is inversely associated with the tendency to be affectionate. This possibility was explored first by Floyd (2010) using digit length measurements as surrogates for baseline testosterone. As mentioned above, multiple studies have established that the ratio of the length of the second digit (index finger) to the length of the fourth digit (ring finger) is associated with both testosterone (Manning, Scutt, Wilson, & Lewis-Jones, 1998) and aggression (Bailey & Hurd, 2005). There is also evidence that absolute second and fourth digit lengths (corrected for height) and the difference in the 2D:4D ratio between the left and right hands are phenotypic markers of testosterone (see Kondo, Zákány, Innis, & Duboule, 1997; Manning et al., 2000).

In a preliminary test of the association between testosterone and trait affectionate communication, Floyd (2010) had 240 young adults complete the TAS and then took a clear photocopy of the ventral (palm-side) surface of each participant's left and right hands (after removal of rings). Using electronic Vernier calipers, accurate to one ten-thousandth of an inch, coders measured the second and fourth digit on each hand from the basal crease – where the finger meets the hand – to the midpoint of the fingertip, exclusive of the fingernail.

After calculating 2D:4D values by dividing the length of the second digit by that of the fourth (see Csathó et al., 2003), Floyd found that, contrary to predictions, trait affectionate communication was nonsignificantly correlated with 2D:4D for either hand. However, absolute digit lengths, corrected for each participant's height, were all significantly correlated with trait affection scores except for the length of the right ring finger. Floyd also found that the 2D:4D ratio *difference* between the right and left hands (D_{r-l}), which was calculated by subtracting the left 2D:4D value from that of the right, showed a significant association with trait affection scores.

Although promising, these results are highly preliminary, for at least three reasons. First, the most commonly measured phenotypic marker of testosterone in this method – 2D:4D – did not show a significant association with trait affectionate behavior, even though almost all of the other markers did. Second, effect sizes for the significant correlations were small (r^2 = .02 to .03). Finally, Floyd did not measure participants' testosterone levels directly, and although there is substantial evidence that digit length and digit length ratio are reliable phenotypic markers for testosterone, measuring testosterone directly would provide a more straightforward test of the hypothesis that it is inversely related to trait affectionate communication.

Such a test was conducted by Hesse, Floyd, Boren, Lee, and Holland (2018), who sampled testosterone directly – although from men only – to examine a predicted negative association with participants' trait affection scores. To control for natural twenty-four-hour variation in testosterone levels, Hesse and colleagues tested the association between trait affection and baseline testosterone while controlling for the time of day when the salivary testosterone sample was taken. Having done so, they found an inverse association (β = −.38), which supports the hypothesis and represents a medium effect size (whereas the effect sizes from the Floyd (2010) digit length study were small).

This finding from Hesse et al. is substantially more promising, both because it was derived from a direct measurement of testosterone and because it reflects a larger effect size. Although limited by an exclusively male sample, it provides a more direct demonstration that baseline testosterone levels are associated with an affectionate disposition.

Cortisol

Another potentially relevant hormone is cortisol. Given that cortisol is thought of as a "stress hormone," and given that exchanging affection can be thought of as a stress-alleviating activity (see Chapter 8), one might expect that higher trait levels of affectionate behavior correlate with lower baseline levels of cortisol. For this hormone, however, the baseline level is actually not a good measure of an individual's stress load. Rather, stress experienced in the moment is indexed by a significant increase in cortisol *over* the baseline level (i.e., *cortisol stress reactivity*; see Dickerson & Kemeny, 2004), and an individual's allostatic load – his or her accumulated "wear and tear" from stress – is indexed by twenty-four-hour variation in cortisol levels (i.e., *diurnal cortisol variation*; see Corbett, Mendoza, Abdullah, Wegelin, & Levine, 2006).

Irrespective of moment-to-moment experiences of acute stress, the diurnal rhythm for cortisol is characterized by peak values within the hour after awakening, a steep decline through the morning and early afternoon, and a slower decrease from the late afternoon to approximately midnight, when elevation begins again (Kirschbaum & Hellhammer, 1989). This pattern appears early in life (Price, Close, & Fielding,

1983) and is indicative of the ability of the hypothalamic-pituitary-adrenal (HPA) axis to regulate the stress response (see Nelson & Kriegsfeld, 2016). When people experience heavy chronic stress, such as from cumulative or repeated stressors related to marital dysfunction (Saxbe, Repetti, & Nishina, 2008) or serious illness (Abercrombie et al., 2004), their diurnal cortisol rhythms often "flatten," evidencing substantially less variation over time.

On the basis of affection exchange theory's claim that affectionate behavior ameliorates stress, Floyd (2006b) reasoned that highly affectionate people would show greater morning-to-evening variance in cortisol than would less affectionate people. As is common in research examining the diurnal cortisol rhythm, Floyd collected four salivary cortisol samples from young adult participants on a typical workday: on awakening, at noon, in the late afternoon, and in the late evening. He also had participants complete the TAS, separating the scores for expressed affection and received affection. Floyd's hypothesis was that trait expressed affection is positively related to diurnal cortisol variation, but he tested that prediction while controlling for the effect of trait received affection so as to rule out the alternate explanation that the benefit of expressing affection is attributable only to the benefit of the affection one receives in return. With trait received affection controlled, trait expressed affection showed a strong positive relationship with diurnal cortisol variation ($r = .56$).

One can conclude from Floyd's finding that twenty-four-hour variation in cortisol accounts for variance in trait affectionate communication – at least, in the trait level of *expressed* affection – and this makes sense given AET's assertion that affectionate behavior functions to attenuate stress. A later dyadic study of spouses that used the Affectionate Communication Index instead of the Trait Affection Scale found that participants' diurnal cortisol variation was predicted by the amount of verbal, nonverbal, and supportive affection they received from their spouses (Floyd & Riforgiate, 2008).

Sex and Sex Composition

Numerous studies have examined the influences of sex and sex composition[1] on the amount of affection people communicate to others, and the findings have been remarkably consistent. For example, nearly every study examining the effect of sex has found that women express more affection in their relationships than men do, and those that have not (e.g., Bombar & Littig, 1996; Carton & Horan, 2014; Floyd, 1997b; McCabe, 1987) have reported null results.[2] Bernhold and Giles (in press) did find that grandfathers were more affectionate with grandchildren than were grandmothers, but only for one specific form of affection – memories and humor, as measured by Mansson's (2013e) GRAS. Otherwise, no known published research has found that men, at any age or in any context, express *more* affection than women do, even though men express affection *earlier* than women do in developing romantic relationships (Ackerman, Griskevicius, & Li, 2011).

Women are often stereotyped as being more affectionate than men (Fabes & Martin, 1991), and research shows that women are cognizant of this sex difference. In his study of affection in the family of origin, Wallace (1981) reported that women perceived themselves as having been more affectionate in their families than men did and that women perceived that they were still more affectionate than men were. In a later diary study of affectionate behavior, Floyd (1997b) also found that women perceived themselves as being more affectionate than men did. Interestingly, this was one of the few studies that did not show a sex difference in *actual* behavior; the significant difference was in *perceived* behavior only.

In addition to expressing more affection than boys and men, do girls and women also receive more? The evidence on this point has thus far been mixed. Some support for this difference comes from research with young children. Botkin and Twardosz (1988) conducted naturalistic observations of daycare teachers' interactions with students, focusing on affectionate behaviors such as smiling, using affectionate words, and displaying affectionate physical contact. These researchers documented that female children received significantly more affection than did male children.

Floyd (2002) measured received affection at a trait level. No sex comparison was reported in that paper, but supplemental analyses of the data show that women report receiving significantly more affection than do men and that the sex difference remains significant even after the effects of expressed affection are controlled. Supplemental analyses of data from Mansson, Floyd, and Soliz (2017) also show that women receive some forms of affectionate communication from their grandparents more than men do, yet Mansson and Booth-Butterfield (2011) showed no sex difference in affection received from grandparents (see also Carton & Horan, 2014).

Some studies have also reported that affectionate behavior within dyads is influenced by their sex composition. In a verbal affection experiment, for instance, Shuntich and Shapiro (1991) found that male–male dyads were significantly less affectionate than female–female or male–female dyads, the latter two of which did not differ from each other.

Moreover, Floyd and Voloudakis (1999a) reported that, in conversations between same-sex friends, women displayed greater nonverbal immediacy, expressiveness, and positive affect (as coded from videotapes) than did men; however, no sex differences in these behaviors were observed in conversations between opposite-sex friends. Although these two experiments presented their findings somewhat differently, they amount to the same pattern: men are less affectionate than women in same-sex interaction but not in opposite-sex interaction. Blier and Blier-Wilson (1989) similarly found that men are less *confident* than women in expressing affection to other men, but not to women.

The same pattern emerged in Bombar and Littig's (1996) questionnaire study about affectionate baby talk; men and women did not differ from each other in their likelihood of using baby talk with opposite-sex friends, but women were more likely than men to use it with same-sex friends. The pattern in Noller's (1978) study with parents and children was only slightly different: boys were less affectionate than girls when interacting with fathers but not with mothers. Father–son dyads (which are male–male pairs) were the least affectionate of the four types, however, which is consistent with the findings of Shuntich and Shapiro, Floyd and Voloudakis, and Bombar and Littig. Fryrear and Thelen (1969) even found that nursery school children imitated observed affectionate behavior most frequently when both they and the adult enacting the affection were female.

Gender

In addition to examining the influence of biological sex, some research has focused on how affectionate communication varies as a function of gender. Gender refers to one's psychological sex role orientation (i.e., masculine, feminine, androgynous) rather than to one's biological sex, and it has been conceptually and operationally defined in a variety of ways. Early approaches to measuring gender dichotomized masculinity and femininity, which implied that the more of one characteristic a person was seen to have, the less he or she had of the other characteristic. Being more masculine thus meant being less feminine, and vice versa (see, e.g., Gough, 1957). Bem (1974) reconceptualized masculinity and femininity as orthogonal, therefore allowing that an individual could actually score high on both (a case she referred to as being *androgynous*) or could score low on both (which she referred to as being *undifferentiated*). In the Bem Sex Role Inventory (BSRI), masculinity is operationally defined as including assertiveness, competitiveness, and aggressiveness, whereas femininity is operationalized as including compassion, responsiveness, and gentleness. Although it eschewed the terms "masculinity" and "femininity," Richmond and McCroskey's (1990) Assertiveness-Responsiveness Scale (ARS) retained largely similar operational indicators of each, whereas Kachel, Steffens, and Niedlich's (2016) Traditional Masculinity-Femininity (TMF) scale eliminated references to specific characteristics and simply asked participants to report how they perceived themselves and their behaviors on a continuum from highly masculine to highly feminine.

The potential influence of gender on interpersonal behavior is of particular interest to those who take a strong social learning theory perspective. Such a perspective suggests that women and men are not inherently different from each other in ways that ought to affect their behaviors (with the obvious exception of reproductive behaviors). Any observed sex differences in social behavior are therefore attributed to differences in role socialization – that is, in the ways that culture and upbringing socialize girls and boys to act. Men act in predominantly "masculine" ways, and women in predominantly "feminine" ways, because (and only because) those differences are prescribed and reinforced at a social and cultural level. According to this perspective, differences that appear to be a function of sex are, in reality, a function of gender.

Morman and Floyd (1999) began looking at the influences of gender on affectionate behavior in a study of fathers and their young adult sons. Given evidence that women are more affectionate (and perceive themselves as more affectionate) than men, Floyd and Morman predicted that affectionate behavior is directly related to psychological femininity and inversely related to psychological masculinity. Indeed, Rane and Draper (1995) had reported that both women and men were judged to be less masculine when described as engaging in nurturant touch with young children than when not engaging in such touch. Morman and Floyd advanced these predictions for verbal affection and direct nonverbal gestures, but because socially supportive behavior may be less recognizable as affectionate, they posed a research question as to whether it would follow the same patterns with respect to gender.

Using the BSRI, Morman and Floyd discovered that sons' femininity was directly associated with their own nonverbal and supportive affection and with their fathers' verbal, nonverbal, and supportive affection. Fathers' femininity was directly related only to their own supportive affection. These results fit the hypotheses and also answered the research question. Surprisingly, however, they also discovered that sons' masculinity was directly (rather than inversely) associated with their own nonverbal affection and with their fathers' verbal, nonverbal, and supportive affection. Moreover, fathers' masculinity was directly associated with their own verbal, nonverbal, and supportive affection.

Those results for masculinity were unanticipated. One would not necessarily expect stereotypically masculine qualities (e.g., aggression, competitiveness) to be positively related to affectionate behavior, *especially* verbal and direct nonverbal affection and *especially* in male–male relationships, such as a father–son pair. Speculating that the results might be an artifact of a potentially outdated measure of gender roles, Floyd and Morman (2000a) replicated the test using Richmond and McCroskey's (1990) ARS. That study elicited only fathers' reports, but the findings again revealed that fathers' verbal, nonverbal, and supportive affection were all directly related to their femininity *and* their masculinity.

This replication suggested that the results were not measurement artifacts; however, because no explanation was evident, the extent to which the findings were unique to male–male relationships (or perhaps to father–son relationships, specifically) was examined in two new replications. The first involved data collected for the Floyd (2002) project, although these data are not reported in that paper. In that project, adults completed the ARS and then reported on their verbal, nonverbal, and supportive affection with three targets: their mothers, their fathers, and a sibling (who was randomly selected if participants had more than one). Results indicated that participants' femininity was directly related to their verbal, nonverbal, and supportive affection for all three targets. Their masculinity was also directly related to their verbal affection with their fathers and to their supportive affection with their siblings. The coefficients for all of these correlations appear in Floyd and Mikkelson (2002).

The second replication was conducted during the Floyd and Tusing (2002) experiment, which involved opposite-sex pairs of adult platonic friends or romantic partners. Using the ARS, Floyd and Tusing found that participants' nonverbal and supportive forms of affection were directly related to their femininity and also to their masculinity (coefficients appear in Floyd & Mikkelson, 2002).

The findings from these four studies yield several conclusions. First, affectionate behavior is positively associated with femininity, which is unsurprising given the tendency of women to be more affectionate than men. Second, affectionate behavior is positively associated with masculinity, which is more puzzling and has not, to date, been adequately explained. Third, the associations between affectionate behavior and masculinity are neither measurement-specific nor relationship-specific. Fourth, masculinity demonstrated fewer significant associations with affectionate behavior than did femininity, and the magnitudes of its correlations were generally smaller than those for femininity. Fifth,

however, all of the significant correlations between affection and masculinity identified in these studies (and, indeed, all of the nonsignificant
ones) were positive; not once did masculinity show an inverse association
with any form of affectionate behavior in any relationship, as Morman
and Floyd (1999) had originally hypothesized.

Age

In the Floyd (2002) study, no relationship emerged between participants'
trait levels of affectionate behavior and their ages; however, other
research has reported associations between age and affectionate communication. In two studies with children and adolescents, Eberly and
Montemayor (1998, 1999) discovered that sixth-grade students were
more affectionate, in general, than eighth- and tenth-grade students
(the latter of whom did not differ significantly from each other), but also
that sixth- and eighth-grade students were less affectionate toward their
parents than were tenth-grade students.

In a study of men's relationships with their preadolescent sons (ages
7–12 years), Salt (1991) reported that the sons' ages were inversely
related to the fathers' self-reported affectionate touch behavior and also
to the number of affectionate touches actually observed in the study. The
same pattern emerged in Floyd and Morman's (2000a) study of men's
relationships with their adolescent and adult sons (sons in that study
ranged in age from 12 to 53 years). That project, which used the ACI
as the operational definition of affectionate communication, found that
sons' age was inversely related to fathers' self-reported affectionate
behavior. These studies both suggest that fathers are more affectionate
with younger than older sons. Floyd and Morman (2000a) also reported
a significant direct relationship between fathers' affectionate communication and fathers' own age. Thus, older fathers communicated more
affection to their sons than did younger fathers.

Age also seems to play a role in people's motives for communicating.
For instance, Rubin, Perse, and Barbato (1988) reported that older
respondents were more likely than younger respondents to report communicating for the purpose of conveying affection.

Attachment Style

Bowlby's (1969, 1973) attachment theory provides that individuals
develop differentiated styles of forming human attachments based on
the manner of nurturing they receive from their primary caregivers –
usually their mothers – in the early days of their lives. The theory posits

that interactions with primary caregivers create cognitive models of attachment, referred to as *attachment styles*, that influence the formation and maintenance of close relationships throughout the life course. Bartholomew and Horowitz (1991) proposed that four attachment styles can be identified in adults, based on the juxtaposition of individuals' views of themselves and their views of others. The *secure* style represents positive views of the self and others, whereas the *fearful-avoidant* style represents negative views of the self and others. Those with a *dismissive* style have a positive view of self but a negative view of others, and those with a *preoccupied* style see themselves negatively but others positively. Some studies categorize individuals according to their primary attachment style (categorical approach), whereas others measure individuals' tendencies toward each style (continuous approach).

Data from Floyd's (2002) study of highly affectionate communicators indicate that adults with different attachment styles differ in their trait-like affectionate communication tendencies. (Scores and effect size estimates are reported here, as they do not appear in this form in the Floyd (2002) paper.) Floyd took a categorical approach to measuring attachment style and found that those with a secure style reported significantly higher trait expressed affection (5.49 on a seven-point scale) than did those with a dismissive style (4.60), with a preoccupied style (4.44), and with a fearful-avoidant style (4.36), the latter three of whom did not differ from each other. Similarly, with respect to trait affection received, those with a secure style (5.44) scored significantly higher than those with a dismissive style (4.81) and with a fearful-avoidant style (4.79), who in turn scored significantly higher than those with a preoccupied style (4.24). Although effect sizes for attachment style were modest (partial η^2 = .18 for affection given and .13 for affection received), these results do indicate that attachment style is one significant source of individual variation in affectionate behavior.

Hesse and Trask (2014) replicated these comparisons but took a continuous approach to measuring attachment style. After controlling for the influence of trait received affection, they found that trait expressed affection is positively associated with the secure style and negatively associated with the other three styles. In a separate study, Dillow, Goodboy, and Bolkan (2014) found that the effects of the fearful-avoidant, preoccupied, and dismissive styles (measured continuously) on affectionate communication in romantic relationships (measured by the ACI) are mediated by the experience of romantic love. Specifically, the preoccupied style was positively associated with love and the fearful-avoidant and dismissive styles were negatively associated with love, and love was a positive predictor of verbal, nonverbal, and supportive affectionate expressions.

Cultural and Familial Influences on Affectionate Behavior

People vary in their affectionate behavior as a function of individual-level differences, such as their gender or genotype, but affectionate behavior is also affected by group-level influences. These influences include people's cultural backgrounds and the norms of the families in which they were raised, as this section details.

Culture, Ethnicity, and Nationality

Affectionate behavior is culturally variant, so several studies have focused on culture as a predictor of affectionate communication. This is not always a straightforward process. As Floyd (2014d) pointed out, many communication studies that aim to address the effects of *culture* are actually measuring the effects of *race* or *ethnicity* (such as by comparing Caucasian and African American samples) or *nationality* (such as by comparing US and Japanese samples). Race/ethnicity and nationality may both be influential, Floyd argued, but neither is a perfect surrogate for culture, which most introductory communication texts define as comprising the symbols, values, and norms that distinguish groups of people.

In research on affectionate communication, therefore, it is instructive to examine the influences of culture, race/ethnicity, and nationality separately. A common way to study culture (as it is formally defined) is to measure the effects of Hofstede's cultural dimensions (Hofstede & Hofstede, 2010). Hofstede proposed that societies vary along several continua. The *individualism/collectivism* continuum represents the extent to which a society teaches people to emphasize either their own needs and ambitions or those of their families, workplaces, and communities. The *masculinity/femininity* dimension reflects either a focus on achievement, acquisition of goods, and strongly differentiated roles for women and men or a focus on nurturing behavior, quality of life, and little differentiation between the sexes. *Uncertainty avoidance* is an index of how much a society tries to avoid situations that are unstructured or unpredictable versus embracing uncertainty as a normal part of life. Finally, *power distance* is a measure of how much a society accepts power inequity; a low power-distance society believes that people are essentially equal and that no one person or group should have excessive power, whereas a high power-distance society accepts that certain people or groups should have great power whereas the average person has much less.

Two studies have explored the influences of these cultural dimensions on people's trait levels of affectionate behavior. Both measured the effects of culture on participants from different countries, thereby examining the influences of culture and nationality – the country with which one identifies as a citizen or resident – in tandem. In the first study, Mansson et al. (2016) recruited 558 undergraduate students from the United States, Russia, and Slovakia to complete Floyd's TAS-G (assessing trait expressed affection) and TAS-R (assessing trait received affection). Mansson and colleagues then input the scores for each country's individualism/collectivism, masculinity/femininity, uncertainty avoidance, and power distance provided by Hofstede.

Regarding cultural influences, expressed affection was highest in cultures that were individualistic (as opposed to collectivistic), feminine (as opposed to masculine), accepting of uncertainty (as opposed to uncertainty avoidant), and of a low (rather than high) power distance. Received affection followed exactly the same pattern except that the association with uncertainty avoidance was nonsignificant. With respect to nationality, Mansson and colleagues found that both expressed and received affection were higher in the United States than in Russia or Slovakia and that the latter countries differed in received affection but not expressed.

A follow-up study by Mansson and Sigurðardóttir (2017) replicated the Mansson et al. procedure using 606 undergraduate students from the United States, Denmark, Iceland, and Poland. Regarding cultural influences, expressed affection was again highest in cultures that were individualistic and accepting of uncertainty, but also in countries that were masculine as opposed to feminine (contrary to what Mansson et al., 2016, had found). Received affection was highest in individualistic and uncertainty-accepting cultures but was unrelated to the other dimensions. With regard to nationality, expressed affection was higher in the United States than in the other countries, which did not differ from each other. However, received affection was highest in the United States, lower in Denmark, lower still in Poland, and lowest in Iceland (all differences were significant).

The findings from these two studies indicate that valuing individualism, accepting rather than avoiding uncertainty, and (to a lesser extent) valuing an equal rather than diffused distribution of power are all related to being more affectionate. They also depict people in the United States as a relatively affectionate people (see also Kline, Horton, & Zhang, 2008; Zhang & Wills, 2016). Both Mansson et al. (2016) and Mansson and Sigurðardóttir (2017) found that individualism was the strongest predictor of expressed affection out of all the cultural dimensions measured, and Hofstede's official website (www.hofstede-insights.com) identifies the United States as the most individualistic country in the world.

That conclusion is in line with research showing that those in the United States are often more emotionally expressive, in general, than are those in other countries (Stephan, Stephan, & de Vargas, 1996; Stephan, Stephan, Saito, & Barnett, 1998).

That national difference raises an intriguing question about the benefits associated with expressing affection. As Chapters 7 and 8 describe in detail, affectionate behavior is related to a wide variety of benefits for both mental health and physical wellness, yet most of these studies have been conducted with exclusively US samples. If people in other countries are less demonstrative of affection, on average, than people in the United States, does that imply that those of other nationalities also benefit less from expressing affection? Wu et al. (2014) proposed that it does not. Their study hypothesized that, irrespective of national differences in mean trait affection level, the strength of associations between trait affection and indices of wellness would not differ by country. Wu and colleagues had college students in the United States and China complete the TAS-G to measure their trait levels of expressed affection, and also had participants complete measures of life satisfaction and mental and relational wellness.

As expected, US students reported having significantly higher trait affection levels than did Chinese students. Given that Hofstede (www .hofstede-insights.com) describes Chinese culture as characterized by high power distance and low individualism, the substantially lower trait affection scores of Chinese students comport with the findings of Mansson et al. (2016) and Mansson and Sigurðardóttir (2017). Moreover, for students in both countries, TAS-G scores were positively related to self-esteem, life satisfaction, positive affect, empathy, resilience in the face of stress, and the likelihood of having close relationships, in line with previous research (Floyd, 2002; Floyd, Hess, et al., 2005).

The most important finding to come from the Wu et al. study, however, is that the correlations between trait affection level and these outcomes were of equally high magnitude for the US and Chinese samples. Even though Chinese students were less affectionate, overall, than their US counterparts, their levels of expressed affection were equally as strongly associated with these indices of mental and relational wellness as was the case for the US students. Being affectionate, in other words, is just as strongly associated with benefits in the collectivistic, high power-distance culture of China as in the individualistic, low power-distance culture of the United States.

Several studies have also focused on differences in affectionate behavior as a function of race or ethnicity.[3] Some have addressed how affection is expressed in interracial couples, regardless of the specific ethnic or racial characteristics of the partners. Using data from the National Longitudinal Study of Adolescent Health, for instance, Vaquera and Kao (2005) examined displays of affection in adolescent romantic couples that were both intraracial and interracial (consisting of various combinations of Caucasian, African American, Hispanic, Native American, and Asian adolescents). Three categories of affectionate displays were measured, which the researchers labeled as *public displays* (holding hands, telling others they are a couple, going out together alone or in a group, meeting each other's parents), *private displays* (exchanging gifts, saying "I love you," thinking of themselves as a couple), and *intimate displays* (kissing, touching each other under clothing, touching each other's genitals, having sexual intercourse). Vaquera and Kao found that intimate displays were equally frequent for inter- and intraracial couples, but that interracial couples engaged in fewer public displays and fewer private displays than their intraracial counterparts. However, in a study of "tie signs" – behaviors used to connote the presence of a relationship, such as holding hands, maintaining proximity, and making verbal references to one's "boyfriend," "girlfriend," "spouse," or "partner" – Mederos (2015) actually found that interracial couples used more tie signs as markers of affection than did intraracial couples. Tie signs would approximate what Vaquera and Kao referred to as public displays, so the findings of these two studies are potentially inconsistent on this point, although Mederos did not differentiate between behaviors enacted in public and private contexts.

It is possible that such an inconsistency reflects differences between specific racial and ethnic groups, insofar as several studies have documented differences between particular groups in affectionate behavior. Many early studies in this vein focused on touch. For example, Regan, Jerry, Narvaez, and Johnson (1999) unobtrusively observed Asian and Latino heterosexual romantic couples on a university campus. Researchers observed each pair for a period of two minutes and recorded any instances of touching behavior. Only half of the couples engaged in any form of touch during the two-minute observation window. Those who did, however, were significantly more likely to be Latino than Asian. With respect to particular forms of touch, the authors found that Latino couples were more likely than Asian couples to engage in "one-arm embracing" (i.e., one person's arm draped across the shoulders of the other as the pair walks), although there was no significant difference in hand-holding. Regan and her colleagues explained their findings as reflecting the difference between the "contact culture" of Latin America (which emphasizes personal proximity and touch) and the "noncontact culture" of Asia (at least, some parts of Asia; see McDaniel &

Andersen, 1998). Similarly, other research has reported that Hispanic parents are considerably more physically affectionate with their children than are Caucasian parents (e.g., Calzada & Eyberg, 2002; Escovar & Lazarus, 1982).

Burleson, Roberts, Coon, and Soto (in press) likewise compared Mexican American and European American college students in their perceptions of the *acceptability* of affectionate touch (rather than their actual enactment of touch). Compared with European Americans, Mexican Americans reported that affectionate touch was more acceptable when enacted in public settings (but not in private settings) and when shared with acquaintances (but not with loved ones). The researchers also reported that, among Mexican American students, greater acculturation to mainstream US culture was related to lower personal comfort with affectionate touch.

Research comparing the touch behaviors of African American and Caucasian participants has produced mixed results. In a review, Halberstadt (1985) reported that eight studies (Hall, 1974; Rinck, Willis, & Dean, 1980; Smith, Willis, & Gier, 1980; Williams & Willis, 1978; Willis & Hoffman, 1975; Willis & Reeves, 1976; Willis, Reeves, & Buchanan, 1976; Willis, Rinck, & Dean, 1978) found African American participants exhibiting more frequent touch than Caucasian participants. Halberstadt suggested that this behavioral difference reflects a difference in the social meaning of touch. Specifically, she contended that African American participants touched each other to convey messages of community and to develop and maintain a sense of pride and solidarity more than did their Caucasian counterparts.

Contrary to these findings, a ninth reviewed by Halberstadt (Reid, Tate, & Berman, 1989) reported that Caucasian preschool children touched, and stood closer to, Caucasian babies than African American preschool children did with African American babies. By way of explanation, Reid and colleagues suggested that expectations for the appropriateness of touch, at least with infants, might be more stringent in African American families than in Caucasian families, causing African American children to shy away from touching infants more than Caucasian children of comparable ages did. To investigate that possibility, Harrison-Speake and Willis (1995) studied differences between African American and Caucasian adults in their ratings of the appropriateness of several kinds of parent–child touch within families. These researchers approached shoppers in a public market and asked them to read eighteen short scenarios depicting various forms of parent–child touch, ranging from a child sitting on a parent's lap to a parent touching the child's genitals while tucking him or her into bed. The children in the scenarios were described as being either two, six, ten, or fourteen years of age, and participants rated the appropriateness of each scenario.

Harrison-Speake and Willis found that Caucasian adults reported higher appropriateness ratings, overall, than did African American adults. This main effect was qualified by numerous interaction effects involving the sex of the parent in the scenarios, the age of the child in the scenarios, and the type of touch being described.[4] Among the findings Harrison-Speake and Willis reported was that touch initiated by fathers was particularly viewed as less appropriate by African American respondents than by Caucasian respondents. However, the differences between racial categories also varied with the age of the child being described. For two-year-old children, African American respondents approved of parental touch more than did Caucasian respondents. That difference reversed for six-year-old and ten-year-old children, and for fourteen-year-old children, no difference between African American and Caucasian adults was observed.

A wider variety of affectionate behaviors was measured by Bernhold and Giles (2017) in their study of grandparent–grandchild relationships. These authors recruited undergraduate students to report on their relationship with one of their grandparents. The students had either Asian American, European American, or Latino grandparents, and the researchers posed questions as to how grandparents from these groups would differ in their expressions of affection to their grandchildren. The authors used Mansson's (2013c) GRAS to assess four forms of affectionate behavior: love and esteem, memories and humor, caring, and celebratory affection.

Some main effects of grandparents' racial/ethnic group emerged. Grandchildren reported receiving more love and esteem affection, and more caring affection, from European American grandparents than Asian American grandparents. Similarly, they reported more celebratory affection from European American than from Latino grandparents. Finally, memories and humor were highest from Latino grandparents, less from European American grandparents, and least from Asian American grandparents (see also Mansson & Sigurðardóttir, in press).

These findings are informative because they go beyond comparisons of *levels* or *frequencies* of affectionate behavior and also consider differences in *form*. It was not the case, for instance, that European American grandparents were more affectionate than Latino grandparents (or vice versa) across the board. Rather, grandparents from each group differed in the ways they showed affection, with memories and humor being most common for Latino grandparents, and love and esteem, caring, and celebratory affection being most common for European American grandparents. Consistent with the findings of Wu et al. (2014), however, Asian American grandparents generally reported less affectionate behavior than did those in the other groups, regardless of form.

Family of Origin

Researchers have known for decades that children resemble their parents in terms of values (Troll, Neugarten, & Kraines, 1969) and personality characteristics (Scarr, Webber, Weinberg, & Wittig, 1981), so it is entirely probable that children resemble their parents in terms of their levels of affection. Few studies have examined this likelihood, but the ones that have demonstrate associations between children's affection (either in childhood or in later adulthood) and the affection they were exposed to in their families of origin.

Using data from the National Surveys of Families and Households, for instance, White (1999) examined 428 mother–father–child triads who reported on their levels of warmth and tension. In each triad, both parents reported on their warmth for the child and the child reported on his or her warmth for the parents. White's interest was in the extent to which warmth in individual dyadic relationships (e.g., mother and child) is predicted by the third triadic member's reports of warmth in the parent–child or marital relationships.

For mother–child pairs, White reported that the mother's warmth toward the child was predicted by the father's warmth toward the child, and the child's warmth toward the mother was predicted by the child's warmth toward the father. The mother's warmth toward the child was also significantly related to her own warmth toward the father. These patterns were nearly identical to those observed in the father–child pairs.

Warmth is not the same as affection, although the operational definition of warmth used in the survey included at least one item specifically referencing affectionate behavior. Nonetheless, the results presented by White illustrate a high level of interdependence in family relationships with respect to warmth, and this suggests the possibility that children who grow up in a loving, affectionate household are more likely to become affectionate adults themselves.

Floyd and Morman (2000a) tested that proposition in a study of fathers and sons. The authors were interested in how the amount of affection a man received from his father while growing up would predict his level of affection with his own sons in adulthood. Two competing hypotheses were adjudicated. First, the *modeling hypothesis* provides that men who experienced high levels of affection from their fathers would become affectionate fathers themselves, because they are modeling the parental affection they observed (see, e.g., Cowan & Cowan, 1987). Second, the *compensation hypothesis* predicts that men who perceived their fathers to be distant and uninvolved would become affectionate fathers themselves, because they are compensating for the lack of paternal affection they received (see Radin, 1988).

Floyd and Morman reasoned that, when combined, these hypotheses predicted a curvilinear relationship between the amount of affection men received from their fathers and the amount they expressed to their own sons. Specifically, men who received either very high or very low levels of paternal affection would become the most affectionate fathers – in the former case, because they are modeling the paternal affection they received, and in the latter case, because they are compensating for it. Conversely, men who received moderate paternal affection would become less affectionate fathers themselves.

The curvilinear relationship emerged as predicted. After dividing men into ten equally sized groups based on the amount of affection they received from their own fathers, Floyd and Morman found that men were more affectionate with their own sons at the low and high ends of the continuum and were least affectionate with their own sons at the midpoint of the scale, just as the combined modeling/compensation hypotheses would predict. This study was cross-sectional, so it cannot support a causal claim. Although the Floyd and Morman (2000a) study does not *prove* that men learn to be affectionate with their sons by modeling or compensating for the affection their own fathers showed them, it is fully consistent with such a proposition. Unlike White (1999), of course, Floyd and Morman examined only the father–son pair, and it is certainly possible that the effects of modeling or compensation are of greater or lesser magnitude in other familial dyads.

In a separate study of familial influence on affectionate behavior, Floyd and Morman (2005) employed the paradigm of the naïve theory of affection (Robey, Cohen, & Epstein, 1988). Heider (1958) coined the term *naïve theory* to refer to implicit beliefs about specific phenomena that are reified through the identification of seemingly confirmatory events in daily life. According to Robey et al., a naïve theory of affection is the implicit belief that affection is a finite resource, meaning that the amount of affection shown to one person necessarily lessens the amount that can be shown to another. Children with this implicit belief would assume, for instance, that the more affection their parents show their siblings, the less they have to show them.

Naïve theories are operative in adulthood, as well, and this led Floyd and Morman to hypothesize that the more siblings a man has, the less affection he reports receiving from his father. If affection is implicitly believed to be finite, that is, then siblings would be seen as competing for that resource. Importantly, however, Floyd and Morman reasoned that this type of naïve theory would shape the sons' reports of affection received from their fathers but not the fathers' reports of affection expressed to their sons. As the providers of affection (rather than the recipients), fathers should be unencumbered by an implicit belief that their affection is finite, so Floyd and Morman predicted no relationship between a father's affection toward his son and the number of siblings the son has. Using 115 pairs of adult men and their adult sons, Floyd and Morman showed that sons reported receiving less paternal affection the more siblings they had (with a stronger effect for the number of brothers than sisters), but that fathers' reports of affection toward their sons were unrelated to how many siblings the sons had. This study adds to the observation of Floyd and Morman (2000a) of an association between fathers' and sons' levels of affection while also demonstrating that the relationship can be influenced by family size.

To the extent that parents' warmth and affection are associated with the same in their children, two different hypotheses are relevant. One is that children of affectionate parents *learn* that behavior through observation and reinforcement, in much the same way they learn their native language and cultural traditions. The second possibility is that children of affectionate parents acquire a *genetic predisposition* for affectionate behavior from those parents, similar to the way they acquire their eye color or a predisposition for certain illnesses. These hypotheses are not mutually exclusive; it is certainly possible that children of affectionate parents acquire a predisposition for that behavior genetically but also find that the behavior is practiced and rewarded in their family of origin. Nonetheless, if an affectionate disposition is exclusively learned – having no genetic component – then one would expect that children's affectionate behavior is equally as strongly related to that of their biological parents as to that of nonbiological parents, such as stepparents or adoptive parents. On the contrary, if some proportion of the variance in children's affection levels is genetic, it is logical to expect that a child's affection level is more strongly related to the affection level of his or her biological parents than nonbiological parents. These hypotheses await direct exploration, but there is ample evidence that child–stepparent relationships are less affectionate, overall, than child–biological parent relationships. Floyd and Morman (2001) demonstrated that men are less affectionate with stepsons than with biological sons, for instance, and White (1999) reported that stepfathers both express and receive less warmth with their children than do biological fathers.

Thus far, this chapter has examined individual differences and cultural/familial effects that are relevant for predicting how affectionate individuals are. A third category of research focuses on aspects of the social context that can affect people's tendencies to behave affectionately.

Contextual Predictors of Affectionate Behavior

Beyond the effects of individual, cultural, and familial characteristics, aspects of communicative contexts or situations can influence affectionate behavior. Research on contextual influences has focused largely on privacy and has produced some mixed findings, depending on the behaviors being examined and on whether reports of behaviors or judgments of their appropriateness have been sought. Bell and Healey (1992), for example, reported that participants in their study were more likely to express affection through the use of idioms – expressions whose meanings are known only to them – in private settings (such as at home) than in public settings (such as at work). Respondents in Bombar and Littig's (1996) study similarly reported that they were more likely to communicate affection to friends or romantic partners through the use of baby talk in private contexts than in public ones. Conversely, however, when Floyd and Morman (1997) asked respondents to report on their perceptions of the *appropriateness* of affectionate behavior with friends or siblings, they discovered that affectionate behaviors were judged to be more appropriate in public settings than in private ones, a finding that was replicated for male respondents in Morman and Floyd (1998).

Why should the privacy level of the context matter, either in terms of people's actual affectionate behavior or in terms of their perceptions of appropriateness? Floyd and Morman (1997) suggested that the answer has partly to do with the risks involved in overtly communicating affection, particularly in nonromantic relationships such as friendships or family relationships. Certain risks, such as embarrassment, are mitigated by saving affection displays for private settings. Other risks, however, are mitigated by expressing affection publicly. If one wonders, for instance, whether a friend's affection display might be a romantic overture, there may be less concern if the display occurs in a public setting, where the friend recognizes that he or she is being seen and heard by others. If the friend appears unconcerned about how onlookers might interpret the affection display, then the recipient may be similarly unconcerned, whereas if the display occurred in private, the recipient may wonder why the friend waited for a private setting before conveying his or her affection.

One other aspect of the context that Floyd and Morman (1997) studied was its emotional intensity. Specifically, they predicted that affectionate behavior in nonromantic relationships ought to be considered less appropriate in emotionally neutral situations than in situations that are emotionally charged in some way. The reasoning was that the emotional intensity of a situation such as a wedding, a graduation, or a funeral would make affection displays more normative – and thus would mitigate potential risks of such displays – than in situations that were not particularly charged emotionally. To test the prediction, they used a scenario method involving descriptions of a positively charged situation (in this case, a wedding), a negatively charged situation (a funeral), and a neutral situation (an interaction in a classroom). As hypothesized, they found that respondents rated affectionate behavior as more appropriate in the emotionally charged situations than in the emotionally neutral one. There was no difference between the positively charged and the negatively charged situations. This finding was replicated with male respondents in Morman and Floyd (1998).

Making Sense of Innate and Environmental Influences

Considered collectively, the research reviewed in this chapter indicates that the tendency to encode affectionate messages is subject to individual, relational, and contextual influences that are numerous and sometimes interact with each other in complex ways. To understand the implications of this research, both alone and in the broader context of work on affectionate behavior, it is useful to attend to at least two observations.

First, research indicates that both innate and environmental influences on affectionate behavior are potent. The discovery of genetic, neurological, and hormonal antecedents of affectionate communication, in particular, may lead some to disregard environmentally acquired influences as negligible, but the science does not support such a conclusion. Both stable (e.g., cultural traditions) and fleeting (e.g., emotional intensity) characteristics of an individual's environment are associated with his or her propensity for affection. Although much research on environmental influences explores how affectionate people are within specific relationships, rather than their trait-like tendencies, these are likely to be strongly related. Thus, an environmental factor that predicts people's affectionate behavior in their marriages, for instance, may also account for variance in their affectionate behavior across the board (i.e., at a trait level).

However potent environmental influences are, a second important observation is that the influence of innate factors is nonzero. No scholar would claim on the basis of existing research that innate influences, such as genetics or hormone levels, can account for *all* the variance in affectionate tendencies; nonetheless, these studies support the claim that environmental influences likewise fail to account for all the variance.

This, then, is not a question of "nature versus nurture" in what accounts for how affectionate people are. The most likely answer to emerge over time is that some variation in affectionate behavior is attributable to biological factors, some is attributable to environmental factors, and some is attributable to their interactions, wherein people may be genetically predisposed toward a high trait affection level but find that the predisposition manifests itself only if specific environmental characteristics (e.g., parental reinforcement, cultural prescriptions) are present. As an example of the latter, Floyd and Denes (2015) reported that trait affection levels were predicted by an interaction between genotypic variation on a single nucleotide polymorphism (a "nature" cause) and attachment security, which attachment theory predicts is formed through interaction with one's primary caregiver in infancy (a "nurture" cause). Rather than illustrating the concept of nature *versus* nurture, this finding exemplifies what Ridley (2003) called nature *via* nurture – the claim that innate influences can predispose an individual toward a particular behavioral pattern but that such a predisposition is activated only under particular environmental circumstances (in the way that genotypic variation on rs53576 was influential when attachment security was weak rather than strong). There are likely to be many such interactions between innate and environmental influences on affectionate behavior that await discovery.

The very idea of innate influences on behavior – particularly genetic ones – has been met with consternation in some of the social sciences. This often reflects a fear that such an idea implies *biological determinism*, the notion that one's biological or genetic characteristics not only influence behavior but determine it. Such a claim would understandably be troubling to communication scholars, whose work often focuses on improving communication skills through direct instruction and practice. Efforts of that nature would seem to be futile if social skills were biologically determined, and because that idea is unpalatable, many communication scholars have rejected wholesale the proposition that social behavior has any innate antecedents.

In point of fact, however, this is a straw man argument to begin with (see Floyd, 2014b; Floyd & Afifi, 2012). "Influence" does not mean "determine," and no serious scholar working in the field of psychophysiology or biological psychology espouses the claim that social behavior is dictated by genetic or biological influences. To be sure, innate characteristics such as genotype, neurological activity, and baseline hormone levels can predispose an individual to behave in a particular manner – such as predisposing someone to be highly affectionate – but such characteristics neither *cause* the behavior to be enacted nor *constrain* the possibility that the individual might behave contrary to his or her predisposition. There is little doubt, for instance, that certain genotypes are associated with the probability of certain behavioral patterns, but genes do not "code for" behaviors. They, and other innate influences, simply elevate the likelihood of some behaviors over others.

There is an irony in the social sciences' fear of biological determinism, insofar as the prospect of *environmental determinism* is all but accepted as axiomatic. There is virtually no controversy in the proposition that individuals behave as they do *because of* their culture, their familial upbringing, their peer influences, their media use, or their exposure to education. The idea, for instance, that teaching students public speaking skills *makes them good speakers* seems self-evident, but the idea that having a specific variant on a SNP makes students good speakers seems inconceivable, even threatening.

On these points, it is useful to bear in mind the concept of accounting for variance. A social behavior, such as affectionate communication, varies both within and between people, and the social sciences seek to identify characteristics that account for at least some of that variation. Research clearly demonstrates that some portions of variance in affectionate behavior are accounted for by environmental factors, such as upbringing, culture, and aspects of the social context. Nonetheless, this research also clearly demonstrates that some portions of the variance are accounted for by innate factors, such as genotype, neurological activity, hormone levels, and biological sex. If the science is sound, it is antiintellectual to embrace one set of findings while rejecting the other as invalid or inconsequential. That is true no matter which set of findings one is embracing. To conclude from the research that only innate factors are relevant for affectionate behavior – and consequently to consider environmental factors to be negligible – would be entirely unwarranted. Similarly, ignoring or discounting innate influences does not render those influences invalid. Genuinely understanding and appreciating what contributes to an individual's social experience, including his or her experience of affectionate communication, requires attending to the breadth of factors that account for variance.

5   Decoding and Responding to Affectionate Messages

As the previous two chapters detailed, individuals use a range of behaviors to encode messages of affection, and their tendencies to do so are influenced by a diversity of innate and environmental factors. Expressions of affection are also provocative events for recipients, however. When individuals receive affectionate behaviors, they are typically motivated to make at least two assessments: Are they correctly decoding these behaviors as affectionate messages? and How should they respond to them? This chapter reviews research that has addressed how people manage each of these tasks.

Decoding Behaviors as Affectionate

Competence in telling friend from foe is one of the most useful human abilities in terms of individual and group survival. Affectionate communication most assuredly plays a part in forming and maintaining pair bonds and other significant relationships, but only to the extent that one's affectionate behaviors are decoded as such by recipients. As Chapter 9 details, incongruence between a sender's intention with an affectionate message and a receiver's interpretation of that message is one of the major sources of risk in communicating affection in the first place. For these reasons, this section reviews research on the decoding of affectionate behaviors.

The body of research on decoding is small, relative to the larger numbers of studies that have addressed how affection is encoded and how people react to affectionate expressions. This could well reflect a "social meaning" assumption, wherein researchers presume congruence between how people encode and decode a given relational message, and thus tend not to examine that congruence in detail (see, e.g., Burgoon & Newton, 1991). That is likely a safe assumption; one can easily imagine how disjointed communication efforts would be if there were frequently large gaps in how the same messages were encoded and decoded. There is still something to be learned by examining the decoding of affectionate behavior in greater detail, however. The few studies that have done so can be divided into two focus areas. Those in the first group have examined congruence between particular behaviors and affectionate interpretations; thus, they indicate *which behaviors are most likely to be decoded as affectionate.* Those in the second group have focused on intensity ratings for affectionate expressions; these studies indicate *which behaviors communicate affection most intensely.* Findings from each group of studies are examined subsequently.

Congruence between Behaviors and Affectionate Interpretations

Chapter 3 described a tripartite model in which expressions of affection are categorized as being verbal statements, direct nonverbal gestures, or provisions of affectionate social support. Research on the congruence between specific behaviors and affectionate interpretations has thus far focused solely on behaviors in the second category, nonverbal gestures. This may be because verbal expressions are relatively unambiguous in their affectionate intentions (statements such as "I like you," "I love you," or "I feel close to you" are easily decodable as gestures of affection) and/or because provisions of social support serve associated instrumental purposes (i.e., meeting whatever need prompted them) and so their affectionate intentions can be secondary. Neither of these is a particularly *good* reason for failing to examine decoding in greater detail. On the contrary, more attention should be paid to decoding, particularly with affectionate social support, given that it is a relatively common means of communicating affection in many relationships.

The most direct examinations of the congruence between particular behaviors and affectionate decoding were provided in studies by Ray and Floyd (2006) and by Palmer and Simmons (1995). In the Ray and Floyd study, pairs of college students (one of whom was induced to be a participant confederate) interacted with each other in two short laboratory conversations. Prior to the second conversation, confederates were instructed either to greatly increase or to greatly decrease the extent to which they communicated messages of liking and affection to their partners. They received no instructions as to the particular behaviors they should use to accomplish this task, except that they should enact the manipulation nonverbally, rather than verbally. The confederates' nonverbal behaviors during the second conversation were extensively coded and compared with their partners' reports of how affectionate the confederates were and also with the reports of third-party observers who were watching the conversations on a closed-circuit television.

Table 5.1 *Correlations between confederates' nonverbal behaviors and participants' and observers' reports of confederates' affection level, from Ray and Floyd (2006)*

Behavior	Participants' Report	Observers' Report
Animation	.34**	.32*
Smiling	.40**	.28*
Head nodding	.32*	.42**
Illustrators	.29*	.47**
Self-adaptors	.01	.11
Other-adaptors	−.22	−.32*
Gaze	.43**	.35**
Proximity	.23	.18
Forward lean	.26*	.14
Postural matching	−.19	−.01
Direct body orientation	.06	.03
Vocal pitch	−.17	−.19
Vocal pitch variance	.47**	.43**
Vocal intensity	−.03	−.04
Vocal intensity variance	.18	.00
Talk time	.06	.20
Pleasantness	.40**	.38**
Friendliness	.37**	.38**
Warmth	.40**	.29*
Involvement	.41**	.48**
Participativeness	.41**	.47**
Interest	.42**	.46**

*$p < .05$; **$p < .01$. Probability values are one-tailed for animation, smiling, gaze, proximity, forward lean, postural matching, vocal pitch variance, pleasantness, friendliness, warmth, involvement, participativeness, and interest, and are two-tailed for the remaining behaviors.

Most of the associations with nonverbal behaviors are reported in the Ray and Floyd (2006) paper. In line with the advice of Burgoon and Le Poire (1999), coding of the confederates included their micro-level behaviors (e.g., smiling, head nodding, body orientation) and also macro-level perceptions of their behaviors (e.g., how friendly, pleasant, and involved the confederates were). Ray and Floyd then examined correlations between these codes and participants' and observers' reports of how affectionate the confederates were being during the second conversation.

Two noteworthy patterns emerged. First, several behaviors were significantly associated with reports of affection. The correlation coefficients, including the nonsignificant correlations, appear in Table 5.1.

With respect to micro-level behaviors, affection was directly related to facial animation, smiling, head nodding (as a type of backchanneling behavior), the use of illustrator gestures, eye contact, and vocal pitch variation. Participants' perceptions of confederates' affection were also directly related to the confederates' forward lean, whereas observers' perceptions of confederates' affection were inversely related to the confederates' use of other-adaptor gestures (behaviors such as picking lint off someone else's clothing). With respect to macro-level perceptions, affection was directly related to pleasantness, friendliness, warmth, involvement, and how participative and interested confederates appeared to be.

For exploratory purposes, Ray and Floyd also examined whether any linear combinations of the behaviors would predict assessments of confederates' affection levels better than the individual behaviors did. They ascertained this by regressing reports of affection level on the behaviors in stepwise regression analyses, which do not presume any hierarchical ordering of the predictor variables but test for all possible linear combinations. The regressions indicated that a combination of vocal pitch variance and warmth best predicted participants' assessment of confederates' affection level (adjusted R^2 = .27), whereas observers' assessment of confederates' affection level was best predicted by a combination of illustrator gestures and pitch variance (adjusted R^2 = .25).

The second aspect of the results that is noteworthy is the degree of correspondence between participants' and observers' reports. This follows from the social meaning orientation to nonverbal behavior, mentioned above. Participants' and observers' points of view diverged for only two behaviors (forward lean and other adaptors), and these differences were only in terms of statistical significance: the correlation between the behavior and the report of affection level was significant for one person but not for the other. In no case (including the nonsignificant correlations) was a behavior directly related to participants' assessments but inversely related to observers', or vice versa. That does not imply that the distinction between participants and observers is a trivial one; as discussed below, the difference between these points of view certainly has implications for reactions to affectionate behavior (especially cognitive reactions). It does, however, lend credence to the idea behind the social meaning orientation to nonverbal behavior by indicating that, with few exceptions, conversational participants and third-party observers converged in their decoding of confederates' behaviors.

Although acoustic analyses of confederates' voices were included in the behaviors reported in the Ray and Floyd (2006) paper, further analyses of vocalic properties appear in papers by Farley et al. (2013) and Floyd and Ray (2003). Floyd and Ray present hierarchical regression analyses using participants' and observers' reports of confederates' affection levels as criterion variables. Control variables were the sex of the confederate and the confederates' talk time, measured in seconds. The predictor variables were confederates' vocalic fundamental frequency (F_0), variance in fundamental frequency, and vocalic loudness. Working from affection exchange theory, Floyd and Ray hypothesized that F_0 and variance in F_0 both would show direct relationships with participants' and observers' reports of confederates' affection levels, whereas loudness would show an inverse relationship with these outcomes.

For F_0, observers' reports manifested the predicted linear relationship. Participants' reports were subject to a sex-by-F_0 interaction effect, however, which indicated that the predicted linear relationship held for female confederates only. For male confederates, F_0 was inversely related to participants' reports of their affection level, which was contrary to the hypothesis. Both participants' and observers' reports of confederates' affection levels were linearly related to confederates' variance in F_0, as hypothesized. Contrary to the prediction, however, neither participants' nor observers' reports were significantly related to confederates' vocal loudness (although both relationships were inverse, as expected).

Floyd and Ray had therefore found that speaking in a higher pitch was decoded as more affectionate for women, whereas the opposite was true for men. When asked to decode the level of love in a verbal expression of the phrase "how are you," however, participants in the Farley et al. (2013) experiment decoded higher-pitched voices as more loving, whether those voices were male or female.

The Palmer and Simmons (1995) experiment was designed to focus on expressions of liking, which is certainly implicated in affection. In their study, participant confederates were induced to show either increased or decreased liking for a naïve partner, using nonverbal behaviors. The partners were then asked to indicate their levels of liking for the confederates. Palmer and Simmons looked to see which nonverbal behaviors were most strongly associated with changes in participants' levels of liking for the confederates. They did not code for as many behaviors as did Ray and Floyd, but they identified similar results.

Specifically, Palmer and Simmons found that participants' judgments of liking for confederates were associated with increases in three of the confederates' behaviors: eye contact, smiling, and the use of object-focused gestures. They had also predicted that liking would be directly associated with head nodding and inversely associated with the use of self-adaptor gestures, but neither of these associations was significant.

Perhaps the most appropriate conclusion to be drawn from these decoding studies is that there is a core set of behaviors that people tend to interpret as expressions of liking, love, or affection. These behaviors tend to be those that convey interest in, and attraction toward, the recipient (e.g., smiling, gaze) and those that convey involvement in the interaction (e.g., facial and vocal animation, head nodding). The idea of a core set of behavioral indicators of affection naturally poses the question of how culturally variant or invariant those behaviors are. Few studies have examined whether affectionate expressions encoded by people from one culture are decoded as such by people from another, but Laukka et al. (2013) explored this question using nonlinguistic vocalizations. The researchers selected recordings from a cross-cultural database featuring professional actors from India, Kenya, Singapore, and the United States enacting nonlinguistic vocalizations of multiple positive and negative emotions. In the study, Swedish adults listened to recordings of nine positive emotions, including affection, and were tasked with matching each sound to the proper emotion. The researchers then calculated accuracy scores – representing the percentage of vocalizations whose emotional meanings were decoded correctly – for each emotion and for the cultural background of each speaker.

Out of nine positive emotions,[1] affection was decoded with the lowest accuracy. Participants were most accurate at decoding affection when listening to actors from Kenya (24 percent) and India (21 percent), but these accuracy scores were far below the averages for other positive emotions. When listening to actors from Singapore (18 percent) and the United States (16 percent), participants did not accurately decode affection at rates significantly greater than chance (see also Jiang, 2017).

The Laukka study was severely limited by its reliance on nonlinguistic vocalizations, a behavior that no previous study had identified as denoting affection.[2] The study was also limited by its use of encoders from only four cultures and decoders from only one. Nonetheless, Laukka and colleagues provide some of the first evidence suggesting that affectionate behavior may not be decoded with high consistency from one cultural context to the next, although much more remains to be discovered before that conclusion is warranted.

Just because multiple behaviors are decoded as expressions of affection, however, that does not suggest that the behaviors are equal in their intensity nor in the magnitude with which they convey affectionate intentions. Research on this point is described subsequently.

Ratings of Intensity for Affectionate Expressions

Although there are numerous ways to encode affectionate expressions, decoders tend not to attribute the same level of intensity to all of them.

The statement "I like you" and the statement "I'm in love with you" are both affectionate verbal behaviors, but they clearly differ from each other in the *magnitude* of affection they convey. Thus, besides looking at which behaviors convey affection in the first place, it is instructive also to look at variation in intensity.

Two studies have elicited ratings of intensity for affectionate expressions. The first, by Shuntich and Shapiro (1991), focused on verbal behaviors only. The researchers constructed a list of ten verbal statements that were meant to convey to the receiver that "the person saying the statement feels positively toward her/him and is trying to convey this feeling" (p. 285). They then presented the list to a group of 102 undergraduate students (46 male, 56 female) and asked the students to rate each statement on a seven-point scale in which high scores meant "high intensity" and low scores meant "low intensity."

The means and standard deviations for each of the ten statements appear in Table 5.2. The most intense statements on Shuntich and Shapiro's list were "I care for you very much" (mean intensity rating = 6.34) and "I like you very much" (mean intensity rating = 6.32). Because they intended to use these statements in later experiments with platonic pairs, Shuntich and Shapiro did not include statements dealing with love or being in love; presumably, these would have elicited higher intensity ratings. The least intense statements on the list were "I think you're OK" (mean = 3.51) and "I think you are sort of nice" (mean = 3.34). In a later experiment, Shuntich and Shapiro found that participants who were the receivers of affectionate statements from their list, as opposed to aggressive or neutral statements, judged the senders as being less hostile, less violent, less aggressive, warmer, and – understandably – more affectionate.

A later study by Floyd (1997b) expanded on Shuntich and Shapiro's efforts by asking participants to rate the intensity of a list of behaviors that included both verbal and nonverbal expressions of affection. The verbal statements included expressions of love, liking, and admiration, and the nonverbal behaviors included hugging, kissing, holding hands, and other affectionate gestures. As in the Shuntich and Shapiro study, undergraduate students (65 male, 71 female) rated each behavior for intensity; however, the Floyd study used a five-point scale instead of a seven-point scale. Means for intensity for all of the behaviors appear in Table 5.2.

Unlike Shuntich and Shapiro, Floyd had not designed the stimuli to be relevant for platonic pairs only, so they reflect a mix of behaviors that might be observed in platonic, romantic, and familial relationships. In this study, the behaviors that elicited the highest intensity ratings were

Table 5.2 *Intensity ratings for verbal and nonverbal expressions of affection from Shuntich and Shapiro (1991) and Floyd (1997b)*

Behavior	Intensity Rating
Verbal Statements from Shuntich and Shapiro (1991)	
"I think you are sort of nice"	3.34
"I think you're OK"	3.51
"I think you are interesting"	4.29
"I think you are pleasant"	4.34
"I like you"	5.31
"I admire you"	5.35
"I value you a great deal"	5.77
"I'm very fond of you"	5.80
"I like you very much"	6.32
"I care for you very much"	6.34
Verbal Statements from Floyd (1997b)	
"I admire you"	1.91
"I value our relationship"	2.46
"I like you"	2.91
"I'm fond of you"	3.18
"I feel close to you"	3.64
"I care for you"	4.27
"I love you"	4.64
Nonverbal Behaviors from Floyd (1997b)	
Shake hands	1.27
Put arm around shoulder	2.00
Hold hands	2.36
Kiss on cheek	3.63
Hug	3.73
Kiss on lips	4.64

Note: Ratings from Shuntich and Shapiro (1991) were made on seven-point scales. Ratings from Floyd (1997b) were made on five-point scales. In both cases, higher mean scores indicate greater intensity of the behavior.

kissing on the lips and saying "I love you." Both earned a mean intensity rating of 4.64 out of a possible 5.00. Shaking hands was judged to be the least intense nonverbal affectionate behavior (mean = 1.27) and saying "I admire you" received the lowest intensity rating among the verbal statements (mean = 1.91).

The question of intensity is consequential because it directly implicates the *value* that decoders place on various affectionate behaviors. Numerous theories in both the evolutionary and social learning paradigms capitalize on the concept of exchange – the give and take of resources of value. Affection often functions as one such commodity; reciprocating one affectionate expression (e.g., "I'm in love with you") with another of lesser intensity (e.g., "I think you're neat") can cause distress for the original speaker, whose positive face is likely to be highly threatened by such a move (see Erbert & Floyd, 2004). The "commodities" being exchanged in such an interaction are of unequal value; specifically, they are of unequal relational value. For this reason, it is important for affection researchers to be cognizant not only of the *amount* of affection being communicated by study participants but also of the *intensity* being conveyed.

The body of research that has examined the decoding and intensity of affectionate behaviors is small, but its findings have been relatively consistent. In contrast, several studies have investigated how decoders react and respond to expressions of affection. This research is described in the next section.

Responding to Expressions of Affection

Expressions of affection are notable communicative events and they rarely fail to elicit some type of reaction from receivers. Certainly, people do not always respond to affectionate behaviors in ways that senders wish, and as Chapter 9 details, uncertainty about a receiver's response is one of the major risks of expressing affection in the first place. What determines how receivers of affectionate messages respond to them? This section reviews research that has addressed this question. Importantly, one must distinguish between two major types of responses: cognitive responses and behavioral responses. The former category concerns judgments and interpretations that receivers make, and the latter concerns the behaviors that receivers enact in response to the message. Although these two types of responses are often complementary, it is useful to discuss them individually because they do not necessarily covary.

Responding Cognitively to Affectionate Expressions

A good deal of research has addressed people's cognitive responses to affectionate behaviors. Participants in some studies acted as receivers, responding to expressions of affection that were directed at them. In other studies, participants acted as observers and responded to behaviors they witnessed. To make sense of this research, one must first distinguish between three types of cognitive responses (these apply to people's cognitive responses to all behaviors, not just affectionate messages). The first are *evaluations*, which deal with the valence of people's judgments about a behavior: Is the behavior positive or negative? The second are *interpretations*, which pertain to people's sense-making judgments about a behavior: What does the behavior mean?[3] Finally, cognitions of the third type, *attributions*, pertain to people's inferences about the cause of a behavior: Why did the behavior occur? Although most of the studies reviewed in this section have examined only one of these types of cognitive responses, those that have included more than one type have tended to find correspondence between them (i.e., positive evaluations coincide with positive interpretations and/or positive attributions).

This section reviews research that has investigated each of these three types of cognitive responses. The focus will be on identifying the antecedents of cognitive responses – that is, on what makes someone evaluate an affectionate expression negatively instead of positively or attribute it to a favorable cause rather than an unfavorable one.

Evaluations

Multiple studies have examined how people evaluate expressions of affection, either as receivers of those expressions or as third-party observers. The question undergirding an evaluative response is one of valence: is the received (or observed) behavior good or bad, positive or negative, appropriate or inappropriate? Approaches to measuring evaluative responses have ranged from single-item bipolar adjective scales (such as a seven-point scale on which the low end signifies "negative" or "inappropriate" and the high end signifies "positive" or "appropriate") to validated, multiple-item measures (such as the four-item evaluation measure developed by Burgoon, Newton, Walther, & Baesler, 1989).

In this section, the discussion of each study will note how evaluation was assessed, because that can influence the appropriate interpretation of the findings. For instance, a rating of appropriateness may be more context-specific than a rating of positivity; some behaviors may be appropriate for certain individuals in certain situations, whereas other behaviors could be judged as inherently negative, regardless of the context. Thus, although ratings of appropriateness and ratings of positivity are both evaluative measures, they may tap different aspects of an evaluation.

Research on the evaluation of affectionate communication can readily be divided into two categories: those studies that have evaluated changes in people's overall levels of affectionate behavior and those studies that have evaluated specific affectionate expressions (and have examined the variables that influence those evaluations). Studies in the former category have generally been laboratory experiments in which participants evaluated the actions of a confederate who behaved in an increasingly engaged, affectionate way during a conversation or else decreased his or her level of engagement and affection. Experiments by Floyd and

Mikkelson (2004), Floyd and Ray (2000), and Floyd and Voloudakis (1999a), each of which used the Burgoon et al. (1989) evaluation scale, have all reported the same overall pattern: participants' evaluations of confederates become more positive as the confederates become more affectionate, and become more negative as the confederates become less affectionate.

That is certainly no surprise; given the importance of affectionate communication in relational interaction, one should generally expect people to evaluate it positively *in the absence of a reason not to*. Notably, this does not mean there are no valid reasons to react negatively to affectionate behavior; indeed, the risks of affectionate communication are examined in detail in Chapter 9. Neither does it suggest that all affectionate behaviors in all contexts will be evaluated positively. Indeed, research has shown that several aspects of affectionate exchanges, including characteristics of the communicators and of the behaviors themselves, influence how those behaviors are evaluated. Research on particular forms of affectionate communication has identified many of those aspects.

Of the studies that have addressed evaluations of specific affectionate behaviors, most have focused on affectionate touch. Some have used the scenario method, wherein participants respond to written descriptions of a situation. Rane and Draper (1995), for instance, used written scenarios to study evaluations of men's and women's nurturant touching of young children. Their scenarios varied according to whether (a) the subject of the scenario was a woman or man; (b) the subject did or did not engage in nurturant touching with children; (c) the children in the scenario were the subject's own children or a neighbor's children; and (d) the context of the scenario was a bedtime setting or a playground setting. Nurturant touching included hugging, giving back rubs, holding a child on one's lap, putting an arm around a child's shoulder, and holding a child to comfort him or her. Participants in the study, who were undergraduate students, each read one of the scenarios and provided an evaluation of the "goodness" of the adult subject in the story. Rane and Draper measured evaluation by summing the ratings participants gave on three bipolar adjective scales: pleasant/unpleasant, well-adjusted/maladjusted, and good/bad.

Two results were particularly noteworthy with respect to evaluation. First, story characters who engaged in nurturant touching were evaluated more positively than those who did not, and this difference was more pronounced for women than for men. Interestingly, although participants evaluated male characters who engaged in nurturant touching more positively than those who did not, they also rated the nurturantly touching males as being less masculine than the nontouchers.[4] The latter result replicated one identified earlier by Draper and Gordon (1986) in a study of men's perceptions of nurturing behavior in other men. Rane and Draper suggested that the inverse relationship between touching and ratings of masculinity could fuel men's unwillingness to engage in nurturant touching out of a fear of appearing feminine. Alternatively, one might speculate that, because men's nurturant touching was judged as *both* less masculine *and* more positive than the absence of touch, masculinity is not an especially useful quality when it comes to men's (and particularly fathers') nurturant interactions with young children.[5]

The second finding of interest was that participants evaluated male story characters with their own children and female story characters with a neighbor's children more positively than they evaluated males with a neighbor's children and females with their own children. Rane and Draper interpreted this finding as reflecting a stereotypical view that women are better suited than men to provide care for young children who are not their own.

Harrison-Speake and Willis (1995) also studied adult-to-child touch within the context of the family using a scenario method. Unlike in Rane and Draper's study, their scenarios depicted adults interacting only with their own children, and they varied the sex of the child as well as the sex of the parent. They also varied the age of the child (2, 6, 10, and 14 years of age), and they separately described four different touch sequences: child sitting on parent's lap, parent kissing child on the lips, parents and child sleeping together in the same bed, and parent giving child a bath. Adult participants read all of the scenarios and provided an evaluation for each, using a single-item bipolar adjective scale with "very appropriate" and "very inappropriate" as the anchors.

Several main and interaction effects achieved significance in the Harrison-Speake and Willis study (see a separate discussion of this study in Chapter 4). Among them, participants evaluated mothers more positively than fathers in the kissing, bathing, and lap-sitting scenarios, and the differences between mothers and fathers were greater for older children than for younger children. Other research has suggested that, as their children age, men decrease their affectionate communication to their children more than women do (see, e.g., Morman & Floyd, 1999; Salt, 1991), and this finding concurs. Harrison-Speake and Willis suggested that men, especially, curtail their affectionate touch as their children age, given the likelihood that male touch could be interpreted as sexual.

Moreover, participants evaluated the touch scenarios involving kissing and lap-sitting more positively when the child depicted was a girl than when it was a boy. That was true regardless of the age of the child or the sex of the parent, and it confirmed Jourard's (1966) earlier finding that daughters receive more parental touch than do sons.

The findings from these two scenario studies are useful in that they identify specific influences on people's evaluative responses to affectionate expressions. Importantly – but perhaps not surprisingly – many of these variables parallel those that influence how affectionate people are in the first place: the sex of the person enacting the behavior, the sex of the person receiving the behavior, the nature of the relationship between them, the form that the affectionate behavior takes, and the context in which it occurs. This point is revisited later.

Additional evidence that the form of an affectionate touch can directly influence evaluations of it comes from an experiment that manipulated the form and duration of an embrace (Floyd, 1999). In that study, participants watched a videotape of two actors enacting one of three forms of an embrace – a "criss-cross" hug, in which each person has one arm over and one arm under the shoulder of the other; a "neck–waist" hug, in which one person's arms are around the other's neck, and the other person's arms are around the other's waist; and an "engulfing" hug, in which one person's arms are pulled to his or her chest and the other's arms completely envelop him or her – for one of three durations (one, three, or five seconds). These conditions were crossed with the sex-pairing of the actors (either male–male or female–female) to create eighteen experimental conditions. Participants evaluated the scenario they watched by completing the four-item evaluation scale developed by Burgoon et al. (1989).

These specific forms of the embrace were chosen to represent differing levels of egalitarianism in the behavior. That is, because the criss-cross hug was the most "balanced" in terms of the relative physical positioning of the two participants, Floyd speculated that it would be judged by observers as being the most egalitarian. He further expected that the neck–waist hug would be seen as less egalitarian and that the engulfing hug would be seen as the least egalitarian of the three. A manipulation check using the equality subscale of Burgoon and Hale's (1987) Relational Communication Scale confirmed these speculations.

Unlike in the Rane and Draper (1995) or Harrison-Speake and Willis (1995) studies, neither the sex of the actors nor the sex of the partici-pants, alone or in combination, exerted any influence on evaluations in the Floyd (1999) study. However, both the form of the embrace and its duration had main effects on participants' evaluations. Specifically, par-ticipants evaluated the criss-cross hug the most positively, followed by the neck–waist hug and then the engulfing hug. Expressed differently, evaluations declined in positivity as the embraces became less egalitarian.

Participants also preferred shorter hugs over longer ones: the one-second embrace was evaluated the most positively, followed (interestingly) by the five-second embrace and then by the three-second embrace (focused contrasts indicated, however, that only the one- and three-second hugs differed significantly from each other, whereas neither differed significantly from the five-second hug).

Do these findings indicate that people are most favorably disposed to brief, egalitarian hugs? Perhaps in this particular context they are, although it is important to note that the actors in the videotapes were all students in their early twenties interacting in same-sex pairs, and so participants probably attributed a good deal of egalitarianism to the relationships between the actors anyway. In fact, when asked to speculate as to what kind of relationship the actors in each videotape had to each other, participants were substantially more likely to conclude that the actors were platonic friends, as opposed to relatives.

Research has also investigated the evaluation of affectionate behaviors other than touch. The Floyd and Morman (2000b) experiment, for instance, looked at evaluative responses to verbal affection, specifically the verbal expression of love. Participants in that study read a short transcript of a conversation occurring either between two women or two men in which one communicator said "I love you" to the other. The transcript stimulus was chosen over an audio or video recording so as to isolate the verbal channel and remove the possibility that nonverbal cues, such as facial expression or tone of voice, would be rival causes for the effects. As in Floyd (1999), participants provided their evaluations of the interaction they read by responding to the evaluation scale created by Burgoon et al. (1989).

Whereas no effects of actor or participant sex were found for evaluations of touch in the Floyd (1999) experiment, the Floyd and Morman (2000b) results indicated that participants' sex interacted with the sex of the communicators depicted in the transcripts to influence the participants' evaluations. The interaction effect is depicted in Figure 5.1. As the figure shows, both male and female participants evaluated the conversations more positively when the expression of affection occurred between two women than when it occurred between two men, and there was almost no difference in the evaluations that male and female participants gave to the female–female conversation. This is similar to the finding, reported by Harrison-Speake and Willis (1995), that women engaging in affectionate touch were evaluated more positively than were men engaging in the same touches.

Male and female participants disagreed more strongly in their evaluations of the male–male affectionate exchange, however. Female participants

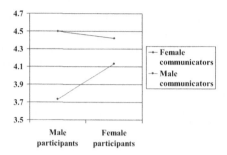

Figure 5.1 Interaction of participant and communicator sex on participants' evaluations of communicators' affection behaviors. (Floyd & Morman, 2000b). Used with permission

evaluated it only slightly more positively than they had evaluated the women's conversation. Male participants, on the other hand, evaluated male–male affection more negatively than they evaluated female–female affection, and much more negatively than the female participants had evaluated either conversation. An earlier experiment (Floyd & Morman, 1997) similarly found that women did not differentiate between female–female and opposite-sex platonic relationships in terms of their evaluation of affection (measured in that experiment using a single-item bipolar adjective scale with "very appropriate" and "very inappropriate" as the anchors). Men, however, reported that affectionate behavior was significantly more appropriate in opposite-sex platonic pairs than in male–male dyads. The 1997 experiment used a battery of verbal and nonverbal behaviors as the operational definition of affection, instead of a single touch or verbal behavior. Also found was that affectionate behavior was evaluated more positively when it occurred between siblings than between unrelated friends, and this difference between relationships was substantially more pronounced for men than for women.

Studying the evaluations that receivers assign to affection expressions provides one barometer for their cognitive reactions. In some ways, the judgment of whether a given behavior is positive or negative is the most fundamental of judgments one can make. However, it is often accompanied by other, more complex cognitive reactions, including interpretations and attributions.

Interpretations

The issue of interpretations concerns the relational meanings that decoders ascribe to communication behaviors. Half a century ago, in one of the foundational works of the human communication discipline,

Watzlawick, Beavin, and Jackson (1967) distinguished between the *content* and *relational* dimensions of messages. A given verbal message, for instance, conveys both a literal meaning and an implied meaning about the relationship in which it is communicated. If one person says to a friend "I feel scared about the future," the content dimension of the statement is its literal message (the speaker feels scared about the future). However, the statement may also implicitly convey relational messages to the hearer, such as "I trust you," "I feel I can be vulnerable with you," or "I want you to protect me." In truth, there are multiple types of relational messages that a given behavior can convey. In their seminal work on relational communication, Burgoon and Hale (1984) proposed that there are as many as a dozen conceptually distinct relational meanings that a specific behavior can express, which include meanings of dominance, emotional arousal, composure, similarity, formality, task versus social orientation, intimacy, depth/familiarity, attraction/liking, inclusion, trust, and involvement. Most studies using Burgoon and Hale's (1987) measure have combined these relational messages, through factor analyses, into a smaller number of more conceptually and empirically orthogonal themes (typically between three and seven).[6] Other meanings that are often examined in this type of research include attraction and credibility.

What kinds of relational meanings do affectionate behaviors convey? One could certainly intuit that they communicate messages of interest, attraction, or intimacy, but do decoders attach other types of relational interpretations to them, as well? Four experiments have examined this question, the earliest of which was the Floyd and Voloudakis (1999a) study of adult platonic friends. In that study, friends interacted in the laboratory and one friend in each pair was induced to increase or decrease his or her affectionate behaviors toward the other. Before and after the manipulation, the naïve participants' relational interpretations of the confederates' behaviors were assessed using Burgoon and Hale's (1987) relational communication scale, McCroskey and McCain's (1974) interpersonal attraction scale (which measures both *social attraction*, or attraction to one's personality, and *task attraction*, or attraction to one's abilities), and McCroskey and Young's (1981) credibility scale (which measures both *competence* and the quality of one's *character*).

Several of these assessments were affected by the confederates' affectionate behaviors. Specifically, confederates who became more affectionate over time were judged by their friends as conveying more immediacy, being more receptive, being more composed, having more positive character, being more informal, and seeing themselves as more similar to the participants. Those confederates who became less affectionate over time received the opposite assessments. There were no significant effects in this study for dominance, equality, or attraction.

In the Floyd and Voloudakis study, the participant confederates were instructed to increase or decrease their affectionate behaviors toward their partners but were not given any instruction as to the specific behaviors to manipulate. Numerous manipulation checks confirmed the efficacy of the manipulation; however, it is difficult to know *which* behaviors, in particular, contributed to changes in participants' relational message interpretations. Ray and Floyd (2006) examined the links between specific affection behaviors and relational message interpretations more directly, although this study looked only at the confederates' social attractiveness as an outcome measure. The design of the Ray and Floyd experiment was nearly identical to that used by Floyd and Voloudakis, except that strangers were used instead of friends and each dyad had a third-party observer who also provided assessments of the confederates. Ray and Floyd found that participants' social attraction to the confederates was directly related to how much the confederates smiled, nodded their heads, maintained eye contact, leaned forward, maintained proximity, and varied the pitch in their voices. Observers' social attraction to the confederates was likewise predicted by head nodding, eye contact, and vocal pitch variation, as well as by how much the confederates talked to the participants.

Expressions of affection often involve a combination of behaviors (e.g., smiling, touching, maintaining eye contact, increasing vocal warmth, and saying "I care about you" all in tandem), rather than single behaviors in isolation. Two other studies have examined relational message interpretations of affectionate behavior using multi-cue manipulations (i.e., those in which confederates manipulate several affection behaviors at once). Unlike the Floyd and Voloudakis study, both of these involved trained confederates interacting with strangers. In the first (Floyd, 1998), confederates were instructed to modify six behaviors during an experimental interaction with a naïve participant: smiling, gaze, touch, proximity, forward lean, and postural matching. Confederates in the "high affection" condition were specifically trained to smile a great deal, maintain moderate gaze with participants, touch participants during the interaction, sit close to participants, lean forward while speaking, and match the way participants were sitting (in terms of their arm and leg positions). Confederates in the "low affection" condition received the opposite instructions. As in the other experiments, participants were asked to rate confederates in terms of their relational messages after the conversations.

In this study, significant differences between the high and low affection groups were observed for only three relational messages: competence, composure, and intimacy. In all cases, confederates in the high affection condition were rated higher than those in the low affection condition, as one might expect. Given the number of associations between affectionate behaviors and relational message interpretations identified in the Floyd and Voloudakis and the Ray and Floyd studies, it was surprising to find differences on only three such messages in the Floyd (1998) study. One methodological characteristic of the Floyd (1998) study that distinguished it from the others, however, was that it used a between-subjects design instead of a repeated-measures design. In the other studies, confederates all began their laboratory conversations without manipulating any of their behaviors, and then changed their behaviors at specified points during the interactions. In the Floyd study, confederates behaved in either affectionate or nonaffectionate ways throughout the conversations. Why should this design difference be consequential? Because confederates and participants in the Floyd study were strangers to each other, it could be that the lack of a baseline (nonmanipulated) portion of the conversations led participants to infer that the behaviors the confederates were enacting reflected their normative levels of immediacy, friendliness, and affection, and, thus, had little value as gauges for how the confederates might feel about them. In other words, without the baseline period for comparison, participants may have concluded that confederates were behaving as they would normally and were not, therefore, sending particular relational messages to the participants (at least, ones that would differ by condition).

This is speculation, of course, but the credibility of this explanation is bolstered by the results of a study by Floyd and Mikkelson (2004) that was nearly identical in design to the Floyd (1998) study, except that it used a repeated-measures design. This study also involved interactions between trained confederates and naïve participants who were strangers, and also manipulated the same behaviors that were manipulated in the Floyd (1998) study. The difference was the inclusion of a baseline period prior to the start of the manipulation, and the comparison of participants' reports of confederates' behaviors during both the baseline and the manipulated portions of the conversation.

Unlike in the Floyd (1998) study, several relational messages in the Floyd and Mikkelson study were influenced by confederates' behaviors. Specifically, those confederates who became more affectionate over time were seen as more socially attractive, more task attractive, more involved, more receptive to participants, more similar and equal to participants, and having more positive character. They were also seen as being less dominant and formal. Those confederates who became less affectionate over time elicited the opposite interpretations of their behavior.

Interpretations are important because they aid receivers in ascertaining the implications that a sender's behavior has for the relationship. When one receives an embrace from a platonic friend and interprets it as a romantic gesture, for instance, such an interpretation has implications for the friendship that are different from those associated with an interpretation of the hug as a social support gesture. Thus, it is in people's best interests to be cognizant of the relational meanings inferred from different behaviors, whether enacted by familiar or unfamiliar others.

Finally, in addition to evaluations and interpretations, humans make attributions about other people's behaviors (as well as about their own). Some studies have examined variation in the attributions made for affectionate behaviors, and that research is described in the next section.

Attributions

Research on attributions for affectionate behaviors has focused on people's inferences for the causes of those behaviors. Attribution-making is a pervasive human activity; people continually make inferences about the reasons why things happen, often for the purpose of deciding on the most appropriate response (see, e.g., Heider, 1958; Weiner, 1985). When snubbed by a friend, for example, people will typically respond differently if they perceive the snub was deliberate than if they perceive it was not. Specifically, they may feel more justified reacting with hurt or anger in the former instance than in the latter, on the presumption that if the friend snubbed them on purpose, then the behavior was malicious and the friend should be held accountable for it. On the contrary, if they infer that the behavior was accidental, they may attribute no malice or personal responsibility to it and feel less justified harboring hurt or anger as a result.

Three studies have focused on attribution-making for affectionate expressions. The first, by Booth-Butterfield and Trotta (1994), investigated the attributions people made for a particular affectionate behavior, the verbal expression of love. Respondents in their survey were asked to think of a romantic relationship they had been in, in which the words "I love you" had been uttered. If they could identify such a relationship, they were asked to describe the first time love was verbally expressed in this way and to indicate *why* they thought the expression had occurred. Booth-Butterfield and Trotta analyzed the responses and grouped them into five categories, the first of which was that *the expression reflected the speaker's true feelings.* Slightly more than half (54.8 percent) of the respondents provided this attribution, characterizing the verbal behavior as an accurate reflection of the speaker's love. The second most common attribution was that *the expression was motivated by situational influences.*

This attribution explained the statements as having been prompted by something in the environment – for instance, that the couple had just made love for the first time or was anticipating a temporary separation. Approximately a fifth (20.8 percent) of the respondents provided this attribution.

A third attribution was that *the expression had an ulterior motive.* The respondents who provided this attribution (13.2 percent of the sample) suggested that the speaker expressed love for an underhanded reason, such as trying to convince them to engage in sexual activity or to conduct a type of "secret test" to find out whether the recipient would reciprocate the gesture or not. (The manipulative use of affectionate behavior, including why it can be effective, is discussed in greater detail in Chapter 9.)

The final two attributions, which were each offered by only 5.5 percent of the sample, were that *the expression was meant to convey comfort or support, rather than love* and that *the speaker was simply confused about his or her feelings.* These attributions are similar in that, in both cases, the recipient does not believe the speaker's expression of love was genuine, even though the speaker may have felt that it was.

Two other studies have examined the form (rather than the content) of people's attributions for affectionate expressions. The first was the Floyd and Voloudakis (1999a) study, although the data on attributions are reported in a separate paper (1999b). In that study, participants were asked to provide causal attributions for the behaviors of confederates who had become either increasingly or decreasingly affectionate over the course of a laboratory interaction. The attribution measure, which had been adapted from an earlier study by Manusov, Floyd, and Kerssen-Griep (1997), first asked participants whether any of the confederates' behaviors "stood out" to them during the experimental conversations; if so, participants were instructed to describe those behaviors. (This initial question had the dual purpose of focusing participants' thoughts onto the specific behaviors they would be asked to explain and also of allowing the researchers to discard attributions made about behaviors that were not manipulated in the study.)

If participants responded affirmatively to the first question, they were then asked to respond to the question, "How would you explain your partner's behavior(s)?" Their written responses were later coded along two dimensions: causality (indicating whether the cause of the behaviors was internal to the confederate or external) and responsibility (indicating whether the confederate was responsible for the behaviors or not; see Bradbury & Fincham, 1992; Karney, Bradbury, Fincham, & Sullivan, 1994; Manusov, 1990).

As hypothesized, participants were significantly more likely to offer attributions about decreases in affectionate behavior than about increases. This difference was predicted on the presumption that, because the dyads in the study were platonic friends, decreases in affection would be more unexpected – and, thus, more likely to invoke causal attributions – than would increases. For those participants (in both conditions) who did offer attributions, however, Floyd and Voloudakis then examined their scores for causality and responsibility, as coded from their written attributions, and two findings were particularly noteworthy.

First, Floyd and Voloudakis had hypothesized that, regardless of whether participants received increased or decreased affectionate behavior from the confederates, they would be more likely to attribute the behavior to external and uncontrollable causes than to internal, controllable ones. The justification for this prediction was that, in both conditions, attributing the change in confederates' affectionate behavior to external, uncontrollable causes would "shield" participants from having to attend to the potential relational implications of those changes. In close but nonromantic friendships, decreases in affectionate behavior could signal decreases in liking or interest, whereas increases in affectionate behavior could signal a desire to make the relationship romantic. Either implication could invoke psychological distress for the recipient (a point discussed in greater detail in Chapter 9). Thus, Floyd and Voloudakis reasoned that participants could avoid this potential distress by concluding that the behaviors were not done intentionally but were instead attributable to causes external to the confederates and beyond their control. The data supported that hypothesis.

Also hypothesized was that the intimacy level of the friendship would be influential, such that participants making external, uncontrollable attributions for changes in their friends' affectionate behavior would be those who were in more intimate friendships than those making internal, controllable attributions. Several previous studies had documented that patterns of attribution-making in established relationships are influenced by the intimacy or satisfaction of those relationships (for review, see Bradbury & Fincham, 1990). The Floyd and Voloudakis findings supported the hypothesis for causality but not for responsibility, although the mean difference for responsibility was in the predicted direction.

It is intriguing that the potential relational implications of affection behaviors might have an influence on the attributions receivers make for them. In the attribution literature, the principle of the *self-serving bias* suggests that individuals make attributions for their own behaviors so as to cast themselves in the most favorable light (see, e.g., Mezulis, Abramson, Hyde, & Hankin, 2004; Shepperd, Malone, & Sweeney, 2008).

In particular, it predicts that individuals attribute their successes to internal, controllable causes (e.g., I got an "A" on my test because I'm smart), and attribute their failures to external, uncontrollable causes (e.g., I got an "F" on my test because my child kept me awake the night before). Assumed in this principle is the idea that attributions matter both to how people see themselves and to how others see them. That is, it is less threatening to one's self-image (or "positive face"; see Brown & Levinson, 1987) to say that good behaviors reflect one's inherent goodness, whereas bad behaviors are anomalies caused by external forces over which one has no control.

The self-serving bias, as it has been applied and studied in the attribution literature, has dealt only with people's attributions for their own behaviors. Floyd (2000b), however, suggested that the principle behind the self-serving bias – that people's attributions for behaviors have implications for themselves – ought also to apply to their attributions for others' behaviors, at least when those behaviors would have implications for the self. For example, if one observes a man acting rudely to someone else, one might attribute his behavior to his personality ("he's a jerk") without engaging in more involved cognitive activity. (Indeed, this is precisely the response predicted by another principle of attribution-making, the *fundamental attribution error*; see Ross, 1977.) However, if the man were a friend and his rude behavior were directed at oneself, then the behavior – and one's attribution for it – could carry personal implications for oneself. If, in this situation, one concludes that "he's a jerk," then one must deal with the attendant questions of what this implies for the friendship, what one has done to deserve this treatment, and indeed, why one is friends with a jerk in the first place. In such a context, one might therefore be motivated, at least subconsciously, to find a more external attribution for the friend's behavior that will allow one to sidestep those implications. If, for instance, the friend's behavior is attributed to a temporary situational influence (e.g., "he's been under a lot of stress at work lately"), then one can forgive and forget the behavior without attending to whatever personal or relational implications it might have.

This idea was the basis for the *extended self-serving bias*, proposed by Floyd (2000b). Floyd tested the model with respect to affectionate behavior, using an augmented version of the Floyd and Burgoon (1999) dataset. In that study, participants interacted with trained confederates whose nonverbal behaviors conveyed either liking or disliking. After the interactions, Floyd and Burgoon elicited participants' attributions for the confederates' behaviors, using the same procedure as in the Floyd and Voloudakis (1999b) study described above. Subsequent to the data collection, Floyd recruited a new sample of participants to watch the videotapes of the laboratory conversations and to provide their own attributions for the confederates' behaviors. He coded the attributions from the participants and observers for causality and responsibility dimensions, and then compared them with each other. Because the participants actually received the expressions of liking or disliking, whereas the observers merely witnessed them, Floyd expected their patterns of attribution-making to differ, on the principle that the behaviors ought to have carried more personal implications for the participants than for the observers.

Two comparisons were of particular interest. First, compared with disliking behaviors, Floyd predicted that participants would attribute liking behaviors to causes that were more internal and controllable. Because affectionate behavior has direct personal implications for receivers, then receivers ought to be motivated to explain those behaviors in the most positive way possible. This prediction was supported with respect to both causality and responsibility. Second, Floyd hypothesized that, for expressions of disliking, observers would make more internal and controllable attributions than participants would. Again, because disliking behaviors would not carry the personal implications for observers that they would for participants, he speculated that observers would opt for the less cognitively demanding route and attribute them to the confederates' personalities ("he's acting that way because he's a mean person"), whereas participants would be motivated to look for external causes that would assuage any negative implications the disliking behaviors might have carried for them. This hypothesis was also supported. As anticipated, observers and participants did not differ from each other in their attributions for liking behavior; they were equally likely to attribute such behavior to internal, controllable causes.

At least two conclusions are warranted from these data. First, people's default mode is to respond to affectionate behavior positively, in terms of their evaluations, interpretations, and attributions. This is unsurprising, given affectionate behavior's numerous and substantial benefits to individuals and their relationships. Referring to this as a "default mode," however, suggests that people respond to affectionate behavior positively *unless there is a compelling reason not to*. That qualifier is important, because although humans need affection, they also have other physical, mental, and emotional needs that may be superordinate. When competing needs are strong enough, individuals will react negatively to expressions of affection if those expressions are seen as interfering with the individuals' abilities to satisfy their competing needs. This was evidenced in the Floyd (1998) study, which demonstrated that threats to the need for negative face – the need to avoid being unduly encumbered – can override affection needs and cause people to evaluate affectionate behaviors negatively.

This is significant in an evolutionary sense because motivations that are adaptive individually can often compete with each other. For example, parents can advance their reproductive success by investing resources in their children, but because such a move diverts resources from the parents themselves, it can actually be detrimental to the parents' own survival. Long-term evolutionary success therefore relies partly on people's abilities to manage competing motivations simultaneously. That explains why people can welcome affectionate behavior under most conditions but can react negatively to it when competing needs take precedence. This idea is embodied in affection exchange theory and will underlie the discussion of the risks of expressing affection appearing in Chapter 9.

A second conclusion is that some of the same characteristics that influence how affectionate people are also influence how they react cognitively to affection displays. Those include the sex of the person enacting the affectionate behavior, the sex of the person receiving it, the point of view of the evaluator (whether a recipient of the affection display or a third-party observer), the form of the behavior itself, and the context in which it is displayed. This similarity in sources of influence may not be surprising, but it, too, may be important from an evolutionary perspective. Adaptations, whether physical or psychological, are often equipped to function only in response to particular environmental triggers. As affection exchange theory suggests, affectionate behavior can serve one's motivations for viability and fertility motivations, but only if enacted in such a way that it elicits favor from others. Affection expressed in a manner that causes negative reactions on the part of the receiver is not likely to be of benefit to the sender (or to the receiver, for that matter). It is strategically useful, therefore, for individuals to be sensitive to the interpersonal and contextual variables that influence receivers' reactions to affectionate behavior. It is thus rather efficient that those variables are similar to the ones that influence individuals' affectionate behavior in the first place.

Responding Behaviorally to Affectionate Expressions

Receivers of affectionate expressions have three principal options for their behavioral responses. The first option is to *reciprocate the expression*. This can take the form of direct reciprocity, wherein the receiver displays the same behavior as was directed to him or her (e.g., hearing "I love you" and saying "I love you, too" in return). It might also take the form of indirect reciprocity, wherein the receiver replies with a similar, but not the same, behavior (e.g., hearing "I love you" and then hugging or kissing the sender in return). In the case of indirect reciprocity, however, mere reciprocation is not necessarily sufficient. Rather, one tends to desire a behavioral response that is of approximately the same intensity as the original expression. Hearing "I'm in love with you" and saying "I really like you a lot" in reply qualifies as indirect reciprocity, but the sentiment implied in the response is clearly of a lesser intensity than that implied in the initial expression. Likewise, one may not desire a response that implies a greater intensity, either. Therefore, although reciprocity is generally the most preferred behavioral response to an affectionate expression, its positivity is likely to be moderated by the extent to which the response matches the intensity level of the original expression.

A second option is to *compensate for the expression*. This consists of responding to the affectionate expression with negatively valenced behaviors. An extreme example is hearing the words "I love you" and saying "Well, I hate you" in reply. A more common example involves a sender acting increasingly affectionate toward a receiver who becomes increasingly withdrawn and disengaged from the conversation in response. Behavioral compensation was a key component of Argyle and Dean's (1965) equilibrium theory, which posits that increases in affiliative behavior (such as eye gaze or proximity) induce the receiver to compensate by reducing the level of affiliation in order to maintain equilibrium. As with reciprocity, compensation can be done directly, by changing the same behaviors that were changed before (e.g., taking a step back in response to a partner's step forward), or indirectly, by changing other behaviors that have a similar effect on the interaction (e.g., frowning or crossing one's arms in response to a partner's step forward). Empirical research has largely failed to support the primacy of compensatory adaptation that equilibrium theory predicts. However, it would be reasonable to hypothesize that compensation for expressions of affection is likely when the expressions are threatening to the receiver and/or when the receiver wants to be clear that the affectionate sentiment is not shared.

Finally, a third option is to *fail to respond to the expression*. In this case, the affectionate expression is simply ignored, at least behaviorally. This may be a common response when the receiver finds the expression to be somehow threatening but does not wish to hurt or embarrass the sender. On receiving a message of romantic interest that one does not share, for example, one may not wish to reciprocate the expression, but one may not wish to compensate for it, either, given the risks of hurting the sender's feelings. A receiver ignoring the expression may provide the sender the opportunity to "take the hint" and save face.

In that example, the failure to respond is used strategically for the purpose of steering the outcome of the interaction. In other cases, receivers may fail to respond simply because they are uncertain about *how* to respond. Receivers might be unsure of their reaction because they haven't yet ascertained the meaning of the affectionate expression or perhaps because they are uncertain whether they share the sender's affectionate sentiments.

Certainly, there is a good deal of variation within each of these three types of behavioral responses. To the extent that they constitute the three principal options for responding behaviorally to affectionate expressions, the variables that predict each type of response can be identified. Thus far, three experiments have addressed that topic. These studies used different theories and therefore examined different types of variables as potential predictors of behavioral responses, but taken together, their results begin to answer the question.

The first of the experiments was that conducted by Floyd and Voloudakis (1999a), which examined affectionate behavior in adult platonic friendships and tested hypotheses drawn from expectancy violations theory (EVT). EVT implies that behaviors constituting a positive expectancy violation ought to be reciprocated, whereas behaviors constituting a negative expectancy violation ought to be compensated for, or at least ignored. In the experiment, pairs of friends reported to a laboratory where they were told they would be engaging in two short conversations with each other. The first conversation served as a baseline, with no behaviors manipulated. In between the conversations, one friend from each pair was made a confederate and was induced either to increase or to decrease his or her affectionate behaviors toward the partner during the second conversation. The conversations were videotaped and were subsequently coded for the participants' and confederates' behaviors.

Floyd and Voloudakis reasoned that, because their participants were friends (which is generally a rewarding relationship), they should judge increases in their friends' affectionate behavior positively and judge decreases negatively. Using EVT, Floyd and Voloudakis predicted behavioral reciprocity (in the form of increased immediacy, expressiveness, and positive affect) in the former condition and behavioral compensation in the latter condition. Importantly, both predictions call for the same behavioral display from the participants; that is, in both conditions, participants were expected to become more affectionate.

The hypothesis received little support. The predicted main effect for time was significant only for positive affect, and an examination of the means revealed that participants actually *decreased* their positive affect from the first conversation to the second one. A post hoc analysis showed, however, that the effect was attributable only to participants who received decreased affection: they decreased their positive affect in response (a reciprocal response), whereas participants who received increased affection had nearly identical levels of positive affect in both conversations (a failure to respond).

A significant interaction effect between time and confederate behavior also emerged. Follow-up tests showed that participants who received decreased affection increased their expressivity from the first conversation to the second (a compensatory response). Participants who received increased affection had nearly identical levels of expressivity in both conversations. There were no significant effects for immediacy.

Clearly, these were not the expected behavioral responses, and there are several reasons why the predictions may have failed. Perhaps not all participants judged increases in affectionate behavior positively and decreases negatively. Perhaps EVT is incorrect in its reasoning, or perhaps Floyd and Voloudakis reasoned from it improperly to arrive at the hypotheses. Two features of the method are particularly suspect, however. First, confederates were not instructed as to the particular behaviors they should modify to manipulate their affection levels. Rather, they were asked to increase or decrease their levels of affection using whichever behaviors seemed most appropriate to them. This feature of the method did allow Floyd and Voloudakis to examine which behaviors confederates enacted in order to convey affection; however, it virtually guaranteed variance in those behaviors, such that participants in the two conditions were not always responding to the same behavioral changes. Second, the coders in the study rated participants' behaviors only once for the first conversation and once for the second conversation. This was done so that the behavioral data would match participants' self-report data (which was elicited once for each conversation) in terms of the size of the "data window." However, both conversations averaged approximately four minutes in length, and levels of immediacy, expressivity, and positive affect can fluctuate considerably in that period of time. Given that likely variation, requiring coders to average in their minds all of the behaviors they witnessed during a four-minute period was likely an unwise strategy.

These two methodological problems (as well as the small number of dyads in the Floyd and Voloudakis study) were remedied in the second experiment, by Floyd and Burgoon (1999). This study differed from the Floyd and Voloudakis study in a number of ways. First, pairs of strangers were used instead of pairs of friends. Second, trained confederates were used instead of participant confederates. Third, participants' and confederates' behaviors were coded in thirty-second windows at eight points in the conversations. Fourth, the design was a between-subjects design, meaning that confederates did not increase or decrease their affection behaviors over time but were either highly affectionate or unaffectionate throughout the laboratory interaction. A fifth difference was that only same-sex pairs were used in the Floyd and Burgoon study, whereas the Floyd and Voloudakis experiment used both same- and opposite-sex dyads.

Perhaps the most important difference is that the Floyd and Burgoon study derived its hypotheses from interaction adaptation theory (IAT), which differs from expectancy violations theory in the specificity with which it predicts patterns of behavioral adaptation. Specifically, IAT proposes that people compare their needs, expectations, and desires with the behaviors of their conversational partners, and reciprocate behaviors that match, or are more positive than, those needs, expectations, and desires. Behaviors that people judge to be more negative than what they need, expect, and want are compensated for. These predictions are relatively straightforward when people's needs, expectations, and desires are identical. However, it is not uncommon for people to desire one thing but expect another, or to need something that is undesired. The Floyd and Burgoon experiment not only tested IAT's ability to predict behavioral responses under conditions of congruent expectations and desires (needs were not manipulated in this experiment), but also examined how people respond to behaviors that match either their expectations or their desires but not both.

In this experiment, naïve participants were paired with trained confederates of the same sex. When a participant reported to the laboratory to check in for the study, a confederate (whom the participant thought was simply another study participant) was already present in the waiting area. During this check-in and orientation period, the confederate was behaving either very positively toward the participant (smiling, maintaining eye contact, sitting close with an open posture, asking the participant questions) or very negatively (not smiling or looking at the participant, sitting far away with a closed posture, not saying anything to the participant). This was intended to manipulate participants' expectations, inducing them to expect either a positive or a negative conversation with the confederate during the interaction portion of the experiment.

Participants and confederates were told that the experiment was about how strangers interact with each other, that they would be taking part in a semi-structured conversation that would be videotaped, and that they would be completing measures afterward that would assess their perceptions of their partner. Prior to the conversations, participants and confederates were briefly separated to complete some pre-measures. During this time, participants were informed that the conversation was being observed by a researcher, unconnected with the current study, who was looking for pairs of new acquaintances to invite as participants in a longitudinal study of relationship development. Specifically, participants were told that the new study would be a long-term, labor-intensive project and that the researcher was particularly looking either for pairs of people who seemed to like each other a great deal during their initial conversation or who seemed to dislike each other quite a bit. This served as the manipulation of participants' desire to be liked or disliked by the confederates. By describing the prospective study as long term and labor intensive, Floyd and Burgoon intended to induce participants to want to avoid being invited to take part in it,[7] and by describing the type of relational interaction the prospective researcher was looking for, they intended to induce participants either to want the confederates to like them or to want the confederates to dislike them.[8] The efficacy of both the expectation and desire manipulations was confirmed in pilot studies.

For the experimental interaction, participants and confederates went through a conversation exercise in which they were presented with descriptions of moral and ethical dilemmas and instructed to discuss options for dealing with them. During the interaction, confederates were trained to behave either as though they especially liked participants (smiling, leaning forward, maintaining eye contact, using facial and vocal animation, sitting with open posture) or especially disliked them (not smiling, maintaining little eye contact, lacking facial and vocal animation, sitting rigidly with a closed posture). Confederates maintained either the "liking" or "disliking" behaviors throughout the interaction.

Thus, the study employed a three-way crossed factorial design with desire, expectation, and behavior manipulations. Drawing on IAT, Floyd and Burgoon hypothesized that participants would behaviorally match confederates when they expected, wanted, and received liking behavior and also when they expected, wanted, and received disliking behavior. However, IAT does not specify the relative potency of desires and expectations, so there was no basis for making directional predictions about the behavioral responses of people who expected to be liked but wished not to be, or of people who wanted confederates to like them but did not expect that they would. There were, therefore, four cells of the design in which directional hypotheses could be advanced and four cells in which only research questions were appropriate. A description of the conditions appears in Table 5.3.

Results indicated that participants with congruent expectations and desires (represented in cells 1–4 of Table 5.3) matched the behavior of confederates who acted in accordance with those expectations and

Table 5.3 *Experimental conditions in Floyd and Burgoon*
(1999) experiment

Cell	Desire	Expectation	Behavior
1	Liking	Liking	Liking
2	Disliking	Disliking	Disliking
3	Liking	Liking	Disliking
4	Disliking	Disliking	Liking
5	Liking	Disliking	Liking
6	Disliking	Liking	Disliking
7	Liking	Disliking	Disliking
8	Disliking	Liking	Liking

Note: "Desire" and "Expectation" refer to the manipulations of naïve participants' desires and expectations for the confederates' behaviors. "Behavior" refers to the confederates' actual manipulated behaviors.

desires but compensated for the behavior of confederates who acted against them. That is, participants who wanted and expected to be liked matched the behavior of confederates who enacted liking behavior and compensated for the behavior of confederates who enacted disliking behavior. Moreover, participants who wanted and expected to be disliked matched the behavior of confederates who enacted disliking behavior and compensated for the behavior of confederates who enacted liking behavior. These findings provided direct support for the hypotheses derived from IAT.

When Floyd and Burgoon examined the behaviors of those participants with incongruent expectations and desires (represented in cells 5–8 of Table 5.3), they discovered that responses to confederates' behaviors were largely in line with participants' desires rather than their expectations. The general pattern was one in which participants matched the behaviors they desired and compensated for the behaviors they did not desire, irrespective of their expectations. That does not imply, of course, that desires are always more potent than expectations in determining people's behavioral adaptation to others; that was simply the case in this experiment.

Although they bolstered the predictive utility of IAT, these findings would otherwise be unremarkable were it not for their demonstration that friendly, affiliative behavior is not always welcomed, considered positive, or reciprocated. Rather, all four groups of participants who had been induced to want to be disliked actually compensated for liking behaviors when they received them, and matched disliking behaviors.

The most important aspect of this finding is not the abstract pattern – people matching behavior that they desire – nor even the fact that people reciprocated negative affect behaviors. What is notable is the demonstration that *people can be induced into compensating for behavioral expressions of liking.* This runs directly counter to the intuitive notion that humans always strive to be liked and appreciated by others (see Goffman, 1959; Maslow, 1970). Instead, as this experiment suggested, when affectionate behaviors have implied obligations (or even potential obligations) attached to them, those obligations may be sufficient to override natural desires for liking and affection. The Floyd and Burgoon study is notable because it was the first to demonstrate a pattern of compensation for affectionate behavior.

Despite the significance of this finding, however, the Floyd and Burgoon experiment was limited in two important ways. First, confederate behavior was a between-cells manipulation only. That is, the confederates in each condition enacted their assigned behaviors (whether expressing liking or disliking) throughout the interactions, rather than starting with a baseline, nonmanipulated period and then changing their behavior over time (as in the Floyd and Voloudakis study). That makes it difficult for the researcher to observe behavioral adaptation occurring, because the comparison of interest is simply between conditions, not over time within conditions. Second, although manipulating expectations and desires provides the researcher with greater experimental control and a greater ability to examine causal relationships than would be gained by simply measuring them, it generally limits the researcher to studying only one type of expectation or desire at a time. As other studies have indicated, people can enter interactions with *multiple* expectations and desires (see Burgoon, Allspach, & Miczo, 1997). Therefore, manipulating only one of each precluded the researchers from examining the effects of other expectations and desires that participants may have had, and also from examining how multiple expectations and desires might operate in tandem. In the Floyd and Burgoon study, for instance, only participants' expectations of how confederates would behave during the laboratory conversations were manipulated. However, other expectations, such as how similar the confederate would be to oneself or how quickly the conversation would go, might also have been influential.

Floyd and Ray (2000) designed an experiment to address these limitations. Their study involved a mix of the elements of the Floyd and Burgoon experiment and the Floyd and Voloudakis experiment. Floyd and Ray used interactions between strangers and induced one of the strangers in each pair to be a participant confederate (instead of using trained confederates). Each pair engaged in a four-minute baseline (nonmanipulated) conversation in which they discussed how they might deal with various moral and ethical dilemmas.[9] After that conversation, the participants were separated and one was instructed to act, during a second conversation, either "as though you really like your partner" or "as though you really dislike your partner." This instruction was similar to that given to the trained confederates in the Floyd and Burgoon study; however, as in the Floyd and Voloudakis study, the confederates were given no instructions about particular behaviors to manipulate, nor were they provided with examples of behaviors that could be used. Rather, Floyd and Ray instructed confederates to express liking or disliking using whichever behaviors they believed would convey that message appropriately.

Like Floyd and Burgoon, Floyd and Ray used IAT to predict behavioral responses to confederates' behaviors. In this study, however, expectations and desires were not manipulated, but were instead measured. Specifically, Floyd and Ray measured the extent to which participants expected the conversations to be pleasant and comfortable, expected themselves to be relaxed, engaged, and extroverted, and expected that they would like their partners (the confederates). They also measured the extent to which participants wanted to manage their images, their relationships with the confederates, and the flow of the conversations themselves. Certainly, these are not all of the expectations and desires one might assess, but other research has suggested that they are among the most pertinent expectations and desires with which strangers enter conversations (see, e.g., Burgoon et al., 1997).

The overall pattern of behavioral response was one in which participants reciprocated confederates' liking behaviors with increases in their own behavioral involvement and pleasantness. In response to disliking behaviors, participants tended not to change their own behaviors, maintaining their previous levels of involvement and pleasantness. Importantly, however, these patterns were moderated by participants' expectations about whether or not they would like the confederates. In particular, participants reciprocated both liking *and* disliking behaviors more if they expected (before the conversation) to like the confederates than if they expected not to. As Floyd and Ray pointed out, the fact that the expectation to like confederates moderated participants' reciprocity of liking behavior is in line with IAT's reasoning that liking behavior, even though it may have some inherent positivity, can be judged negatively by people who are not expecting it.

IAT's reasoning was contradicted, however, by the finding that the expectation to like confederates also moderated participants' reactions to disliking behavior. If participants expected that they would like the confederates, then disliking behavior on the part of the confederate should have been judged less positively than the expected behavior and should have, according to IAT, elicited compensatory behavior from participants (in the form of increased, not decreased, pleasantness and involvement).

One conclusion to be drawn from these three experiments is that several factors influence whether individuals reciprocate, compensate for, or fail to respond to affectionate behavior. It is too simplistic to predict that people reciprocate positive behavior and compensate for negative behavior, as a number of factors can moderate that outcome, including the extent to which the behavior supports or contradicts people's expectations. A second important conclusion is that, although affectionate behaviors may carry some inherent positivity, their valence is also determined by the extent to which they are congruent with a recipient's desires. If affection is expressed in an inappropriate manner or in an inappropriate situation, for instance, it may contradict the receiver's desires and be more likely to evoke compensatory than reciprocal responses.

6 Communicating Affection in Various Relationships

Although affectionate communication is influenced by aspects of individuals, it is also influenced by the types and characteristics of the relationships in which people interact. In turn, it covaries with – and, at times, exerts influence on – the qualities of those relationships. This chapter begins with a review of research comparing relationship types in terms of their tendencies to communicate affection in particular ways. It then addresses why, and in what ways, affectionate behavior is associated with multiple indices of relational quality, including relationship satisfaction, love, closeness, commitment, relational maintenance, and sexual satisfaction, among others.

Relationship Types and Affectionate Behavior

The range of individual-level antecedents of affectionate behavior notwithstanding, expressing affection is inherently a relational activity. It therefore stands to reason that it is influenced by the nature of the relationships in which it occurs. To appreciate how, it is instructive first to identify the consequential characteristics on which relationship types are distinguished from one another, and then to determine why, from the perspective of relevant theory, such characteristics should matter for affectionate expression.

Two Approaches to Categorizing Relationship Types

The variety of close human relationships can be categorized in at least two ways that are relevant for understanding affectionate behavior. One approach is to differentiate romantic and/or sexual relationships from those that are platonic, a term denoting a nonsexual form of love (Calvo, Brown, & Scheding, 2009). This distinction is not without its conceptual problems. For one, the adjectives *romantic* and *sexual* are not synonyms. Some romantic relationships (even long-term marriages) are nonsexual (Donnelly & Burgess, 2008), and many sexual relationships – such as "friends with benefits" relationships – are nonromantic (Mongeau, Knight, Williams, Eden, & Shaw, 2013). Thus, to the extent that affectionate emotions embody experiences of love and fondness, they may be more relevant for romance than sexuality, even though sexual behavior is a common means of expressing affection (see Debrot, Meuwly, Muise, Impett, & Schoebi, 2017). Moreover, the adjective *platonic* encompasses a broad range of social and intimate relationships, including those with family members (parents, grandparents, children, siblings, etc.), friends, coworkers, neighbors, and acquaintances. One would naturally expect substantial variation in the experience and expression of affection among these types of relationships, necessitating a further categorization of platonic relationships into those that represent, for instance, friendships, familial bonds, social or workplace bonds, and so on.

Aside from differentiating romantic/sexual and platonic relationships, a second relevant discrimination is between genetic and nongenetic relationships. More than 99 percent of an individual's DNA is shared with every other human being, so less than 1 percent of DNA varies from individual to individual (National Human Genome Research Institute, 2017). When one speaks of two people being *genetically related*, one is actually referring to the probability that, among that 1 percent of DNA that varies from person to person, a given gene present in one person is also present in the other. Genetic relatedness is therefore conceptualized along a probability continuum that indexes, primarily, the degree of consanguinity, or genetic kinship, between two individuals. Identical (monozygotic) twins[1] have the highest degree of kinship, having come from the same zygote and therefore sharing the same genetic inheritance from their biological parents. Identical twins are therefore said to be 100 percent genetically related. Parents and their biological children, and full biological siblings (including fraternal, or dizygotic, twins), are said to be 50 percent genetically related. Grandparents and grandchildren, half biological siblings, and aunts/uncles and nieces/nephews all share a 25 percent genetic relationship, and relationships between first cousins and great grandparents/great grandchildren have a 12.5 percent genetic overlap. In contrast, individuals tend to have virtually no genetic relationship with their spouses, their step-relatives (step-parents, step-children, step-siblings), their in-laws (parents-in-law, children-in-law, siblings-in-law), and their adoptive relatives (adoptive parents, adopted children, adoptive siblings).

These two approaches to categorizing relationships – distinguishing between romantic and platonic relationships, and between genetic and nongenetic relationships – certainly have some conceptual overlap. In modernity, at least, sexual/romantic relationships tend to occur between nongenetically related individuals, due to the genetic risks involved in procreating with a genetic relative.[2] Some platonic relationships – including those between biological siblings and parents and their biological children – are genetic, whereas others – including between step-relatives, in-laws, neighbors, and friends – generally are not. When it comes to the experience and expression of affection, however, the consequential question is why the type of relationship should matter in the first place, and theories from the socio-cultural and bio-evolutionary paradigms tend to answer that question differently. Specifically, socio-cultural theories tend to give greater weight to the romantic/platonic distinction, whereas the genetic/nongenetic distinction is generally of much greater import to bio-evolutionary theories.

Why Relationship Types Vary in Affectionate Behavior

Regarding the distinction between romantic and platonic relationships, theories reflecting a socio-cultural or social learning orientation would posit differences in social behavior based on differing social and cultural expectations for those relationships, as well as differing levels of investment, commitment, and closeness within them. From that perspective, spouses would be expected to be more affectionate with each other than would siblings because the marital relationship carries a greater expectation for love and feelings of affection than a sibling relationship does, and because people are usually more invested in and committed to their spouses than their siblings. People would be expected to be more affectionate with personal friends than with casual acquaintances for the same reasons. Whether romantic or platonic, positive relationships that involve a greater frequency of interaction and a higher degree of emotional closeness would be expected to be more affectionate that those that do not.

In comparison, the degree of genetic relatedness is not, per se, particularly consequential for socio-cultural theories. Theories such as social exchange theory, expectancy violations theory, and politeness theory take little account of whether social actors share a genetic bond with each other, except insofar as the genetic bond is associated with their relational histories and anticipated patterns of behavior. Two individuals may be emotionally close because their degree of genetic relatedness has caused them to grow up together and spend a great deal of time in each other's company – and because of their closeness, they may have established an expected pattern of reciprocity. No theories from the socio-cultural paradigm would posit that genetic relatedness is either a necessary or sufficient condition for the formation of emotional closeness, however, nor would they automatically accord greater importance to genetic than nongenetic bonds.

Theories in the bio-evolutionary paradigm – including affection exchange theory – pay greater attention to genetic relatedness. These theories recognize that humans have evolved to attend to consanguinity cues, because they enhance their own reproductive success by helping genetic relatives. A finite resource (such as time, attention, or money) given to a genetic relative furthers the probability of that relative's own survival and reproduction – and, therefore, the reproduction of one's own genetic material. Throughout evolutionary history, it has behooved individuals more to help their kin than to help their nonkin, so from this perspective, the degree of genetic overlap between two individuals is consequential for understanding social behavior.

An important clarification is that, in bio-evolutionary theories, the degree of genetic relatedness matters not for its own sake but for its contribution to reproductive success, which explains why affection exchange theory would also predict high degrees of affectionate behavior in marriage, even though spouses usually have no genetic overlap. To the extent that it is a sexual and procreative relationship (as opposed to an exclusively romantic but nonsexual one), marriage offers a context for directly furthering one's reproductive success. Affection exchange theory posits that affectionate behavior is a consequential resource and recognizes that reproductive success can be advanced by sharing affection with one's nongenetically related sexual partner as well as with one's genetically related kin.

However relationship types are conceptualized, therefore, socio-cultural and bio-evolutionary theories offer different explanations as to why they matter for affectionate behavior. Importantly, though, theories from these two paradigms do not always lead to competing hypotheses. Marital affection is illustrative, insofar as both socio-cultural and bio-evolutionary theories would predict that people are more affectionate with their spouses, on average, than in any other relationship, even though they offer different theoretic reasoning as to why. As discussed below, some studies grounded in affection exchange theory have measured and controlled for explanatory mechanisms springing from socio-cultural or social learning theories – such as proximity, frequency of contact, and degree of emotional closeness – when comparing relationship types with each other. The point in doing so is not to show that such influences are irrelevant; in fact, these and similar factors often account for significant proportions of the variance in affectionate behavior. Rather, the purpose in controlling for such variables is to determine whether relationship type or degree of genetic relatedness account for significant variation above and beyond those factors, which lends support to a bio-evolutionary approach.

Multiple studies have now compared types of relationships in terms of their affectionate behavior. For simplicity's sake, these are organized below according to whether the study examined relational differences in the *frequency* of affectionate behavior or in its *form* or *evaluation.*

Relational Differences in Frequency of Affectionate Communication

As one might expect, relationships differ in their levels or frequencies of affectionate communication. One may intuit that affectionate behavior is more common in marriages than in other relationships, but the validity of that assertion depends on the nature of the relationships to which marriage is being compared. Floyd and Morr (2003) examined affection exchange in the marital/sibling/sibling-in-law system. They collected data from triads consisting of a married couple and the biological sibling of one of the spouses. Using the ACI, all three participants in each triad reported on the extent to which they communicated affection to the other two. The reports for verbal, nonverbal, and supportive affection were averaged within each relationship to form an affection score for that relationship (e.g., the two siblings' scores were averaged to form a score for the sibling dyad). When they analyzed these scores by relationship type, Floyd and Morr discovered a clear pattern in which people communicated the most affection within their marriages, less affection within their sibling relationships, and the least affection within their sibling-in-law relationships. All of the relationship-type differences were statistically significant for each of the three forms of affectionate communication.

Punyanunt-Carter (2004), however, compared 100 individuals who were part of a married couple with 100 individuals who were part of a dating couple. Each participant completed the ACI with respect to his or her relationship. Nearly all of the nonverbal indicators of affection measured – holding hands, kissing on the lips, kissing on the cheek, exchanging massage, putting an arm around another's shoulder, hugging, and sitting in close proximity – were significantly more frequent in dating relationships than in marriages. Saying "you're a good friend" was also more common for dating partners than for spouses. Tellingly, no specific affectionate behavior was reported more often by spouses than by dating partners, suggesting that although marriages are more affectionate than many other relationships, they perhaps do not exceed dating relationships in their frequency of affectionate behavior.

Table 6.1 *Means and standard deviations for affectionate communication with mothers and fathers from Floyd (2002) study*

	Men		Women	
Affection Type	Fathers	Mothers	Fathers	Mothers
Support	4.96 (1.50)	5.54 (1.21)	5.13 (1.32)	5.84 (1.11)
Verbal	3.88 (1.72)	4.64 (1.59)	3.90 (1.55)	4.97 (1.53)
Nonverbal	2.51 (1.16)	3.98 (1.61)	3.43 (1.39)	4.04 (1.34)

Note: Means are on a seven-point scale wherein higher scores indicate greater amounts of affectionate communication. Standard deviations are in parentheses.

Multiple other studies have examined the frequency of affectionate communication in various configurations of the parent–child relationship. For instance, as part of the data collection for the Floyd (2002) study, participants were asked to report on their affectionate behavior with their fathers and mothers. These data are not reported in the Floyd (2002) paper, so more detail on the analyses is provided here. The reports of affectionate communication were analyzed by parent type (father, mother), affection type (verbal, nonverbal, support), and sex of the participant, and a significant three-way interaction effect emerged, $F (2, 346) = 22.96$, $p < .001$, partial $\eta^2 = .12$. The interaction effect was completely ordinal, indicating that one can interpret the significant main effects for parent type, $F (1, 346) = 120.40$, $p < .001$, partial $\eta^2 = .41$; for affection type, $F (2, 346) = 313.75$, $p < .001$, partial $\eta^2 = .65$; and for participant sex, $F (1, 173) = 5.86$, $p = .017$, partial $\eta^2 = .03$.

The means and standard deviations, which appear in Table 6.1, indicate that participants were more affectionate with their mothers than with their fathers. Moreover, participants were most likely to communicate affection through supportive behaviors, less likely to communicate affection through verbal behaviors, and least likely to communicate affection through nonverbal behaviors. Finally, women reported being more affectionate than men.

Two studies have also examined differences between genetic and non-genetic parent–child relationships in terms of their levels of affectionate communication. On the basis of affection exchange theory, Floyd and Morman (2001) reasoned that, if affection is a resource that contributes to long-term viability and fertility, then parents ought to give more affection to their biological children, on average, than to their stepchildren, because such discrimination will further the parents' own reproductive success.

Although adopted children are typically not genetically related to their adoptive parents, there is some disagreement in the literature on parental solicitude as to whether predictions made for stepchildren should necessarily generalize to adopted children. Daly and Wilson (1995), among others, have reasoned that the practice of adoption requires willing investments on the part of the adoptive parents that mirror those involved in biological child-rearing, so the evolutionary mechanisms that make it adaptive to invest in biological offspring might also motivate adoptive parenting, even in the absence of a genetic parent–child relationship.

On the basis of these theoretic arguments, Floyd and Morman predicted that men are more affectionate with biological *and* adopted sons than they are with stepsons, and they tested this prediction in two surveys. The first survey included only fathers' self-reports, whereas the second included the reports of both fathers and sons about the fathers' affectionate behavior. Both surveys had an adequate distribution of biological, step-, and adoptive father–son relationships to allow for comparisons between these relationship types. Using the ACI as the operational definition of affectionate communication, Floyd and Morman found that fathers were more affectionate with biological and adoptive sons than with stepsons, but that biological and adoptive relationships did not differ significantly from each other. In a later survey of nearly 500 US fathers who reported on their affectionate communication with either a biological or a nonbiological son, Floyd and Morman (2003) again found that fathers communicated more verbal, nonverbal, and supportive affection to biological sons than to nonbiological sons. (The subsamples of stepsons and adopted sons were too small in that survey to analyze separately, so they were combined for purposes of the comparison.)

Differences in sons' ability to contribute to fathers' procreative success also led Floyd (2001) to predict that heterosexual sons receive more affection from their fathers than do homosexual or bisexual sons. Men of all sexual orientations can produce genetic offspring, of course, but Floyd reasoned that gay and bisexual men are less likely than straight men, on average, to do so. Based on AET, Floyd hypothesized that homosexual and bisexual men's lower likelihood of reproduction translates to receiving less affection from fathers, compared with heterosexual men, and the prediction was confirmed for verbal, nonverbal, and supportive forms of affectionate behavior.

More recent research has examined affectionate communication in various configurations of the grandparent–grandchild relationship. Using Mansson's (2013e) GRAS as the operational definition of affectionate communication, Mansson and Booth-Butterfield (2011) reported that grandparents express equal levels of affection to grandsons and granddaughters, but also that biological grandparents express more affection than nonbiological grandparents, which is in line with Floyd and Morman's (2001, 2003) finding regarding biological and stepfathers. Giarrusso, Feng, Silverstein, and Bengtson (2011) compared affection shown by grandparents with that shown by grandchildren among European-American and Mexican-American participants. Among European-Americans, grandparents showed more affection for their granddaughters than the granddaughters showed for them (a finding that mirrors Morman & Floyd's 2002 finding that men are more affectionate with their sons than with their own fathers), but no such difference was identified for grandsons. Among Mexican-Americans, however, grandsons showed greater affection to their grandfathers than their grandfathers showed to them.

The grandparental relationship comes in both maternal and paternal forms, and Bernhold and Giles (in press) compared the levels of affection that adults received from all four types of grandparents, using the GRAS as the operational definition. The significant findings related to the form of affection comprising memories and humor. A main effect for sex emerged, wherein grandfathers communicated more affection via memories and humor than did grandmothers. More specifically, paternal grandfathers communicated the most affection, whereas maternal grandmothers communicated the least (no other forms of affection showed a difference by relationship type). These findings are intriguing because they are in contrast to the frequent finding that women are more affectionate than men, on average (see Chapter 4), even though the significant difference was for one form of affectionate behavior only.

The research on frequency therefore illustrates that both the romantic/platonic and the genetic/nongenetic distinctions are relevant. Some romantic relationships (such as dating relationships) are more affectionate than others (such as marriages), and marriages are more affectionate than the platonic relationships of siblings and in-laws. Similarly, relationships with genetic ties (such as biological parent–child or grandparent–grandchild relationships) are generally more affectionate than those with nongenetic ties, although not without exception, insofar as men are equally affectionate with biological sons and adopted sons.

Relational Differences in Form and Evaluation of Affectionate Communication

Compared with research examining relational differences in the frequency of affectionate communication, fewer studies have investigated how relationships compare in (1) the types of behaviors they use to convey affection and (2) their evaluation of the appropriateness of affectionate acts. One certainly might expect that intimate behaviors such as kissing and sexual contact are used to express affection more commonly in romantic than platonic relationships (see, e.g., Gulledge, Gulledge, & Stahmann, 2003; Wlodarski & Dunbar, 2013), but other studies have explored how different forms of affectionate behavior vary across relationship types. In their study of baby talk between adults, for instance, Bombar and Littig (1996) predicted that people were more likely to use baby talk as a form of affectionate communication in their romantic relationships than in their platonic friendships. Although that hypothesis was supported, slightly more than half of their respondents (50.4 percent) reported having used baby talk in a platonic friendship, which suggests that the behavior is by no means exclusive to romantic pairs. Bombar and Littig also found that women were more likely than men to use baby talk with same-sex friends, but among opposite-sex friends no such difference was observed.

Two studies have examined differences *between* forms of affectionate communication within the same relationship. Reasoning on the basis of the gendered closeness perspective that masculine role prescriptions encourage men to be wary of overt affectionate gestures with other men – even genetically related men, such as fathers and sons – Morman and Floyd (1999) predicted that men communicate affection to their sons more through the use of socially supportive behaviors than through direct verbal or nonverbal expressions. In a dyadic study comprising fifty-five father–adult son pairs, Morman and Floyd found that supportive activities – including, as measured by the ACI, helping someone with a problem, praising his or her accomplishments, sharing private thoughts, and providing compliments – were significantly more common means of expressing affection than were verbal statements or direct nonverbal gestures. This was true for both fathers' and sons' reports, and the effect sizes (partial η^2) were substantial, ranging from .77 to .87. The authors concluded that even in a familial relationship, men are subject to norms for masculinity that make more overt forms of affectionate expression (hugging, saying "I love you") potentially identity threatening.

Floyd (2001) replicated the comparisons from the Morman and Floyd study using a sample of both heterosexual and homosexual fathers with sons. As in the earlier study, Floyd found that supportive activities were substantially more common means of expressing affection than were verbal statements or direct nonverbal gestures. That was true for fathers of both sexual orientations, and effect sizes were again substantial, ranging from .56 to .85.

Other studies have examined the influence of relationship type on people's evaluations of the *appropriateness* of affectionate behavior.

All have compared adults' relationships to their platonic friends with their relationships to their siblings – as a comparison of familial and nonfamilial peer-like relationships – and all have found that the difference between these relationships is more consequential for men than for women. An initial study by Floyd (1997c) used the verbal and direct nonverbal subscales of the ACI and asked participants to report on how appropriate they thought each behavior was as a means of expressing affection with either a close platonic friend or a full biological, nontwin sibling. A main effect of relationship type was not observed for the appropriateness of affectionate behavior (averaged across the verbal and nonverbal subscales), but relationship type interacted with the sex of the participant to affect evaluations. Specifically, women reported that affectionate behavior was equally appropriate in their relationships with siblings and friends. Men, on the other hand, considered affectionate behavior to be significantly more appropriate between siblings than between friends.

Two experimental investigations have also compared friendships and sibling relationships in terms of the appropriateness of affectionate behavior. Floyd and Morman (1997) replicated the interaction effect observed by Floyd (1997c) and again found that men considered it significantly more appropriate to be affectionate with siblings than with friends. Women again reported that affectionate behavior was equally appropriate for friends and siblings. On the same note, men in the Morman and Floyd (1998) experiment reported believing that it was more appropriate for them to communicate affection to their brothers than to their male friends.

Considered collectively, these studies on the form and evaluation of affectionate behavior support the contention that although both familial relationships and those with friends are affectionate, men in particular negotiate a tension between conveying affection that they feel and conforming to masculine role prescriptions. Floyd and Morman have suggested elsewhere that men are cognizant that overt affection displays with other men may be interpreted as sexual overtures (see, e.g., Morman & Floyd, 1998). Because of equally strong cultural proscriptions against incest, however, men appear to be less concerned about the risks of expressing overt affection to family members than to unrelated friends, *even if they actually feel more affection for their friends.* This reasoning, consistent with the gendered closeness perspective, explains why men favor less-overt forms of affection in their father–son relationships and why they evaluate affectionate behavior as more appropriate with their brothers than with their male friends. Similar differences are not observed among women, however, which is also consistent with the gendered closeness perspective (see also Floyd, 1995, 1996b).

Situating the study of affectionate communication within the context of close relationships is informed not only by examining differences between relationships in their level of affectionate behavior but also by exploring how affectionate interaction covaries with perceptions of the quality of those relationships. Research on that topic is addressed subsequently.

Associations with Relationship Quality

A formidable literature demonstrates that affection exchange is associated with the quality of people's close relationships, and even if that conclusion seems intuitive, the reasons behind it are not necessarily obvious. This section begins with a discussion of why affectionate behavior ought to show associations with relational quality in the first place, and then reviews extensive findings regarding how it does.

Why Affectionate Behavior Is Associated with Relationship Quality

Later chapters will address the question of how and why affectionate communication is beneficial to individuals, but ample evidence shows that it also promotes the development of pair bonds (whether romantic or platonic), which entail a number of physical, financial, emotional, and psychological advantages for individuals (see Hu & Goldman, 1990; Umberson & Montez, 2010; Waite & Lehrer, 2003). Affection exchange theory provides that affectionate behavior is efficient and effective at establishing, maintaining, and nurturing pair bonds because it serves higher-order needs that have evolved to be adaptive in human mate selection, and because many of the qualities that are valuable in a potential mating partner are also valuable for other close personal bonds.

Specifically, according to AET, affectionate communication may facilitate pair bonding by conveying intentions of relational commitment and emotional investment, qualities that are adaptive to seek in a potential mate. According to such a perspective, it is advantageous to concern oneself with commitment and emotional investment when pair bonding because the evolutionary purpose of a pair bond is procreation, and the ability to rear healthy children who survive to sexual maturity is enhanced when both partners in a pair bond are committed to that task. It is beneficial, therefore, to be alert to signs of commitment and investment in a potential partner and wary of their absence. In the long term, in fact, one would expect that those who are more attuned to those signs are better positioned to select apt partners and exclude poorer options and should therefore accrue more procreative success than those who are less cognizant of such signals.

There is ample evidence that humans do, indeed, discriminate in the selection of long- and short-term romantic partners. Buss (1989) investigated patterns of mate selection among more than 10,000 people in thirty-seven societies worldwide and reported a high degree of consistency in the qualities people seek in potential mates and sexual partners. Specifically, he found that, when seeking potential mates, men across cultures look for physical attractiveness and cues to health and youth, whereas women across cultures seek cues to wealth, status, and commitment. In a review of the research on mate preference, Grammer (1989) also noted that women typically consider a larger number of cues than men do when choosing potential mates.

When selecting short-term sexual partners as opposed to long-term pair bonds, however, men appear willing to adjust their standards fairly dramatically. Buss and Schmidt (1993) asked college students to indicate what would matter to them in selecting a short-term sexual partner as opposed to a long-term mate. Their results indicated that men were substantially more willing than women to relax their typical standards when choosing a short-term sexual partner. Specifically, men relaxed their standards with respect to age, educational achievement, level of honesty and independence, intelligence, and emotional stability, along with a number of other characteristics. Conversely, Buss and Schmidt found that men were less willing than women to accept sex partners who were physically unattractive, who had a high need for commitment, who had high amounts of body hair, and/or who had a low sex drive. On all of the other sixty-one characteristics Buss and Schmidt measured, however, men showed relaxed standards for sex partners as opposed to long-term mates more so than did women (see also Dawson & McIntosh, 2006; Smiler, 2011).

The differences in what men and women seek in mating partners may reflect a sex difference in minimal parental investment (Bjorklund & Shackelford, 1999). Bearing even one healthy child and raising it to sexual maturity requires a substantial investment of time, labor, energy, and other resources on the part of a woman. At minimum, she must carry the fetus in utero for approximately nine months, incurring the accompanying costs of the physical strain on her body, the mental and emotional strain associated with her hormonal fluctuations, and the physical and financial stress of her restricted mobility and activity. Those who then rear their child must also attend to his or her substantial and oft-changing physical, emotional, and financial needs for many more years, if the child is to reach sexual maturity and be able to pass on his or her mother's genes to succeeding generations.

In stark contrast, a man's minimum investment consists of the time and energy required to impregnate the woman and the resources he spent in the pursuit of that mating opportunity. His required part in this process is then complete. Certainly, most men invest enormous emotional and financial resources in rearing and caring for their children, and one should not minimize the significant role that fatherhood plays in human family dynamics (Floyd & Morman, 2007; Tichenor, McQuillan, Greil, Contreras, & Shreffler, 2011). The point, however, is that the *minimum* investment of resources required to produce and raise a child to sexual maturity is substantially different for men and women.[3]

In humans and many other species, this difference manifests itself in different strategies used by men and women to attract mates. In his theory of parental investment, Trivers (1972) suggested that the sex whose minimum investment in offspring is greater will be the most selective when choosing sexual partners, because a poor decision is more consequential for that sex than for the other. Because women's minimum parental investment is so substantially greater than men's, therefore, Trivers predicted that women would be more selective than men when choosing mating partners, and indeed that is the case (see also Bateman, 1948).

Importantly, however, differential minimum investment also suggests that the sexes ought to emphasize different *qualities* when seeking mates. Indeed, as mentioned, Buss's research has found that, in numerous cultures, men seeking mates value physical attractiveness more than women do, whereas women seeking mates value markers of both status and commitment more than men do. In his sexual strategies theory, Buss (1994) explained this robust sex difference within the framework of differential minimum investment. Specifically, he proposed that men emphasize women's physical attractiveness because attractiveness signals health and youth, which are phenotypic markers of fertility. By mating with attractive women, men therefore increase the chances that any resulting offspring will be healthy enough to survive to sexual maturity. This strategy thus maximizes the evolutionary return on men's investment. Buss's theory suggested that women, in contrast, emphasize status because status typically translates into economic resources for the woman and her offspring; further, he suggested that women emphasize markers of relational commitment due to the greater efficacy in raising a healthy child *with* the father's involvement as opposed to *without*. Women's attunement to signs that men have resources to invest in them and their offspring – and are committed to actually providing those resources in the long term – is therefore adaptive. Importantly, Buss's theory suggests neither that women are indifferent to physical attractiveness nor that men are indifferent to signs of status or commitment; rather, it provides only that women and men will favor those traits differentially.

Expressing affection to a potential partner may not make individuals appear wealthy or physically attractive (although that possibility has yet to be empirically explored). In contrast, however, it is efficient at conveying relational commitment. The use of verbal statements such as "I love you" and "I care about you," accompanied by nonverbal gestures that signal intimacy (such as kissing) and relational exclusivity (such as hand-holding), can encode messages of commitment in new or ongoing relationships, perhaps more effectively and more efficiently than any other types of behavior. Because it is adaptive for individuals to be attuned to signals of commitment when forming new pair bonds (and to attend to *continued* signals of commitment in ongoing relationships), displays of affection often play a substantial role in relationship development and relationship maintenance. Indeed, as King and Christensen (1983) reported, using affectionate names and making verbal declarations of love are two significant turning points in new romantic relationships (see also Owen, 1987).

This discussion suggests that affection displays are beneficial to relationships because they convey something that is adaptive for humans to seek in pair bonds, and therefore contribute to the formation and maintenance of such bonds, exposing the partners to the benefits of pair bonding. Whether affection displays convey *genuine* relational commitment or not is, of course, a different matter. As AET provides, the experience of affection and the expression of affection do not necessarily covary. This, coupled with the importance of affection in newly developing relationships, creates the possibility that one could use affectionate communication in a manipulative way, perhaps to elicit sexual interaction or premature relational commitment. These possibilities receive more detailed attention in Chapter 9.

Given this understanding of *why* affectionate communication covaries with relationship quality, it is instructive to explore *how* affectionate behavior and relational quality are associated.

How Affectionate Behavior Is Associated with Relationship Quality

Multiple studies, conducted by researchers in multiple fields, attest to the variety of relationship qualities associated with affectionate communication. This section details research linking affectionate behavior with relational satisfaction; communication and life satisfaction; relationship formation and maintenance; love, liking, closeness, and commitment; sexual interaction and satisfaction; and relational negativity.

Relationship Satisfaction

The relational quality most often studied with respect to affectionate communication is relationship satisfaction, or the degree to which individuals feel happy, content, and fulfilled in their close relationships (Hendrick, 1988). Dainton (1998) and Parrot and Bengtson (1999) have both suggested that affectionate behavior is the interactional type that has the greatest influence on marital satisfaction. Indeed, research conducted over several decades has shown that affectionate communication has significant associations with relational satisfaction in marriages (Punyanunt-Carter, 2004; Schultz & Schultz, 1987; Spanier, 1976; Waring, McElrath, Lefcoe, & Weisz, 1981), families (Hesse, Rauscher, Roberts, & Ortega, 2014), cohabiting romantic relationships (Floyd et al., 2009), parent–child relationships (Barber & Thomas, 1986; MacDonald, 1992; Morman & Floyd, 1999; Russell, 1997), friendships (Floyd & Morman, 1998; Floyd & Voloudakis, 1999a), sibling and sibling-in-law relationships (Floyd & Morr, 2001), caregiver relationships (Parsons, Cox, & Kimboko, 1989), small-group relationships (Anderson & Martin, 1995), and even among those meeting for the first time (Floyd & Burgoon, 1999).

Gulledge et al. (2003) looked extensively at the associations between relationship satisfaction and multiple forms of physical affection in romantic relationships. In their study, satisfaction was measured by the level of agreement with four statements: "I am happy/satisfied in my current relationship," "My romantic partner is happy/satisfied in our relationship," "I am happy/satisfied with my romantic partner," and "My romantic partner is happy/satisfied with me." Both the total amount of physical affection respondents gave their partners and the total amount they received from their partners were positively correlated with their own relational satisfaction and their perception of their partners' relational satisfaction. Moreover, all four indices of satisfaction were positively correlated with the amount or frequency of five specific forms of physical affection: backrubs/massages, cuddling/holding, hugging, kissing on the lips, and kissing elsewhere on the face. Participants were also in high agreement that physical affection is important for relationship satisfaction and that they feel more loved when their partners show them physical affection (see also Jakubiak & Feeney, 2017). Similarly, Muise, Giang, and Impett (2014) demonstrated that the duration of romantic couples' post-sex affection is linearly related to relationship satisfaction and also has an indirect association with relationship satisfaction via sexual satisfaction.

Other research has examined satisfaction within particular familial dyads. Floyd and Morman have studied affectionate behavior in the relationships of fathers and their adult sons extensively. In three studies involving nearly 500 men, these researchers have demonstrated that verbal, direct nonverbal, and socially supportive forms of affectionate interaction are linearly related to satisfaction in the father–son relationship for both fathers and sons (Floyd & Morman, 2001; Morman & Floyd, 1999). Similarly, Curran and Yoshimura (2016) recruited mother–adult child dyads for a survey of affectionate communication in the mother–father and child–father dyads within their families. In that study, relationship satisfaction was measured as satisfaction with the family as a whole, rather than with a discrete familial pair. Curran and Yoshimura showed that mothers' family satisfaction was significantly associated with their level of affection in the mother–father relationship and that adult children's family satisfaction was associated with their level of affection with their fathers.

Whereas most research assessing relational satisfaction has been cross-sectional, two experiments have manipulated affectionate behavior to ascertain its effect on satisfaction. Floyd et al. (2009) recruited fifty-two healthy adults in marital or cohabiting relationships, and half were assigned to a six-week treatment condition in which they were induced to kiss more frequently than normal. Relational satisfaction was measured before and after the trial. As hypothesized, those in the treatment group reported a significant increase in relational satisfaction, whereas satisfaction scores for those in the control group were unchanged over time (see also Welsh, Haugen, Widman, Darling, & Grello, 2005). Van Raalte (2017) replicated the Floyd et al. procedure with eighty adults and induced participants in the treatment condition to cuddle more often than normal. Like Floyd and colleagues, van Raalte also documented a significant increase in relational satisfaction.

Communication Satisfaction and Life Satisfaction

Hecht (1978) conceived of communication satisfaction as one's level of contentment with a specific interpersonal encounter (rather than with one's relationship as a whole). Two studies have documented associations between affectionate behavior and communication satisfaction in specific relationships. In her study of married and dating couples, Punyanunt-Carter (2004) found a substantial relationship (β = .75) between communication satisfaction and socially supportive forms of affection (as measured by the ACI). Verbal and direct nonverbal expressions of affection had no association with communication satisfaction in that study. On the contrary, in Morman and Floyd's (1999) study of father–adult son dyads, fathers' nonverbal and supportive affection were linearly related to both fathers' and sons' reports of communication satisfaction. Sons' verbal, nonverbal, and supportive affection were also linearly related to both fathers' and sons' communication satisfaction, except that the association between sons' communication satisfaction and sons' nonverbal affection was nonsignificant.

In comparison to communication satisfaction, life satisfaction indexes contentment with one's life as a whole. Diener, Emmons, Larsen, and Griffin (1985) operationalized life satisfaction in the form of a scale measuring agreement with items including "In most ways my life is close to my ideal," "I am satisfied with my life," and "If I could live my life over, I would change almost nothing." Using Diener et al.'s measure, Debrot, Meuwly, Muise, Impett, and Schoebi (2017, Study 1) reported that affectionate touch in romantic relationships is linearly related to life satisfaction. The study also found that affectionate touch mediates the association between sexual frequency and life satisfaction, suggesting that the frequency of sexual interaction is related to life satisfaction partially because sexual interaction leads to affectionate touch.

Curran and Yoshimura's (2016) study of family relationships also addressed overall life satisfaction, as measured by two items: "Overall, how satisfied are you with life as a whole these days?" and "Overall, to what extent do you feel the things you do in your life are worthwhile?" As with relationship satisfaction, Curran and Yoshimura found that mothers' reports of mother–father affection were associated with their own life satisfaction, whereas adult children's life satisfaction was associated with their affectionate communication with their fathers.

Relationship Formation and Maintenance

Some research indicates that trait levels of affectionate communication are correlated with success in forming and maintaining relationships. Both the Floyd (2002) and the Floyd, Hess, et al. (2003) studies predicted that people who are highly affectionate (as a trait) are more likely to be in an ongoing romantic relationship than are people who are less affectionate. In both studies, as hypothesized, individuals' trait affection levels reliably discriminated between those who were in an ongoing romantic relationship (going steady, engaged, cohabiting, or married) and those who were not, with more affectionate people being more likely to be in such a relationship. Moreover, among those participants in both studies who did have a romantic relationship, their trait affection levels showed direct linear associations with their satisfaction in those relationships.

Other research has drawn connections between affectionate communication and the ways in which close relationships are maintained.

Research on relationship maintenance often utilizes Canary and Stafford's (1992) typology, which identifies five principal maintenance strategies: (1) positivity, (2) openness, (3) use of assurances, (4) network support (i.e., relying on people known to both partners), and (5) the completion of tasks necessary for the relationship to function. On the basis of affection exchange theory's claim of a connection between affectionate behavior and pair-bonding success, Pauley et al. (2014) hypothesized that in married couples, individuals' trait affection levels are positively associated with their own and their spouses' enactment of these five relationship maintenance strategies. Using dyadic data from 143 heterosexual married couples, the researchers found that husbands' and wives' trait affection levels – operationalized as a combination of trait affection expressed and trait affection received – were significantly and positively associated to all five of their own relational maintenance strategies (excepting a nonsignificant correlation between husbands' trait affection and task completion). In addition, husbands' trait affection levels were significantly related to their wives' positivity, use of assurances, and network support, whereas wives' trait affection levels were associated with their husbands' use of assurances. The authors also found that the relative effects of trait affection on the enactment of these maintenance strategies were not significantly different between husbands and wives.

In a similar study of the grandparent–grandchild relationship, Mansson (2014b) proposed that affection received from grandparents predicts grandchildren's use of relational maintenance behaviors and that that association is mediated by grandchildren's trust in their grandparents. Mansson used a modified measure of relational maintenance strategies that included conflict management and advice sharing in addition to Canary and Stafford's five strategies. As predicted, he found that the amount of affection participants received from their grandparents was associated with their enactment of relational maintenance strategies in those relationships. Further, this association was fully mediated by trust for some maintenance strategies and partially mediated for others.

Pauley et al. and Mansson were the first to document significant associations between affectionate behavior and Canary and Stafford's relational maintenance strategies, but an earlier study by Myers et al. (2011) suggested that affectionate behaviors can serve as relational maintenance strategies in and of themselves. The Myers et al. investigation focused on the adult sibling relationship and addressed the question of how the three forms of affectionate communication from Floyd and Morman's (1998) typology (verbal statements, direct nonverbal gestures, and socially supportive behaviors) function as relational maintenance behaviors.

Of particular interest was whether siblings use these forms of affectionate expression more as strategic maintenance strategies – that is, done intentionally and specifically for the purpose of sustaining the relationship – than as routine strategies (done in a perfunctory, often subconscious manner). To address that question, Myers and colleagues asked nearly 500 young adults to report on their relationship with an adult sibling. Participants indicated how often they used each item on Floyd and Morman's affectionate communication index strategically for the purpose of maintaining their sibling relationship, and how often they used each item routinely (nonstrategically). As hypothesized, participants used all three forms of affectionate behavior strategically more often than routinely for the purpose of maintaining their adult sibling relationships.

Love, Liking, Closeness, and Commitment

Other research has looked at the experiences of love, liking, closeness, and commitment in close relationships. These are distinct but overlapping relational constructs. In line with Sternberg's (1986) triangular theory, love is often defined conceptually and operationally as encompassing feelings of intimacy/bondedness, passion/attractiveness, and commitment to a specific partner. Rubin's (1969, 1970) work distinguished liking as an attitude of attraction toward and admiration for another, a perception of similarity with the other, and an opinion that most people ought also to like the other. Closeness is a perception of connectedness that includes high interdependence (Berscheid et al., 1989) and an awareness that the other is included in one's conception of the self (Aron, Aron, & Smollan, 1992; see also Mashek & Aron, 2004). Finally, commitment (which Sternberg included as a component of love) indexes a perception of cohesion and solidarity with a partner and a lack of perceived alternatives to that relationship (e.g., Sabatelli & Cecil-Pigo, 1985).

Perhaps unsurprisingly, early examinations of the contributions of affectionate behavior to these outcomes tended to focus on romantic relationships. In their investigation of idioms for affection in heterosexual pair bonds, Bell et al. (1987) discovered that, for both men and women, the number of idioms for expressing affection was linearly related to reported levels of love, closeness, and commitment in the relationship (see also Hopper, Knapp, & Scott, 1981). Similarly, Dainton, Stafford, and Canary (1994) examined satisfaction with physical affection – including hugging, touching, and kissing – in 200 married couples. They found that, for wives, satisfaction with physical affection was a significant predictor of liking, but not of love. No associations between affection, liking, and love emerged for husbands, however.

Other studies have focused on nonromantic relationships. For instance, Floyd and Parks (1995) examined verbal interaction in the relationships of adult platonic friends and adult siblings and found that verbal behavior contributed to perceptions of closeness more strongly for friends than for siblings. In a study of young adult grandchildren, Mansson (2013a) found that commitment to the grandparent–grandchild relationship was predicted by a combination of the grandparents' love and esteem affection and caring affection (as assessed by Mansson's 2013e GRAS) toward grandchildren. A later study by Mansson et al. (2017) focused instead on closeness in the grandparent–grandchild relationship and found that closeness was predicted by a combination of grandparents' love and esteem affection, caring affection, celebratory affection, and memories and humor.

Floyd and Mikkelson (2002) looked across multiple datasets to identify average correlations between relational affection, love, and closeness. They found that closeness manifests average correlations of .51 with verbal affection, .46 with direct nonverbal affection, and .58 with supportive affection. Love manifests even stronger average correlations of .77 with verbal affection, .79 with nonverbal, and .82 with supportive. The authors noted, however, that the studies that produced these associations varied not only in the type of relationship on which they focused but also in their methodology and sometimes in their operational definitions of the outcomes.

Sexual Interaction and Satisfaction

Recent studies have explored the connections between affectionate communication, sexual behavior, and satisfaction. Debrot et al. (2017) noted a well-established association between the frequency of sexual interaction and general well-being (see, e.g., Blanchflower & Oswald, 2004; Laumann et al., 2006) and speculated that that association could be accounted for partially by the frequency of affectionate interactions in romantic couples. Debrot and colleagues conducted four studies involving nearly 900 Swiss and US adult participants. The first study found that the frequency of affectionate touch was significantly associated with the frequency of sexual behavior and that affectionate touch mediated the relationship between sexual frequency and life satisfaction, in line with hypotheses. The second study likewise found that affectionate touch mediated an association between sexual frequency and positive emotions for both women and men. An experience-sampling method in Study 3 found that sexual activity predicted heightened positive affect and that this association was mediated by experiences of affection. Finally, a longitudinal method in Study 4 showed that when couples engaged in sexual or erotic encounters at one point in time, they were more likely to report experiencing affection within the subsequent four hours.

Considered collectively, these findings suggest that the experience and/or expression of affection not only covary with sexual interaction but are partially responsible for why sexual interaction contributes to well-being. In other words, sex contributes to wellness partly because sex induces affection and affection contributes to wellness (a point receiving extensive attention in the next two chapters). Additional research has explored the effects of affectionate behavior shared during the postsex period, specifically. In two studies, for instance, Muise et al. (2014) examined how the duration and quality of postsex affectionate communication contributed to both sexual and relational satisfaction. Cross-sectional analyses in the first study established a significant association between the duration of postsex affection and relational satisfaction, an association that was mediated by sexual satisfaction. Thus, engaging in affection after sex was related to increased sexual satisfaction, which in turn predicted increased relational satisfaction. The direct effect of postsex affection on relational satisfaction was significant only for women, however.

Using an experience-sampling method in their second study, Muise and colleagues found a direct effect of postsex affection on sexual satisfaction and replicated the mediational model wherein postsex affection contributed to relational satisfaction via sexual satisfaction. Moreover, the perceived *quality* of postsex affection also had direct associations with both sexual and relational satisfaction. Finally, the researchers documented that both the duration and the quality of postsex affection at the time of the study were directly predictive of sexual and relational satisfaction at a three-month follow-up.

Denes (2012) has examined a specific form of postsex affectionate expression – the sharing of *pillow talk*, or the verbal exchange of positive, intimate disclosures – and has hypothesized that it is more common in committed than in casual relationships; that it contributes to feelings of trust, closeness, and satisfaction with a relationship; and that, for women, it is more common when they achieve orgasm than when they do not. In a study of 200 young sexually active adults, Denes confirmed all three predictions (see also Denes, Afifi, & Granger, 2017). These results, along with those of Dubrot et al. and Muise et al., not only replicate and confirm the previously discussed correlations between affectionate behavior and relational and life satisfaction; they also identify affectionate behavior as consequential for the benefits of sexual interaction. That intimate touch, pillow talk, and other forms of affectionate communication help to make sex fulfilling and relationally beneficial supports

AET's contention that affectionate behavior contributes to reproductive success by helping to fortify romantic relationships.

Relational Negativity

Finally, there is some evidence that affectionate communication contributes to relational quality partly through a buffering effect in which it helps to attenuate the effects of otherwise adverse influences. In a two-year longitudinal study of 105 newlywed couples, for instance, Huston and Chorost (1994) found that affectionate communication communicated from husbands to wives buffered the effects of their negativity on their wives' marital satisfaction. That is, when husbands were highly affectionate, their emotional negativity was uncorrelated with their wives' relational satisfaction. On the contrary, when husbands were low in affection, their negativity was inversely associated with their wives' satisfaction (the same associations were not observed between wives' affection and husbands' satisfaction, however). Gulledge et al. (2003) likewise reported that physical affection in romantic relationships – in particular, kissing, hugging, and cuddling – is associated with the ease of conflict resolution, despite being unrelated to the amount of conflict. Both studies suggest that, in addition to whatever relational benefits affectionate communication may be directly associated with, affectionate behaviors also convey benefits via indirect relational pathways, by attenuating the effects of negativity or easing the process of conflict resolution. Unsurprisingly, these effects are influential in the long-term stability of marital relationships. As Huston, Caughlin, Houts, Smith, and George (2001) reported, overt expressions of affection shared between spouses during the first two years of marriage significantly predicted lower rates of divorce thirteen years later.

Summary

Extensive evidence supports the contention that affectionate behavior is associated with benefits for personal relationships. This is likely intuitive and unsurprising, given that affection is a valued behavior in many marriages, families, and other interpersonal bonds, yet two caveats are worth noting. First, there is considerable conceptual (and, at times, operational) overlap between many of the constructs reviewed in this section. Relational satisfaction, sexual satisfaction, communication satisfaction, and life satisfaction, for instance, all share a focus on fulfillment and gratification, albeit with different specific referents. Liking, love, and closeness all index a perception of care for, and connection to, another, and these variables show considerable empirical overlap (e.g., Floyd, 1997a). Commitment reflects cohesion and solidary with a relational partner, which does not necessarily presume positive affect, yet it is also included as a principal component of one of the most commonly used measures of love (Sternberg, 1997). To some extent, then, virtually all of these relational constructs index an assessment that one's relationship is *good*, so from an empirical standpoint, the fact that affectionate behavior is positively associated with one construct should make it unsurprising that it is associated with another.

None of that is to suggest that conceptual distinctions between these constructs lack meaning. There is value in understanding commitment separate from closeness, for instance, and sexual satisfaction separate from love. The caveat is only that the associations between these constructs and affectionate communication are not orthogonal, and there would also be value in exploring the proportions of variance explained by affectionate behavior in one measure of relational quality while controlling for the influence of related measures.

A second caveat is that with many – perhaps most – of these outcomes, the causal connection with affectionate behavior is unclear. Prospective designs, such as those used by Muise et al. (2014) and Debrot et al. (2017), demonstrate how affectionate behavior at one point in time affects relational quality at a later point. However, only experimental designs, such as those used by Floyd et al. (2009) and van Raalte (2017), confirm that affectionate behavior *leads to* changes in relational quality, and both of those studies focused on relationship satisfaction, specifically. How affectionate communication actually influences other markers of relational quality, such as relational maintenance or liking, remains to be determined.

7   Affectionate Communication and Mental Wellness

In recent years, much of the most provocative research on affectionate communication has focused on its benefits for mental and physical health. As Floyd (2006a) surmised, sharing affection *feels good* – at least, under most circumstances – raising the possibility that sharing affection *is good for us*. This and other theoretic observations have prompted many researchers to investigate the connections between affectionate behavior and human well-being.

Most of the research on wellness has focused on physical health, which is the topic of the next chapter. Nonetheless, a substantial literature attests to the associations between affectionate communication and various indices of mental health and wellness. This chapter begins by considering the question of why affectionate behavior might be related to mental health, revisiting the need to belong and speculating about the relative effects of expressed and received affection. The discussion then turns to how affectionate behavior relates to mental health, and a variety of outcomes – from stress and depression to self-esteem, loneliness, and autism – is explored. The chapter concludes with some important caveats as well as speculation about potential therapeutic applications.

Why Is Affectionate Behavior Related to Mental Wellness?

If affectionate behavior relates to mental wellness, from whence do these benefits come? This is among the most important questions posed in this book, because an understanding of why affectionate behavior is therapeutic is not only informative to social scientists but could also be useful in clinical settings. Proposed here is that the principal answer to that question rests in the connection between affectionate behavior and the need to belong. That likelihood is explored in this section, as well as the possibility that the benefits of expressing affection are largely accounted for by the benefits of the affection one receives in return.

Revisiting the Need to Belong

In a general sense, it is traumatic for humans to be denied social contact with others (whether affectionate or not) for prolonged periods. Research on solitary confinement in prisons (Bonta & Gendreau, 1995; Zinger, 1999) and on political imprisonment or captivity (Bauer, Priebe, Häring, & Adamczak, 1993; Sanchez-Anguiano, 1999) confirms that their damaging psychological and psychopathological effects can be swift and severe. Even short-term solitary confinement can produce perceptual distortions, illusions, hallucinations, panic attacks, paranoia, cognitive impairments, and problems with impulse control (Grassian, 1983, 2006). Prolonged isolation is associated with a high prevalence of ruminations, irrational anger, oversensitivity to stimuli, confusion, depression, and dramatic mood swings (Haney, 2003). Not surprisingly, isolation is also associated with increases in self-harm and attempted suicide (Kaba et al., 2014). To be certain, social disconnection alone does not fully account for the damaging outcomes of solitary confinement; duration of confinement, conditions of treatment, and even prisoners' individual characteristics all mediate its effects (Smith, 2006). Nonetheless, as Baumeister and Leary (1995) made clear in their explication of the need to belong, the human requirement for frequent and meaningful social contact is formidible.

Imprisonment and solitary confinement are obviously dramatic examples of social disconnection, but one need not be incarcerated to experience its effects. The much more common condition known as loneliness can emerge any time individuals perceive that their social and intimate needs are not being adequately met (Cacioppo & Patrick, 2008). Situational loneliness can occur, for instance, when people move to an unfamiliar neighborhood or city or begin working for a new employer or attending a new school (Shiovitz-Ezra & Ayalon, 2010). Chronic loneliness results from prolonged perceived disconnection and is generally more common among adolescents and the elderly than among other age groups (Hawkley & Cacioppo, 2010). Objective isolation, such as might result from living or traveling alone, can contribute to loneliness, but it is the *perception* of social isolation – rather than any objective measure of disconnectedness – that is primarily problematic (Cacioppo & Cacioppo, 2014).

In their evolutionary theory of loneliness, Cacioppo et al. (2006) proposed that if the need for social inclusion is indeed fundamental, then a predisposition to experience discomfort and distress during episodes of perceived social isolation is adaptive because such feelings motivate a return to the group and to the benefits of group inclusion, such as protection, shared resources, and reproductive opportunity. Because social inclusion is such a substantial need, feelings of loneliness cause psychological (and even physical) distress until they are alleviated. Specifically, Cacioppo's theory suggests that experiencing loneliness increases feelings of vulnerability, anxiety, and surveillance of potential threats (see Bangee, Harris, Bridger, Rotenberg, & Qualter, 2014; Floyd, 2017b). From this perspective, it is unsurprising that loneliness and related conditions such as social exclusion (Baumeister, Brewer, Tice, & Twenge, 2007), bullying (Hansen et al., 2006), stigmatization (Smart Richman & Leary, 2009), and ostracism (Oaten, Williams, Jones, & Zadro, 2008) – when sufficiently chronic and/or intense – are associated with problems ranging from social anxiety (Leary, 1990) and depression (Donovan et al., 2017) to eating disorders (Levine, 2012), substance abuse (Åkerlind & Hörnquist, 1992), pathological gambling (McQuade & Gill, 2012), and suicide ideation (Stravynski & Boyer, 2001).

Along with Baumeister and Leary's claims about the need to belong, Cacioppo's theory explains why social disconnection, whether caused by incarceration or by less traumatic circumstances, is associated with impairments in mental wellness. Insofar as affectionate behavior contributes to the establishment and maintenance of social bonds (as the previous chapter detailed), therefore, there is a sound theoretic basis for predicting that affectionate communication is associated with enhanced, rather than impaired, mental well-being. Several findings relevant to this contention are described in this chapter, but before those are explored, it is useful to consider one further question related to the association between affection and mental health. If affectionate behavior is connected to mental wellness, is there value both in expressing and receiving affection, or do the apparent benefits of expressed affection reside only in the affection it elicits in response?

The Respective Influence of Affection Given and Affection Received

To the extent that a lack of social connection is detrimental to mental health, one might hypothesize that socially connecting behaviors such as affectionate communication are beneficial, but perhaps mainly when received rather than expressed. Whereas saying "I love you" to another conveys a wish to create or reinforce a social bond, receiving the expression "I love you" from another is perhaps more compelling evidence that one has been selected or preferred by the other and, therefore, truly *belongs*. Although speculative, this idea suggests that the benefits of affectionate communication reside principally in the receipt of affection, specifically. If true, then benefits that covaried with expressed affection may be largely attributable only to the affection that is received in return.

This possibility merits consideration because the relationship between expressed and received affection is strongly reciprocal. It is unsurprising that it should be; Gouldner's (1960) moral norm of reciprocity explains that humans expect one good turn to be followed by another, and theories of behavioral adaptation, such as interaction adaptation theory (Burgoon, Stern, et al., 1995), acknowledge that dyadic communication operates in a patterned manner that tends, more often than not, to elicit behavioral reciprocity. The relationship between affection given and affection received was investigated in two studies that were pivotal to the development of separate measures for expressed and received affection (TAS-G and TAS-R, respectively). In both data sets, expressed and received affection were strongly correlated ($r = .65$ and $.70$; see Floyd, 2002; Floyd, Hess, et al., 2005).

This correspondence is important because of the possibility that received affection moderates, or even accounts for, the effects of expressed affection on various benefits. For instance, some of the benefits of communicating affection that Floyd's (2002) study of trait expressed affection identified could have been dependent on the amount of affection participants received from others. Floyd, Hess, et al. (2005) took up this issue in a study that used data from an online survey of more than a thousand undergraduates from schools around the United States. They first looked at the correlations between trait expressed affection and several individual and relational benefits; they then reexamined those correlations after having controlled for trait received affection.

All of the correlations with expressed affection that were significant when received affection *was not* controlled continued to be significant when received affection *was* controlled. Specifically, expressed affection showed linear associations with social activity, extraversion, comfort with interpersonal closeness, the likelihood of being in a romantic relationship, and relational satisfaction (for those in romantic relationships), and an inverse association with fear of intimacy. Most (but not all) of the correlations decreased in magnitude when received affection was controlled for, however, indicating that *some* of the variance in the beneficial effects of giving affection was accounted for by the effects of receiving affection, but not *all* of it.

To investigate the issue further, Floyd examined correlations between trait affection given and a number of wellness variables from the Floyd (2002) data set (more variables were measured in this study than in the Floyd, Hess, et al., 2003, study), and then reconfigured the correlations having controlled for trait affection received. Both sets of correlation

Table 7.1 *Bivariate and partial correlations between various mental wellness outcomes and trait affection given, from Floyd (2002) data*

Variable	Bivariate Correlation with Affection Given	Correlation Controlling for Affection Received
Depression	−.26***	−.15*
Self-esteem	.40***	.25**
Social activity	.38***	.14*
Stress	−.39***	−.31***
Comfort with closeness	.67***	.50***
Fear of intimacy	−.53***	−.37***
Happiness	.53***	.37***
General mental health	.42***	.20***

Note: Probability estimates are one-tailed. df = 126. *$p < .05$; **$p < .01$; ***$p < .001$.

coefficients appear in Table 7.1. As in the Floyd, Hess, et al. (2003) paper, significant linear associations emerged between expressed affection, social activity, and comfort with closeness, and an inverse association emerged between expressed affection and fear of intimacy. Direct associations also emerged with self-esteem, happiness, and general mental health, and inverse associations were observed with stress and depression. Importantly, all of the correlations with expressed affection that were significant before controlling for received affection remained significant afterward.

To investigate the possibility that the benefits of receiving affection are likewise moderated by the amount of affection given, Floyd computed correlations between affection received and the various individual and relational benefits from the Floyd (2002) and the Floyd, Hess, et al. (2003) data sets, and then recomputed them after controlling for affection given. Both sets of correlations appear in Table 7.2. From the Floyd (2002) data, received affection was directly related to self-esteem, social activity, happiness, comfort with closeness, and mental health, and inversely associated with depression, stress, and fear of intimacy. When expressed affection was covaried out, these correlations remained significant, with the exceptions of depression, stress, and fear of intimacy. The significant partial correlations were all reduced in magnitude relative to the original bivariate correlations. Similar results emerged from the Floyd, Hess, et al. (2003) data. In that study, affection received was directly related to social activity, comfort with closeness, extraversion, likelihood of being in a romantic relationship, and satisfaction with that relationship. All of these correlations, although attenuated, remained significant when expressed affection was controlled.

Table 7.2 *Bivariate and partial correlations between various mental wellness outcomes and trait affection received, from Floyd (2002) data*

Variable	Bivariate Correlation with Affection Received	Correlation Controlling for Affection Given
Depression	−.24***	−.06
Self-esteem	.42***	.20*
Social activity	.48***	.33***
Stress	−.32***	−.11
Comfort with closeness	.53***	.19*
Fear of intimacy	−.39***	−.11
Happiness	.52***	.32***
General mental health	.42***	.22**

Note: Probability estimates are one-tailed. $df = 126$. *$p < .05$; **$p < .01$; ***$p < .001$.

One can conclude from these findings that affection given and affection received share some variance in the benefits with which they are associated, but also retain statistically significant, independent proportions of that variance in many cases. Contrary to the speculation that only received affection is beneficial, the benefits associated with received and expressed affection are at least partly orthogonal – that is, one can benefit from receiving gestures of affection even if one does not give them and can benefit from giving gestures of affection even if one does not receive them.

Based on theories of social exchange and the norm of reciprocity, one might posit that the *similarity* between one's levels of expressed and received affection should be influential in predicting benefit. In other words, are people who give and receive approximately the same amounts of affection advantaged over those who give more than they receive, or receive more than they give? To investigate this possibility, using the Floyd (2002) and Floyd, Hess, et al. (2005) data sets, Floyd computed deviation scores by taking the absolute value of the difference between participants' scores for affection given and affection received, and correlated those deviation scores with all of the individual and relational benefits measured. Significant inverse correlations would have suggested that people are better off giving and receiving approximately the same levels of affectionate communication, whereas significant direct correlations would have suggested that giving more than one receives, or receiving more than one gives, are advantageous strategies. None of the correlations with any of the benefits measured in either of the two data sets was significant, however, suggesting that although the *absolute levels* of affection given and affection received are associated with various benefits, their *relative levels* are not.

This discussion has theorized about *why* affectionate behavior is associated with mental wellness (and why giving and receiving account for both shared and nonshared proportions of the variance). The subsequent section, in turn, explores *how* affectionate behavior relates to mental well-being.

Connections to Individual Mental Wellness Indices

Mental health is a complex and multifaceted construct. Just as physical health encompasses a broad range of organ systems with virtually innumerable potential impairments, mental health is subject to multiple, diverse pathologies. The current version of the *Diagnostic and Statistical Manual of Mental Disorders*, the DSM-5 (American Psychiatric Association, 2013), differentiates nineteen categories of psychopathology, including addictive disorders, dissociative disorders, sexual dysfunctions, anxiety disorders, eating disorders, and personality disorders. The vast majority of diagnosable impairments have not been studied in relation to affectionate communication – and in truth, many psychopathologies are likely unrelated to affectionate behavior. Nonetheless, research has examined a variety of indices of mental well-being (or impaired well-being), and relevant findings are detailed in this section. This description begins with studies measuring general subjective wellness and then explores anxiety and depression; stress; self-esteem; loneliness; alexithymia, Asperger syndrome, and autism spectrum disorders; and alcohol abuse.

General Subjective Wellness

General subjective wellness is a broad category of mental well-being outcomes that includes global perceptions of psychological wellness as well as assessments of positive and negative affect. Of the studies that have investigated links between affectionate behavior and general subjective wellness, most have focused on affectionate touch, and for good reason. Touch is a provocative and intimate form of human contact (Gallace & Spence, 2010) with multiple links to both physical and emotional well-being (Field, 2010). Recently, Jakubiak and Feeney (2017) articulated a theoretical model wherein the receipt of touch interpreted by the receiver as affectionate (as opposed to touch that conveys instrumental caregiving, power, control, or aggression, or touch that is purely ritualistic; see Floyd, 2017a) initiates a relational-cognitive pathway leading to subjective wellness outcomes including a sense of social inclusion, felt security, and an expectation of support when needed. Those, in turn, are posited to increase general psychological and relational well-being.[1]

Several empirical findings have lent support to the proposed connection between affectionate touch and wellness. In an early experimental investigation, Clipman (1999) randomly assigned college students to treatment and comparison conditions for a four-week trial. Those in the treatment group were instructed either to proactively give or passively receive at least five hugs per day. Students were told specifically that the hugs should be front-to-front encounters involving both arms of both participants, but hand placement, amount of body contact, and hug duration and intensity were uncontrolled. Students assigned to the comparison group were asked to record the number of hours they spent reading each day.

Before and after the intervention, participants completed an eighteen-item subjective well-being scale created for the study. Although the measure asked about self-perceptions of physical health, the majority of questions referenced perceptions of emotional wellness, life satisfaction, connectedness, and general happiness, constituting at least a rough approximation of general subjective wellness. Clipman hypothesized that students in the hugging condition would experience a significant increase in their wellness over the course of the trial, whereas those in the comparison group would show no change.

Students in the treatment condition reported giving or receiving an average of seven hugs per day with an average of five different people. As hypothesized, treatment participants experienced a significant increase in wellness over the course of the four-week intervention, whereas wellness for comparison participants did not change. Based on the means and standard deviations reported by Clipman (1999), the repeated measures effect size (d_{ppc2}; Morris, 2008) for the experiment equals .38. Neither the average number of daily hugs given/received nor the average number of people hugged per day accounted for variance in the experimental participants' increases in wellness.

More contemporary diary studies have confirmed the positive associations between affectionate touch and wellness. Debrot, Schoebi, Perrez, and Horn (2013) had both partners in 102 dating couples complete electronic diaries four times per day for one week. At each data collection point, participants reported their frequency of responsive touch with their partner, defined as affectionate touch enacted in response to the partner's affective state. They also reported on their own affective state at the time, using two bipolar scales anchored with the descriptors "unwell/well" and "discontent/content." Their analyses showed that responsive affectionate touch was significantly associated with greater positivity both in participants' own affective states and in their partners' affective states.

Similarly, in a national sample of pre- and perimenopausal women, Burleson, Trevathan, and Todd (2007) had participants complete a daily diary every morning for thirty-six weeks. Each diary measure assessed, among other outcomes, participants' experiences of physical (nonsexual) affection and their levels of positive and negative mood. Like Debrot et al., Burleson and colleagues found that physical affection was directly associated with positive mood and inversely associated with negative mood on the same day (so, participants felt more positive and less negative on days when they experienced more physical affection). Notably, however, physical affection on one day also predicted less negative mood on the following day, so participants who engaged in physical affection felt less negative not only on the same day but also a day later. Physical affection did not predict positive mood on the following day, but the reverse was true: a more positive mood on one day predicted more physical affection on the subsequent day.

Other studies have not focused on touch, specifically, but have included broader assessments of affectionate interaction. Mansson (2014a), for instance, examined affectionate communication in the grandparent–grandchild relationship and its association with general mental wellness. One hundred four grandparents completed the GRAS indicating the extent to which they showed affection to their grandchildren in the form of love and esteem, caring, memories and humor, and celebration. All four forms of affectionate behavior were significantly correlated with general mental health, with correlation coefficients ranging in magnitude from .33 to .38 (but see Schrodt et al., 2007).

In sum, these results reflect positive associations between affectionate behavior (especially affectionate touch) and individuals' general subjective wellness. Mental well-being takes many more specific forms, however, so subsequent sections address the associations of affectionate communication with specific dimensions of mental health.

Anxiety and Depression

Two of the most commonly diagnosed categories of mental health disorders are mood disorders (a category including major depressive disorder) and anxiety disorders (a category including generalized anxiety disorder; Steel et al., 2014), and many more people suffer from subclinical levels of both conditions (see, e.g., van Zoonen et al., 2015). Although these two conditions are often mentioned in the same breath – and although their comorbidity is high (Lamers et al., 2011) – they are not the same experience. In general, depression is characterized by feelings of sadness and hopelessness, pessimism and listlessness, low self-esteem, and a diminished ability to concentrate (as well as with physical symptoms such as sleep disturbances and significant weight changes; Comer, 2017). Depression is also a major risk factor for suicide ideation and attempted suicide (Brown, Beck, Steer, & Grisham, 2000). Importantly, excessive worry is not a characteristic of (or a diagnostic criterion for) depression, but it is the principal diagnostic criterion for generalized anxiety disorder. Unlike depression, this disorder is characterized by frequent, excessive, and typically long-lasting worry (often about a variety of topics) that is difficult to control and interferes with daily functioning (Comer, 2017).

Floyd, Hess, et al. (2005) provided early correlational evidence of a connection between affectionate behavior and the symptoms of (although not necessarily diagnosis for) depression. The first study in that paper reanalyzed data from Floyd (2002), in which adults reported on their trait affection scores (given and received), using the Trait Affection Scale. Participants also completed a battery of measures that included the Center for Epidemiologic Studies Depression (CES-D) scale, a commonly used brief self-report of depressive symptoms (see Vilagut, Forero, Barbaglia, & Alonso, 2016). On the basis of AET, Floyd and colleagues predicted that trait expressed affection is inversely correlated with depressive symptoms, and that correlation was significant, although the correlation was diminished when trait received affection was controlled (see Table 7.1). The attenuated partial correlation suggests that, to the extent that affectionate communication mitigates depressive symptoms, it is the *receipt* of affection, rather than the *expression*, that is primarily instrumental. One replication in the Floyd, Hess, et al. paper (Study 2) produced the same finding, wherein depression was negatively correlated with expressed affection at a bivariate level ($r = -.29$), but not when received affection was controlled ($r = .01$). A second replication in the same paper (Study 3) again found a significant bivariate correlation with expressed affection ($r = -.48$); however, that study found that the magnitude of the correlation actually increased substantially ($r = -.84$) once received affection was controlled, in contradiction to the first two results.

What is clear from these findings is that affectionate communication is inversely associated with depressive symptoms. The preponderance of the evidence suggests that received rather than expressed affection is responsible for that association, but the evidence to the contrary implies that this issue is not yet definitively resolved.

Much of the other research related to depression and anxiety has concentrated on affection received from family members. In a random sample of Dutch adults, for instance, Kerver, van Son, and de Groot (1992) found that the amount of affection participants reported receiving from their fathers during their upbringing was inversely associated with their likelihood of suffering clinical depression at the time of the study (although it was not significantly predictive of depression symptoms experienced one year later). Similarly, in a sample of more than 2,400 Australian adults, Jorm, Dear, Rodgers, and Christensen (2003) reported that affection received from both mothers and fathers during upbringing was significantly associated with lower anxiety and less susceptibility to depression, as well as lower neuroticism. Maselko, Kubzansky, Lipsitt, and Buka (2011) even found that mothers' affection shown toward their children during infancy inversely predicted their children's anxiety during adulthood (but see Francis, 2010). These collective findings suggest that receiving affectionate behavior, particularly from parents, can serve a protective effect against the symptoms of depression and anxiety.

Koole, Sin, and Schneider (2014) examined anxiety related to dying, specifically. They demonstrated that receiving a brief touch on the shoulder by a female experimenter was associated with lower levels of death anxiety following a reminder of mortality. Similarly, reminding participants of their own mortality was associated with an increased desire for touch. Importantly, however, these patterns emerged only for individuals with low self-esteem, who, according to research, exhibit greater anxiety about their mortality than their high-self-esteem counterparts (Routledge et al., 2010).

There is some evidence that the connections of affectionate behavior to depression and anxiety are mediated by need fulfillment. Prager and Buhrmester (1998, Study 2) had participants from 133 cohabiting couples keep a daily diary record of their intimate interactions over the course of a week. The intimacy measure was not specific to affectionate communication, but assessed more broadly the levels of interactional positivity, self-disclosure, and attentive listening that characterized participants' encounters during the week. Participants also completed global measures of their anxiety, depression, and their ratings of the importance and fulfillment of multiple individual ("agentic") and relational ("communal") needs. Agentic needs included needs for autonomy, self-esteem, meaning and purpose, and approval by others; communal needs included needs for companionship, affection, sexual fulfillment, and support. For both women and men, higher levels of intimacy were associated with lower levels of depression and anxiety. Importantly, however, these effects were mediated by need fulfillment, suggesting that intimacy contributes to lower depression and anxiety partly by fulfilling individuals' agentic and communal needs.

Whereas higher affection tends to be beneficial with respect to depression and anxiety, at least one study has suggested that the *lack of affection* is also associated with these outcomes. Floyd (2014) measured adults' levels of affection deprivation, a variable indexing the discrepancy between an individual's desired and received levels of affectionate communication. On the basis of AET, Floyd predicted that affection deprivation is positively associated with the number of mood disorders (the category that includes major depressive disorder) and/or anxiety disorders (the category that includes generalized anxiety disorder) with which individuals have been formally diagnosed. The prediction was supported. Importantly, participants were not asked to indicate the specific mood or anxiety disorders with which they had been diagnosed, if any. Rather, they were presented with a list of the psychopathologies that belong in each category and were simply asked to report how many of them, if any, they had been diagnosed with. It is therefore possible that participants' affection deprivation was associated with mood disorders other than depression, such as seasonal affective disorder or bipolar disorder, and/or with anxiety disorders other than generalized anxiety disorder, such as phobias or panic disorder. As a result, this finding must be interpreted cautiously, although it is consistent with the other evidence that affectionate communication is associated with a lower risk of anxious and depressive symptoms.

Mental Stress

Selye (1936, 1956) conceived of stress as comprising the body's regulatory responses to environmental threats. Such threats – referred to as *stressors* – represent any type of perceived challenge to an individual's mental, emotional, physical, financial, relational, or existential well-being. Although stress is experienced physiologically (including, for instance, cardiovascular, muscular, and hormonal responses; Everly & Lating, 2013), it is also experienced mentally. As it is typically operationalized, mental stress embodies feelings of worry or nervousness, a lack of self-confidence or control over one's circumstances, the perception that one's difficulties are insurmountable, an inability to cope with threats, and feelings of upset over unexpected events (Cohen, Kamarck, & Mermelstein, 1983).

To the extent that humans crave social inclusion (Baumeister & Leary, 1995), it is reasonable to expect that a lack of inclusion is mentally stressful, and therefore that behaviors signifying social inclusion are inversely associated with stress. Multiple studies detailed in the next chapter have demonstrated that pattern with respect to physiological stress, but it has also been documented with mental stress. For instance, Floyd, Hess, et al. (2005) reanalyzed data from Floyd (2002) showing that mental stress is inversely correlated with trait expressed affection and that the correlation remains significant even after the influence of trait received affection is partialled out (see Table 7.1). These results were replicated in Study 3 of the same paper, which again showed that expressed affection was negatively related to stress ($r = -.56$), even net of the effects of received affection ($r = -.75$).

Although the Floyd, Hess, et al. (2005) findings are purely correlational, at least two experiments have shown that inducing affectionate behavior produces a reduction in stress. Floyd et al. (2009) recruited fifty-two healthy adults in marital or cohabiting relationships to take part in a six-week trial. Participants assigned randomly to the treatment condition were instructed to kiss their romantic partner more frequently for the duration of the study, whereas control participants were given no specific instructions regarding their behavior. Mental stress was measured at the beginning and end of the trial, and, as hypothesized, the treatment group experienced a significant decrease in stress (Cohen's $d = .78$), whereas stress levels were unchanged for the control group.

The second experiment, by Coan, Schaefer, and Davidson (2006), focused on hand-holding instead of kissing. In that study, sixteen married women were subjected to the threat of an electric shock while undergoing functional magnetic resonance imaging (fMRI), a radiological technique used for imaging brain activity by detecting changes in blood in various regions of the brain. During the procedure, participants were holding their husband's hand, the hand of an anonymous male researcher, or no hand at all, and the researchers focused on how hand-holding attenuated the stress associated with the threat of shock.

This study is seminal for two reasons. First, stress was measured not via self-report (as in all of the other research reported in this section), but as a function of activation in neural systems associated with emotional and behavioral threat responses. Although the fMRI procedure itself may be more closely related with physiological stress, the researchers' focus was on the psychological stress caused by the threat of electric shock, and they used neural imaging, instead of self-report, to assess that outcome.

To the extent that the findings of this study align with those of others, this approach offers the potential for valuable corroboration of the self-report method used to assess mental stress in other studies.

Second, the Coan et al. experiment was among the first to address a fundamental question about the benefits (mental or otherwise) of affectionate behavior: How much does the *source* of the behavior matter? If receiving affection ameliorates mental stress (or provides any other mental or physical health benefit, for that matter), how much of that benefit is resident in the behavior itself, and how much depends on the nature of the receiver's relationship with the sender? If a hug is stress alleviating, for instance, is it just as beneficial to receive a hug from a stranger as from a spouse? Is a hug from a stranger any more beneficial than no hug at all? Few studies prior to Coan et al. provided an opportunity to parse out the variance associated with the behavior and with the relationship.

With respect to stress amelioration, Coan and colleagues hypothesized an additive model wherein any hand-holding (whether from a spouse or a stranger) was better than none, and wherein hand-holding from a spouse was more beneficial than from a stranger. The researchers examined activity in several neural regions of interest, including the ventral anterior cingulate cortex, dorsolateral prefrontal cortex, caudate-nucleus accumbens, superior colliculus, and supramarginal gyrus, and both predictions were supported. Holding a spouse's hand produced the greatest stress-protective effect, followed by holding a stranger's hand, and finally by holding no hand at all. These findings are in accord with those of other studies showing that affectionate behavior is associated with reduced self-reported stress, and they further suggest a type of ordinal interaction effect wherein the behavior itself is beneficial, and even more so when enacted in a positive personal relationship.

There is evidence, too, that the association between affectionate behavior and stress has a temporal element. Burleson et al.'s (2007) longitudinal study of pre- and perimenopausal women, for instance, reported that the amount of physical affection experienced on a given day was uncorrelated with the amount of stress experienced on the same day. Nonetheless, physical affection experienced on one day was negatively associated with stress experienced the following day. Moreover, in a multiwave longitudinal study, Schwartz and Russek (1998) reported that the amount of love and caring college students had expressed to them by their parents significantly, and inversely, predicted both their physical and psychological stress as many as forty-two years later (but see Christopher, Bauman, & Veness-Meehan, 2000).

Self-Esteem

Self-esteem indexes the extent to which individuals value, prize, like, or approve of themselves (Blascovich & Tomaka, 1991); it is commonly also referred to as self-regard, self-worth, and self-respect. Although some caution that its benefits may be overstated (Baumeister, Campbell, Krueger, & Vohs, 2003), research has shown self-esteem to be correlated with higher academic achievement (Hansford & Hattie, 1982), higher-quality relationships with friends (Keefe & Berndt, 1996) and work associates (Frone, 2000), greater likelihood of romantic success (Hendrick, Hendrick, & Adler, 1988), and (among adolescents) a reduced likelihood of delinquency (Trzewniewski, Donnellan, Robins, Moffitt, & Caspi, 2002). Although low self-esteem is not in itself a mental disorder, it is a characteristic of various psychopathologies, including depression and anxiety (Orth & Robins, 2013; Sowislo & Orth, 2012), eating disorders (Cervera et al., 2003), psychosis (Silverstone, 1991), borderline and avoidant personality disorders (Lynum, Wilberg, & Karterud, 2008), attention deficit hyperactivity disorder (ADHD; Shaw-Zirt, Popali-Lehane, Chaplin, & Bergman, 2005), and schizophrenia (Barrowclough et al., 2003).

Researchers have known for some time that children's self-esteem is strongly associated with the level of affection and love they receive from their parents (see, e.g., Gecas & Seff, 1990; McLeod & Shanahan, 1993; Scott, Scott, & McCabe, 1991). Although the benefits of parental affection appear to wane as daughters and sons enter adulthood (Amato, 1994; Roberts & Bengtson, 1993; Umberson, 1992), parental affection is still predictive of adults' self-esteem. For instance, Roberts and Bengtson (1996) showed that affection with parents during adolescence and young adulthood is predictive of self-esteem over a twenty-year period. Similarly, Barber and Thomas (1986) showed that undergraduate women's (but not men's) self-esteem was predicted by the amount of physical affection they received from their fathers.

Among adults, self-esteem is also associated with the amount of affection expressed to others. In two studies, Floyd, Hess, et al. (2005) reported moderate to large correlations between self-esteem (as measured by the Rosenberg (1965) self-esteem scale) and trait expressed affection ($r = .40$ and $.54$). To examine whether expressed affection continued to account for variance in self-esteem after the potential effects of received affection were partialled out, Floyd and colleagues computed partial correlations and found that the coefficients remained statistically significant. This suggests that, when considering one's trait-like levels of affectionate communication (rather than affection shared in a specific social or familial relationship), self-esteem is positively associated with affection that is expressed, to a degree that cannot be fully accounted for by the affection one receives in return.

Loneliness

As described above, loneliness is a discrepancy between one's desired and perceived levels of social engagement (Cacioppo & Patrick, 2008). Like low self-esteem, loneliness is not a psychopathology. Nonetheless, it is comorbid with multiple diagnosable mental disorders, including depression (Donovan et al., 2017), social anxiety (Leary, 1990), disordered eating (Levine, 2012), pathological gambling (McQuade & Gill, 2012), and substance abuse (Åkerlind & Hörnquist, 1992), as well as with suicide ideation (Stravynski & Boyer, 2001).

If humans need social connection, if affectionate behavior contributes to connection, and if loneliness reflects a lack of connection, then it is logical to deduce that affectionate behavior is negatively associated with the experience of loneliness. Mansson (2014a) examined that hypothesis in the grandparent–grandchild relationship. Grandparents reported on the extent to which they showed affection to their grandchildren in the form of love and esteem, caring, memories and humor, and celebration. The latter three forms (but not love and esteem) were negatively associated with the grandparents' own loneliness, with correlations ranging from $-.21$ to $-.37$. In a separate study of 214 young adult grandchildren, Mansson (2013b) reported that the grandchildren's loneliness was negatively associated with the celebratory affection they received from their grandparents ($r = -.18$) as well as with their grandparents' affection in the form of memories and humor ($r = -.17$).

Simply communicating for the *purpose* of affection is inversely associated with loneliness. In a study involving 100 senior citizens (ranging in age from 55 to 85), Downs and Javidi (1990, Study 2) explored the relationship between loneliness and the extent to which affection is a motivation for communication. Rubin et al. (1988) had conceptualized multiple common motives for interpersonal communication, including the motives to communication for pleasure, for inclusion, for escape, for relaxation, for control, and for affection. Downs and Javidi discovered that the more participants reported communicating for the purpose of exchanging affection, the less lonely they were ($r = -.25$).

A lack of affection, in contrast, appears to correlate positively with loneliness. Green and Wildermuth (1993) explored loneliness in a population of undergraduate students. They found that loneliness in women was predicted by a lack of expressed affection and that loneliness in men was predicted by a lack of expressed inclusion. Similarly, in a study of more than 500 adults, Floyd (2014) reported a moderate association (β = .45) between loneliness and the perception that one receives less affection than one desires.

Alexithymia, Asperger Syndrome, and Autism Spectrum Disorders

This category of disorders reflects deficits in social interaction, social communication, and emotional expression. Alexithymia, a term coined by Sifneos (1973), is a personality construct rather than a psychopathology. The term *alexithymia* means a lack of words for emotions (Taylor, Bagby, & Parker, 1997), and individuals who score high on this trait have a difficult time recognizing and communicating their own emotions, as well as recognizing emotional signals from others (see Hesse et al., 2013). Highly alexithymic individuals also find it difficult to distinguish between the emotional and physiological components of arousal (see Bagby, Parker, & Taylor, 1994).

Until 2013, Asperger syndrome was a diagnosable developmental disorder, but with the release of the DSM-5, it (along with childhood disintegrative disorder and pervasive developmental disorder not otherwise specified) has been incorporated into a single diagnosis of autism spectrum disorder. The symptoms of Asperger syndrome, which typically appear early in life (Schnur, 2005), include (among others) an impaired ability to use nonverbal behavior (eye contact, facial expressions, gestures) to facilitate social interaction, repetitive motor movements, and a lack of emotional reciprocity (Toth & King, 2008).[2] Autism is also an early-onset condition (Baxter et al., 2015) characterized by problems such as deficits in social communication and social interaction (including impaired nonverbal ability and emotional reciprocity), difficulty maintaining or understanding relationships, repetitive motor movements, and insistence on routines (see Lord & Bishop, 2015).

Hesse and Floyd (2008) provided initial data regarding the relationship between alexithymia and affectionate communication. Reasoning that because alexithymia impairs emotional communication ability, it would also make it difficult for individuals to give and receive affection, the researchers expected that alexithymia would be inversely associated with affectionate communication. They further speculated, however, that affectionate communication may mediate the associations between alexithymia and mental and relational outcomes, including happiness, nonverbal immediacy, depression, stress, and the levels of closeness and affectionate communication in an individual's closest personal relationship.

In their study of 349 undergraduate students, Hesse and Floyd measured affectionate communication in two ways: trait-level affectionate behavior was assessed using the combined expressed and received subscales of the TAS, and communication in a specific relationship with a loved one was assessed using the ACI. Results showed that alexithymia had the expected inverse relationships with trait affectionate communication ($r = -.56$) as well as affectionate communication in a close relationship ($r = -.23$). In addition, mediation analyses showed that trait affectionate communication partially mediated the associations between alexithymia and happiness, nonverbal immediacy, and depression, and fully mediated the associations between alexithymia and the levels of closeness and affectionate communication in individuals' closest relationship (the mediation effect for stress was nonsignificant).

A larger follow-up study by Hesse and Floyd (2011a) again reported a strong inverse relationship between trait affectionate communication and alexithymia ($r = -.81$). The researchers further found that trait affectionate communication partially mediated the association between alexithymia and a tendency toward an anxious-avoidant attachment style, and fully mediated the associations of alexithymia with the need for relationships and the number of close relationships (see also Hesse & Floyd, 2011b; Frye-Cox & Hesse, 2013).

Affectionate communication research regarding Asperger syndrome and autism spectrum disorders has focused primarily on developing and testing interventions to help children with those impairments to understand and express affection more effectively. Attwood (2007) reported that children with these disorders often have great difficulty initiating, interpreting, and responding to affectionate expressions, which is understandable given their difficulties in interpreting and reacting to emotional expressions, more generally. In a 2011 study, Sofronoff, Eloff, Sheffield, and Attwood developed and tested a cognitive behavioral intervention called "Exploring Feelings: Affection," which was designed to improve understanding and expression of affection among twenty-three children with Asperger syndrome. The intervention comprised five two-hour sessions in which children participated in small groups while their parents took part in a separate large group. Each session focused on a specific skill, such as constructing a story about how loving someone can affect one's thoughts and feelings and role-playing appropriate ways of showing love to others. In a pretest–posttest design, Sofronoff et al. found that the intervention significantly improved children's appropriateness of affectionate behavior with others (as measured by parental reports) and their understanding of the purpose of affection (as measured by children's reports). Parents also reported a substantial increase in the amount of affection shown by their children after the intervention. Importantly, all three of these improvements were maintained at a three-month follow-up.

Besides the relatively small sample, the Sofronoff et al. (2011) study was also limited by the lack of a control group. These limitations were addressed in a later experiment by Andrews, Attwood, and Sofronoff (2013), which enrolled fifty-eight children who had been diagnosed with Asperger syndrome, high-functioning autism, or pervasive developmental disorder not otherwise specified. This study employed a waitlist-control design, which allowed the researchers to compare the scores of children who had completed the intervention with those of children who had yet to do so. As in the earlier study, the authors found that the intervention improved children's appropriateness of affectionate behavior with others and their understanding of the purpose of affection and that these improvements were maintained at a three-month follow-up.

The findings related to alexithymia, Asperger disorder, and autism spectrum disorder suggest that all three experiences are associated with impairments in the tendency or ability to share affectionate communication, but that both the tendency and the ability to communicate affection can be improved with cognitive-behavioral intervention, at least for children with Asperger disorder and autism spectrum disorders (see also Twardosz & Jozwiak, 1981). Whether a similar intervention would be successful for alexithymic children or adults is unknown, but the results of Sofronoff and colleagues' research are promising.

Alcohol Abuse

Finally, one study has demonstrated associations between affectionate communication and alcohol abuse. The DSM-5 recognizes alcohol use disorder as a psychopathology, but, of course, individuals can and do abuse alcohol to a subclinical degree (see, e.g., Gunzerath, Faden, Zakhari, & Warren, 2004). Over the course of three separate surveys, Shuntich, Loh, and Katz (1998) asked more than 500 undergraduate students how often their parents showed affection to each other and to them. Participants also reported their perception of how frequently their parents drank alcohol to excess. Across all three surveys, the authors found that parental abuse of alcohol was inversely associated with parents' overall affectionate communication toward each other and with parents' physical and verbal affection toward their children (correlation coefficients ranged from −.12 to −.52). Floyd (2015) later speculated that alcohol use and abuse may be a common coping strategy (albeit a maladaptive one) for dealing with affection deprivation, a speculation that is in line with the inverse associations observed between parental affection and excessive alcohol consumption.

Table 7.3 *Mental wellness markers associated with affectionate communication*

Marker	Associations with Affectionate Communication
General subjective wellness	Positively associated with relational affection; increased by hugging; positively related to affectionate touch
Anxiety	Inversely related to intimacy; parental affection inversely associated with anxiety; touch reduces death-related anxiety; affection deprivation positively related to likelihood of diagnosis for anxiety disorder
Depression	Inversely related to trait affectionate communication and intimacy; parental affection inversely related to likelihood of clinical depression; affection deprivation positively related to likelihood of diagnosis for mood disorder
Mental stress	Inversely related to trait expressed affection; reduced by kissing and hand-holding; reduced by affection received on previous day; inversely associated with parental affection
Self-esteem	Positively associated with trait expressed affection and affection received from parents
Loneliness	Inversely related to affection between grandparents and grandchildren; inversely related to communicating for the purpose of affection; positively related to affection deprivation
Alexithymia, Asperger syndrome, and autism spectrum disorders	Alexithymia inversely related to trait affectionate communication and relational affectionate communication; affection mediates associations between alexithymia and negative outcomes; interventions improve affectionate behavior for children with Asperger syndrome and/or autism spectrum disorders
Alcohol abuse	Inversely associated with spousal affection and affection toward children

A summary of the mental wellness indices associated with affectionate communication appears in Table 7.3.

Conclusion

Considered in concert, the findings reported in this chapter reflect a rather clear pattern in which affectionate communication is associated with mental wellness across a range of indices. The more affection people give and receive, the higher their general subjective wellness and self-esteem, and the lower their likelihood of experiencing anxiety, depression, stress, loneliness, social and emotional communication impairments, and alcohol abuse. It is critical to reiterate that most of the research described in this chapter is cross-sectional, which does not allow for causal inferences. Perhaps it is the case that communicating affection engenders the rewards of better mental wellness; perhaps it is instead (or also) the case that experiencing mental well-being prompts people to be more affectionate with others. Without controlled experimental studies it is impossible to determine the causal connections between affection and mental wellness, but their varied and often strong associations would warrant such investigations.

It is instructive to point out, too, that many of the conditions described in this chapter are comorbid, both with each other and with additional pathologies. As a result, their associations with affectionate communication cannot be presumed to be orthogonal. On the basis of relevant empirical findings, it would be reasonable to expect, for example, not only that a lack of affection is related to conditions such as depression, loneliness, and alcohol abuse, but also that a lack of affection influences loneliness, which in turn influences depression and alcohol abuse.

That caveat notwithstanding, the connections between affectionate behavior and mental well-being raise the possibility that promoting affectionate communication in personal relationships may have some clinical benefit. As a complement to pharmacological and/or psycho-therapeutic treatments, for instance, would there be value for therapists in "prescribing" greater attention to and practice of affection exchange? L'abate (2008) has introduced a therapeutic homework activity to pro-mote affectionate behavior in intimate relationships. The intervention, dubbed 3HC (for hugging, holding, huddling, and cuddling), is designed to improve emotional communication in couples or family pairs as an adjunct to marital and family therapy. The activity, which is prescribed by a therapist for engagement at home, calls for participants to schedule uninterrupted time together in which they begin by forming a huddle, making sure they are hugging and holding each other as much as pos-sible. The huddle should morph into a cuddling session that is purely nonverbal, with the focus on touch rather than talking. The activity should last from ten to fifteen minutes and can be performed daily, weekly, or twice weekly, depending on the therapist's suggestion.

Evidence for the intervention's effects is still only clinical (rather than based on systematic research), but L'abate (2008) offers a compelling case study attesting to its utility in a family therapy setting. He also notes that the intervention is contraindicated for enmeshed families or those with extremely rigid boundaries, and also in cases of incest or sexual or verbal abuse, unless those conditions have already been successfully treated. (See also Migdat (2016), who found that therapy with marital partners increased levels of physical affection, albeit only for husbands.)

Another possibility is that interventions focused on increasing the quality or frequency of affection exchange may be useful in the counseling of suicidal individuals. Although suicide has myriad causes, Joiner's interpersonal theory of suicide (Joiner, 2005; Van Orden et al., 2010) suggests that two predictors are especially potent. The first is a belief that one is a burden to others, but the second is a thwarted sense of social inclusion or belonging (Joiner points out that the influence of both states is enhanced when one feels hopeless that those states will ever improve). Thus, when one has the capability to attempt suicide, the perceptions that one is alone and a burden to others interact to predict lethal or near-lethal suicide attempts, according to the theory.

In this chapter, a common theme linking affectionate behavior to mental wellness is the ability of affectionate behavior to create or reinforce the perception of belongingness. It is reasonable to propose that the more affection one gives and receives with others, the less likely one is to feel alone or socially excluded in life. To the extent that is true, then affectionate behavior may have a protective effect on suicidality by thwarting the perception that one is alone (one of the two key predictors of suicide in Joiner's theory).

Quinnett (2009) references this idea in his explication of therapeutic techniques for counseling suicidal people. One technique, which he has nicknamed "Being Someone's Teddy Bear," focuses specifically on encouraging hugging as a means of reinforcing social and relational inclusion and the perception that one matters to others. Rabinowitz (1991) points out that hugging is not easy for everyone – especially not for men hugging other men, given male–male touch taboos – but he also touts its benefits in the therapeutic context. The possibility that affectionate behavior may be a useful adjunct to counseling for suicidal individuals remains to be adjudicated systematically, but there is certainly an adequate theoretic basis for making that prediction.

In sum, compelling evidence exists for the associations between affectionate communication and mental wellness. The links between affectionate behavior and physical wellness are perhaps even stronger, however, as the next chapter details.

8   Affectionate Communication and Physical Health

Perhaps the most groundbreaking research to be done on affectionate communication is the work demonstrating its associations with physical health and wellness. Floyd (2006a) offered multiple speculations about the physical and physiological components of affectionate behavior, but scholarship adjudicating those speculations was relatively sparse at the time. Since then, however, the research has proliferated, offering a much more complete picture of how affectionate communication in close relationships contributes to physical well-being. Like the previous chapter, this one begins by considering why affectionate behavior is related to physical health. It then details research linking affectionate communication to health benefits involving the cardiovascular system, the endocrine system, allergy and immunology, metabolism, and susceptibility to infection and pain. The chapter concludes with a summary that acknowledges some of the health detriments of affectionate interaction.

Why Is Affectionate Behavior Related to Physical Health?

The argument connecting affectionate communication to physical health is similar to the one connecting it to mental health. In both cases, the important causal factor is the need to belong. In his explication of affection exchange theory, Floyd (2006a) argued that because social inclusion is such a fundamental human need, humans evolved a propensity to express affection as a means of meeting that need. As with other fundamental needs – such as for food, water, and sleep – the need for close relationships is physically rewarding when met and physically aversive when thwarted. It is therefore understandable why giving and receiving expressions of affection – at least in the context of positive relationships – are associated with sensations of physical reward, such as increased calm and reduced pain and stress (see, e.g., Denes, Bennett, & Winkler, 2017; Floyd & Deiss, 2012; Floyd, Hesse, & Pauley, 2009; Floyd & Ray, 2016). In the same way that physical reward follows eating when one is hungry and sleeping when one is fatigued, communicating affection feels physically rewarding because it serves the fundamental human need for close interpersonal connections. For these reasons, therefore, it is reasonable to argue that affectionate behavior *feels good to people* because it *is good for them*.

Like mental health, physical health is a complex and multifaceted construct. The wellness of the human organism is indexed by hundreds of individual outcomes (or *markers*) from a diverse range of physiological systems. Whereas mental health is typically assessed through some manner of self-report (whether on a questionnaire, in a diary, or in psychotherapy), however, evaluations of physical health (other than for the subjective experiences of symptoms) typically require the measurement of physiological markers, such as one's levels of blood pressure, stress hormones, immunoglobulins, or lipids.

In the communication field, this endeavor has required not only the use of novel methodologies (Afifi & Floyd, 2015; Floyd, 2004; Floyd, Hesse, & Pauley, 2013) but also a paradigm shift allowing for consideration of communication behaviors' physiological antecedents, consequences, and correlates. Whereas physiological markers are commonly measured in association with social behavior in disciplines such as health psychology, psychophysiology, and nursing, the communication discipline has been markedly slower to embrace a biological frame for understanding human behavior. Floyd and Ray (2016) speculated that this is based in part on a fear that calling a behavior "biological" equates to claiming that it is biologically determined. That conclusion would appear to suggest that individuals have little control over their social behaviors and that environmental influences such as parenting, enculturation, education, and media are benign. As noted earlier, however, that conclusion was inaccurate to begin with. Arguing that communication and biology are inseparably related in no way implies that communication is biologically determined. Biology certainly affords humans the ability to communicate, but as Floyd and Afifi (2012) pointed out, "The ability to communicate does not dictate the *manner* in which we communicate, however, any more than the ability to write dictates the words we use or the ability to sing dictates the songs we enjoy" (p. 95; emphasis in original).

As psychophysiological methods have gained traction in communication research (see, e.g., Aloia, Denes, & Crowley, in press; Beatty, McCroskey, & Floyd, 2009; Floyd, Mikkelson, & Hesse, 2007), scholars have been able to document multiple ways in which affectionate behavior influences physical health and wellness. As one might expect, given the fundamental human need that affectionate interaction serves, the majority of influences on health are positive. The research detailed in this chapter will demonstrate, for instance, that sharing affection buffers individuals from the negative effects of stressors and helps them recover more quickly from elevated stress; supports cardiovascular, immune, and metabolic function; and promotes calm, among other effects. Not all influences of affectionate behavior on health are positive, however. Because sharing affection often involves highly intimate behaviors done in close proximity, such as kissing and sexual interaction, it can also promote the transmission of viral and bacterial pathogens that facilitate infectious illness. Research on the health detriments of affectionate behavior is therefore also reviewed in this chapter.

This discussion has theorized about why affectionate communication is associated with physical health. The subsequent section, in turn, explores what those specific associations are.

Connections to Individual Physical Health Indices

Physical health is a multifaceted construct, as noted above, and research has thus far explored its associations with affectionate behavior for a variety of indices. This section details research on the connections of affectionate communication with cardiovascular activity, endocrine activity, immunological activity, metabolic activity, and susceptibility to infection and pain.

Cardiovascular Activity

The cardiovascular system – also called the circulatory system – is an organ system that facilitates the transport of oxygen, carbon dioxide, nutrients, hormones, and blood cells via the circulation of blood. Along with blood, its principal components are the heart and the blood vessels, including arteries, veins, capillaries, and sinusoids (McKinley, O'Loughlin, Pennefather-O'Brien, & Harris, 2015). In both research and clinical practice, cardiovascular health is typically assessed with two outcomes: heart rate and blood pressure.

Heart Rate

To facilitate the circulation of blood, the heart engages in a continuously repeating cardiac cycle that consists of two periods. Systole occurs when the heart muscle contracts to force blood through the arteries and into circulation, and diastole occurs when the heart muscle relaxes and refills with blood carried from the veins. Heart rate (or pulse rate) indexes the number of completed cardiac cycles the heart undergoes within a fixed period of time, usually a minute. Thus, heart rate is usually measured in beats per minute (BPM), although some studies instead measure the interbeat interval (IBI), or the number of milliseconds elapsed between beats of the heart (see, e.g., Costa, Davis, & Goldberger, 2017). Healthy adults exhibit resting heart rates of approximately 64–72 BPM for men and 72–80 BPM for women (Marieb & Hoehn, 2015). Heart rate is affected by metabolic demand and is also responsive to illness, stress, medications, body temperature, hydration, and other factors.

Two studies have found that trait affectionate communication is associated with a lower resting heart rate (HR). Floyd, Pauley, et al. (2014) found that resting HR was negatively related to trait expressed affection, and to a moderately strong degree ($\beta = -.40$). Similarly, Floyd, Mikkelson, Tafoya, et al. (2007b) measured affectionate communication in participants' closest personal relationships, specifically, and found that resting HR was negatively related to affection expressed verbally ($\beta = -.38$) and through socially supportive behaviors ($\beta = -.35$), although the association with nonverbal affectionate expressions was nonsignificant. Thus, individuals who tend to be affectionate in general, and also in their close relationships (via verbal and socially supportive behaviors) tend to exhibit lower resting HR.

Multiple studies have also demonstrated a stress-buffering effect of affectionate behavior, such that sharing affection prior to exposure to a stressful event reduces the extent to which HR is elevated in response to that stressor. In a laboratory study by Grewen et al. (2003), for instance, participants were separated into two groups prior to being assigned to deliver a speech. Those in the experimental group held hands with their romantic partner for ten minutes and then shared a ten-second hug, whereas those in the control group had no tactile contact. In reaction to the public speaking stressor, participants who held hands and hugged beforehand evidenced significantly lower increases in HR compared with controls. Similarly, Ditzen et al. (2007) found that women who engaged in affectionate touch with a romantic partner demonstrated lower HR reactivity to a subsequent public speaking stressor, and Pauley et al. (2015) demonstrated that sharing affection with either a romantic partner or a platonic friend ameliorated HR reactivity to a series of laboratory stressors.

These experimental findings suggest that, regardless of how much affection one *typically* gives or receives, sharing affectionate behavior immediately before a stressful event has a protective effect with respect to physiological reactivity to that stressor. That outcome is beneficial because exaggerated physiological responses to stressors are detrimental to health (see, e.g., Jennings et al., 2014). As noted below, research has also documented the stress-buffering effect of affectionate behavior with other physiological outcomes.

Blood Pressure

Blood pressure (BP) is the level of pressure exerted against the arterial walls by the circulation of blood. It is most commonly assessed as a function of two separate outcomes: systolic blood pressure (SBP) is the level of arterial pressure when the heart muscle is contracting (i.e., in systole), and diastolic blood pressure (DBP) is the level of arterial pressure when the heart muscle is relaxing (i.e., in diastole). A resting blood pressure of 120 mmHg for SBP and 80 mmHg for DBP is typically considered healthy, with higher rates predicting hypertension and cardiovascular disease (Chobanian et al., 2003). As with HR, many factors influence both resting and moment-to-moment BP, including blood volume, diet, cardiac output/HR, and genetic variants.

As far back as the 1920s, researchers noticed that BP is also influenced by emotion (see Marston, 1924). More specifically, the emotional and behavioral experience of affection appears to be associated with lower resting SBP and DBP. In a study of forty-eight undergraduate students, Floyd, Hesse, et al. (2007) measured participants' trait expressed affection and, controlling for the effects of received affection, found that expressed affection had strong negative relationships with both resting SBP ($\beta = -.55$) and resting DBP ($\beta = -.48$). In an earlier study of fifty-nine premenopausal women, Light, Grewen, and Amico (2005) also reported that the number of hugs participants reported receiving from their romantic partners was inversely associated with both resting SBP ($r = -.29$) and resting DBP ($r = -.34$).[1]

There is some evidence that interventions designed to induce affectionate behavior are associated with reductions in SBP, but the results are inconsistent. In a four-week trial, Holt-Lunstad et al. (2008) recruited both partners from thirty-four married couples and instructed the treatment participants to share affectionate touch on three occasions per week for thirty minutes at a time. Before and after the trial, participants underwent twenty-four-hour measurement of their ambulatory BP. Although there was no main effect of the intervention on ambulatory SBP or DBP levels, there was an interaction effect with the sex of the participant, such that the intervention significantly reduced SBP values for men (relative to controls) but not for women. Similarly, Grewen et al. (2005) had romantic partners engage in a "warm contact" intervention in which they sat close to each other on a loveseat, held hands if they were comfortable doing so, talked about an occasion that made them feel close to each other, then watched and discussed a five-minute segment of a romantic movie. Grewen and colleagues also asked participants to report on the level of support they received from each other. As in the Holt-Lunstad et al. study, the intervention did not have a main effect on BP. An interaction effect revealed that women's SBP decreased after the intervention, but only for women who received high levels of relational support from their romantic partners.

Finally, as with HR, there is evidence that affectionate behavior has a stress-buffering effect on BP. After sharing affection with either a romantic partner or a platonic friend, participants in the Pauley et al. (2015) experiment were subjected to a series of standard laboratory stressors. Compared with control participants who did not engage in affectionate interaction, experimental participants had significantly lower increases in both SPB and DPB in response to the stressors (see also Grewen et al., 2003).

With respect to cardiovascular indices, therefore, the evidence consistently shows that resting HR, SBP, and DBP are inversely associated with trait expressed affection and that all three outcomes show ameliorated stress-induced elevation in the wake of affectionate interaction. No affectionate behavior interventions have yet been tested for their effects on HR, however, and those focused on BP have produced results for SBP only, with contradictory results based on participant sex. Whereas affectionate behavior is *associated with* cardiovascular health, therefore, there is limited evidence that it *affects* cardiovascular health.

Endocrine Activity

The endocrine system regulates and integrates the body's metabolic activities and is responsible, among other tasks, for the production and secretion of hormones. Hormones are chemical substances introduced into the circulatory system by various endocrine glands to regulate the physiology of target organs and tissues (Neal, 2016). Major glands of the endocrine system include, among others, the thyroid gland, pituitary gland, adrenal gland, pancreas, hypothalamus, and gonads (testes or ovaries). Each gland produces and secretes specific hormones in response to various stimuli (Nelson & Kriegsfeld, 2016).

As with physiological markers in general, the communication discipline has embraced the study of endocrine markers only relatively recently (see, e.g., Floyd, 2011; Floyd & Roberts, 2009). Although affectionate communication research has measured a variety of hormones, two that have received the lion's share of attention are cortisol and oxytocin, each detailed subsequently.

Cortisol

Cortisol is a steroid hormone produced by the adrenal cortex and released in response to both low blood glucose and stress (Dickerson & Kemeny, 2004). Cortisol is measured in affectionate communication research primarily due to its associations with stress, as a means of studying the effects of affectionate behavior on the stress response. As Chapter 4 explained, cortisol is elevated in the bloodstream in response to acute stressors via activation of the hypothalamic-pituitary-adrenal (HPA) axis, and it also follows a diurnal (twenty-four-hour) rhythm in which it peaks shortly after awakening, drops sharply during the first half of the day, then wanes more slowly until reaching its lowest point around midnight (Giese-Davis, Sephton, Abercrombie, Durán, & Spiegel, 2004). Chronic stress (or repeated acute stress) reduces diurnal variation, making the amount of twenty-four-hour variation a useful marker of stress load.

With respect to cortisol, affectionate communication research has documented multiple specific patterns. First, highly affectionate people have more differentiated diurnal rhythms than do their less affectionate counterparts. On the basis of AET, Floyd (2006b) hypothesized an inverse association between trait expressed affection and chronic stress load, as indexed by diurnal cortisol variation. In that preliminary study, twenty healthy adults provided saliva samples taken at four points in time throughout a typical workday: on awakening, at noon, in the late afternoon, and at bedtime. After analyzing the saliva samples for cortisol levels and examining variance in their values over time, Floyd reported a strong correlation ($r = .56$) between diurnal cortisol variation and trait expressed affection, with the effect of trait received affection controlled. A later study by Floyd and Riforgiate (2008) examined the association between diurnal cortisol variation and levels of verbal, nonverbal, and socially supportive affection in marital relationships. In that study, one spouse in each couple provided saliva samples, and both spouses reported their level of affectionate behavior with the other. No actor effects emerged; in other words, participants' diurnal cortisol rhythms were unrelated to the levels of affection they showed their spouses. Strong partner effects were evident, however; variation in participants' cortisol levels was associated with their spouses' verbal affection ($\beta = -.55$), nonverbal affection ($\beta = -.40$), and supportive affection ($\beta = -.51$) toward them.[2]

Second, engaging in affectionate behavior is associated with lower momentary and daily levels of cortisol. After inducing warm contact between romantic partners, Grewen et al. (2005) found that cortisol levels were reduced for both women and men (see also Matsunaga et al., 2009). Sumioka, Nakae, Kanai, and Ishiguru (2013) later showed that the same cortisol-reducing effect of affection can manifest even if the affection is shared with a nonhuman entity. Participants in their study engaged in fifteen-minute telephone conversations with a stranger. Those assigned to the treatment group enacted the conversation while embracing a huggable robotic cushion called a Hugvie. Treatment participants experienced a significant decrease in both salivary and plasma cortisol levels as a result of the conversation, a decrease not shared by control participants. (More detail on the use of technology in affectionate communication appears in Chapter 10.)

Regarding daily cortisol levels, Ditzen, Hoppmann, and Klumb (2008) asked romantic partners from fifty-one couples to complete relationship questionnaires and to collect saliva samples six times per day for one week. At each time point, they reported their total duration of time spent engaged in "physical affection, such as holding hands, touching, hugging, kissing, or having sexual intercourse" (p. 884), and took a saliva sample that was later analyzed for cortisol. Ditzen and colleagues hypothesized that participants would display lower levels of cortisol on days with longer durations of physical affection, and that was the pattern that emerged.

Third, as with cardiovascular outcomes, affectionate communication buffers the effects of acute stress on cortisol. After measuring the verbal, nonverbal, and supportive affectionate communication characterizing participants' closest personal relationship, Floyd, Mikkelson, Tafoya, et al. (2007b) subjected participants to a series of standard laboratory stressors to determine how relational affection would predict levels of cortisol elevation. Floyd and colleagues reported that cortisol reactivity to the stressor was significantly inversely associated with verbal affection ($r = -.46$) and supportive affection ($r = -.33$), although the inverse association with nonverbal affection was nonsignificant. Similarly, Ditzen et al. (2007) found that physical affection (in the form of a neck and shoulder massage from their romantic partner) suppressed women's cortisol reactivity to a public speaking stressor (see also Heinrichs, Baumgartner, Kirschbaum, & Ehlert (2003), who demonstrated the same pattern for emotional and instrumental support rather than affection).

Fourth, affectionate communication accelerates cortisol recovery (return to baseline levels) after stressful episodes. The rate of recovery from an acute stressor is clinically significant because a prolonged stress response can damage muscle tissue and bone density, among other effects (Sapolsky, 2002). Floyd, Mikkelson, Tafoya, et al. (2007a) exposed participants to laboratory stressors and then assigned them randomly into one of three groups. Participants in the treatment group were instructed to spend twenty minutes writing an affectionate letter to someone about whom they cared deeply. Those in the comparison group spent twenty minutes thinking about someone they loved, and those in the control group spent twenty minutes sitting quietly. Stress recovery was indexed by participants' cortisol levels (relative to their baseline levels) at the end of the twenty-minute period. Results indicated that those who wrote affectionate letters recovered from the stressor most efficiently, whereas those in the comparison and control groups did not differ from each other in their rate of recovery.

These findings attest to a strong association between affectionate communication and stress. At both state and trait levels, affectionate behavior correlates with lower cortisol levels and greater variation in their twenty-four-hour rhythm and serves to protect individuals from over-reacting to stressors or experiencing prolonged acute stress responses. Although not all of these studies were based specifically on AET, their results are in line with its proposition that affectionate interaction – and the social and emotional inclusiveness it implies – is instrumental in managing the body's stress response.

Oxytocin

Oxytocin is a peptide hormone produced by the hypothalamus (Hedge, Colby, & Goodman, 1987). It is released into the circulatory system via the pituitary gland and is also sent to other parts of the brain, including the amygdala, striatum, other parts of the hypothalamus, and the vagal motor and sensory nuclei (see Argiolas & Gessa, 1991). Oxytocin is perhaps best known for the two important functions that it serves with respect to childbirth (Uvnäs-Moberg, 2003). First, it initiates the delivery process by stimulating uterine contractions. (The word *oxytocin* in fact means *swift birth*, and synthetic oxytocin, called *pitocin*, can be administered to initiate contractions.) Second, it is responsible for the let-down reflex in lactating women (McCarthy & Becker, 2002).

Oxytocin is also secreted during human sexual interaction and appears to play a role in making sex rewarding. Several studies have found that oxytocin is released into the circulatory systems of both men and women at sexual orgasm (Carmichael et al., 1987; Murphy, Seckl, Burton, Checkley, & Lightman, 1990; Richard, Moos, & Freund-Mercier, 1991). Moreover, the amount of oxytocin released into the bloodstream is linearly related to the subjective intensity of orgasm, at least for women (Carmichael, Warburton, Dixen, & Davidson, 1994). Oxytocin is also elicited by touch and massage, even when the touch is nonsexual (Turner, Altemus, Enos, Cooper, & McGuinness, 1999).

Oxytocin's primary effect on the body (besides initiating delivery and lactation in women) is a long-term reduction in stress: it reduces blood pressure and resting heart rate, increases anabolic metabolism, and inhibits the production of cortisol (Altemus, Deuster, Carter, & Gold, 1995; Amico, Johnston, & Vagnucci, 1994). When elevated in the bloodstream, it promotes a feeling of calmness, pleasantness, and mild euphoria (Carter & Altemus, 1997; Chiodera et al., 1991).

Floyd (2006a) speculated that oxytocin plays a role in making the communication of affection a rewarding experience. If oxytocin is elevated by loving interaction, then its physiological effects on the body can partially explain why affectionate behavior elicits such positive feelings, both physically and emotionally. Were that to be true, then it would stand to reason both that one's overall receipt of affection is positively correlated with circulating levels of oxytocin and that engaging in affectionate behavior can increase oxytocin levels in the moment.

Thus far the only direct evidence for a correlation between overall affection and oxytocin comes from Light et al. (2005), who studied fifty-nine premenopausal women. For participants in that study, baseline plasma oxytocin levels were positively related ($r = .31$) to the frequency with which their romantic partners hugged them. Associations between oxytocin and other affectionate behaviors, such as kissing and hand-holding, were nonsignificant, so the link between overall affection and oxytocin appears to be specific to the embrace.

Two experiments have demonstrated that engaging in affectionate behavior can elicit increases in oxytocin. As described above, Grewen et al. (2005) had heterosexual romantic couples engage in a ten-minute affectionate interaction. Using an indwelling catheter, the researchers drew blood samples during a baseline period prior to the affectionate interaction and again three times during a recovery period afterward. Each participant also provided a self-report of the level of support he or she received from the romantic partner.

Two findings were particularly noteworthy with respect to oxytocin. First, for both men and women, baseline levels of oxytocin were directly related to the amount of support participants reported receiving from their spouses, suggesting that those with more satisfying, supportive relational bonds have higher average levels of blood oxytocin than do those in less supportive relationships. This finding is in line with Light et al.'s (2005) discovery that baseline oxytocin is related to the receipt of hugs from a romantic partner, but because the correlate was support rather than affection, it does not speak to the affection–oxytocin relationship specifically. Second, and more important to the current discussion, plasma oxytocin levels in the Grewen et al. study increased over baseline levels following the affectionate interaction, but for women only.

Both Light et al. and Grewen et al. found that affectionate behavior was associated with oxytocin only for women, but a later experiment documented that increasing affectionate behavior increases oxytocin for both sexes. As described above, Holt-Lunstad et al. (2008) taught spouses to conduct a "warm touch enhancement" procedure that involved massage to the neck, shoulders, and hands. Participants learned the procedure in a laboratory training session and then practiced the technique at home during a four-week intervention. Compared with spouses in an attention comparison group, both women and men who practiced warm touch experienced significant increases in oxytocin over the course of the four-week trial.

Although it is difficult to know which aspect of the affectionate inter-action in the Grewen et al. or Holt-Lunstad et al. studies had the greatest effect on oxytocin levels, these findings are the first to demonstrate that affectionate, warm contact between romantic partners increases plasma levels of oxytocin. As noted, this causal association may be a key factor in explaining why affectionate interaction in close relationships is physically and emotionally rewarding, and why it can be antagonistic to stress.

Research by Floyd et al. (2010) further illuminated the connections between affection, oxytocin, and stress. As described above with respect to HR, BP, and cortisol, several studies have documented a stress-buffering effect of affectionate behavior, wherein exchanging affection prior to exposure to a stressful event dampens physiological reactivity to that event. The physiological mechanisms responsible for the stress-buffering effect have not been well articulated, but Floyd and colleagues speculated that oxytocin is a viable candidate. They hypothesized that higher levels of affectionate communication – both as a trait and in the week prior to exposure to a stressor – would be associated with higher levels of oxytocin in reaction to that stressor. Their argument was that oxytocin is elevated in response to a stressor as a means of antagonizing the stress response, but much more so for affectionate people than for their nonaffectionate counterparts. In other words, their speculation was that oxytocin may be one of the reasons why affectionate communication buffers the stress response.

After reporting on their trait affectionate communication (a combin-ation of trait-level expressed and received affection) as well as recording their received affection for one week in a diary format, 100 healthy adults were subjected to a series of standard laboratory stressors. During the stress induction, participants' levels of cortisol and oxytocin were moni-tored. A significant increase in cortisol confirmed the stress-inducing effects of the laboratory activities. After controlling for participant sex, the researchers found that people with higher trait affection scores had higher increases in oxytocin in the wake of the stressor (β = .24). Similarly, regardless of their trait affection levels, those who received more affectionate communication during the preceding week had higher increases in oxytocin during the stressor (β = .24). The researchers suggested that the elevated levels of oxytocin may have buffered the stress reactions of participants who received higher levels of affection.

Cortisol and oxytocin are not the only hormones measured in affectionate communication research; other studies have examined, for instance, testosterone (Hesse et al., 2018) and dehydroepiandrosterone sulfate (Floyd & Riforgiate, 2008). Because of their connections to stress and reward, however, cortisol and oxytocin have received greater scholarly attention in the literature on affectionate behavior, and the accumulated findings suggest that affectionate communication – at least when enacted in positive relationships – has important stress-protective and stress-alleviating effects for individuals.

Immunological Activity

The immune system comprises a network of cells, proteins, organs, and tissues that interact to protect the body from infection and disease (Sompayrac, 2016). Indexing the strength of the immune system – its *immunocompetence* – is challenging because there is no single global marker representing the potency of the immune response (Farnè, Boni, Corallo, Gnugnoli, & Sacco, 1994). In research, immunocompetence is sometimes assessed by measuring levels of particular markers, such as immunoglobulins, B cells, or T cells, or the cytotoxicity of particular cells, such as natural killer (NK) cells. Some research also assesses antibody levels, such as antibodies for the Epstein-Barr virus, or measures antibody response to the introduction of specific antigens. Importantly, these and other markers can produce conflicting results, wherein a behavior or characteristic is shown to be positively associated with immunocompetence according to some outcome but unrelated or even negatively related to immunocompetence according to other outcomes. For that reason, it is important to know *how* immunocompetence is being indexed in any given study.

Three studies thus far have directly examined the association between immunocompetence and affectionate communication. Floyd, Pauley, et al. (2014) measured trait expressed affection in a group of healthy volunteers and collected blood samples for immune measures. That study focused on NK cells, which are lymphocytes (a subtype of white blood cell) that attack virally infected cells and impede tumor formation. Although trait affectionate communication was unrelated to the number of NK cells in study participants, it was positively related (β = .43) to NK cell cytotoxicity, a measure of the efficacy in killing target cells. The researchers also found that trait affection was linearly related (β = .36) to circulating levels of immunoglobulin M (IgM), an antibody that provides immediate response to infection and leads other immune cells to destroy invading substances.

Whereas Floyd, Pauley, et al. (2014) measured trait-level affectionate communication, Floyd et al. (in press) looked specifically at the level of socially supportive affection participants expressed in their closest relationship. They again found a significant association with IgM, as well as with immunoglobulin G (IgG), an antibody that binds to antigens and aids in antibody synthesis. Socially supportive affection was also correlated with three T cells: CD3+, CD4+, CD8+, and one B cell, CD19+ (correlations ranged in magnitude from .28 to .46). Of those outcomes, associations between expressed supportive affection and IgG, CD3+, CD4+, and CD19+ remained significant even when the effects of received support were controlled, illustrating AET's contention that expressing affection is beneficial even net of the effects of received affection.

The findings of both studies suggest that communicating affection is associated with greater immunocompetence, at least as indexed by these specific markers. However, Floyd, Hesse, et al. (2014) arrived at the opposite conclusion when measuring another marker of immunocompetence, antibody levels to latent Epstein-Barr virus (EBV). EBV is a human herpesvirus that is perhaps best known as the cause of infectious mononucleosis. Most adults harbor the virus in a latent state. When EBV becomes virally active, the immune system responds by elevating the level of EBV antibodies. Thus, lower levels of antibodies reflect greater immunocompetence by indicating the immune system's ability to hold the virus in a latent state.

After measuring trait expressed affection and collecting blood samples from healthy adults, Floyd, Hesse, et al. found that trait affection was directly related to the number of EBV antibodies (Spearman's ρ = .24). In contrast to Floyd, Pauley, et al. (2014) and Floyd et al. (in press), this finding suggests a negative association between affectionate communication and immunocompetence. Further discussion of this finding appears in the conclusion to this chapter.

Thus far, therefore, research has produced findings that largely – although not without exception – support a positive association between affectionate communication and immunocompetence. Two further studies have addressed that association somewhat differently, by examining the effects of kissing on the allergic response. When individuals inhale or ingest allergens – substances to which they are allergic – the immune system responds by producing antibodies to attack those allergens. In clinical settings, when individuals are tested for allergies, it is often by means of a skin test in which the skin is pricked and allergens are introduced to see if the skin reacts. The first reaction to an allergen is a skin wheal response, in which a pale raised welt appears on the skin. In research, allergic responses are also indexed by the levels of immune markers such as immunoglobulin E (IgE), nerve growth factor (NGF), brain-derived neurotrophic factor (BDNF), neurotrophin-3 (NT-3), and neutrophin-4 (NT-4).

Speculating that romantic kissing might confer protective effects with respect to the allergic response, Kimata (2003) had adult patients with either allergic rhinitis or atopic dermatitis kiss their romantic partner for thirty minutes while alone in a closed room. All of the patients were allergic to house dust mites and Japanese cedar pollen. Before and after the kissing intervention, Kimata performed skin prick tests using those two allergens and simultaneously measured plasma levels of NGF, BNDF, NT-3, and NT-4. He found that kissing significantly reduced the skin wheal responses to dust mites and cedar pollen, and also significantly reduced plasma levels of NGF, BNDF, NT-3, and NT-4, whereas the same effects of kissing were not observed in non-patient controls. In a later (2006) study, Kimata repeated the kissing induction using patients with mild atopic eczema and allergic rhinitis and found that it inhibited allergen-specific IgE production. Kimata concluded from these experiments that for allergic patients, kissing can alleviate some allergic symptoms, a finding that is also supportive of a positive association between affectionate behavior and immunocompetence (see also Liccardi, Senna, Rotiroti, D'Amato, & Passalacqua, 2007).

Metabolic Activity

Metabolism consists of ongoing chemical transformations at the cellular level that facilitate the maintenance of the organism. In research on affectionate communication, two metabolic markers that have received attention are blood lipids and blood glucose.

Blood Lipids
Lipids are fat-soluble organic molecules that are essential for the formation of cell membranes; the provision of energy to cells; cellular growth, maintenance, and repair; and the synthesis of steroid hormones and bile

acids (Shier, Butler, & Lewis, 2015). Lipids occur in multiple forms, but the specific form that has been measured in affectionate communication research is cholesterol. Cholesterol is a sterol most commonly assessed in the form of total cholesterol, which is the sum of high-density lipoproteins (HDL, often called "good cholesterol"), low-density lipoproteins (LDL, or "bad cholesterol"), and very-low-density lipoproteins (VLDL). Cholesterol levels are responsive to multiple factors, including diet, the use of alcohol or tobacco, hydration, vitamin consumption, recent infectious illness, and history of heart problems (Stoney, 2008). Importantly, cholesterol is also elevated in response to stressors (Bacon, Ring, Lip, & Carroll, 2004), whether chronic or acute (Stoney, Niaura, Bausserman, & Metacin, 1999).

Two studies have directly examined the association between affectionate behavior and total cholesterol. Reasoning that because stress elevates cholesterol and because expressing affection in close relationships reduces stress, Floyd, Mikkelson, Hesse, and Pauley (2007) hypothesized that communicating affection would reduce total cholesterol. In two five-week interventions, healthy undergraduates wrote affectionate letters to their close friends, relatives, and/or romantic partners for twenty minutes on three separate occasions. Compared with controls who wrote on the same schedule about innocuous topics, treatment participants experienced a significant reduction in total cholesterol. In the first trial, the treatment effect was moderated by the use of third-person pronouns in participants' writing but not by any other linguistic features; in the second trial, no linguistic features were influential.

In a subsequent study, Floyd et al. (2009) measured total cholesterol from healthy adults who were cohabiting with a romantic partner. Treatment participants in that study were instructed to kiss more frequently than normal during a six-week trial. After ruling out multiple potential control variables (including demographic characteristics, caffeine and alcohol consumption, use of tobacco, change in body mass index, and change in exercise habits), Floyd and colleagues found that treatment participants experienced a decrease in total cholesterol that was not experienced by controls.

These findings suggest that the communication of affection exerts an influence on lipid levels, perhaps via its ameliorating effects on stress. It is important to note, however, that some attempts from the Floyd laboratory to replicate these patterns have produced null results. Compared with other physiological associations with affectionate behavior, therefore, the findings of Floyd, Mikkelson, Hesse, et al. (2007) and Floyd et al. (2009) should be interpreted with greater caution.

Although not a direct replication, a later study by Floyd, Veksler, et al. (2017) examined the effects of social inclusion, a construct indexing how socially engaged and active individuals are. Social inclusion is not the same construct as affectionate communication, of course, although both are related to fulfilling the need to belong. In this study, the researchers looked at HDL and LDL, specifically, rather than total cholesterol, predicting that social inclusion is directly related to HDL and inversely related to LDL. Although the association with HDL was nonsignificant, the study found a significant inverse relationship between social inclusion and LDL, indicating that people who feel more socially connected and engaged exhibit healthier levels of so-called bad cholesterol.

Blood Glucose

Blood glucose, or blood sugar concentration, refers to the amount of glucose present in the bloodstream at any given time. Glucose is a critical source of energy for cellular and muscle function and for cerebral metabolism (Huang et al., 1980). At the cellular level, glucose absorption is regulated by the hormone insulin, making glucose clinically relevant for diabetes mellitus, a metabolic disorder reflecting a failure to produce adequate insulin (type 1 diabetes mellitus) or cellular resistance to insulin (type 2). Blood glucose can be measured in the form of fasting glucose, an index of the amount of glucose in the blood at the time of measurement (independent of the effects of recent food consumption), and also in the form of glycated hemoglobin (also referred to as HbA_{1c}), which is a nonfasting measure of an individual's average blood glucose concentration over the preceding three months.

Like blood lipids, blood glucose is also elevated in response to stressors (Netterstrøm, Danborg, & Olesen, 1988; Schuck, 1998). During periods of increased stress, cortisol and epinephrine increase blood glucose to fuel the body's fight-or-flight response. On the basis that affectionate communication reduces stress and stress elevates blood glucose, Floyd, Hesse, and Haynes (2007) hypothesized that trait expressed affection is inversely related to glycated hemoglobin. In that study, thirty healthy adults reported on their trait levels of expressed and received affection, and then provided blood samples for analysis. With the influence of trait received affection controlled, trait expressed affection exhibited a strong negative association ($\beta = -.85$) with glycated hemoglobin, meaning that the more affection individuals typically expressed, the lower their average blood glucose levels over the previous three-month period. Floyd, Veksler, et al. (2017) also reported a negative association ($r = -.27$) between fasting glucose and social inclusion.

Is it possible that the experience of love and affection can increase stress, rather than decrease it? Stanton, Campbell, and Loving (2014) offered the argument that the experience of romantic love can trigger activation of both the HPA axis and the sympathetic-adrenal-medullary (SAM) pathway of the endocrine system, such that experiencing love produces physiological effects comparable to those of stress. Specifically, they argued that love can produce *eustress*, a positive or euphoric form of stress (Selye, 1956) that is typically accompanied by positive affect but whose physiological effects (such as increased cortisol or blood pressure) mimic those of negative stress (or *distress*; see Loving, Crockett, & Paxson, 2009). Their study randomly assigned adults to complete one of three guided imagery tasks. Those in the partner condition were asked to visualize their romantic partner and to think about their feelings and experiences of love for that person. Those in the friend condition did the same for an opposite-sex platonic friend, and those in a comparison group visualized going through their daily morning routine. Blood glucose was assessed at baseline and again after the visualization task, and participants also reported on their levels of positive and negative affect after the task.

Those who visualized a platonic friend or their morning routine experienced declines in glucose over time, which were statistically significant for the comparison group and nearly significant for the friend condition. Those in the partner condition experienced a slight (nonsignificant) increase in glucose, but the researchers also found that those in the partner condition who reported high positive affect after the visualization task experienced a significant increase in glucose. (The same was not true for those in the friend or comparison groups.) Stanton and colleagues concluded that when visualizing a romantic partner produces highly positive affect, this experience induces eustress, causing a corresponding increase in blood glucose.

Although it would appear that the findings of Stanton et al. are at odds with those of Floyd, Hesse, and Hayes, that is not necessarily the case. The apparent difference lies in the distinction between eustress and distress, as both experiences can elevate blood glucose. What remains unknown from the findings of both studies is how actual affectionate *interaction* would influence glucose levels. Participants in the Floyd study simply reported on their trait levels of affectionate behavior, and those in the Stanton study merely visualized interacting with their romantic partner. Neither study induced actual affectionate contact, so it is as yet unknown how such interpersonal contact – such as in the form of touch, verbal interaction, etc. – would affect blood glucose levels, if at all.

Susceptibility to Infection and Pain

Finally, some research has documented associations between affectionate behavior and individuals' susceptibility to infection and pain. Various scholars have argued that certain affectionate behaviors – particularly kissing – are implicated in neurological and biochemical processes that can aid not only mating and reproductive success but also protection from illness (see, e.g., Kort et al., 2014; Müller & Lindenberger, 2014; Nicholson, 1984). Hendrie and Brewer (2010), for instance, proposed the hypothesis that mouth-to-mouth kissing is an evolutionary adaptation protecting women against microbial disease that could threaten critical stages of embryonic development in their offspring.

Aside from that speculation, there has been little research documenting actual effects of affectionate behavior on the susceptibility to illness, but a notable exception is the study of Cohen, Janicki-Deverts, Turner, and Doyle (2015). In an ambitious experiment, Cohen and colleagues measured the frequency of hugs shared with others on a daily basis for fourteen consecutive days, as well as outcomes related to social support, conflict, and personality, for 406 healthy adults. The researchers then exposed participants (via nasal drops) to either a rhinovirus or influenza virus, and subsequently quarantined participants for either five days (rhinovirus group) or six days (influenza group) to monitor the progress of infection.

Among their findings was that the percentage of days on which participants had received at least one hug in the previous two weeks was inversely related to the risk of developing infection in response to the viruses (odds ratio = .39). Similarly, the percentage of days with hugs was associated with more efficient nasal clearance ($\beta = -.13$), although it was unrelated to mucus production.

Although Cohen and colleagues examined only one specific affectionate behavior, they reported convincingly that receiving frequent hugs is associated with a reduced risk of infection on exposure to rhinovirus or influenza virus. Moreover, they found that the frequency of hugging moderated an effect of interpersonal conflict on infection. This finding adds to the evidence that affectionate behavior serves a stress-buffering effect, in this instance by reducing the likelihood that the stress of conflict would lead to infection.

This is only one study, but to the extent that affectionate communication has protective effects against illness, it stands to reason that lacking adequate affection would be associated with an increased risk of illness. Floyd (2014c) examined this hypothesis in a study of affection deprivation, the discrepancy between an individual's desired and received levels of affectionate behavior. Among other hypotheses, Floyd predicted that the extent to which people feel deprived of affection is positively associated with their likelihood of having been diagnosed with a secondary immune disorder. Whereas primary immune disorders – such as herpes simplex encephalitis, hyper-IgE syndrome, and Kostmann syndrome – are inherited genetically (and therefore unlikely to be influenced by aspects of the social environment, such as affectionate communication), secondary immune disorders – such as multiple myeloma and AIDS – are acquired as a result of exposure to environmental conditions (which can include conditions of the social environment). Given that affectionate communication is associated with immunocompetence (at least according to most measures; see above), Floyd hypothesized that the deprivation of affection would correlate positively with the number of diagnosed secondary immune disorders, and this prediction was supported (β = .12). More detail on the outcomes of affection deprivation appears in the next chapter.

In addition to its relationships with susceptibility to illness, some evidence suggests that affectionate behavior is also associated with susceptibility to pain. A common example is the phenomenon of holding another's hand to lessen the potency of a pain-inducing event. Weekes, Kagan, James, and Seboni (1993) explored that phenomenon with adolescents undergoing painful medical treatments, such as blood draws, lumbar punctures, peripheral chemotherapy, and bone marrow aspirations. The adolescents, who had been diagnosed with either cancer or renal disease, perceived hand-holding to be highly effective at ameliorating treatment-related pain. Participants preferred overwhelmingly to hold their mother's hand or, if their mother was unavailable, the hand of a specific nurse.

Studying affection's influence on pain is different from studying its influence on infection, because pain is a purely subjective experience that can be assessed only via self-report, rather than through any objective indicators. Therefore, if the participants in the Weekes et al. study *perceived* less pain as a result of hand-holding, one can accept this as evidence that hand-holding has that effect. In a later experiment, Floyd, Ray, van Raalte, Stein, and Generous (2017) tested the effects of a different form of touch – hands placed on another person's shoulders – on pain sensitivity. That study induced pain via cold pressor, a procedure in which participants submerge their forearm into a galvanized steel bucket filled with very cold water (in this study, the average water temperature was 38.43°F). During the cold pressor procedure, participants in the touch condition had the hands of an opposite-sex romantic partner, platonic friend, or stranger on their shoulders. Those in the presence condition had an opposite-sex romantic partner, friend, or stranger with them in the room, but not touching them, and those in the absence condition were alone with the experimenter. Once participants submerged their forearm into the water, they were asked to indicate how long it took before the water caused pain (*pain threshold*) and how much pain (on a scale of 1–9) they experienced in that moment (*pain sensitivity*).

Neither the experimental condition (touch, presence, absence) nor the relationship type (romantic partner, friend, stranger) affected pain threshold, but touch had effects on pain sensitivity that differed by relationship type. For participants paired with a romantic partner, touch dampened pain sensitivity (compared with presence and absence), allowing participants to tolerate a higher degree of intensity before labeling the stimulus as painful. This finding is in line with a stress-buffering effect of affectionate behavior (with the cold pressor serving as the stressor). For participants paired with a friend or stranger, however, the opposite effect emerged: touch heightened pain sensitivity (compared with presence or absence).

Although the effect of relationship type on the association between touch and pain sensitivity had not been hypothesized, the authors noted that it is consistent with the findings of Coan et al. (2006), who reported that the stress-alleviating benefit of touch was most pronounced in romantic relationships (see Chapter 7). It is perhaps understandable that touch from a stranger might induce psychological discomfort that could translate into heightened sensitivity to pain, but why touch from a platonic friend would be similarly detrimental remains unknown.

As with susceptibility to illness, the connection between affectionate behavior and pain implies that lacking adequate affection would be positively associated with the experience of pain. Across three studies, Floyd found small but significant relationships between affection deprivation and reports of chronic pain, with beta values of .12, .15, and .15, respectively.

A summary of health benefits associated with affectionate communication appears in Table 8.1.

This chapter began with the observation that physical health is a multidimensional construct. Although research certainly has not investigated every possible health outcome that may be related to affectionate behavior, the literature has thus far demonstrated associations with a variety of health indices, from resting blood pressure and diurnal cortisol variation to glycated hemoglobin, natural killer cell cytotoxicity, and susceptibility to viral infection. These studies show that affectionate

Table 8.1 *Beneficial physical health markers associated with affectionate communication*

Marker	Associations with Affectionate Communication
Resting heart rate	Negatively related to trait expressed affection; HR response to stressors buffered by received affection
Blood pressure	Negatively related to trait expressed affection and received hugs; women's SBP lowered by receiving affection; BP reactivity to stressors buffered by received affection
Cortisol	Variance in diurnal variation associated with trait expressed affection and marital affection; engaging in affectionate behavior lowered cortisol; affectionate behavior buffers cortisol response to stressors and accelerates cortisol recovery from stressors
Oxytocin	Baseline oxytocin negatively related to received hugs for women; received affection increases oxytocin; oxytocin elevated in response to stressors for highly affectionate people
Natural killer cell cytotoxicity	Positively related to trait expressed affection
IgM	Positively related to trait expressed affection and to socially supportive affectionate communication within a specific relationship
IgG, CD3+, CD4+, CD8+, CD19+	Positively related to socially supportive affectionate communication within a specific relationship
Skin wheal responses, NGF, BNDF, NT-3, NT-4	Reduced by kissing
Cholesterol	Total cholesterol reduced by kissing and affectionate writing (although some replications failed); LDL inversely related to social inclusion
Blood glucose	Glycated hemoglobin negatively related to trait expressed affection; fasting glucose negatively related to social inclusion but elevated by visualizing a romantic partner (if accompanied by positive affect)
Susceptibility to illness	Hugging protects against infection from rhinovirus and influenza virus; deprivation of affection related to number of diagnosed secondary immune disorders
Susceptibility to pain	Hand-holding reduces treatment-related pain; shoulder touch from romantic partner buffers pain sensitivity

communication is related to more positive health outcomes, but they are not without exception. It is instructive to consider not only how affectionate behavior can enhance physical health but also how it can impede it, and studies documenting negative associations between affection and health are described subsequently.

Health Detriments of Affectionate Communication

In contradistinction to the evidence of affectionate communication's health-supportive effects, several studies have found negative relationships between affectionate behavior and physical health. Nearly all of these studies focus on kissing, specifically. This focus is understandable, in that, beyond sexual behaviors involving oral-genital contact or penetrative intercourse, kissing is likely the affectionate behavior posing the greatest risk for disease transmission.[3]

Research on the health risks of kissing has focused largely on the implications of salivary exchange and potential blood exchange (via trace amounts of blood in saliva) in romantic kissing. For instance, kissing can facilitate the transmission of viral infections such as influenza (Schoch-Spana, 2000), herpes simplex viruses (Cowan et al., 2002), and infectious mononucleosis, commonly known as the "kissing disease" (Carbary, 1975; Ödegaard, 1967). In a matched cohort study of adolescents fifteen to nineteen years of age, for example, Tully et al. (2006) reported that intimate kissing quadrupled the risk of meningococcal meningitis. People certainly curtail kissing when they feel ill, but kissing can facilitate viral transmission even in the absence of symptoms. Scientists have even warned of the potential for HIV transmission from romantic kissing if microlesions are present on the oral mucosa of the infected partner (Piazza et al., 1989).

A second risk of kissing is that it can elicit allergic reactions. For instance, those allergic to specific foods can react with allergic symptoms after contact with the saliva of someone who has eaten a nontolerated food (Maloney, Chapman, & Sicherer, 2006). In a study of patients with food allergies, for instance, Eriksson, Möller, Werner, Magnusson, and Bengtsson (2003) found that 12 percent reported having experienced allergic symptoms after kissing someone who had eaten something to which participants were allergic. Hallett, Haapanen, and Teuber (2002) reported an allergic reaction rate of 5.3 percent for those with IgE-mediated allergies to nuts or seeds, specifically. Similar kissing-induced allergic responses can occur with medications. In particular, allergic reactions after kissing have been reported to the antibiotics bacampicillin (Liccardi, Gilder, D'Amato, & D'Amato, 2002) and amoxicillin (Mancuso & Berdondini, 2006).

Whereas most evidence for the health risks of affectionate behavior implicates kissing, specifically, Floyd, Hesse, et al. (2014) measured trait expressed affection in order to examine its association with antibody levels for Epstein-Barr virus (see above). A lower number of circulating antibodies for EBV is indicative of the immune system's ability to keep the virus in a latent state (and therefore reflects immunocompetence). However, Floyd and colleagues found that higher levels of trait expressed affection corresponded to higher antibody counts, suggesting a negative association between trait affectionate communication and immunocompetence. The authors speculated that behaviors such as kissing facilitate viral transmission and elevate the likelihood of infectious disease, which would certainly be in line with research demonstrating that effect, but because the measure in Floyd et al. was of overall, trait-level affection rather than of kissing behavior in particular, that speculation awaits verification.

9   The Dark Side of Affectionate Communication

Perhaps the least intuitive aspect of affectionate communication is the fact that it sometimes produces negative outcomes. Everyday experience suggests that affectionate behavior characterizes our most positive, intimate relationships; that it is a pleasing aspect of those relationships; and that it advances the welfare of those relationships and their participants. It is largely counterintuitive, therefore, to think of affectionate behavior as an instigator of distress, one that could even precipitate the demise of an otherwise positive relationship. Counterintuitive though it may be, there are very real risks and problems associated with the communication of affection, and an adequate understanding of affection exchange would elude researchers who failed to acknowledge them (Floyd & Pauley, 2011).

This chapter is divided into four sections. The first examines some of the salient risks associated with expressing affectionate messages to others, which include the risks of nonreciprocity, misinterpretation, social censure, and disease transmission. The following section examines instances in which affectionate behavior is deceptive and even manipulative. Third, the chapter explores the problem of not receiving adequate affection – a concept referred to as affection deprivation – and its problematic individual and relational correlates. The final section explores the possibility – as yet quite understudied – that people can actually receive *too much* affection for their own good. Each of these topics belies the intuitive notion that affectionate communication is always positive, revealing instead its darker side.

Risks Associated with Expressing Affection

Floyd and others (e.g., Floyd & Burgoon, 1999; Floyd & Morman, 1997) have suggested that senders of affectionate messages must negotiate, to varying degrees, at least three types of risks: the risk of nonreciprocity, the risk of misinterpretation, and the risk of social censure. To this list can be added a fourth, equally potent risk associated with physical affection: the risk of disease transmission. This section addresses each of these risks, offering speculation as to when each might be salient and how each might be managed by senders. Floyd (2006a) pointed out that nearly all of the research on these negative outcomes of affectionate behavior has addressed the topic from the vantage of receivers rather than senders – and that remains true – so the discussion of these risks is still somewhat speculative.

The Risk of Nonreciprocity

Perhaps the most evident risk of expressing affection is that receivers will fail to reciprocate. This is actually two separate risks masquerading as one. First, there is the risk that the *expression* will not be reciprocated, and second, there is the risk that, even if the expression is reciprocated, the actual *sentiment* will not be. Both involve potential threats to senders' positive face (see Brown & Levinson, 1987; Lim & Bowers, 1991), as well as their need to belong (Baumeister & Leary, 1995; Baumeister et al., 2007).

One might speculate that this risk is at its most intense during early stages of relationship development. Indeed, the initial expression of affection – whether it be an embrace, a kiss, or a verbal declaration of love – is often a critical turning point for a new relationship (Owen, 1987). It is reasonable to speculate that when the initial expression of affection is not reciprocated, it becomes a negative turning point, rather than a positive one. In newly forming relationships, a declaration of affection (whether verbal or nonverbal) is, in part, a sender's invitation for the receiver to make his or her own feelings known. As such, it could operate as a type of "secret test" for gaining information on a partner's feelings about a new relationship (see Baxter & Wilmot, 1984). If the receiver fails to reciprocate the expression, senders may interpret that failure as an indication that the affectionate sentiment is not shared.

Adding insult to injury in cases of nonreciprocity is the strong social expectation that expressions of affection *will* be reciprocated. Gouldner's (1960) moral norm of reciprocity provides that one beneficial behavior ought to elicit another in response; or, in this case, that one expression of affection ought to elicit another. Evolutionary psychologists have concurred; Trivers (1971) suggested that humans practice *reciprocal altruism* by expecting that their good deeds will be reciprocated in kind and by feeling wronged when they are not. Specifically, Cosmides and Tooby (1992) have argued that humans are so attuned to principles of equity and reciprocity of positive behaviors as to have evolved cognitive "detection mechanisms" to draw their attention to instances of cheating. If one does a favor for a friend, for instance, then Gouldner, Trivers, Cosmides, and Tooby would argue that both oneself and one's friend would expect that favor to be repaid at some future point when one is in need of help. If such a time comes when one needs the friend's help and he or she refuses it, the reciprocity principle suggests that one should feel cheated and that the friend should feel guilty. Cosmides and Tooby argue that these emotions are adaptive in that they make "cheating" (by not reciprocating favors) aversive, particularly for the cheater.

Indeed, people have overwhelming tendencies to reciprocate positive feelings and evaluations that are directed to them by others (Jones & Wortman, 1973; Kenny & Nasby, 1980). Under typical circumstances, one would expect both senders and receivers to share this expectation. Therefore, if a receiver fails to reciprocate an affectionate message, *even despite the strong social expectation to do so*, then the offense to the sender may be particularly poignant.

Although senders of affectionate messages may risk nonreciprocity, a correlated risk for *receivers* of affectionate gestures is that they may immediately feel obligated to reciprocate the expression, whether they would elect to or not. As noted above, when one person receives, for instance, a verbal expression of affection (e.g., "I love you"), both the receiver and the sender will, under normal circumstances, expect the expression to be reciprocated in kind. This expectation can place the receiver in the undesirable position of feeling obligated to reciprocate the expression – and to reciprocate it in kind, with an expression of similar intensity – whether or not he or she actually possesses feelings of affection for the sender.

Research on unrequited love supports the claim that receiving an expression of affectionate feelings that one does not share is a psychologically distressing experience. In a study that examined that experience from the standpoints of both "would-be lovers" (those who conveyed feelings of romantic love to another) and "rejecters" (those who failed to reciprocate the emotions), Baumeister, Wotman, and Stillwell (1993) found that rejecters actually described greater distress than did would-be lovers. Baumeister and colleagues offered several observations by way of explanation. For one, they noted that rejecting love may go against basic, innately prepared motives for attachment (Bowlby, 1969, 1973; Hazan & Shaver, 1987; Shaver, Hazan, & Bradshaw, 1988) and the need to belong (Baumeister & Leary, 1995), causing psychological turmoil and internal conflict for rejecters. Second, rejecters commonly reported feeling guilt as a result of their failure to reciprocate the would-be lovers' affections. Indeed, in the Baumeister et al. study, rejecters' guilt was significantly more likely to be reported in their own accounts than in the would-be lovers' accounts, suggesting that rejecters felt guilty more often than the rejected believed.

Importantly, as Baumeister and his colleagues noted, rejecters have the option of reciprocating (or, at least, failing to reject overtly) a would-be lover's expression of affection even if they do not share the emotion. This option may temporarily relieve the rejecter of guilt or other negative emotions, but it runs the long-term risks of obligating the rejecter to spend time unwillingly with the would-be lover and of encouraging the would-be lover's affectionate feelings and overtures. Paradoxically, then, this short-term solution to the rejecter's problem can have the long-term effect of making the eventual overt rejection far more traumatic for both parties than it would have been initially.

Erbert and Floyd (2004) reasoned that reciprocating a sender's affectionate expression in kind – regardless of one's actual feelings for the sender – would be especially likely for those with a strong positive face need (or the need for social approval and inclusion). In a study of 235 undergraduate students reporting on either a same- or opposite-sex friend, Erbert and Floyd found that, after controlling for the sex of the participant and the sex composition of the dyad, participants' positive face need was a significant predictor of their intention to respond in kind to an affectionate expression from a platonic friend.

The Risk of Misinterpretation

A second risk for senders of affectionate messages is the risk that receivers will misinterpret them. The specific threat is that a receiver may interpret an affectionate behavior as a romantic gesture when it was intended to convey platonic affection, or vice versa. This is a salient risk, for two reasons. First, with many types of affectionate behavior, there is ample opportunity for such misinterpretation to occur. As noted in Chapter 3, even a straightforward verbal statement such as "I love you" can be decoded in multiple ways (e.g., "I love you in a romantic way," "I love you as a platonic friend," "I love you like a family member," "I am in love with you"). This risk is magnified as the ambiguity of the gesture increases. For instance, the phrase "I love you" might be more ambiguous when written than when spoken, because vocal and facial cues in the latter situation can aid in clarifying its meaning (see, e.g., Floyd & Morman, 2000b). Likewise, the risk of misinterpretation may be greater for nonverbal expressions of affection than for verbal (see Floyd, 1999, 2000a).

The second reason that misinterpretation is such a salient risk is that it can lead to relational boundary ambiguity. In a platonic relationship, for instance, misinterpreting an expression such as "I love you" can raise questions and expectations as to whether the sender intended the message to convey romantic feelings. This type of relational boundary ambiguity may be most common in relationships that are not especially close. Erbert and Floyd (2004) asked participants in their study to think of a particular platonic friend and to imagine receiving one of three different affectionate messages from that friend.[1] The messages were constructed to correspond to three politeness strategies identified by Brown and Levinson (1987). These were: (1) *bald-on-record*, in which the expression is straightforward and unqualified (e.g., "I really care about you; you're very important to me"); (2) *negative politeness*, in which the expression is qualified in order to mitigate potential negative face threats (e.g., "I don't mean this in a romantic way, but I really care about you"); and (3) *off-the-record*, in which the expression is crafted in such a way that the sentiment is implied rather than directly stated (e.g., "You're pretty cool"). The researchers asked participants to report on the extent to which receiving these affectionate expressions from their specified platonic friends would cause them to wonder whether those friends were making a romantic overture.[2] In other words, the study examined whether these types of affectionate behaviors, enacted in platonic relationships, might cause ambiguity in participants' conceptions of their friendships.

Erbert and Floyd found that the type of affectionate expression (bald-on-record, negative politeness, off-the-record) was influential in predicting receivers' likelihood of experiencing relational boundary ambiguity. Importantly, however, this effect was moderated by the closeness of the friendship. Specifically, participants reporting on friendships that were not highly close indicated that they would experience the greatest relational boundary ambiguity if they received the bald-on-record message, less if they received the negative politeness message, and the least if they received the off-the-record message. In comparison, participants in closer friendships reported no difference among the three messages in terms of the likelihood that they would experience relational boundary ambiguity.

The Risk of Social Censure

A third risk for senders of affectionate expressions is related to variation in receivers' and observers' perceptions of appropriateness, expectancies, and decorum. As discussed in detail in Chapter 4, characteristics of the sender, his or her relationship to the receiver, and the social and environmental context in which they interact can influence people's evaluations of affectionate behaviors. If senders engage in affectionate behaviors that

receivers and/or observers judge as inappropriate for the type of relationship or the type of context, they risk censure from others in the form of
disapproval or, in extreme cases, retaliatory action.

An example of the latter consequence would be an instance of sexual
harassment in the professional workplace. Let us suppose that Stephen is
a bank manager and Chris is a teller who reports to him. Stephen and
Chris are friends as well as co-workers. One afternoon at work, Stephen
decides to express his affection by hugging Chris in the lobby of the bank.
Given the social context in which the gesture occurs – a professional work
environment, with clients and other employees present – most who
witness this display, including Chris, deem it inappropriate. Whereas
clients and other employees might convey their disapproval mildly
(e.g., via facial expressions of concern), Chris may decide to convey it
through formalized means, such as by filing a grievance with the bank or
accusing Stephen of sexual harassment.

Importantly, Stephen and Chris (due to their friendship) may have
been used to embracing each other in more private, nonprofessional
contexts. Thus, in this example, it was not the behavior itself that elicited
censure from others but, rather, the context in which it was enacted. In
other situations, it may be the case that the behavior itself is deemed
inappropriate for a given relationship, regardless of the social environment. For instance, a man attempting to convey affection for his sister by
kissing her intimately would, in all typical circumstances, incur the
disapproval of others no matter the social situation. No such censure
would typically be expected if he attempted to show affection in a similar
manner to his spouse, however, provided he was enacting the behavior in
a social context in which it was appropriate.

What determines the perceived appropriateness of affectionate behaviors? Preliminary research, such as that conducted by Floyd and Morman
(1997), has already identified some of the aspects of communicators,
their relationships, and social contexts that are influential, including the
sexes of the sender and receiver, the fundamental nature of their relationship (whether romantic, platonic, or familial), and the privacy and
emotional intensity of the environment. Additional research on this topic
will contribute to increased understanding about these influences and
may also illuminate the manner in which receivers' perceptions of appropriateness differ from those of third-party observers.

The Risk of Disease Transmission

For those suffering from communicable diseases – or even diseases
believed to be communicable through casual contact – affectionate

expressions involving physical contact or proximity carry a fourth risk, that of disease transmission. As Chapter 8 explained, it is common for those with acute disorders, such as a cold or flu, to curtail physically affectionate behaviors such as kissing while their condition is contagious. Research suggests that some with chronic disorders, even if they cannot be transmitted through casual contact, may similarly curtail physical affection out of fear that the disease will be transmitted to the receiver.

For instance, Schuster, Beckett, Corona, and Zhou (2005) interviewed 344 US parents drawn from a nationally representative probability sample of human immunodeficiency virus (HIV)-infected adults regarding their beliefs about HIV and their affectionate behavior with their children. Although the authors asked about only three affectionate behaviors – hugging, kissing on the lips, and kissing on the cheek – they found that more than a third (36.1 percent) of the parents avoided at least one of those behaviors with their children out of fear of transmitting HIV to the children via that behavior. Avoidance was more common for kissing on the lips than for hugging or kissing on the cheek. The authors also found that the fear of transmitting HIV to a child through affectionate behavior was substantially more common for Hispanic parents than for African American or Caucasian parents and moderately more common for fathers than for mothers. Self-reported knowledge about HIV was also inversely associated with the fear of transmitting it to children. Later qualitative research by Cowgill, Bogart, Corona, Ryan, and Schuster (2008) also identified hugging and kissing as behaviors that intensified fears of HIV transmission for infected parents. Notably, 42 percent of the Schuster et al. sample reported avoiding at least one of the affectionate behaviors with children, not out of fear of transmitting HIV to the child but out of fear of catching an opportunistic infection *from* the child that would be prove challenging for an HIV-infected adult to handle.

Although this is a risk of greater gravity than nonreciprocity, misinterpretation, or social censure (at least, theoretically), it is also one that is relatively isolated by circumstance, affecting only those who believe themselves likely to transmit or contract illness via physical contact. The risks of nonreciprocity, misinterpretation, and social censure should be comparatively more prevalent in their effects on senders of affectionate messages.

As noted, there is still relatively little research on these risks, making them more speculative than empirical. Research is gaining traction, however, on the ways in which affectionate behavior can be deceptive or even manipulative.

Affectionate Behavior as Deception and Manipulation

One characteristic that makes affectionate communication potentially challenging is that it can be faked. As AET makes clear, *experiencing* affection and *expressing* affection are independent, and do not necessarily co-occur. Rather, individuals have the ability to feel affection that they do not express, as well as to express affection that they do not actually feel. In a program of research, Horan and others (Carton & Horan, 2014; Gillen & Horan, 2013; Horan, 2013a, b; Horan, Parker-Raley, & Cafferty, 2015) has dubbed these behaviors instances of *deceptive affection.* According to Horan, deceptive affection is enacted in two separate but related ways. First, individuals can communicate deceptive affectionate messages (DAMs), which are verbal or nonverbal expressions of affection that is not actually felt by the sender at the time. Second, they can withhold affection by declining to convey affectionate feelings they actually are experiencing.

The subsequent section first explores how common deceptive affection is, how it is usually enacted, and how it varies among relationship types. It then describes the most common motives people report for using it and concludes with a discussion of the individual and relational correlates of deceptive affection.

Frequencies and Forms of Deceptive Affection

In an early study on the prevalence of deceptive affection, Floyd, Erbert, et al. (2005) recruited 1,032 undergraduate students from universities and community colleges throughout the United States. Participants completed an online questionnaire that asked whether they had ever expressed affection to someone when they did not really feel it, but when they were, instead, using the affectionate expression for some other motive. Those who responded affirmatively were instructed to describe the situation, including the relationship they had with the target and what their actual motive was. Importantly, the descriptions were of times when participants had expressed affection that they *did not actually feel*, as opposed to situations when they simply reaffirmed genuine affection for a manipulative purpose.

Results indicated that 86 percent of the respondents (888 of 1,032 people) had conveyed nongenuine affection on at least one occasion. More than half of these participants reported having done so at least once within the previous month, suggesting that the use of deceptive affection is relatively common.

There was no sex difference in the tendency to use nongenuine affection manipulatively, nor were there any effects of ethnicity or marital status. However, compared with those who had not done so, participants who had used affectionate communication manipulatively were younger, more extraverted, more neurotic, more psychotic, more socially active, more fearful of intimacy, and more affectionate overall. The three most common targets that participants identified in association with their manipulative use of affection were a platonic friend (34.2 percent), a current boyfriend/girlfriend (24.4 percent), or a former boyfriend/girlfriend (11.5 percent). Together, these three relationships accounted for just over 70 percent of the instances described.

Two later diary studies explored the frequencies of DAMs and withheld affection, respectively, in romantic relationships. Horan and Booth-Butterfield (2013) had fifty-seven undergraduate students complete a journal entry daily for seven days in which they recorded each time they expressed a DAM to a romantic partner, how they expressed it, and why. Six participants reported no use of DAMs during the week-long study. Those who did use DAMs reported an average of 3.3 instances over the seven-day period. As in the study of Floyd, Erbert, et al. (2005), there was no difference in frequency based on participant sex, nor did the seriousness of the romantic relationship have an effect.

To understand *how* participants used DAMs, Horan and Booth-Butterfield content analyzed their diary reports. They found that verbal behaviors and nonverbal behaviors were roughly equally common. Among nonverbal behaviors, the most commonly described was the use of touch (such as hugging, kissing, and putting one's arm around another), but kinesic behaviors (including smiling or playful physical teasing) and proxemic behaviors (sitting or lying close to another) were also reported.

In a follow-up study, Carton and Horan (2014) asked adults to keep a seven-day diary about their use of withheld affection. Participants reported withholding affection an average of 5.67 times during the week-long study. When asked what they expressed in lieu of affection, participants were most likely to say they communicated a less-intense form of affection than they felt (such as touching the arm instead of kissing); expressed nonchalance (such as acting aloof); or took no action at all.

Although deceptive affection has been studied primarily in the context of romantic pair bonds, there is some evidence that it occurs with varying frequency in other relationships as well. Trask, Horstman, and Hesse (2016) explored the use of deceptive affection in various opposite-sex relationship types. Intensified affection, wherein behaviors connote more affection than is actually felt, was more commonly reported between friends with benefits than between platonic friends or romantic partners.

Similarly, friends and friends with benefits were more likely to report deintensified affection (behaviors that convey less affection than is actually felt) than were romantic partners. Zhong and Dailey (2017) also reported that DAMs were more frequently reported for casual daters than for those who were seriously dating, engaged, or married, although the latter three groups did not differ from each other.

Motives for Using Deceptive Affection

When individuals have been asked to describe *why* they engage in deceptive affection, their responses reflect a combination of prosocial, antisocial, and innocuous motives. For instance, participants in the Floyd, Erbert, et al. (2005) study described a variety of reasons for communicating affection that they did not feel (what Horan calls a DAM). Some were *relationship-focused motives*, such as sustaining a relationship or avoiding interpersonal conflict. Others were *target-centered motives*, in which the goal was to do something for the target of the affectionate behavior. These included making the other person feel cared for, providing emotional comfort, expressing sympathy, or avoiding hurting the other person's feelings. Still other motives were *self-centered motives*, in which the goal was to obtain something from the target of the affectionate message. These included the goals of eliciting instrumental help (such as assistance with a project or task), eliciting material help (such as money), eliciting forgiveness for a past indiscretion in order to appease one's own guilt, and eliciting sexual interaction.

Similar motives were reported by participants in the Horan and Booth-Butterfield (2013) study. Among those participants, the most commonly reported motive was face-saving. Some participants reported using DAMs to support their own face needs, such as to mask embarrassing or vulnerable feelings. Twice as many participants, however, reported using DAMs to support their partner's face needs, such as to avoid embarrassing their partners or hurting their feelings (which Floyd, Erbert, et al. characterized as a target-focused motive). A second motive was conflict management, in which participants reported expressing affection for the purpose of avoiding or curtailing an argument (which Floyd, Erbert, et al. included in their category of relationship-focused motives). Finally, some participants reported using DAMs out of habit or routine, such as saying "I love you" at the end of a telephone conversation because that is what one always says in order to end the conversation on a positive note.

In contrast, the most frequently expressed motives for *withholding* affection identified by Carton and Horan (2014) were largely self-oriented.

The most commonly cited was a concern for how the partner or others would perceive oneself; for instance, one participant reported, "I felt very affectionate, but held back because I didn't want to seem clingy" (p. 233). Participants also withheld affection because they felt it would be inappropriate in their current circumstances, because they were feeling negative emotions about the partner, or because they feared the effects of the affectionate behavior on the relationship, among other reasons.

Individual and Relational Correlates of Deceptive Affection

To the extent that DAMs and withheld affection (or intensified and deintensifed affection, as Trask et al. labeled them) represent forms of deception, it is reasonable to expect their effects and correlates to be largely negative. Horan has pointed out, however, that they have a combination of positive and negative effects on individuals and their relationships. With respect to relationship maintenance, for instance, the use of DAMs is negatively related to assurances and positivity and (along with withholding affection) is positively related to control (Horan, 2013b), yet it appears to have no effect on relational partners' satisfaction with or commitment to their relationship (Gillen & Horan, 2013). Moreover, Trask et al. found that relational health (a composite of relationship satisfaction, commitment, and closeness) was negatively associated with deintensified affection for friends with benefits, but positively associated with both intensified and deintensified affection for romantic partners.

Moreover, engaging in deceptive affection does not appear to be stress-inducing, the way that enacting other forms of deception can be (Horan & Booth-Butterfield, 2011). In some contexts, in fact, deceptive affection appears to be associated with a reduction in stress. In two studies, Horan and Parker-Raley investigated the use of DAMs and withheld affection among medical staff working in a hospital's emergency department (Horan, Parker-Raley, & Cafferty, 2015; Parker-Raley & Horan, 2014). Their studies suggested (although did not conclusively prove) that emergency department staff risk burnout and compassion fatigue if they communicate authentic affection all the time, so DAMs and withheld affection can be strategies for avoiding those outcomes.

Redlick and Vangelisti (in press) tied the use of DAMs in romantic relationships to partners' perceptions of mate value. The authors argued that when perceived mate value is high, relational partners may use DAMs as a mate-retention strategy; that is, they may express affection, even when unfelt, as a tactic for sustaining the relationship. Their study therefore hypothesized a positive association between perceived mate value and the use of DAMs. Respondents in their study were US adults currently involved in a romantic relationship. Results indicated that mate value and the use of DAMs were indeed significantly correlated, but contrary to the hypothesis, the correlation was inverse. People who perceive that their romantic partners have high mate value are therefore *less* likely to use DAMs in those relationships, not *more* likely. The authors speculated that people with high-value mates may shy away from using DAMs out of fear of harming the relationship, or they may simply feel affection from the partners more often, producing fewer opportunities to express affection deceptively.

Deceptive affection, then, might be most accurately characterized as having both a dark and a light side, in that its motives and correlates are often negative, but not exclusively. One condition whose effects tend to be exclusively negative, however, is that of affection deprivation, described subsequently.

Affection Deprivation

AET posits a range of optimal tolerance for affectionate communication, such that individuals have a minimum amount of affection that they desire and require, and also a maximum. Affectionate behavior that occurs within that range is generally associated with positive relational and health indices, as earlier chapters have detailed, but Floyd (2014c) proposed that people experience *affection deprivation* when they lack an adequate level of affectionate interaction in their lives. This section describes how affection deprivation is defined (including how it is differentiated conceptually and empirically from loneliness), and then details its individual and relational correlates.

Defining Affection Deprivation

Floyd's (2014c) original articulation of affection deprivation focused specifically on the lack of affectionate touch. Specifically, he defined affection deprivation as "the condition of wanting more tactile affectionate communication than one receives" (p. 383). Drawing on pioneering research on touch deprivation from Prescott (1976b, 1979, 1980) – who found that deficits in affectionate touch in children were associated with developmental delays, violence, and drug abuse later in life – the concept of affection deprivation originally proposed that lacking sufficient affectionate touch would be associated with deficits in physical and mental health, as well as social and relational wellness. Later, Floyd (2016) reconceptualized affection deprivation as a deficit in any form of affectionate behavior, not simply touch, and his eight-item Affection Deprivation Scale now reflects that broader focus.

Given that affection deprivation indexes a deficit in one's desired level of affectionate behavior, one might question whether the construct is sufficiently distinct from loneliness. That question is worth considering, for at least two reasons. First, loneliness is routinely associated with many of the same problems identified as correlates of affection deprivation (see later). For instance, loneliness predicts sleep disturbances (Kurina et al., 2011), pain and fatigue (Jaremka, Fagundes, Glaser, et al., 2013), depression (Aylaz, Aktürk, Erci, Öztürk, & Aslan, 2012), alexithymia (Qualter, Quinton, Wagner, & Brown, 2009), and relationship dissatisfaction (Frye-Cox & Hesse, 2013), as well as lack of physical activity (Shankar, McMunn, Banks, & Steptoe, 2011), hypertension (Momtaz et al., 2012), and inflammatory responses to stress (Jaremka, Fagundes, Peng, et al., 2013). A second reason it is useful to consider the distinction between affection deprivation and loneliness is that these experiences correlate strongly with each other. Hesse (2015) identified a significant relationship between affection deprivation and loneliness ($\beta = .28$), as did Floyd (2014c; $\beta = .45$). To the extent that measures of these variables share variance, therefore, it is useful to ask how distinct they are from each other.

Floyd and Hesse (2017) argued that affection deprivation is conceptually distinct from loneliness on two grounds. First, whereas loneliness describes a broad deficit in social connectedness, writ large, affection deprivation focuses specifically on a shortage of affectionate behavior received from other people. Second, although both constructs are perceptual, loneliness is more affective and affection deprivation is more behavioral. On these bases, Floyd and Hesse hypothesized that items on the Affection Deprivation Scale and on the UCLA Loneliness Scale (the most commonly used operational definition of loneliness; Russell, 1996) would comprise largely separate factors when factor analyzed together. Across three studies, Floyd and Hesse found this to be true; although the factors were correlated, there was a clear empirical distinction between items used to measure affection deprivation and those used to measure loneliness.

On the basis of AET's claim that individuals require a minimum amount of affection, several studies have now documented that being deprived of affection is associated with individual and relational problems.

Correlates of Affection Deprivation

In an initial survey of 509 adults from the United States and sixteen foreign countries, Floyd (2014c) measured affection deprivation as a lack of affectionate touch, specifically. He found that affection deprivation was positively related to mental health deficits, including depression, stress, loneliness, insecure attachment, alexithymia, and the number of diagnosed mood/anxiety disorders. It was also positively associated with the number of diagnosed secondary immune disorders and negatively related to general health, life happiness, received social support, relationship satisfaction, and attachment security. These initial results suggest that being deprived of affectionate touch correlates with indices of wellness across people's mental, physical, and social experiences.

In three studies involving a total of 1,368 adults, Floyd (2016) found that a broadened definition of affection deprivation (focused on inadequate affection in all forms, rather than just touch) predicted experiences of chronic physical pain, as well as disturbances in sleep quality, sleep latency, sleep duration, and daytime dysfunction. Other research has identified associations with various social and relational experiences. For example, Hesse and Mikkelson (2016) studied the connections between affection deprivation and romantic relationship quality. Their study found that affection deprivation was inversely associated with relationship satisfaction ($\beta = -.28$) and closeness ($\beta = -.16$) in romantic pairs. Hesse and Mikkelson also reported that both relational uncertainty and relational maximization moderated those associations, with most of the associations gaining strength at higher levels of both moderating variables. This included a significant inverse association between affection deprivation and commitment when maximization was high ($\beta = -.38$). Mederos (2015) also reported a small but significant negative association between affection deprivation and the use of tie signs in romantic relationships ($r = -.12$).

In a different study, Hesse (2015) reported that affection deprivation was inversely related to family satisfaction ($\beta = -.19$) and directly associated with loneliness ($\beta = .28$), depression ($\beta = .37$), and attachment anxiety ($\beta = .35$). Hesse theorized that people who feel affection deprived may cope with that deficit by consuming pornography, and he showed that affection deprivation was significantly associated with the frequency of pornography use ($\beta = .44$). Hesse and Floyd (2018) later offered additional evidence that affection-deprived adults may consume pornography as a coping mechanism.

Like loneliness, therefore, affection deprivation is associated with a range of mental, physical, relational, and social problems. There is certainly more research to be done to illuminate its correlates and perhaps even to test interventions to reduce affection deprivation, but the existing evidence is squarely in line with AET's contention that failing to receive an adequate level of affectionate behavior is problematic.

Whereas that contention may seem somewhat intuitive, the associated contention – that receiving *too much* affection is also problematic – is perhaps less so. Thus far only one study has investigated the problem of excessive affection, but its results and implications are described next.

Excessive Affection

AET's concept of the range of optimal tolerance implies that it is problematic to receive not only too little affection but also too much. Floyd and Burgoon (1999) demonstrated that under certain circumstances, affection can be undesired, and indeed, excessive affectionate attention in inappropriate relationships or circumstances can constitute sexual harassment or even sexual abuse (see, e.g., Fitzgerald, Gelfand, & Drasgow, 1995).

One need not experience harassment or abuse to perceive excessive levels of affection, however. Hesse, Mikkelson, and Saracco (2018) argued that a parenting style known as helicopter parenting, which is characterized by high parental warmth, overinvolvement, and excessive control (Padilla-Walker & Nelson, 2012), exemplifies AET's concept of excessive affection. Whereas children of helicopter parents report high levels of parental affection, they also report excessive levels of enmeshment, representing a lack of boundary differentiation between parent and child that can impede adjustment in later life (see, e.g., Schiffrin et al., 2014; Segrin, Givertz, Swiatkowski, & Montgomery, 2015; Segrin, Woszidlo, Givertz, Bauer, & Taylor Murphy, 2012).

On the basis of AET, Hesse and colleagues hypothesized that excessive affection received from parents is negatively associated with individuals' life satisfaction and self-esteem, as well as with their relational satisfaction and closeness with their parent. They further proposed that excessive affection is characteristic of the helicopter parenting style. They recruited 149 undergraduate students to report on their experiences of helicopter parenting and excessive parental affection, as well as the individual and relational outcomes. As expected, the helicopter parenting style was associated with excessive affection (r = .20). Moreover, excessive affection was inversely associated with life satisfaction (β = $-$.18), self-esteem (β = $-$.22), and parent–child relational satisfaction (β = $-$.33), although it was unrelated to parent–child closeness.

These results are among the first to confirm AET's claim that receiving more affection than one desires from a given relationship is significantly associated with negative outcomes for individuals and relationships. Whereas multiple studies have demonstrated that appropriate levels of affection are beneficial for the parent–child relationship (see Chapter 6), the findings of Hesse et al. suggest that the association between affection and benefit is nonlinear, turning from positive to negative at a certain level of affectionate behavior. There is certainly much more to be done to illuminate the characteristics of excessive affection, but the Hesse et al. study is a promising start.

Much of this book has touted the benefits of affectionate behavior. Those benefits are plentiful, but they are not without exception. Just as affectionate communication can impair physical health under certain circumstances (see Chapter 8), it can also precede negative outcomes for individuals and relationships, particularly when it invites risk, when it is enacted deceptively, and when it is beneath or above one's optimal range of tolerance.

10 Looking Back and Looking Ahead

The preceding chapters have explored multiple dimensions of affection exchange in human social interaction. Several theoretic treatments of affectionate behavior have been detailed, and a large body of empirical findings has been synthesized around several fundamental questions concerning why, how, to whom, and with what effects people convey affection to each other. The research on affectionate communication is indeed eclectic in terms of its focus, its methodology, and its theoretic underpinnings. Although eclecticism serves the purposes of ensuring that diverse ideas are considered and that observed patterns are not conceptually or operationally bound, it can have the additional effect of making the literature appear not to support any general conclusions.

Such is not the case with affectionate communication, however. To bring this volume to a close, this chapter begins by identifying some important observations about affectionate communication that have found support in the empirical literature. Some of these conclusions may appear relatively intuitive, whereas others will not, a testament to the provocative and often paradoxical nature of affectionate communication. After looking back at what is known, this chapter looks ahead to some of the most intriguing and promising questions currently being investigated in the affectionate communication literature. Although this work is in its infancy, it has the potential to illuminate aspects of human affection exchange in ways as yet unseen.

Looking Back: Some Qualified Conclusions about Affectionate Communication

As noted, research on affectionate communication supports a diverse range of conclusions, some of the most important of which are identified and discussed here. Where appropriate, qualifiers are identified and discussed so that each conclusion can be appreciated with proper evaluation of the research that generated it.

Affection Is a Fundamental Human Need

This text began with the assertion – formalized in AET – that both the experience and the expression of affection are fundamental human needs. In the critical early days and years of their lives, humans rely almost exclusively on conspecifics to meet their other fundamental needs, including for food, water, shelter, and medical care, and the most potent motivator for parents to make such substantial investments in their offspring is their love for them. Both that emotional experience and their expressions of it therefore contribute substantially to infant survival.

Because humankind is such a highly social species, with a pervasive need to belong, the exchange of affectionate communication characterizes a wide range of intimate, personal, and social relationships throughout the life course. In developing relationships, people often use affectionate behavior to signal their desires for relational escalation, and the enactment of significant affectionate gestures – such as the first kiss or the first exchange of the words "I love you" – is frequently considered a turning point in relationship development. On the contrary, shifts toward less frequent or less intense forms of affection display may coincide with, and serve as evidence of, relational deterioration.

If the need for affection is fundamental, then it is unsurprising that affectionate communication is linearly and strongly related to a number of positive qualities in personal relationships. Relationships characterized by frequent affectionate behavior also tend to be closer, more satisfying, and more engaging than those that are not. People who frequently communicate affection to a relational partner (whether a romantic, platonic, or familial partner) also tend to like, love, and be socially attracted and committed to that partner more than those who do not. Highly affectionate relationships are more stable over time, and involve more intimacy and self-disclosure, than less affectionate relationships. In short, affectionate human relationships tend to be *good* human relationships.

Additional evidence on the importance of affection is found in the research on affection deprivation. When individuals are deprived of a fundamental physical need – such as water, food, or sleep – their bodies react by signaling that need – such as through thirst, hunger, or fatigue. If those signals are not attended to properly, negative outcomes can ensue, such as pain, immunosuppression, and cognitive difficulties. A similar process may be operative for affection deprivation, wherein the lack of sufficient affection initiates an emotional signaling process (loneliness, perhaps) that, if unattended, produces negative outcomes associated with that deprivation, including those identified in the literature: pain, disordered sleep, depression, acquired immune disorders, psychiatric disorders, and the like.

Even if the ubiquity and positivity of affectionate communication are intuitive, they are nonetheless consequential because of the importance of personal relationships themselves. It is difficult to exaggerate the importance of human interpersonal bonds; like many species, humans are inherently social beings, and their satisfaction with their relationships is among the strongest predictors of their satisfaction with life. By implication, then, understanding better those communicative behaviors that demonstrate reliable and substantial associations with relationship success holds much promise for improving the human condition, and it is clear that affectionate communication is among those.

Affectionate Communication Overlaps Only Partially with Affectionate Emotion

Researchers have recognized for quite some time that although the internal experience and the external expression of emotion frequently coincide, they are somewhat independent. Indeed, Ekman and Friesen's (1975) display rules acknowledge that communicators can fail to express emotions they are feeling and can express emotions that they fail to feel. The imperfect connection between emotion and expression is particularly important for affection, given that affection is an externally oriented emotion (i.e., one feels affection *for* someone or something else). It may be relatively inconsequential to one individual whether a conversational partner is accurately displaying his or her happiness, fear, or surprise. If that partner is feeling and/or displaying affection for the individual, however, that has direct implications for the nature of the relationship between the individual and the partner. Therefore, to the extent that the partner is hiding the affection he or she is feeling or is communicating affection that he or she is not feeling, these have consequences for the individual that other emotions or emotion displays may not.

There are several reasons why individuals may elect not to convey (or, at least, to downplay the intensity of) affection they are experiencing. For instance, they may fear putting the receiver "on the spot," making him or her feel obligated to reciprocate, or they may worry that the receiver will fail to reciprocate the expression. Likewise, they may be concerned that a recipient would misinterpret the affectionate gesture as more or less intense than intended, or that the recipient would believe the expression was insincere. They may also fail to express felt affection if doing so would violate the norms of the relationship or the social context.

Similarly, research indicates that people can and do express affection in the absence of the emotion (or, at least, express affection more intensely than they are feeling it). Several motives can be served by such a move. For instance, communicators may falsely convey affection in order to garner favor or elicit instrumental support from another. They may do so in the service of politeness (e.g., reciprocating another's affectionate expression) or as a means of comforting or consoling another. People may also express false affection as a means of initiating sexual interaction, a strategy with an evident potential to succeed, given the extent to which people need and desire affection.

The somewhat orthogonal relationship between affection and affectionate behavior suggests, among other things, that the ability to discriminate accurately between affectionate expressions that are genuine and those that are not would be characteristic of socially skilled communicators.

Affectionate Communication Is Strongly Influenced by Social and Cultural Norms

That affectionate behavior should be affected by social or cultural norms may seem entirely self-evident. Indeed, the communication of a range of emotions is encouraged, constrained, or proscribed by the normative demands of the social context and the gender roles of the participants, the nature and developmental stage of their relationship, and the cultural prescriptions for when and how emotion is to be displayed, among other influences (see, e.g., Metts & Planalp, 2011). As detailed in earlier chapters, the expression of affection is likewise influenced by norms of propriety associated with the type of relationship in which it is occurring (e.g., intimate affection is considered more appropriate in romantic than platonic relationships), the sex composition of the relationship (e.g., direct affectionate expressions are more expected in female–female than male–male pairs, on average), and aspects of the social context, such as privacy or emotional intensity. Direct expressions of affection, particularly nonverbal ones, are also observed more frequently among those from high-contact cultures than among those from medium- or low-contact cultures. Importantly, those in the latter types of culture may not necessarily convey less affection than their high-contact counterparts; rather, they may simply be more inclined to communicate their affection via more indirect means.

One of the social institutions that clearly exerts influence not only on how affectionate people are, but also on how they convey their affection, is the family (see, e.g., Floyd & Morman, 2014). Research on the effects

of early family environment appears to suggest that people learn a repertoire for affectionate behavior from the behaviors they observed their
parents using with them and with each other. As Floyd and Morman
(2000a) showed, people sometimes replicate these patterns with their
own children, and sometimes compensate for them. It is important to
note, however, that the designs of many studies of early family environment have not allowed for the parceling out of variance associated with
heritable personality traits. That is, children may communicate the way
their parents do because they learned those communicative behaviors
through observation and reinforcement; they may also replicate their
parents' communication because they have genetically inherited the
same predispositions that their parents had. For instance, parents who
are prone to act aggressively may pass that predisposition on to their
offspring genetically *and* they may teach their children aggressive behaviors by enacting their own behavioral predispositions. Importantly, neither explanation precludes the other, but studies that fail to account for
heritability may easily overestimate the proportion of variance accounted
for by learning and reinforcement. Research suggesting that affectionate
tendencies have a partially genetic basis (e.g., Floyd & Denes, 2015)
makes this a relevant consideration. This is not an issue with other social
or cultural institutions (e.g., school, media, government), but it is an
important methodological consideration when studying families.

Affectionate Communication Is Strongly Linked to Mental and Physical Health

Perhaps the most substantial contribution of affectionate communication
research over the past decade has been to illuminate the ways in which
affectionate behavior is correlated with – and, in some instances, contributes to – mental and physical wellness. Multiple mental and psychological states – including depression, anxiety, distress, low self-esteem,
and loneliness – share significant proportions of the variance with affectionate behavior at either the state or trait level. Similarly, affection
exchange correlates with cardiovascular health and immunocompetence
and appears to be instrumental in the body's stress response. Specifically,
affectionate communication acts as a buffer against the negative effects of
stressors, aids in the regulation of the stress reaction, and accelerates the
body's recovery from stress.

One implication of these findings is that affectionate behavior may
comprise a component of clinically effective nonpharmacological interventions for various acute and chronic conditions. As noted in Chapter 7,
some interventions have already been proposed for use in psychotherapeutic

settings, and others, such as affectionate writing (Floyd, Mikkelson, Tafoya, et al., 2007a), could be useful adjuncts in treatment strategies for anxiety or stress (the use of affectionate communication as an intervention is discussed in more detail later).

One important limitation of this research, as yet undiscussed, is its inability to rule out the placebo effect as a possible explanation for observed benefits. Placebo effects are observable or perceived improvements in health that are not attributable to the treatment. In pharmacological trials, for instance, control group participants are unknowingly given a substance (in the same regimen as those in the experimental group) that looks and tastes identical to the treatment but is biologically inert. Despite not receiving the treatment, however, those in the placebo group routinely see clinically significant improvements in their conditions. Indeed, a meta-analysis of the placebo effect in nineteen double-blind clinical trials of antidepressant medication found that the effect sizes produced by experimental and placebo groups were substantially correlated ($r = .90$; Kirsch & Sapirstein, 1998).[1] Although various explanations for the placebo effect have been offered, most focus on the possibility that it is patients' expectation of improvement that leads their condition to improve, despite not being treated medically.

A critical aspect of the placebo effect, however, is that patients must not know whether they are taking the biologically active treatment or the placebo (i.e., they must be blind to the condition), and that is virtually impossible with many behavioral interventions. That is, it would be difficult, if not impossible, to design a study of the health benefits of affectionate behavior that included a placebo condition, since there are few if any instances in which people would be unaware of whether they were receiving affectionate expressions from others (indeed, unlike with pharmacological treatments, one could argue that knowledge of an affectionate gesture is absolutely necessary to its effects). This feature of affectionate communication (and of other nonpharmacological treatments, such as Pennebaker's 2017 therapeutic writing interventions) effectively prevents research from ruling out the alternative explanation that it is people's belief in the power of affectionate behavior, and not the affectionate behavior itself, that leads to their observed improvements. To the extent that people can efficiently manage the risks of affectionate communication, however, the question of whether its benefits derive from the behaviors themselves or from people's *attitudes about* the behaviors may be substantially less compelling than it would be for a pharmacological treatment.

Although most research on affection and health has focused on how affectionate communication may influence health, fewer studies have identified health conditions that influence affectionate behavior. Chapter 7 reported that psychopathologies such as autism and Asperger syndrome (now classified together under the term *autism spectrum disorders*) impair the ability to give and receive affection properly, and that interventions designed to overcome these limitations have shown promise. Similarly, Chapter 8 reported that parents infected with HIV curtailed their physical affection for their children (relative to noninfected controls) out of concern for sharing infection. It is certainly reasonable to predict that physical affection is similarly curtailed by adults with contagious acute conditions, such as influenza, herpes, or contagious skin conditions such as scabies.

Affectionate Communication Benefits Those Who Give It as Well as Those Who Receive It

Prior to the last decade, much of the research on the health benefits of affectionate behavior focused on recipients, rather than providers, of affectionate expressions. A resource orientation to affectionate communication would certainly suggest this focus; to the extent that affectionate behavior is conceived of as a resource (similar to money or time), it is logical to focus on the benefits of receiving it. One of the innovative aspects of more recent affection research, however – particularly in the health arena – has been its demonstration that affectionate communication is beneficial not only when it is received but also when it is given.

This can be a distinction without a difference in routine relational interaction, given the strongly reciprocal nature of expressed and received affection. (That is true both in established relationships, in which affectionate expressions are often reciprocated because the underlying emotion is shared, and in less intimate social relationships, in which expressions of affection may be reciprocated out of politeness.) Theories such as AET and tend and befriend theory provide, however, that people benefit not only by receiving affectionate gestures but also by offering them, perhaps particularly during periods of acute distress. Indeed, empirical research on people's trait-like tendencies to give and receive affection has demonstrated that although expressed and received affection overlap in their abilities to account for variance in individual and relational benefits, expressed affection accounts for significant variance above and beyond that accounted for by received affection.

One way in which this observation can potentially be applied is in the development of therapeutic interventions, such as those discussed above. For instance, to the extent that befriending others can help to attenuate the effects of acute or chronic stress (as tend and befriend theory suggests), behavioral interventions involving increased expressions of affection to loved ones could be designed and their stress-attenuation effects tested clinically. Similarly, the affectionate writing exercise used by Floyd, Mikkelson, Tafoya, et al. (2007a) to study reductions in cortisol following acute stress could be tested against other forms of writing – including Pennebaker's traumatic writing treatment and appropriate controls – for its efficacy in effecting short-term and long-term benefits to physical or mental health. What is particularly noteworthy about writing interventions is that they preclude the possibility that their benefits are caused in any manner by affectionate communication received in return, because neither in Floyd, Mikkelson, Tafoya, et al.'s study nor in the typical Pennebaker therapeutic writing experiment are the written products given to anyone other than the researchers. Consequently, one can have greater confidence that observed benefits are those of having *expressed*, rather than of having *received*, the affectionate or traumatic emotions.

Affectionate Communication Is Associated with Negative as Well as Positive Outcomes

A consistent theme through much of the research described in this text is that, although affectionate communication is normally perceived to be positive (or, at the very least, innocuous), there are particular situations in which its risks outweigh its benefits and it produces negative individual or relational outcomes. Several of the most evident risks for communicators of affection were described in the previous chapter, including risks of nonreciprocity, misinterpretation, social censure, and disease transmission. Moreover, Chapter 8 reviewed multiple health risks of affectionate behavior, including immunosuppression, viral transmission, and the initiation of allergic responses.

Although it is by no means normative that affectionate behavior is detrimental, the relational risks to senders and receivers warrant further investigation, particularly insofar as insincere or deceptive affectionate expressions (DAMs) can be successfully used as manipulation attempts. Whereas some motives for expressing unfelt affection may be benevolent (e.g., to provide comfort) or innocuous (e.g., to reciprocate an affectionate gesture in the service of politeness), others can be malicious and can expose their victims to other forms of risk, such as expressing insincere affection to elicit money or sexual contact. What is perhaps most important to understand about the expression of insincere affection as a manipulation strategy is not why people adopt this strategy but why it is sometimes successful. AET offers that this tactic may succeed because people are motivated to invest in those who love them; therefore, being shown that one is loved initiates such a motivation. More specifically, AET would explain the strategy's success in eliciting sexual access as also involving connotations of the communicator's parental fitness. To the extent that people, particularly adolescents and young adults, are sufficiently vulnerable to the seductions of insincere affection as to agree to sexual contact with the communicator, then this risk of affectionate communication is far from a trivial one.

Existing Theory Is Still Limited

Prior to the formal articulation of AET (Floyd, 2006a), no existing theory attempted to explain affectionate communication per se. Rather, perspectives such as tend and befriend theory implied that affection exchange may have benefit during times of distress, and the need to belong implied that relationship formation and maintenance are important human goals that affectionate behavior may help people to achieve. AET was the first social scientific theory specifically to address the communication of affection writ large, rather than simply during times of stress, and as this book has detailed, it has generated a formidable program of research with substantial empirical support.

AET is nonetheless still limited in particular ways. As Floyd, Hesse, and Generous (2018) pointed out, some limitations were by design and others were not. For example, AET intentionally includes little detail specifying the cultural, political, economic, or environmental variables that account for variance in affectionate behavior. This omission was not because AET conceives of those sources of variation as inconsequential but because it privileges the explication of evolutionary and physiological causes over socially constructed ones. This necessarily limits the theory's predictive ability, however, just as exclusively social learning–oriented theories are similarly limited.

A second limitation of AET is that it speaks more to *why* people communicate affection than to *how* they do. AET is not necessarily useful, for instance, in generating predictions about whether hugging, kissing, hand-holding, or verbal gestures are going to be more common in some relationships than in others, or in identifying hypotheses about how cultural groups vary in their means of encoding affection. The goal of AET was to explain why individuals communicate affection, and with what effects, but this necessarily leaves the "how" largely unspecified.

Perhaps the most consequential limitation of AET is the lack of detail it presently offers about the specific pathways through which affectionate behavior contributes to physical well-being. Generalized pathways are described, including the body's systems for stress response and reward, but these provide only broad bases for predicting specific physiological effects. As research matures on the specific biochemical markers responsible for the benefits of affectionate behavior, it would be worthwhile to attempt to bring greater precision to the theory's predictive ability.

These certainly are not the only broad conclusions that the affectionate communication literature would support, but they are among the most important for understanding this behavioral phenomenon. Like most conclusions in social science, each of these is qualified by the specifics of the studies that produced them (i.e., not necessarily generalizable to all populations or circumstances), and also conditional on future findings that may call their validity into question. In short, these are among the things that are currently known about affectionate communication – but what is left to learn?

Looking Ahead: Important Questions for the Future of Affectionate Communication Research

Especially over the last few decades, research has added immeasurably to our understanding of affectionate behavior in close relationships. There is still much to be discovered, however, and work along three particular lines of inquiry has notable promise for further illuminating the value of affectionate communication in the coming years.

The Question of Inheritance

Several studies have established that individuals vary in their trait-like tendency to communicate affection, but what proportion of the variance in that tendency is inherited genetically? Thus far, only Floyd and Denes (2015) have identified a genetic basis for trait affection level (in that case, based on variation in the rs53576 single-nucleotide polymorphism on the oxytocin receptor gene). Not only does that finding await replication, but *OXTR* is only one out of some 20,000 protein-coding genes in the human genome. Whereas the vast majority of genes code for proteins that cannot reasonably be expected to have any influence on social behavior, research has shown that variations in other receptor genes – including the serotonin (Canli & Lesch, 2007) and dopamine (Bakerman-Kranenburg & van Ijzendoorn, 2006) receptor genes – account for variance in social cognition and interpersonal behavior. Those would therefore be reasonable candidates to investigate in future attempts to understand better the proportion of variance in trait affection level that is accounted for genetically.

The prospect that trait affection level has at least a partially genetic basis should not be controversial. Indeed, all five principal dimensions of personality – openness, conscientiousness, extraversion, agreeableness, and neuroticism – are heritable, with between 41 and 61 percent of the variance attributable to genetic rather than environmental factors (Lang, Livesly, & Vemon, 1996; see also Floderus-Myrhed, Pedersen, & Rasmuson, 1980). Other traits, such as intelligence (Trzaskowski, Yang, Visscher, & Plomin, 2014), empathy (Davis, Luce, & Kraus, 1994), and aggressiveness (Rushton, Fulker, Neale, Nias, & Eysenck, 1986), are also heritable. Importantly, in none of these traits do genetic factors account for 100 percent of the variance, but in each of them, the proportion of variance attributable to genetic influences is significantly greater than zero. If the tendencies to be open, outgoing, and empathic have a genetic basis, it would therefore be surprising if the tendency to be affectionate did not.

Whereas some portion of the variance is attributable to environmental factors and some portion is likely attributable to genetic factors, remaining variance may also be explained by gene–environment interactions, wherein a genetic predisposition is expressed more strongly under certain environmental conditions than under others (see Krueger, South, Johnson, & Iacono, 2008). A genetic predisposition to be highly affectionate, for instance, may manifest itself more strongly in a home environment characterized by loving, affectionate parenting – in which affectionate expression is both modeled and rewarded – than in an environment characterized by more distant parenting. Future research might explore variation on candidate genes (such as polymorphisms on the oxytocin, serotonin, and dopamine receptor genes) in relation to, for instance, family communication patterns (Fitzpatrick, 2004), to ascertain whether genotype interacts with family type to account for variation in trait affection levels.

Technological Means of Meeting Affection Needs

Multiple authors, including Putnam (2000) and Turkle (2017), have warned that advances in technology and mediated communication platforms, although often designed to increase connectedness and shrink social distance, have paradoxically reduced intimacy and connection at the interpersonal level. Whereas social media use can facilitate communication with a geographically dispersed community, it can simultaneously discourage communication in face-to-face settings. It is perhaps unsurprising, therefore, that even as social media use has accelerated, the perception of social isolation has increased dramatically (McPhearson,

Smith-Lovin, & Brashears, 2006), and more Americans are living alone than at any point in history (Vespa, Lewis, & Kreider, 2013).

These observations raise questions about how individuals can effectively meet their needs for affection. Research still in its infancy is showing promise that emerging technologies can assist people in exchanging affection, even when they are not in physical proximity. Exemplary in this regard is research on the Hugvie, a small, human-shaped pillow equipped with built-in cellular communication technology. Users can hold and embrace the Hugvie while speaking over the wireless connection with a partner who is not physically present, but they must actually hug the device in order to communicate (Nakanishi et al., 2014). Using this device can help people create or maintain a sense of affective connection with a partner, even if the partner is not close by.

Research has demonstrated the effects of using Hugvie on a variety of outcomes. For instance, it encourages more attentive listening to one's partner (Nakanishi et al., 2014), and it fosters the maintenance of trust in situations when trust might be threatened (Takahashi et al., 2017). Like person-to-person hugging, using Hugvie also decreases anxiety (Yamazaki et al., 2016) and salivary cortisol (Sumioka et al., 2013). Kuwamura, Sakai, Minato, Nishio, and Ishiguro (2014) showed that male undergraduates reported more intense feelings of love for female partners after using Hugvie to converse, compared with controls who conversed by cell phone. Costa, Chisik, and Faria (2018) even demonstrated the device's efficacy in improving interaction skills among children with developmental deficits.

Users of Hugvie appear to benefit by embracing the device while talking with a partner, but the user's embrace is not actually transmitted to the partner. Other mechanisms, however, allow one user to send forms of affectionate touch to a receiver as long as both have an Internet connection. For instance, Cabibihan and Chauhan (2017) described a tele-touch device that enables one person to send affective touch to a receiver in another location. In their study, receivers watched an emotionally arousing movie while receiving in-person touch, tele-touch, or no touch. Participants in the three conditions did not differ in their heart rate responses to the movie, but compared with the no-touch controls, those who received interpersonal touch or tele-touch had lower electrodermal activity, a measure of sympathetic nervous system arousal. Just as in-person touch promotes relaxation and calm, therefore, the researchers demonstrated that tele-touch can do the same. Similarly, Zhang and Cheok (2016) described a kissing device that allows users to share the haptic sensations of kissing with partners in other locations, although no research has yet been published on its effects.

Some of this technology is actually wearable (Angelini, Caon, Lalanne, Khaled, & Mugellini, 2014). For instance, Teh et al. (2008) described the Huggy Pajama, a two-component device for transmitting the physical sensations of a hug between distant partners. The sender embraces a small, mobile doll with embedded touch and pressure-sensing circuits. This device is connected via the Internet to a wearable pajama top with embedded air pockets and heating elements. When the sender embraces the doll, a receiver wearing the pajama top feels the warmth and pressure of the hug.

Huggy Pajama was originally designed to facilitate affection between parents and their young children, specifically, but a later iteration introduced an adult-sized wearable jacket with the same capabilities as the original pajama top. Using the jacket device, Teh, Tsai, Koh, and Cheok (2012) showed that receiving a "virtual hug" increases recipients' positive affect.

These are only a few examples of technologies currently in development that can facilitate the transmission and/or exchange of experiences approximating the physical sensations of affectionate touch. Additional research has the potential to verify whether affection shared through these modalities has effects on mental health, physical health, and relational health similar to those of affection shared in person, although initial results on this point (e.g., Cabibihan & Chauhan, 2017; Sumioka et al., 2013) are promising. If virtual affection is beneficial, then technologies such as these have the potential to facilitate affection exchange and perhaps reduce feelings of loneliness or isolation, particularly for groups at elevated risk of loneliness, such as adolescents or the elderly (see, e.g., Victor & Yang, 2012).

Affectionate Communication as Intervention

Given the range of mental and physical health benefits associated with affectionate behavior, it is reasonable to consider its potential as an intervention with possible therapeutic benefit. Chapter 7 discussed how "prescribing" affection exchange may be useful in couple therapy as well as in counseling sessions with suicidal people, and Chapter 8 described affectionate writing interventions that may be useful for stress management. Importantly, these interventions are complementary to other therapeutic modalities rather than constituting therapies in and of themselves. However, they have the potential to provide mental, physical, and/or relational benefit, and that potential warrants systematic exploration in future research.

Some affection-based practices already exist in the nonclinical realm and may show promise for providing benefit to practitioners. One is the Buddhist practice of hugging meditation described by Hanh (2000). Like many meditative practices, hugging meditation begins with recognizing others in one's presence. It next prescribes hugging another person and holding the embrace for three complete breaths. With the first breath, participants are encouraged to focus on their own presence and their own happiness. The second breath encourages awareness of the partner's presence and happiness. During the third breath, participants focus on their gratitude at being together, and as the third breath ends, they release their embrace.

This practice shares conceptual space with loving-kindness meditation, which has been shown to increase social connectedness (Hutcherson, Seppälä, & Gross, 2008), to elevate positive affect (Fredrickson, Cohn, Coffey, Pek, & Finkel, 2008), and to decrease intergroup bias (Kang, Gray, & Dovidio, 2014). Whether hugging meditation can elicit similar benefits remains to be seen, but there would be value in exploring the efficacy of an existing practice such as this.

A somewhat analogous practice is the cuddle party, an organized event that facilitates nonsexual physical affection through shared touch, hugging, and cuddling (Cross, 2006). Participants at a cuddle party may be acquainted but are often strangers, and they typically lie next to each other while a facilitator guides them through introductions and games designed to induce comfort with touch and to reinforce boundaries. Participants are then offered time for "freestyle" cuddling in which they can explore touching and hugging other participants. Cuddle parties occur throughout North America, Europe, and Australia, as well as in parts of Asia and Africa. There is speculation that cuddling in this manner may promote benefits such as increased oxytocin and reduced blood pressure (Women's Health, 2016), but no systematic research on the benefits of participating in cuddle parties has yet been conducted. As they gain popularity, this would be a fruitful area of inquiry for future research.

Floyd (2006a) proposed a number of research questions about affectionate communication that were, at the time, unexplored. Many of those questions have now received empirical attention, which contributes to a more complete understanding of affectionate behavior but also raises important new questions that perhaps had not been evident before. Questions about heritability, technology, and interventions are certainly not the only ones left to answer, but given the promise of initial research in these areas, these are fertile questions for continued research over the next several years.

Afterthoughts

Few communicative behaviors are more consequential to the quality and satisfaction of human relationships than the communication of affection. Indeed, it is little exaggeration to suggest that, without affectionate behavior to initiate and maintain them, many of the most important relationships in the life course would be forsaken. In spite of its centrality – or perhaps, in part, because of it – affectionate communication often seems to occur in a perfunctory manner, without much conscious attention being paid to its intricacies. Even so, it influences so many diverse aspects of individual and relational life that humans would be hard pressed to do without it. In this way, affectionate behavior can truly be considered a fundamental component of the human communicative experience.

Endnotes

Chapter 1

1 Some might argue that these outcomes are one and the same – that is, that children's survival *equates* to parental reproductive success. The truth is that direct procreation is only one route to reproductive success. In evolutionary terms, reproductive success is defined as replication of one's genetic material (see Nettle, 2009). This task can certainly be accomplished by producing genetic offspring, but it can also be achieved by supporting the health and viability of nieces, nephews, first cousins once removed, and others in succeeding generations who carry one's own genes. Thus, reproductive success benefits from direct procreation but does not require it, making the self's reproductive success and the survival of one's offspring related but nonredundant outcomes.

2 As nonhuman species, pets obviously cannot benefit humans' reproductive success in a direct manner. Research has shown, however, that having a pet – especially a domestic dog – increases men's attractiveness to women and women's willingness to date those men (see Gray, Volsche, Garcia, & Fisher, 2015; Guéguen & Ciccotti, 2008). Pet keeping therefore can contribute to reproductive success indirectly by increasing the likelihood of mating opportunities for pet owners.

3 Although it likely seems natural for humans to love their own children more than the children of others – and although this practice is clearly adaptive, because it helps ensure the survival of one's genetic material and its representation in future generations – Chiang (2017) provocatively questioned whether this practice is inevitable or even desirable.

Chapter 2

1 None of the theories described in the first part of this chapter was developed for the purpose of explaining and predicting affectionate behavior. Rather, each was developed to account for other phenomena (e.g., behavioral adaptation, politeness), and its tenets have been applied to the study of human affection. This caveat is important because some critiques of these theories *as*

they have been applied in affection research do not necessarily implicate the utility of the theories in total, but only of their abilities to account for affectionate behavior.

2 Importantly, this is true only to the extent that the advantageous characteristic is *heritable*, meaning transmitted from parent to offspring genetically rather than environmentally. Although Darwin observed that certain characteristics were passed from parents to children, he was unaware of the mechanism by which this occurred. It was not until Mendel's (1866) groundbreaking research on plant hybridization was fully appreciated that genes were understood to be that mechanism. Any physical (e.g., height) or mental (e.g., intelligence) characteristic that is at least partially heritable is subject to natural selection pressures, but environmentally acquired characteristics, such as education or wealth – even if they are advantageous for survival or procreation – are not.

3 Individual differences are undoubtedly manifested in the ability to convey and receive expressions of affection. Some variation is developmental. As children acquire linguistic and paralinguistic abilities, for instance, they consequently expand their behavioral repertoires for giving and reciprocating affectionate expressions. Later development of empathic accuracy (Hodges, Lewis, & Ickes, 2015), perspective-taking ability (Van der Graaff et al., 2014), self-monitoring (Tyler, Kearns, & McIntyre, 2016), and interpersonal sensitivity (Bech, Bille, Møller, Hellström, & Østergaard, 2014) should similarly aid in decoding affectionate behavior. Nondevelopmental individual variation is also observed, as in the cases of those suffering from alexithymia (Hesse & Floyd, 2011a, b) or Asperger syndrome (Sofronoff et al., 2011).

4 Importantly, this subpostulate applies only to affection communicated to one's *biological* children. Affection, or any resource, given to nonbiological children (such as stepchildren or adopted children) does not directly contribute to one's own procreation goal at all, because nonbiological children do not carry one's genetic material. In conjunction with subpostulate 4b, this observation suggests that parents communicate more affection to biological than nonbiological children (a principle theoretically supported, if affection is counted as a resource, by Daly and Wilson's theory of discriminative parental solicitude; see Daly & Wilson, 1983, 1985, 1988, 1995, 1996).

Chapter 4

1 While recognizing that these are culturally contested concepts, this book uses the term *sex* to distinguish between genetic males and females, and the term *gender* to refer to the socially and culturally prescribed role orientations of masculinity, femininity, and androgyny. By *sex composition*, this text refers to the pairing or grouping of individuals within relationships by sex (e.g., male–male, female–female, etc.).

2 It may be tempting to interpret these null results as evidence that women and men do not differ from each other in their affectionate behaviors. One must recall, however, that statistical probability is strongly biased in favor

of null results. "Not finding a difference" is therefore not the same as "finding no difference"; rather, null results appropriately call for the suspension of judgment.

3 The US Census Bureau considers individuals of African, Asian, Native American, Caucasian, and other backgrounds to comprise different *racial* categories, and people of Hispanic and non-Hispanic backgrounds to comprise different *ethnic* categories. Most published studies of affectionate behavior conflate the two distinctions methodologically by, for instance, comparing groups of African American, Hispanic, Asian, Native American, and Caucasian participants with each other. In its discussion of this research, this book therefore does not attempt to distinguish the effects of ethnicity from the effects of racial identity.

4 Genital touches were excluded from analysis due to a lack of variance; nearly every respondent rated them as highly inappropriate, regardless of racial identity, the sex of the parent, or the age of the child.

Chapter 5

1 The positive emotions were affection, amusement, happiness, interest, lust, pride, relief, serenity, and positive surprise. The emotion of relief was most accurately perceived, followed by lust, interest, serenity, and surprise.

2 Nonlinguistic vocalizations are actual vocal sounds that simply do not comprise words, so they are distinguished from vocal *characteristics* (such as pitch, volume, etc.) that previous studies had identified as having affectionate meaning.

3 In this context, *interpretation* refers not to the act of decoding (e.g., waving means "hello") but rather to the act of assigning broader relational meaning to a given behavior (e.g., waving means friendliness).

4 The masculinity score was the sum of participants' ratings on two adjective pairs: masculine/feminine, and manly/womanly.

5 There is evidence that at least one physiological marker associated with masculinity, average testosterone level, decreases in men as they become fathers. Gray, Kahlenberg, Barrett, Lipson, and Ellison (2002) reported such a decrease, speculating that it reflects nature's way of preparing men for the more nurturant role they would be required to play if their children were to have the best chances for survival (see also Storey, Walsh, Quinton, & Wynne-Edwards, 2000). Testosterone even declines in women when they marry and become mothers (Barrett et al., 2013).

6 In fact, Dillard, Solomon, and Palmer (1999) proposed that relational meanings can be collapsed into two superordinate factors: dominance and affiliation.

7 This part of the manipulation was tested by asking participants if they wanted to go ahead and volunteer for the prospective study, on the understanding that if participants were actually interested in the study, this would reverse the effect of the desire manipulation. No participants volunteered.

8 Certainly, it is not difficult to induce people to want to be liked by others; researchers such as Brown and Levinson (1987), Goffman (1959), and Maslow (1970) have pointed out that this is a fairly fundamental human

desire. The challenge was in inducing people to want to be disliked. The manipulation drew on the principle of negative face, or the desire to avoid obligation. We reasoned that if one's negative face were sufficiently threatened, one's desire to be liked could be overridden.

9 The dilemmas, adapted from Hale and Burgoon (1984), dealt with (1) the theft of a friend's valuables by a sibling, (2) one's Catholic friend who is contemplating abortion, (3) the infidelity of a best friend's fiancée, and (4) the impending visit of a cohabiting couple's unsuspecting parents. The topics were presented in a cyclical, counterbalanced order within conditions.

Chapter 6

1 The same is true for all monozygotic multiples, including triplets, quadruplets, and so on.

2 Countries, and even individual states within the United States, vary in the *degree* of genetic overlap required to prohibit or proscribe a legally or socially sanctioned sexual relationship, such as marriage. At present, fully half of the states in the United States allow first cousins (who have a degree of genetic overlap of 12.5 percent) to marry, although a few states limit such marriages to instances in which both parties are over a certain age or at least one party is infertile. Only eight US states criminalize sexual relationships between first cousins, and only four prohibit marriage between first cousins once removed (who have a 6.25 percent degree of genetic overlap).

3 The same is also true for males and females of many other species, particularly those characterized by internal gestation.

Chapter 7

1 Jakubiak and Feeney's (2017) model also proposes a neurobiological pathway by which touch contributes to neurochemical changes that reduce stress and contribute to physical well-being, but the focus in this chapter is on the model's implications for mental and psychological health.

2 The lists of symptoms for Asperger syndrome and autism spectrum disorder are illustrative, not exhaustive. Complete diagnostic criteria for autism spectrum disorder (which now encompasses what used to be diagnosed as Asperger syndrome) appear in the DSM-5.

Chapter 8

1 Light et al. (2005) also reported that the frequency of partner hugs was inversely related ($r = -.33$) with mean arterial pressure, an index of average arterial pressure that is calculated by doubling DBP, adding SBP, and dividing the sum by 3.

2 Due to the manner in which cortisol change was indexed in Floyd and Riforgiate (2008), significant negative beta scores support the hypothesis that diurnal cortisol change is positively related to affectionate communication.

3 This discussion of health detriments associated with affectionate communication specifically excludes the risks of sexual behavior, for two reasons. First, although oral, vaginal, and anal sexual contact can, and often do, denote affectionate feelings, they are also enacted in the absence of such emotions, so to group all sexual contact under the umbrella of affectionate communication would be inaccurate. Second, the health risks of sexual interaction are widely known and not necessary to reiterate here.

Chapter 9

1 Participants were instructed to select one platonic friend whom they considered a *close friend* but not their *best friend* and who was neither a relative nor a current or former romantic partner.
2 Relational boundary ambiguity items were: "I would wonder if my friend was trying to 'come on' to me," "I would think that my friend might be wanting something different from our friendship than I want," and "I would wonder whether my friend meant this in a romantic way."

Chapter 10

1 It should be noted that not all scientists agree that the placebo effect exists; some have suggested that it becomes clinically nonsignificant when compared with no-treatment control groups (see, e.g., Hróbjartsson & Gøtzsche, 2001).

References

Abercrombie, H. C., Giese-Davis, J., Sephton, S., Epel, E. S., Turner-Cobb, J. M., & Spiegel, D. (2004). Flattened cortisol rhythms in metastatic breast cancer patients. *Psychoneuroendocrinology*, *29*, 1082–1092. doi: 10.1016/j.psyneuen.2003.11.003

Acker, L. E., Acker, M. A., & Pearson, D. (1973). Generalized imitative affection: Relationship to prior kinds of imitation training. *Journal of Experimental Child Psychology*, *16*, 111–125. doi: 10.1016/0022-0965(73)90067-2

Acker, L. E., & Marton, J. (1984). Facilitation of affectionate-like behaviors in the play of young children. *Child Study Journal*, *14*(4), 255–269.

Ackerman, J. M., Griskevicius, V., & Li, N. P. (2011). Let's get serious: Communicating commitment in romantic relationships. *Journal of Personality and Social Psychology*, *100*, 1079–1094. doi: 10.1037/a0022412

Afifi, T. D., & Floyd, K. (2015). Communication, biology, and physiology: An introduction to the special issue. *Communication Monographs*, *82*, 1–3. doi: 10.1080/03637751.2015.1005964

Ainsworth, M., Blehar, M., Waters, E., & Wall, S. (2015). *Patterns of attachment: A psychological study of the strange situation*. New York: Routledge.

Åkerlind, I., & Hörnquist, J. O. (1992). Loneliness and alcohol abuse: A review of evidences of an interplay. *Social Science & Medicine*, *34*, 405–414. doi: 10.1016/0277-9536(92)90300-F

Aloia, L. S., Denes, A., & Crowley, J. C. (Eds.). (in press). *The Oxford handbook of the physiology of interpersonal communication*. Oxford: Oxford University Press.

Altemus, M., Deuster, E. G., Carter, C. S., & Gold, P. (1995). Suppression of hypothalamic-pituitary-adrenal axis responses to stress in lactating women. *Journal of Clinical Endocrinology and Metabolism*, *80*, 2954–2959. doi: 10.1210/jcem.80.10.7559880

Amato, P. R. (1994). Father–child relations, mother–child relations, and offspring psychological well-being in early adulthood. *Journal of Marriage and the Family*, *56*, 1031–1042. doi: 10.2307/353611

Amato, P. R., & Previti, D. (2003). People's reasons for divorcing: Gender, social class, the life course, and adjustment. *Journal of Family Issues*, *24*, 602–626. doi: 10.1177/0192513X03254507

American Psychiatric Association. (2013). *Diagnostic and statistical manual of mental disorders* (5th edn.). Washington, DC: Author.

Anderson, C. M., & Martin, M. M. (1995). The effects of communication motives, interaction involvement, and loneliness on satisfaction: A model of small groups. *Small Group Research*, 26, 118–137. doi: 10.1177/1046496495261007

Andreassi, J. L. (2006). *Psychophysiology: Human behavior and physiological response* (5th edn.). New York: Taylor & Francis.

Andrews, L., Attwood, T., & Sofronoff, K. (2013). Increasing the appropriate demonstration of affectionate behavior in children with Asperger syndrome, high functioning autism, and PDD-NOS: A randomized controlled trial. *Research in Autism Spectrum Disorders*, 7, 1568–1578. doi: 10.1016/j.rasd.2013.09.010

Angelini, L., Caon, M., Lalanne, D., Khaled, O. A., & Mugellini, E. (2014). Hugginess: Encouraging interpersonal touch through smart clothes. In *Proceedings of the 2014 ACM International Symposium on Wearable Computers, Adjunct Program*, 155–162. doi: 10.1145/2641248.2641356

Archer, J. (1997). Why do people love their pets? *Evolution and Human Behavior*, 18, 237–259. doi: 10.1016/S0162-3095(99)80001-4

Argiolas, A., & Gessa, G. L. (1991). Central functions of oxytocin. *Neuroscience Biobehavioral Reviews*, 15, 217–231. doi: 10.1016/S0149-7634(05)80002-8

Argyle, M., & Dean, J. (1965). Eye contact, distance, and affiliation. *Sociometry*, 28, 289–304. doi: 10.2307/2786027

Aron, A., Aron, E. N., & Smollan, D. (1992). Inclusion of Other in the Self Scale and the structure of interpersonal closeness. *Journal of Personality and Social Psychology*, 63, 596–612. doi: 10.1037/0022-3514.63.4.596

Aron, A., & Westbay, L. (1996). Dimensions of the prototype of love. *Journal of Personality and Social Psychology*, 70, 535–551. doi: 10.1037/0022-3514.70.3.535

Attwood, T. (2007). *The complete guide to Asperger's syndrome*. London: Jessica Kingsley Publishers.

Aylaz, R., Aktürk, Ü., Erci, B., Öztürk, H., & Aslan, H. (2012). Relationship between depression and loneliness in elderly and examination of influential factors. *Archives of Gerontology and Geriatrics*, 55, 548–554. doi: 10.1016/j.archger.2012.03.006

Bacon, S. L., Ring, C., Lip, G. Y., & Carroll, D. (2004). Increases in lipids and immune cells in response to exercise and mental stress in patients with suspected coronary artery disease: Effects of adjustments for shifts in plasma volume. *Biological Psychology*, 65, 237–250. doi: 10.1016/S0301-0511(03)00113-3

Bagby, R. M., Parker, J. D. A., & Taylor, G. J. (1994). The twenty-item Toronto Alexithymic Scale – I. Item selection and cross-validation of the factor structure. *Journal of Psychosomatic Research*, 38, 23–32. doi: 10.1016/0022-3999(94)90005-1

Bailey, A. A., & Hurd, P. L. (2005). Finger length ratio (2D:4D) correlates with physical aggression in men but not in women. *Biological Psychology*, 68, 215–222. doi: 10.1016/j.biopsycho.2004.05.001

Bakerman-Kranenburg, M. J., & van Ijzendoorn, M. H. (2006). Gene–environment interaction of the dopamine D4 receptor (DRD4) and observed maternal insensitivity predicting externalizing behavior in preschoolers. *Developmental Psychobiology, 48,* 406–409. doi: 10.1002/dev.20152

Bandura, A. (1971). *Social learning theory.* Morristown, NJ: General Learning Press.

Bangee, M., Harris, R. A., Bridger, N., Rotenberg, J. J., & Qualter, P. (2014). Loneliness and attention to social threat in young adults: Findings from an eye tracker study. *Personality and Individual Differences, 63,* 16–23. doi: 10.1016/j.paid.2014.01.039

Banham, K. M. (1950). The development of affectionate behavior in infancy. *Journal of Genetic Psychology, 76,* 283–289. doi: 10.1080/08856559 .1950.10534079

Barber, B. K., & Thomas, D. L. (1986). Dimensions of fathers' and mothers' supportive behavior: The case for physical affection. *Journal of Marriage and the Family, 48,* 783–794. doi: 10.2307/352571

Baron-Cohen, S., Wheelwright, S., Hill, J., Raste, Y., & Plumb, I. (2001). The "Reading the Mind in the Eyes" Test revised version: A study with normal adults, and adults with Asperger syndrome or high-functioning autism. *Journal of Child Psychology and Psychiatry and Allied Disciplines, 42,* 241–251. doi: 10.1017/S0021963001006643

Barrett, E. S., Tran, V., Thurston, S., Jasienska, G., Furberg, A.-S., Ellison, P. T., & Thune I. (2013). Marriage and motherhood are associated with lower testosterone concentrations in women. *Hormones and Behavior, 63,* 72–79. doi: 10.1016/j.yhbeh.2012.10.012

Barrowclough, C., Tarrier, N., Humphreys, L., Ward, J., Gregg, L., & Andrews, B. (2003). Self-esteem in schizophrenia: Relationships between self-evaluation, family attitudes, and symptomatology. *Journal of Abnormal Psychology, 112,* 92–99. doi: 10.1037/0021-843X.112.1.92

Bartels, A., & Zeki, S. (2000). The neural basis of romantic love. *NeuroReport, 11,* 3829–3834. doi: 10.1097/00001756-200011270-00046

Bartholomew, K. (1990). Avoidance of intimacy: An attachment perspective. *Journal of Social and Personal Relationships, 7,* 147–158. doi: 10.1177/ 0265407590072001

Bartholomew, K., & Horowitz, L. M. (1991). Attachment styles among young adults: A test of a four-category model. *Journal of Personality and Social Psychology, 61,* 226–244. doi: 10.1037/0022-3514.61.2.226

Bateman, A. J. (1948). Intra-sexual selection in Drosophila. *Heredity, 2,* 349–368. doi: 10.1038/hdy.1948.21

Bauer, M., Priebe, S., Häring, B., & Adamczak, K. (1993). Long-term mental sequelae of political imprisonment in East Germany. *Journal of Nervous and Mental Disease, 181,* 257–262. doi: 10.1097/00005053-199304000-00007

Baumeister, R. F., Brewer, L. E., Tice, D. M., & Twenge, J. M. (2007). Thwarting the need to belong: Understanding the interpersonal and inner effects of social exclusion. *Social and Personality Psychology Compass, 1,* 506–520. doi: 10.1111/j.1751.9004-2007.00020.x

Baumeister, R. F., Campbell, J. D., Krueger, J. I., & Vohs, K. D. (2003). Does high self-esteem cause better performance, interpersonal success, happiness, or healthier lifestyles? *Psychological Science in the Public Interest, 4,* 1–44. doi: 10.1111/1529-1006.01431

Baumeister, R. F., & Leary, M. R. (1995). The need to belong: Desire for interpersonal attachments as a fundamental human motivation. *Psychological Bulletin, 117,* 497–529. doi: 10.1037/0033-2909.117.3.497

Baumeister, R. F., Wotman, S. R., & Stillwell, A. M. (1993). Unrequited love: On heartbreak, anger, guilt, scriptlessness, and humiliation. *Journal of Personality and Social Psychology, 64,* 377–394. doi: 10.1037/0022-3514.64.3.377

Baxter, A. J., Brugha, T. S., Erskine, H. E., Scheurer, R. W., Vos, T., & Scott, J. G. (2015). The epidemiology and global burden of autism spectrum disorders. *Psychological Medicine, 45,* 601–613. doi: 10.1017/S003329171400172X

Baxter, L. A., & Wilmot, W. W. (1984). "Secret tests": Social strategies for acquiring information about the state of the relationship. *Human Communication Research, 11,* 171–202. doi: 10.1111/j.1468-2958.1984.tb00044.x

Beaton, D. E., Bombardier, C., Guillemin, F., & Ferraz, M. B. (2000). Guidelines for the process of cross-cultural adaptation of self-report measures. *Spine, 25,* 3186–3191. doi: 10.1097/00007632-200012150-00014

Beatty, M. J., McCroskey, J. C., & Floyd, K. (Eds.). (2009). *Biological dimensions of communication: Perspectives, methods, and research.* Creskill, NJ: Hampton Press.

Bech, P., Bille, J., Møller, S. B., Hellström, L. C., & Østergaard, S. D. (2014). Psychometric validation of the Hopkins Symptom Checklist (SCL-90) subscales for depression, anxiety, and interpersonal sensitivity. *Journal of Affective Disorders, 160,* 98–103. doi: 10.1016/j.jad.2013.12.005

Bell, R. A., Buerkel-Rothfuss, N. L., & Gore, K. E. (1987). "Did you bring the yarmulke for the Cabbage Patch Kid?" Idiomatic communication of young lovers. *Human Communication Research, 14,* 47–67. doi: 10.1111/j.1468-2958.1987.tb00121.x

Bell, R. A., & Healey, J. G. (1992). Idiomatic communication and interpersonal solidarity in friends' relational cultures. *Human Communication Research, 18,* 307–335. doi: 10.1111/j.1468-2958.1992.tb00555.x

Belsky, J., & Pensky, E. (1988). Marital change across the transition to parenthood. *Marriage & Family Review, 12,* 133–156. doi: 10.1300/J002v12n03_08

Bem, S. L. (1974). The measurement of psychological androgyny. *Journal of Consulting and Clinical Psychology, 42,* 155–162. doi: 10.1037/h0036215

Bernhardt, P. C., Dabbs, J. M., Fielden, J. A., & Lutter, C. D. (1998). Testosterone changes during vicarious experiences of winning and losing among fans at sporting events. *Physiology & Behavior, 65,* 59–62. doi: 10.1016/S0031-9384(98)00147-4

Bernhold, Q. S., & Giles, H. (2017, November). Ethnic differences in grandparent–grandchild affectionate communication. Paper presented at the annual meeting of the National Communication Association, Dallas, TX.

(in press). Paternal grandmothers benefit the most from expressing affection to grandchildren: An extension of evolutionary and sociological research. *Journal of Social and Personal Relationships.* Advance online publication. doi: 10.1177/0265407517734657

Bernstein, I. H., & Nunnally, J. C. (1994). *Psychometric theory*. New York: McGraw-Hill.

Berscheid, E., Snyder, M., & Omoto, A. M. (1989). The relationship closeness inventory: Assessing the closeness of interpersonal relationships. *Journal of Personality and Social Psychology, 57*, 792–807. doi: 10.1037/0022-3514.57.5.792

Bjorklund, D. F., & Shackelford, T. K. (1999). Differences in parental investment contribute to important differences between men and women. *Current Directions in Psychological Science, 8*, 86–89. doi: 10.1111/1467-8721.00020

Blanchflower, D. G., & Oswald, A. J. (2004). Money, sex and happiness: An empirical study. *Scandinavian Journal of Economics, 106*, 393–415. doi: 10.1111/j.0347-0520.2004.00369.x

Blascovich, J., & Tomaka, J. (1991). Measures of self-esteem. In J. P. Robinson, P. R. Shaver, & L. S. Wrightsman (Eds.), *Measures of personality and social psychological attitudes* (Vol. 1, pp. 115–160). San Diego, CA: Academic Press.

Blier, M. J., & Blier-Wilson, L. A. (1989). Gender differences in self-rated emotional expressiveness. *Sex Roles, 21*, 287–295. doi: 10.1007/BF00289908

Blum, D. (2002). *Love at Goon Park: Harry Harlow and the science of affection*. Cambridge, MA: Perseus.

Bombar, M. L., & Littig, L. W. (1996). Babytalk as a communication of intimate attachment: An initial study in adult romances and friendships. *Personal Relationships, 3*, 137–158. doi: 10.1111/j.1475-6811.1996.tb00108.x

Bond, B. J., & Calvert, S. L. (2014). A model and measure of U.S. parents' perceptions of young children's parasocial relationships. *Journal of Children and Media, 8*, 286–304. doi: 10.1080/17482798.2014.890948

Bonta, J., & Gendreau, P. (1995). Re-examining the cruel and unusual punishment of prison life. In T. J. Flanagan (Ed.), *Long-term imprisonment: Policy, science, and correctional practice* (pp. 75–84). Thousand Oaks, CA: Sage.

Booth, A., Shelley, G., Mazur, A., Tharp, G., & Kittok, R. (1989). Testosterone, and winning and losing in human competition. *Hormones and Behavior, 23*, 556–571. doi: 10.1016/0018-506X(89)90042-1

Booth-Butterfield, M., & Trotta, M. R. (1994). Attributional patterns for expressions of love. *Communication Reports, 7*, 119–129. doi: 10.1080/08934219409367594

Botkin, D., & Twardosz, S. (1988). Early childhood teachers' affectionate behavior: Differential expression to female children, male children, and groups of children. *Early Childhood Research Quarterly, 3*, 167–177. doi: 10.1016/0885-2006(88)90020-8

Bowlby, J. (1969). *Attachment and loss*, Vol. 1: *Attachment*. New York: Basic Books.

(1973). *Attachment and loss*, Vol. 2: *Separation anxiety and anger*. New York: Basic Books.

Bradbury, T. N., & Fincham, F. D. (1990). Attributions in marriage: Review and critique. *Psychological Bulletin, 107*, 3–33. doi: 10.1037/0033-2909.107.1.3

(1992). Attributions for behavior in marital interaction. *Journal of Personality and Social Psychology, 63*, 613–628. doi: 10.1037/0022-3514.63.4.613

Brown, G. K., Beck, A. T., Steer, R. A., & Grisham, J. R. (2000). Risk factors for suicide in psychiatric outpatients: A 20-year prospective study. *Journal of Consulting and Clinical Psychology*, *68*, 371–377. doi: 10.1037/0022-006X.68.3.371

Brown, P., & Levinson, S. C. (1987). *Politeness: Some universals in language usage.* Cambridge: Cambridge University Press.

Brown, S. L., Fredrickson, B. L., Wirth, M. M., Poulin, M. J., Meier, E. A., Heaphy, E. D., ... Schultheiss, O. C. (2009). Social closeness increases salivary progesterone in humans. *Hormones and Behavior*, *56*, 108–111. doi: 10.1016/j.yhbeh.2009.03.022

Burgoon, J. K. (1978). A communication model of personal space violations: Explication and an initial test. *Human Communication Research*, *4*, 129–142. doi: 10.1111/j.1468-2958.1978.tb00603.x

(1995). Cross-cultural and intercultural applications of expectancy violations theory. In R. L. Wiseman (Ed.), *International and intercultural communication annual*, Vol. 19: *Intercultural communication theory* (pp. 194–214). Thousand Oaks, CA: Sage.

Burgoon, J. K., Allspach, L. E., & Miczo, N. (1997, February). Needs, expectancies, goals, and initial interaction: A view from interaction adaptation theory. Paper presented at the annual meeting of the Western States Communication Association, Monterey, CA.

Burgoon, J. K., Coker, D. A., & Coker, R. A. (1986). Communicative effects of gaze behavior: A test of two contrasting explanations. *Human Communication Research*, *12*, 495–524. doi: 10.1111/j.1468-2958.1986.tb00089.x

Burgoon, J. K., Dillman, L., & Stern, L. A. (1993). Adaptation in dyadic interaction: Defining and operationalizing patterns of reciprocity and compensation. *Communication Theory*, *4*, 293–316. doi: 10.1111/j.1468-2885.1993.tb00076.x

Burgoon, J. K., & Hale, J. L. (1984). The fundamental topoi of relational communication. *Communication Monographs*, *51*, 193–214. doi: 10.1080/03637758409390195

(1987). Validation and measurement of the fundamental themes of relational communication. *Communication Monographs*, *54*, 19–41. doi: 10.1080/03637758709390214

(1988). Nonverbal expectancy violations: Model elaboration and application to immediacy behaviors. *Communication Monographs*, *55*, 58–79. doi: 10.1080/03537758809376158

Burgoon, J. K., & Le Poire, B. A. (1993). Effects of communication expectancies, actual communication, and expectancy disconfirmation on evaluations of communicators and their communication behavior. *Human Communication Research*, *20*, 67–96. doi: 10.1111/j.1468-2958.1993.tb00316.x

(1999). Nonverbal cues and interpersonal judgments: Participant and observer perceptions of intimacy, dominance, composure, and formality. *Communication Monographs*, *66*, 105–124. doi: 10.1080/03637759909376467

Burgoon, J. K., Manusov, V., Mineo, P., & Hale, J. L. (1985). Effects of eye gaze on hiring, credibility, attraction, and relational message interpretation. *Journal of Nonverbal Behavior*, *9*, 133–146. doi: 10.1007/BF01000735

Burgoon, J. K., & Newton, D. A. (1991). Applying a social meaning model to relational message interpretations of conversational involvement: Comparing observer and participant perspectives. *Southern Communication Journal, 56*, 96–113. doi: 10.1080/10417949109372822

Burgoon, J. K., Newton, D. A., Walther, J. B., & Baesler, E. J. (1989). Nonverbal expectancy violations and conversational involvement. *Journal of Nonverbal Behavior, 13*, 97–120. doi: 10.1007/BF00990793

Burgoon, J. K., Stern, L. A., & Dillman, L. (1995). *Interpersonal adaptation: Dyadic interaction patterns.* New York: Cambridge University Press.

Burgoon, J. K., & Walther, J. B. (1990). Nonverbal expectancies and the evaluative consequences of violations. *Human Communication Research, 17*, 232–265. doi: 10.1111/j.1468-2958.1990.tb00232.x

Burgoon, J. K., Walther, J. B., & Baesler, E. J. (1992). Interpretations, evaluations, and consequences of interpersonal touch. *Human Communication Research, 19*, 237–263. doi: 10.1111/j.1468-2958.1992.tb00301.x

Burleson, M. H., Roberts, N. A., Coon, D. W., & Soto, J. A. (in press). Perceived cultural acceptability and comfort with affectionate touch: Differences between Mexican Americans and European Americans. *Journal of Social and Personal Relationships.* doi: 10.1177/0265407517750005

Burleson, M. H., Trevathan, W. R., & Todd, M. (2007). In the mood for love or vice versa? Exploring the relations among sexual activity, physical affection, affect, and stress in the daily lives of mid-aged women. *Archives of Sexual Behavior, 36*, 357–368. doi: 10.1007/s10508-006-9071-1

Buss, D. M. (1989). Sex differences in human mate preferences: Evolutionary hypotheses tested in 37 cultures. *Behavioral and Brain Sciences, 12*, 1–49. doi: 10.1017/S0140545X00023992

(1994). The strategies of human mating. *American Scientist, 82*(3), 238–249.

(2006). The evolution of love. In R. J. Sternberg & K. Weis (Eds.), *The new psychology of love* (pp. 65–86). New Haven, CT: Yale University Press.

(2015). *Evolutionary psychology: The new science of the mind* (5th edn.). New York: Routledge.

Buss, D. M., & Schmidt, D. P. (1993). Sexual strategies theory: An evolutionary perspective on human mating. *Psychological Review, 100*, 204–232. doi: 10.1037/0033-295X.100.2.204

Cabibihan, J.-J., & Chauhan, S. S. (2017). Physiological responses to affective tele-touch during induced emotional stimuli. *IEEE Transactions on Affective Computing, 8*, 108–118. doi: 10.1109/TAFFC.2015.2509985

Cacioppo, J. T., & Cacioppo, S. (2014). Social relationships and health: The toxic effects of perceived social isolation. *Social and Personality Psychology Compass, 8*, 58–72. doi: 10.1111/spc3.12087

Cacioppo, J. T., Hawkley, L. C., Ernst, J. M., Burleson, M., Berntson, G. G., Nouriani, B., & Spiegel, D. (2006). Loneliness within a nomological net: An evolutionary perspective. *Journal of Research in Personality, 40*, 1054–1085. doi: 10.1016/j.jrp.2005.11.007

Cacioppo, J. T., & Patrick, W. (2008). *Loneliness: Human nature and the need for social connection.* New York: W. W. Norton.

Cacioppo, J. T., Tassinary, L. G., & Berntson, G. G. (Eds.). (2017). *Handbook of psychophysiology* (4th edn.). Cambridge: Cambridge University Press.

Calvo, R. A., Brown, I., & Scheding, S. (2009). Effects of experimental factors on the recognition of affective mental states through physiological measures. *Proceedings of the 22nd Australasian Joint Conference on Artificial Intelligence*, *5866*, 62–70. doi: 10.1007/978-3-642-10439-8_7

Calzada, E. J., & Eyberg, S. M. (2002). Self-reported parenting practices in Dominican and Puerto Rican mothers of young children. *Journal of Clinical Child and Adolescent Psychology*, *31*, 354–363. doi: 10.1207/S15374424JCCP3103_07

Canary, D. J., & Stafford, L. (1992). Relational maintenance strategies and equity in marriage. *Communication Monographs*, *59*, 243–267. doi: 10.1080/03637759209376268

Canli, T., & Lesch, K.-P. (2007). Long story short: The serotonin transporter in emotion regulation and social cognition. *Nature Neuroscience*, *10*, 1103–1109. doi: 10.1038/nn1964

Caraway, S. J. (1998). Sexual coercion: Factors associated with women's reported experience of verbal coercion. (Doctoral dissertation, University of North Dakota.) *Dissertation Abstracts International*, *58*(9-B), 5109.

Carbury, L. J. (1975). Infectious mononucleosis: The kissing disease. *Nursing Care*, *8*(1), 22–24.

Carmichael, M. S., Humbert, R., Dixen, J., Palmiana, G., Greenleaf, W., & Davidson, J. M. (1987). Plasma oxytocin increase in the human sexual response. *Journal of Clinical Endocrinology and Metabolism*, *64*, 27–31. doi: 10.1210/jcem-64-1-27

Carmichael, M. S., Warburton, V. L., Dixen, J., & Davidson, J. M. (1994). Relationships among cardiovascular, muscular, and oxytocin responses during human sexual activity. *Archives of Sexual Behavior*, *23*, 59–79. doi: 10.1007/BF01541618

Carroll, J. E., Gruenewald, T. L., Taylor, S. E., Janicki-Deverts, D., Matthews, K. A., & Seeman, T. E. (2013). Childhood abuse, parental warmth, and adult multisystem biological risk in the Coronary Artery Risk Development in Young Adults study. *Proceedings of the National Academy of Sciences*, *110*, 17149–17153. doi: 10.1073/pnas.1315458110

Carter, C. S., & Altemus, M. (1997). Integrative functions of lactational hormones in social behavior and stress management. In C. S. Carter, I. I. Lederhendler, & B. Kirkpatrick (Eds.), *The integrative neurobiology of affiliation* (pp. 361–372). New York: Annals of the New York Academy of Sciences.

Carton, S. T., & Horan, S. M. (2014). A diary examination of romantic and sexual partners withholding affectionate messages. *Journal of Social and Personal Relationships*, *31*, 221–246. doi: 10.1177/0265407513490587

Cervera, S., Lahortiga, F., Martínez-González, M. A., Gual, P., de Irala-Estévez, J., & Alonso, Y. (2003). Neuroticism and low self-esteem as risk factors for incident eating disorders in a prospective cohort study. *International Journal of Eating Disorders*, *33*, 271–280. doi: 10.1002/eat.10147

Chang, D. (2017). Gratifications associated with Snapchat usage among young people: Uses and gratifications analysis. (Master's thesis, Iowa State University.) Retrieved from ProQuest Dissertations and Theses database (UMI No. 10268038).

Chiang, T. (2017, December 31). What if parents loved strangers' children as much as their own? *The New Yorker* (online). Retrieved January 3, 2018, from www.newyorker.com/tech/elements/what-if-parents-loved-strangers-children-as-much-as-their-own.

Chiodera, P., Salvarani, C., Bacchi-Modena, A., Spallanzani, R., Cigarini, C., Alboni, A., ... Coiro, V. (1991). Relationship between plasma profiles of oxytocin and adrenocorticotropic hormones during suckling or breast stimulation in women. *Hormone Research*, *35*, 119–123. doi: 10.1159/000181886

Chobainai, A. V., Bakris, G. L., Black, H. R., Cushman, W. C., Green, L. A., Izzo, J. L., ... the National High Blood Pressure Education Program Coordinating Committee. (2003). The seventh report of the Joint National Committee on Prevention, Detection, Evaluation, and Treatment of High Blood Pressure. *Journal of the American Medical Association*, *289*, 2560–2572. doi: 10.1001/jama.289.19.2560

Christopher, S. E., Bauman, K. E., & Veness-Meehan, K. (1999). Measurement of affectionate behaviors adolescent mothers display toward their infants in neonatal intensive care. *Issues in Comprehensive Pediatric Nursing*, *22*, 1–11. doi: 10.1080/014608699265356

(2000). Perceived stress, social support, and affectionate behaviors of adolescent mothers with infants in neonatal intensive care. *Journal of Pediatric Health Care*, *14*, 288–296. doi: 10.1067/mph.2000.106136

Clipman, J. M. (1999, March). A hug a day keeps the blues away: The effect of daily hugs on subjective well-being in college students. Paper presented at the annual meeting of the Eastern Psychological Association, Boston, MA.

Coan, J. A., & Allen, J. J. B. (2003). Frontal EEG asymmetry and the behavioral activation and inhibition systems. *Psychophysiology*, *40*, 106–114. doi: 10.1111/1469-8985.00011

Coan, J. A., Allen, J. J. B., Malone, S., & Iacono, W. G. (2003). The heritability of trait midfrontal EEG asymmetry and negative emotionality: Sex differences and genetic nonadditivity. *Psychophysiology*, *40*, S34. doi: 10.1111/1469-8986.40.s1.1

Coan, J. A., Schaefer, H. S., & Davidson, R. J. (2006). Lending a hand: Social regulation of the neural response to threat. *Psychological Science*, *17*, 1032–1039. doi: 10.1111/j.1467-9280.2006-01832.x

Coe, C. L., & Lubach, G. R. (2001). Social context and other psychological influences on the development of immunity. In C. D. Ryff & B. H. Singer (Eds.), *Emotion, social relationships, and health* (pp. 243–261). Oxford: Oxford University Press.

Cohen, S., Janicki-Deverts, D., Turner, R. B., & Doyle, W. J. (2015). Does hugging provide stress-buffering social support? A study of susceptibility to upper respiratory infection and illness. *Psychological Science*, *26*, 135–147. doi: 10.1177/0956797614559284

Cohen, S., Kamarck, T., & Mermelstein, R. (1983). A global measure of perceived stress. *Journal of Health and Social Behavior, 24,* 386–396. doi: 10.2307/2136404

Comer, R. J. (2017). *Abnormal psychology* (9th edn.). New York: Worth.

Compton, M. V., & Niemeyer, J. A. (1994). Expressions of affection in young children with sensory impairments: A research agenda. *Education and Treatment of Children, 17*(1), 68–85.

Corbett, B. A., Mendoza, S., Abdullah, M., Wegelin, J. A., & Levine, S. (2006). Cortisol circadian rhythms and response to stress in children with autism. *Psychoneuroendocrinology, 31,* 59–68. doi: 10.1016/j.psyneuen.2005.05.011

Cosmides, L. L., & Tooby, J. (1992). Cognitive adaptations for social exchange. In J. Barkow, L. L. Cosmides, & J. Tooby (Eds.), *The adapted mind* (pp. 163–228). New York: Oxford University Press.

Costa, D. L. G., Chisik, Y., & Faria, A. L. D. S. (2018). Hugvie as a therapeutic agent in the improvement of interaction skills in children with developmental disabilities: An exploratory study. In A. D. Cheok, M. Inami, & T. Romão (Eds.), *Advances in computer entertainment technology* (pp. 117–127). Cham: Springer International.

Costa, M. D., Davis, R. B., & Goldberger, A. L. (2017). Heart rate fragmentation: A new approach to the analysis of cardiac interbeat interval dynamics. *Frontiers in Physiology, 8,* article 255. doi: 10.3389/fphys.2017.00255

Cowan, C. P., & Cowan, P. A. (1987). Men's involvement in parenthood: Identifying the antecedents and understanding the barriers. In P. W. Berman & F. A. Pedersen (Eds.), *Men's transitions to parenthood: Longitudinal studies of early family experience* (pp. 145–174). Hillsdale, NJ: Lawrence Erlbaum Associates.

Cowan, F. M., Copas, A., Johnson, A. M., Ashley, R., Corey, L., & Mindel, A. (2002). Herpes simplex virus type 1 infection: A sexually transmitted infection of adolescence? *Sexually Transmitted Infections, 78,* 346–348. doi: 10.1136/sti.78.5.346

Cowgill, B. O., Bogart, L. M., Corona, R., Ryan, G., & Schuster, M. A. (2008). Fears about HIV transmission in families with an HIV-infected parent: A qualitative analysis. *Pediatrics, 122,* e950–e958. doi: 10.1542/peds.2008-0390

Cross, A. (2006, March 29). Rise of the "cuddle party." *The Tyee.* Retrieved from https://thetyee.ca/Life/2006/03/29/CuddleParty/.

Csathó, A., Osváth, A., Bicsák, E., Karádi, K., Manning, J., & Kállai, J. (2003). Sex role identity related to the ratio of second to fourth digit length in women. *Biological Psychology, 62,* 147–156. doi: 10.1016/S0301-0511(02)00127-8

Curran, T. M., & Yoshimura, S. M. (2016). Mother–child reports of affectionate communication with fathers: Associations with family satisfaction and life satisfaction. *Communication Reports, 29,* 163–174. doi: 10.1080/08934215.2016.117071

Dabbs, J. M., Frady, R. L., Carr, T. S., & Besch, N. F. (1987). Saliva testosterone and criminal violence in young adult prison inmates. *Psychosomatic Medicine, 49,* 174–182. doi: 10.1097/00006842-198703000-00007

Dabbs, J. M., Ruback, R. B., Frady, R. L., Hopper, C. H., & Sgoutas, D. S. (1988). Saliva testosterone and criminal violence among women. *Personality and Individual Differences*, *9*, 269–275. doi: 10.1016/0191-8869(88)90088-8

Dainton, M. (1998). Everyday interaction in marital relationships: Variations in relative importance and event duration. *Communication Reports*, *11*, 101–109. doi: 10.1080/08934219809367692

Dainton, M., Stafford, L., & Canary, D. J. (1994). Maintenance strategies and physical affection as predictors of love, liking, and satisfaction in marriage. *Communication Reports*, *7*, 88–98. doi: 10.1080/08934219409367591

Daly, M., & Wilson, M. (1983). *Sex, evolution, and behavior* (2nd edn.). Belmont, CA: Wadsworth.

(1985). Child abuse and other risks of not living with both parents. *Ethology and Sociobiology*, *6*, 197–210. doi: 10.1016/0162-3095(85)90012-3

(1988). *Homicide*. Hawthorne, NY: Aldine.

(1995). Discriminative parental solicitude and the relevance of evolutionary models to the analysis of motivational systems. In M. S. Gazzaniga (Ed.), *The cognitive neurosciences* (pp. 1269–1286). Cambridge, MA: MIT Press.

(1996). Violence against stepchildren. *Current Directions in Psychological Science*, *5*, 77–81. doi: 10.1111/1467-8721.ep10772793

Darwin, C. (1859). *On the origin of species*. London: J. Murray.

(1872/1965). *The expression of the emotions in man and animals*. Chicago, IL: University of Chicago Press.

Davidson, R. J. (1993). Parsing affective space: Perspectives from neuropsychology and psychophysiology. *Neuropsychology*, *7*, 464–475. doi: 10.1037/0894-4105.7.4.464

(1995). Cerebral asymmetry, emotion, and affective style. In R. J. Davidson & K. Hugdahl (Eds.), *Brain asymmetry* (pp. 361–387). Cambridge, MA: MIT Press.

(1998). Affective style and affective disorders: Perspectives from affective neuroscience. *Cognition and Emotion*, *12*, 307–330. doi: 10.1080/026999398379628

Davis, M. H., Luce, C., & Kraus, S. J. (1994). The heritability of characteristics associated with dispositional empathy. *Journal of Personality*, *62*, 369–391. doi: 10.1111/j.1467-6494.1994.tb00302.x

Dawson, B. L., & McIntosh, W. D. (2006). Sexual strategies theory and Internet personal advertisements. *CyberPsychology & Behavior*, *9*, 614–617. doi: 10.1089/cpb.2006.9.614

Debrot, A., Meuwly, N., Muise, A., Impett, E. A., & Schoebi, D. (2017). More than just sex: Affection mediates the association between sexual activity and well-being. *Personality and Social Psychology Bulletin*, *43*, 287–299. doi: 10.1177/0146167216681247

Debrot, A., Schoebi, D., Perrez, M., & Horn, A. B. (2013). Touch as an interpersonal emotion regulation process in couples' daily lives: The mediating role of psychological intimacy. *Personality and Social Psychology Bulletin*, *39*, 1373–1385. doi: 10.1177/0146167213497592

Denes, A. (2012). Pillow talk: Exploring disclosures after sexual activity. *Western Journal of Communication*, *76*, 91–108. doi: 10.1080/10570314.2011.651253

Denes, A., Afifi, T. D., & Granger, D. A. (2017). Physiology and pillow talk: Relations between testosterone and communication post sex. *Journal of Social and Personal Relationships, 34,* 281–308. doi: 10.1177/0265407516634470

Denes, A., Bennett, M., & Winkler, K. L. (2017). Exploring the benefits of affectionate communication: Implications for interpersonal acceptance–rejection theory. *Journal of Family Theory & Review, 9,* 491–506. doi: 10.1111/jftr.12218

Dickerson, S. S., & Kemeny, M. E. (2004). Acute stressors and cortisol responses: A theoretical integration and synthesis of laboratory research. *Psychological Bulletin, 130,* 355–391. doi: 10.1037/0033-2090.130.3.355

Diego, M. A., Field, T., Hernandez-Reif, M., Shaw, K., Friedman, L., & Ironson, G. (2001). HIV adolescents show improved immune function following massage therapy. *International Journal of Neuroscience, 106,* 35–45. doi: 10.3109/00207450109149736

Diener, E., Emmons, R. A., Larsen, R. J., & Griffin, S. (1985). The Satisfaction with Life Scale. *Journal of Personality Assessment, 49,* 71–75. doi: 10.1207/s15327752jpa4901_13

Dillard, J. P., Solomon, D. H., & Palmer, M. T (1999). Structuring the concept of relational communication. *Communication Monographs, 66,* 49–65. doi: 10.1080/03637759909376462

Dillow, M. R., Goodboy, A. K., & Bolkan, S. (2014). Attachment and the expression of affection in romantic relationships: The mediating role of romantic love. *Communication Reports, 27,* 102–115. doi: 10.1080/08934215.2014.900096

Ditzen, B., Hoppmann, C., & Klumb, P. (2008). Positive couple interactions and daily cortisol: On the stress-protecting role of intimacy. *Psychosomatic Medicine, 70,* 883–889. doi: 10.1097/PSY.0b013e318185c4fc

Ditzen, B., Neumann, I. D., Bodenmann, G., von Dawans, B., Turner, R. A., Ehlert, U., & Heinrichs, M. (2007). Effects of different kinds of couple interaction on cortisol and heart rate responses to stress in women. *Psychoneuroendocrinology, 32,* 565–574. doi: 10.1016/j.psyneuen.2007.03.011

Doherty, W. J. (1991). Beyond reactivity and the deficit model of manhood: A commentary on articles by Napier, Pittman, and Gottman. *Journal of Marital and Family Therapy, 17,* 29–32. doi: 10.1111/j.1752-0606.1991.tb00860.x

Donnelly, D. A., & Burgess, E. O. (2008). The decision to remain in an involuntarily celibate relationship. *Journal of Marriage and Family, 70,* 519–535. doi: 10.1111/j.1741-3737.2008.00498.x

Donovan, N. J., Wu, Q., Rentz, D. M., Sperling, R. A., Marshall, G. A., & Glymour, M. M. (2017). Loneliness, depression and cognitive function in older U.S. adults. *International Journal of Geriatric Psychiatry, 32,* 564–573. doi: 10.1002/gps.4495

Doss, B. D., Simpson, L. E., & Christensen, A. (2004). Why do couples seek marital therapy? *Professional Psychology: Research and Practice, 35,* 608–614. doi: 10.1037/0735-7028.35.6.608

Downs, V. C., & Javidi, M. (1990). Linking communication motives to loneliness in the lives of older adults: An empirical test of interpersonal needs and gratifications. *Journal of Applied Communication Research*, *18*, 32–48. doi: 10.1080/00909889009360313

Draper, T. W., & Gordon, T. (1986). Men's perceptions of nurturing behavior in other men. *Psychological Reports*, *59*, 11–18. doi: 10.2466/pr0.1986.59.1.11

Drescher, V. M., Whitehead, W. E., Morrill-Corbin, E. D., & Cataldo, M. F. (1985). Physiological and subjective reactions to being touched. *Psychophysiology*, *22*, 96–100. doi: 10.1111/j.1469-8986.1985.tb01565

Eberly, M. B., & Montemayor, R. (1998). Doing good deeds: An examination of adolescent prosocial behavior in the context of parent–adolescent relationships. *Journal of Adolescent Research*, *13*, 403–432. doi: 10.1177/0743554898134003

(1999). Adolescent affection and helpfulness toward parents: A 2-year follow-up. *Journal of Early Adolescence*, *19*, 226–248. doi: 10/1177/27243169002005

Ehrenkranz, J., Bliss, E., & Sheard, M. H. (1974). Plasma testosterone: Correlation with aggressive behavior and social dominance in men. *Psychosomatic Medicine*, *36*, 469–475. doi: 10.1097/00006842-197411000-00002

Eibl-Eibesfeldt, I. (1972). Similarities and differences between cultures in expressive movements. In R. A. Hinde (Ed.), *Non-verbal communication* (pp. 294–314). New York: Cambridge University Press.

Ekman, P., & Friesen, W. V. (1969). The repertoire of nonverbal behavior: Categories, origins, usage, and coding. *Semiotica*, *1*, 49–98. doi: 10.1515/semi-1969.1.1.49

(1975). *Unmasking the face: A guide to recognizing emotions from facial expressions.* Los Altos, CA: Malor Books.

Ekman, P., Friesen, W. V., & Ellsworth, P. (1972). *Emotion in the human face.* New York: Pergamon.

Erbert, L. A., & Floyd, K. (2004). Affectionate expressions as face-threatening acts: Receiver assessments. *Communication Studies*, *55*, 230–246. doi: 10.1080/10510970409388618

Eriksson, N. E., Möller, C., Werner, S., Magnusson, J., & Bengtsson, U. (2003). The hazards of kissing when you are food allergic: A survey on the occurrence of kiss-induced allergic reactions among 1139 patients with self-reported food hypersensitivity. *Journal of Investigational Allergology & Clinical Immunology*, *13*(3), 149–154.

Escovar, P. L., & Lazarus, P. J. (1982). Cross-cultural child-rearing practices: Implications for school psychologists. *School Psychology International*, *3*, 143–148. doi: 10.1177/0143034382033003

Everly, G. S., & Lating, J. M. (2013). *A clinical guide to the treatment of the human stress response.* New York: Springer.

Fabes, R. A., & Martin, C. L. (1991). Gender and age stereotypes of emotionality. *Personality and Social Psychology Bulletin*, *17*, 532–540. doi: 10.1177/01461667291175008

Farley, S. D., Hughes, S. M., & LaFayette, J. N. (2013). People will know we are in love: Evidence of differences between vocal samples directed toward lovers and friends. *Journal of Nonverbal Behavior*, *37*, 123–138. doi: 10.1007/s10919-013-0151-3

Farnè, M. A., Boni, P., Corallo, A., Gnugnoli, D., & Sacco, F. L. (1994). Personality variables as moderators between hassles and objective indicators of distress (S-IgA). *Stress & Health*, *10*, 15–20. doi: 10.1002/smi.2460100104

Fehr, B., & Russell, J. A. (1991). The concept of love viewed from a prototype perspective. *Journal of Personality and Social Psychology*, *60*, 425–438. doi: 10.1037/0022-3514.60.3.425

Feingold, A. (1992). Gender differences in mate selection preferences: A test of the paternal investment model. *Psychological Bulletin*, *122*, 125–139. doi: 10.1037/0033-2909.112.1.125

Feldman, R., Gordon, I., Influs, M., Gutbir, T., & Ebstein, R. P. (2013). Parental oxytocin and early caregiving jointly shape children's oxytocin response and social reciprocity. *Neuropsychopharmacology*, *38*, 1154–1162. doi: 10.1038/npp.2013.22

Fernald, A. (1989). Intonation and communicative intent in mothers' speech to infants: Is the melody the message? *Child Development*, *60*, 1497–1510. doi: 10.2307/1130938

(1993). Approval and disapproval: Infant responsiveness to vocal affect in familiar and unfamiliar languages. *Child Development*, *64*, 657–674. doi: 10.2307/1131209

Fernald, A., & Simon, T. (1984). Expanded intonation contours in mothers' speech to newborns. *Developmental Psychology*, *20*, 104–113. doi: 10.1037/0012-1649.20.1.104

Field, T. (2010). Touch for socioemotional and physical well-being: A review. *Developmental Review*, *30*, 367–383. doi: 10.1016/j.dr.2011.01.001

Field, T., Cullen, C., Diego, M., Hernandez-Reif, M., Sprinz, P., Beebe, K., . . . Bango-Sanchez, V. (2001). Leukemia immune challenges following massage therapy. *Journal of Bodywork and Movement Therapies*, *5*, 271–274. doi: 10.1054/jbmt.2001.0228

Field, T., Henteleff, T., Hernandez-Reif, M., Martinez, E., Mavunda, K., Kuhn, C., & Schanberg, S. (1998). Children with asthma have improved pulmonary functions after massage therapy. *Journal of Pediatrics*, *132*, 854–858. doi: 10.1016/S0022-3476(98)70317-8

Field, T., & Hernandez-Reif, M. (2001). Sleep problems in infants decrease following massage therapy. *Early Child Development and Care*, *168*, 95–104. doi: 10.1080/0300443011680106

Field, T., Hernandez-Reif, M., LaGreca, A., Shaw, K., Schanberg, S., & Kuhn, C. (1997). Massage therapy lowers blood glucose levels in children with diabetes mellitus. *Diabetes Spectrum*, *10*, 237–239.

Fink, B., & Penton-Voak, I. (2002). Evolutionary psychology of facial attractiveness. *Current Directions in Psychological Science*, *11*, 154–158. doi: 10.1111/1467-8721.00190

Fisher, R. A. (1930). *The genetical theory of natural selection*. Oxford: Oxford University Press.

Fitzgerald, L. F., Gelfand, M. J., & Drasgow, F. (1995). Measuring sexual harassment: Theoretical and psychometric advances. *Basic and Applied Social Psychology*, *17*, 425–445. doi: 10.1207/s15324834basp1704_2

Fitzpatrick, M. A. (2004). Family communication patterns theory: Observations on its development and application. *Journal of Family Communication, 4,* 167–179. doi: 10.1080/15267431.2004.9670129

Floderus-Myrhed, B., Pedersen, N., & Rasmuson, I. (1980). Assessment of heritability for personality, based on a short-form of the Eysenck Personality Inventory: A study of 12,898 twin pairs. *Behavior Genetics, 10,* 152–162. doi: 10.1007/BF01066265

Floyd, K. (1995). Gender and closeness among friends and siblings. *Journal of Psychology, 129,* 193–202. doi: 10.1080/0023980.1995.9914958

(1996a). Brotherly love I: The experience of closeness in the fraternal dyad. *Personal Relationships, 3,* 369–385. doi: 10.1111/j.1475-6811.1996.tb00122.x

(1996b). Communicating closeness among siblings: An application of the gendered closeness perspective. *Communication Research Reports, 13,* 27–34. doi: 10.1080/08824099609362067

(1997a). Brotherly love II: A developmental perspective on liking, love, and closeness in the fraternal dyad. *Journal of Family Psychology, 11,* 196–209. doi: 10.1037/0893-3200.11.2.196

(1997b). Communicating affection in dyadic relationships: An assessment of behavior and expectancies. *Communication Quarterly, 45,* 68–80. doi: 10.1080/01463379709370045

(1997c). Knowing when to say "I love you": An expectancy approach to affectionate communication. *Communication Research Reports, 14,* 321–330. doi: 10.1080/08824099709388675

(1998). Evaluative and behavioral reactions to nonverbal liking behavior. (Doctoral dissertation, University of Arizona, Tucson.)

(1999). All touches are not created equal: Effects of form and duration on observers' perceptions of an embrace. *Journal of Nonverbal Behavior, 23,* 283–299. doi: 10.1023/A:1021602926270

(2000a). Affectionate same-sex touch: The influence of homophobia on observers' perceptions. *Journal of Social Psychology, 140,* 774–788. doi: 10.1080/00224540009600516

(2000b). Attributions for nonverbal expressions of liking and disliking: The extended self-serving bias. *Western Journal of Communication, 64,* 385–404. doi: 10.1080/10570310009374683

(2001). Human affection exchange: I. Reproductive probability as a predictor of men's affection with their sons. *Journal of Men's Studies, 10,* 39–50. doi: 10.3149/jms.1001.39

(2002). Human affection exchange: V. Attributes of the highly affectionate. *Communication Quarterly, 50,* 135–154. doi: 10.1080/01463370209385653

(2004). An introduction to the uses and potential uses of physiological measurement in the study of family communication. *Journal of Family Communication, 4,* 295–318. doi: 10.1080/15267431.2004.9670137

(2006a). *Communicating affection: Interpersonal behavior and social context.* Cambridge: Cambridge University Press. doi: 10.1017/CBO9780511606649

(2006b). Human affection exchange: XII. Affectionate communication is associated with diurnal variation in salivary free cortisol. *Western Journal of Communication, 70,* 47–63. doi: 10.1080/10570310500506649

(2010, March). Propensity for affection is predicted by second- and fourth-digit length and ratio discrepancy. Paper presented at the annual meeting of the Western States Communication Association, Anchorage, AK.

(2011). Endocrinology in communication research. *Communication Research Reports, 28,* 369–372. doi: 10.1080/08824096.2011.616246

(2014a). Empathic listening as an expression of interpersonal affection. *International Journal of Listening, 28,* 1–12. doi: 10.1080/10904018.2014.861293

(2014b). Humans are people, too: Nurturing an appreciation for nature in communication research. *Review of Communication Research, 2,* 1–29. doi: 10.12840/issn.2244-3165.201402.01.001

(2014c). Relational and health correlates of affection deprivation. *Western Journal of Communication, 78,* 383–403. doi: 10.1080/10570314.2014.927071

(2014d). Taking stock of research practices: A call for self-reflection. *Communication Monographs, 81,* 1–3. doi: 10.1080/03637751.2014.892670

(2015). *The loneliness cure: Six strategies for finding real connections in your life.* Holbrook, MA: Adams Media/Simon & Schuster.

(2016). Affection deprivation is associated with physical pain and poor sleep quality. *Communication Studies, 67,* 379–398. doi: 10.1080/10510974.2016.1205641

(2017a). *Interpersonal communication* (3rd edn.). New York: McGraw-Hill.

(2017b). Loneliness corresponds with politically conservative thought. *Research in Psychology and Behavioral Sciences, 5,* 13–21. doi: 10.12691/rpbs-5-1-3

Floyd, K., & Afifi, T. D. (2012). Biological and physiological perspectives on interpersonal communication. In M. L. Knapp & J. A. Daly (Eds.), *The handbook of interpersonal communication* (4th ed., pp. 87–127). Thousand Oaks, CA: Sage.

Floyd, K., Boren, J. P., Hannawa, A. F., Hesse, C., McEwan, B., & Veksler, A. E. (2009). Kissing in marital and cohabiting relationships: Effects on blood lipids, stress, and relationship satisfaction. *Western Journal of Communication, 73,* 113–133. doi: 10.1080/10570310902856071

Floyd, K., & Burgoon, J. K. (1999). Reacting to nonverbal expressions of liking: A test of interaction adaptation theory. *Communication Monographs, 66,* 219–239. doi: 10.1080/03637759909376475

Floyd, K., & Deiss, D. M. (2012). Better health, better lives: The bright side of affection. In T. J. Socha & M. Pitts (Eds.), *The positive side of interpersonal communication* (pp. 127–142). New York: Peter Lang.

Floyd, K., & Denes, A. (2015). Attachment security and oxytocin receptor gene polymorphism interact to influence affectionate communication. *Communication Quarterly, 63,* 272–285. doi: 10.1080/01463373.2015.1039718

Floyd, K., & Erbert, L. A. (2003). Relational message interpretations of nonverbal matching behavior: An application of the social meaning model. *Journal of Social Psychology, 143,* 581–598. doi: 10.1080/00224540309598465

Floyd, K., Erbert, L. A., Davis, K. L., & Haynes, M. T. (2005). Human affection exchange: XV. An exploratory study of affectionate expressions as manipulation attempts. Unpublished manuscript, Arizona State University, Tempe.

Floyd, K., & Generous, M. A. (in press). Trait affection scale. In D. L. Worthington & G. D. Bodie (Eds.), *The sourcebook of listening methodology and measurement*. Hoboken, NJ: Wiley-Blackwell.

Floyd, K., Generous, M. A., Clark, L., McLeod, I., & Simon, A. (2017). Cumulative risk on the oxytocin receptor gene (*OXTR*) predicts empathic communication by physician assistant students. *Health Communication, 32,* 1210–1216. doi: 10.1080/10410236.2016.1214225

Floyd, K., Generous, M. A., Clark, L., Simon, A., & McLeod, I. (2015). Empathic communication by physician assistant students: Evidence of an inflation bias. *Journal of Physician Assistant Education, 26,* 94–98. doi: 10.1097/JPA.0000000000000016

Floyd, K., Hess, J. A., Miczo, L. A., Halone, K. K., Mikkelson, A. C., & Tusing, K. J. (2005). Human affection exchange: VIII. Further evidence of the benefits of expressed affection. *Communication Quarterly, 53,* 285–303. doi: 10.1080/01463370500101071

Floyd, K., & Hesse, C. (2017). Affection deprivation is conceptually and empirically distinct from loneliness. *Western Journal of Communication, 81,* 446–465. doi: 10.1080/10570314.2016.1263757

Floyd, K., Hesse, C., Boren, J. P., & Veksler, A. E. (2014). Affectionate communication can suppress immunity: Trait affection predicts antibodies to latent Epstein-Barr virus. *Southern Communication Journal, 79,* 2–13. doi: 10.1080/1041794X.2013.858178

Floyd, K., Hesse, C., & Generous, M. A. (2018). Affection exchange theory: A bio-evolutionary look at affectionate communication. In D. O. Braithwaite, E. A. Suter, & K. Floyd (Eds.), *Engaging theories in family communication: Multiple perspectives* (2nd ed., pp. 312–323). New York: Routledge.

Floyd, K., Hesse, C., & Haynes, M. T. (2007). Human affection exchange: XV. Metabolic and cardiovascular correlates of trait expressed affection. *Communication Quarterly, 55,* 79–94. doi: 10.1080/01463370600998715

Floyd, K., Hesse, C., & Pauley, P. M. (2009). Hug me, heal me: Affectionate communication and health. In M. J. Beatty, J. C. McCroskey, & K. Floyd (Eds.), *Biological dimensions of communication: Perspectives, methods, and research* (pp. 93–113). Creskill, NJ: Hampton Press.

(2013). Psychophysiological methods in family communication research. In A. L. Vangelisti (Ed.), *The handbook of family communication* (2nd ed., pp. 496–511). New York: Routledge.

Floyd, K., & Mikkelson, A. C. (2002, November). Psychometric properties of the affectionate communication index in family communication research. Paper presented at the annual meeting of the National Communication Association, New Orleans, LA.

(2004, May). Human affection exchange: IX. Neurological hemispheric dominance as a discriminator of behavioral reactions to expressed affection. Paper presented at the annual meeting of the International Communication Association, New Orleans, LA.

(2005). The affectionate communication index. In V. Manusov (Ed.), *The sourcebook of nonverbal measures: Going beyond words* (pp. 47–56). Mahwah, NJ: Lawrence Erlbaum Associates.

Floyd, K., Mikkelson, A. C., & Hesse, C. (2007). *The biology of human communication* (2nd edn.). Florence, KY: Thomson Learning.

Floyd, K., Mikkelson, A. C., Hesse, C., & Pauley, P. M. (2007). Affectionate writing reduces total cholesterol: Two randomized, controlled trials. *Human Communication Research, 33,* 119–142. doi: 10.1111/j.1468-2958.2007.00293.x

Floyd, K., Mikkelson, A. C., Tafoya, M. A., Farinelli, L., La Valley, A. G., Judd, J., … Wilson, J. (2007a). Human affection exchange: XIII. Affectionate communication accelerates neuroendocrine stress recovery. *Health Communication, 22,* 123–132. doi: 10.1080/10410230701454015

(2007b). Human affection exchange: XIV. Relational affection predicts resting heart rate and free cortisol secretion during acute stress. *Behavioral Medicine, 32,* 151–156. doi: 10.3200/BMED.32.4.151-156

Floyd, K., & Morman, M. T. (1997). Affectionate communication in nonromantic relationships: Influences of communicator, relational, and contextual factors. *Western Journal of Communication, 61,* 279–298. doi: 10.1080/10570319709374578

(1998). The measurement of affectionate communication. *Communication Quarterly, 46,* 144–162. doi: 10.1080/01463379809370092

(2000a). Affection received from fathers as a predictor of men's affection with their own sons: Tests of the modeling and compensation hypotheses. *Communication Monographs, 67,* 347–361. doi: 10.1080/03637750009376516

(2000b). Reacting to the verbal expression of affection in same-sex interaction. *Southern Communication Journal, 65,* 287–299. doi: 10.1080/10417940009373177

(2001). Human affection exchange: III. Discriminative parental solicitude in men's affectionate communication with their biological and non-biological sons. *Communication Quarterly, 49,* 310–327. doi: 10.1080/01463370109385631

(2003). Human affection exchange: II. Affectionate communication in father–son relationships. *Journal of Social Psychology, 143,* 599–612. doi: 10.1080/00224540309598466

(2005). Fathers' and sons' reports of fathers' affectionate communication: Implications of a naïve theory of affection. *Journal of Social and Personal Relationships, 22,* 99–109. doi: 10.1177/0265407505049323

(2007). What does it mean to be a good father? In L. B. Arnold (Ed.), *Family communication* (pp. 86–89). Boston: Allyn & Bacon.

Floyd, K., & Morman, M. T. (Eds.). (2014). *Widening the family circle: New research on family communication* (2nd edn.). Thousand Oaks, CA: Sage.

Floyd, K., & Morr, M. C. (2003). Human affection exchange: VII. Affectionate communication in the sibling/spouse/sibling-in-law triad. *Communication Quarterly, 51,* 247–261. doi: 10.1080/01463370309370155

Floyd, K., & Parks, M. R. (1995). Manifesting closeness in the interactions of peers: A look at siblings and friends. *Communication Reports, 8,* 69–76. doi: 10.1080/08934219509367612

Floyd, K., & Pauley, P. M. (2011). Affectionate communication is good, except when it isn't: On the dark side of expressing affection. In B. Spitzberg & W. R. Cupach (Eds.), *The dark side of close relationships* (2nd ed., pp. 145–174). New York: Routledge.

Floyd, K., Pauley, P. M., & Hesse, C. (2010). State and trait affectionate communication buffer adults' stress reactions. *Communication Monographs, 77,* 618–636. doi: 10.1080/03537751.2010.498792

Floyd, K., Pauley, P. M., Hesse, C., Eden, J., Veksler, A. E., & Woo, N. T. (in press). Supportive communication is associated with markers of immunocompetence. *Southern Communication Journal.*

Floyd, K., Pauley, P. M., Hesse, C., Veksler, A. E., Eden, J., & Mikkelson, A. C. (2014). Affectionate communication is associated with markers of immune and cardiovascular system competence. In J. M. Honeycutt, C. Sawyer, & S. Keaton (Eds.), *The influence of communication on physiology and health status* (pp. 115–130). New York: Peter Lang Publishing.

Floyd, K., & Ray, C. D. (2016). The biology of affection. In J. Nussbaum (Ed.), *Oxford research encyclopedia of communication* (pp. 1–26). Oxford: Oxford University Press. doi: 10.1093/acrefore/9780190228613.013.157

Floyd, K., Ray, C. D., van Raalte, L. J., Stein, J. B., & Generous, M. A. (2017, November). Interpersonal touch buffers pain sensitivity in romantic relationships but heightens sensitivity between strangers and friends. Paper presented at the annual meeting of the National Communication Association, Dallas, TX.

Floyd, K., & Ray, G. B. (2000, February). Patterns of adaptation to nonverbal expressions of liking and disliking in initial interactions. Paper presented at the annual meeting of the Western States Communication Association, Sacramento, CA.

(2003). Human affection exchange: IV. Vocalic predictors of perceived affection in initial interactions. *Western Journal of Communication, 67,* 56–73. doi: 10.1080/10570310309374758

Floyd, K., & Riforgiate, S. (2008). Affectionate communication received from spouses predicts stress hormone levels in healthy adults. *Communication Monographs, 75,* 351–368. doi: 10.1080/03637750802512371

Floyd, K., & Roberts, J. B. (2009). Principles of endocrine system measurement in communication research. In M. J. Beatty, J. C. McCroskey, & K. Floyd (Eds.), *Biological dimensions of communication: Perspectives, methods, and research* (pp. 249–264). Cresskill, NJ: Hampton Press.

Floyd, K., Sargent, J. E., & Di Corcia, M. (2004). Human affection exchange: VI. Further tests of reproductive probability as a predictor of men's affection with their fathers and their sons. *Journal of Social Psychology, 144,* 191–206. doi: 10.3200.SOCP.144.2.191-206

Floyd, K., & Tusing, K. J. (2002, July). "At the mention of your name": Affect shifts induced by relationship-specific cognitions. Paper presented at the annual meeting of the International Communication Association, Seoul, South Korea.

Floyd, K., & van Raalte, L. J. (in press). Affectionate communication index. In D. L. Worthington & G. D. Bodie (Eds.), *The sourcebook of listening methodology and measurement.* Hoboken, NJ: Wiley-Blackwell.

Floyd, K., Veksler, A. E., McEwan, B., Hesse, C., Boren, J. P., Dinsmore, D. R., & Pavlich, C. A. (2017). Social inclusion predicts lower blood glucose and low-density lipoproteins in healthy adults. *Health Communication, 32,* 1039–1042. doi: 10.1080/10410236.2016.1196423

Floyd, K., & Voloudakis, M. (1999a). Affectionate behavior in adult platonic friendships: Interpreting and evaluating expectancy violations. *Human Communication Research*, *25*, 341–369. doi: 10.1111/j.1468-2958.1999.tb00449.x

(1999b). Attributions for expectancy-violating changes in affectionate behavior in platonic friendships. *Journal of Psychology*, *133*, 32–48. doi: 10.1080/00223989909599720

Francis, A. J. P. (2010). Mothers' affection at 8 months predicts emotional distress in adulthood: Errors in interpretation. *Journal of Epidemiology & Community Health*, *65*, 384. doi: 10.1136/jech.2010.122804

Fredrickson, B. L. (2013). *Love 2.0: How our supreme emotion affects everything we feel, think, do, and become*. New York: Hudson Street Press.

Fredrickson, B. L., Cohn, M. A., Coffey, K. A., Pek, J., & Finkel, S. M. (2008). Open hearts build lives: Positive emotions, induced through loving-kindness meditation, build consequential personal resources. *Journal of Personality and Social Psychology*, *95*, 1045–1062. doi: 10.1037/a0013262

Freese, J., Li, J.-C. A., & Wade, L. D. (2003). The potential relevances of biology to social inquiry. *Annual Review of Sociology*, *29*, 233–256. doi: 10.1146/annurev.soc.20.010202.100012

Frone, M. R. (2000). Interpersonal conflict at work and psychological outcomes: Testing a model among young workers. *Journal of Occupational Health Psychology*, *5*, 246–255. doi: 10.1037/1076-8998.5.2.246

Frye-Cox, N. E., & Hesse, C. (2013). Alexithymia and marital quality: The mediating roles of loneliness and intimate connection. *Journal of Family Psychology*, *27*, 203–211. doi: 10.1037/a0031961

Fryrear, J. L., & Thelen, M. H. (1969). Effect of sex of model and sex of observer on the imitation of affectionate behavior. *Developmental Psychology*, *1*, 298. doi: 10.1037/h0027329

Gallace, A., & Spence, C. (2010). The science of interpersonal touch: An overview. *Neuroscience & Biobehavioral Reviews*, *34*, 246–259. doi: 10.1016/j.neubiorev.2008.10.004

Gangestad, S. W., & Simpson, J. A. (2000). The evolution of human mating: Trade-offs and strategic pluralism. *Behavioral and Brain Sciences*, *23*, 309–338. doi: 10.1017/S0140525X0000337X

Gangestad, S. W., & Thornhill, R. (2003). Facial masculinity and fluctuating asymmetry. *Evolution and Human Behavior*, *24*, 231–341. doi: 10.1016/S1090-5138(03)00017-5

Gangestad, S. W., Thornhill, R., & Yeo, R. A. (1994). Facial attractiveness, developmental stability, and fluctuating asymmetry. *Ethology and Sociobiology*, *15*, 73–85. doi: 10.1016/0162-3095(94)90018-3

Garber, M. C., Nau, D. P., Erickson, S. R., Aikens, J. E., & Lawrence, J. B. (2004). The concordance of self-report with other measures of medication adherence: A summary of the literature. *Medical Care*, *42*, 649–652. doi: 10.1097/01.mlr.0000129496.05898.02

Gecas, V., & Seff, M. A. (1990). Families and adolescents: A review of the 1980s. *Journal of Marriage and the Family*, *52*, 941–958. doi: 10.2307/353312

Gerhardt, S. (2006). Why love matters: How affection shapes a baby's brain. *Infant Observation*, *9*, 305–309. doi: 10.1080/13698030601074476

Giarrusso, R., Feng, D., Silverstein, M., & Bengtson, V. L. (2011). Grandparent–adult grandchild affection and consensus: Cross-generational and cross-ethnic comparisons. *Journal of Family Issues*, *22*, 456–477. doi: 10.1177/019251301022004004

Giese-Davis, J., Sephton, S. E., Abercrombie, H. C., Durán, R. E. F., & Spiegel, D. (2004). Repression and high anxiety are associated with aberrant diurnal cortisol rhythms in women with metastatic breast cancer. *Health Psychology*, *23*, 645–650. doi: 10.1037/0278-6133.23.6.645

Gillen, H., & Horan, S. M. (2013). Toward an understanding of the relationships among deceptive affection, deceptive beliefs, and relational qualities. *Communication Research Reports*, *30*, 352–358. doi: 10.1080/08824096.2013.836629

Goffman, E. (1959). *The presentation of self in everyday life*. New York: Doubleday. (1967). *Interaction ritual: Essays in face-to-face behavior*. New York: Doubleday.

Goldsmith, D. J. (2008). *Communicating social support*. Cambridge: Cambridge University Press.

Golinkoff, R. M., Can, D. D., Soderstrom, M., & Hirsh-Pasek, K. (2015). (Baby)talk to me: The social context of infant-directed speech and its effects on early language acquisition. *Current Directions in Psychological Science*, *24*, 339–344. doi: 10.1177/0963721415595345

Goodson, J. L., & Bass, A. H. (2001). Social behavior functions and related anatomical characteristics of vasotocin/vasopressin systems in vertebrates. *Brain Research Reviews*, *35*, 246–265. doi: 10.1016/S0165-0173(01)00043-1

Gosserand, R. H., & Diefendorff, J. M. (2005). Emotional display rules and emotional labor: The moderating role of commitment. *Journal of Applied Psychology*, *90*, 1256–1264. doi: 10.1037/0021-9010.90.6.1256

Gough, H. G. (1957). *Manual for the California Psychological Inventory*. Palo Alto, CA: Consulting Psychologists Press.

Gouldner, A. W. (1960). The norm of reciprocity: A preliminary statement. *American Sociological Review*, *25*, 161–178. doi: 10.2307/2092623

Grammer, K. (1989). Human courtship behaviour: Biological basis and cognitive processing. In A. E. Rasa, C. Vogel, & E. Voland (Eds.), *The sociobiology of sexual and reproductive strategies* (pp. 147–169). London: Chapman and Hall.

Grassian, S. (1983). Psychopathological effects of solitary confinement. *American Journal of Psychiatry*, *140*, 1450–1454. doi: 10.1176/ajp.140.11.1450 (2006). Psychiatric effects of solitary confinement. *Journal of Law & Policy*, *22*, 325–383.

Gray, J. A. (1994). Three fundamental emotion systems. In P. Ekman & R. J. Davidson (Eds.), *The nature of emotion* (pp. 243–247). New York: Oxford University Press.

Gray, P. B., Kahlenberg, S. M., Barrett, E. S., Lipson, S. F., & Ellison, P. T. (2002). Marriage and fatherhood are associated with lower testosterone in males. *Evolution and Human Behavior*, *23*, 193–201. doi: 10.1016/S1090-5138(01)00101-5

Gray, P. B., Volsche, S. L., Garcia, J. R., & Fisher, H. E. (2015). The roles of pet dogs and cats in human courtship and dating. *Anthrozoös*, *28*, 673–683. doi: 10.1080/08927936.2015.1064216

Green, V. A., & Wildermuth, N. L. (1993). Self-focus, other-focus, and inter-personal needs as correlates of loneliness. *Psychological Reports, 73*, 843–840. doi: 10.2466/pr0.1993.73.3.843

Grewen, K. M., Anderson, B. J., Girdler, S. S., & Light, K. C. (2003). Warm partner contact is related to lower cardiovascular reactivity. *Behavioral Medicine, 29*, 123–130. doi: 10.180/08964280309596065

Grewen, K. M., Girdler, S. S., Amico, J., & Light, K. C. (2005). Effects of partner support on resting oxytocin, cortisol, norepinephrine, and blood pressure before and after warm partner contact. *Psychosomatic Medicine, 67*, 531–538. doi: 10.1097/01.psy.0000170341.88395.47

Gross, J. J., John, O. P., & Richards, J. M. (2000). The dissociation of emotion expression from emotion experience: A personality perspective. *Personality and Social Psychology Bulletin, 26*, 712–726. doi: 10.1177/0146167200268006

Guéguen, N., & Ciccotti, S. (2008). Domestic dogs as facilitators in social interaction: An evaluation of helping and courtship behaviors. *Anthrozoös, 21*, 339–349. doi: 10.2752/175303708X371564

Gulledge, A. K., Gulledge, M. H., & Stahmann, R. F. (2003). Romantic physical affection types and relationship satisfaction. *American Journal of Family Therapy, 31*, 233–242. doi: 10.1080/01926180390201936

Günindi, Y. (2015). Preschool children's perceptions of the value of affection as seen in their drawings. *International Electronic Journal of Elementary Education, 7*(3), 371–382.

Gunzerath, L., Faden, V., Zakhari, S., & Warren, K. (2004). National Institute on Alcohol Abuse and Alcoholism report on moderate drinking. *Alcoholism: Clinical & Experimental Research, 28*, 829–847. doi: 10.1097/01.ALC.0000128382.79375.B6

Gurevitch, Z. D. (1990). The embrace: On the element of non-distance in human relations. *The Sociological Quarterly, 31*, 187–201. doi: 10.1111/j.1533-8525.1990.tb00324.x

Halberstadt, A. G. (1985). Race, socioeconomic status, and nonverbal behavior. In A. W. Siegman & S. Feldman (Eds.), *Multichannel integrations of nonverbal behavior* (pp. 227–266). Hillsdale, NJ: Lawrence Erlbaum Associates.

(1986). Family socialization of emotional expression and nonverbal communication styles and skills. *Journal of Personality and Social Psychology, 51*, 827–836. doi: 10.1037/0022-3514.51.4.827

Hale, J. L., & Burgoon, J. K. (1984). Models of reactions to changes in nonverbal immediacy. *Journal of Nonverbal Behavior, 8*, 287–315. doi: 10.1007/BF00985984

Hall, E. T. (1974). *Handbook for proxemics research*. Washington, DC: Society for the Anthropology of Visual Communication.

Hallett, R., Haapanen, L. A., & Teuber, S. S. (2002). Food allergies and kissing. *New England Journal of Medicine, 346*, 1833–1834. doi: 10.1056/NEJM200206063462320

Hamilton, W. D. (1964). The genetical evolution of social behavior. I and II. *Journal of Theoretical Biology, 7*, 1–52. doi: 10.1016/0022-5193(64)90039-6

Haney, C. (2003). Mental health issues in long-term solitary and "supermax" confinement. *Crime & Delinquency*, *49*, 124–156. doi: 10.1177/0011128702239239

Hanh, T. N. (2000). *Plum Village chanting and recitation book*. Berkeley, CA: Parallax Press.

Hansen, Å. M., Hogh, A., Persson, R., Karlson, B., Garde, A. H., & Ørbæk, P. (2006). Bullying at work, health outcomes, and physiological stress response. *Journal of Psychosomatic Research*, *60*, 63–70. doi: 10.1016/j.psychores.2005.06.078

Hansford, B. C., & Hattie, J. A. (1982). The relationship between self and achievement/performance measures. *Review of Educational Research*, *52*, 123–142. doi: 10.2307/1170275

Harlow, H. F. (1958). The nature of love. *American Psychologist*, *13*, 673–685. doi: 10.1037/h0047884

Harlow, H. F., & Zimmermann, R. R. (1958). The development of affectional responses in infant monkeys. *Proceedings of the American Philosophical Society*, *102*(5), 501–509.

Harris, J. A., Rushton, J. P., Hampson, E., & Jackson, D. N. (1996). Salivary testosterone and self-report aggressive and pro-social personality characteristics in men and women. *Aggressive Behavior*, *22*, 321–331. doi: 10.1002/(SICI)1098-2337(1996)22:5<321::AID-AB1>3.0.CO;2-M

Harrison-Speake, K., & Willis, F. N. (1995). Ratings of the appropriateness of touch among family members. *Journal of Nonverbal Behavior*, *19*, 85–100. doi: 10.1007/BF02173168

Hart, S., Field, T., Hernandez-Reif, M., Nearing, G., Shaw, S., Schanberg, S., & Kuhn, C. (2001). Anorexia symptoms are reduced by massage therapy. *Eating Disorders*, *9*, 289–299. doi: 10.1080/106402601753454868

Hawkley, L. C., & Cacioppo, J. T. (2010). Loneliness matters: A theoretical and empirical review of consequences and mechanisms. *Annals of Behavioral Medicine*, *40*, 218–227. doi: 10.1007/s12160-010-9210-8

Hazan, C., & Shaver, P. (1987). Romantic love conceptualized as an attachment process. *Journal of Personality and Social Psychology*, *52*, 511–524. doi: 10.1037/0022-3514.52.3.511

Heaton, T. B. (1990). Marital stability throughout the child-rearing years. *Demography*, *27*, 55–63. doi: 10.2307/2061552

Hecht, M. L. (1978). The conceptualization and measurement of interpersonal communication satisfaction. *Human Communication Research*, *4*, 253–264. doi: 10.1111/j.1468-2958,1978.tb00614.x

Hedge, G. A., Colby, H. D., & Goodman, R. L. (1987). *Clinical endocrine physiology*. Philadelphia: W. B. Saunders.

Heider, F. (1958). *The psychology of interpersonal relations*. New York: Wiley.

Heinrichs, M., Baumgartner, T., Kirschbaum, C., & Ehlert, U. (2003). Social support and oxytocin interact to suppress cortisol and subjective response to psychosocial stress. *Biological Psychiatry*, *54*, 1389–1398. doi: 10.1016/S0006-3223(03)00465-7

Hendrick, S. S. (1988). A generic measure of relationship satisfaction. *Journal of Marriage and the Family*, *50*, 93–98. doi: 10.2307/352430

Hendrick, S. S., Hendrick, C., & Adler, N. L. (1988). Romantic relationships: Love, satisfaction, and staying together. *Journal of Personality and Social Psychology*, *54*, 980–988. doi: 10.1037/0022-3514.54.6.980

Hendrie, C. A., & Brewer, G. (2010). Kissing as an evolutionary adaptation to protect against human cytomegalovirus-like teratogenesis. *Medical Hypotheses*, *74*, 222–224. doi: 10.1016/j.mehy.2009.09.033

Hernandez-Reif, M., Field, T., & Hart, S. (1999). Smoking cravings are reduced by self-massage. *Preventive Medicine*, *28*, 28–32. doi: 10.1006/pmed.1998.0372

Hernandez-Reif, M., Field, T., Krasnegor, J., Theakston, H., Hossain, Z., & Burman, I. (2000). High blood pressure and associated symptoms were reduced by massage therapy. *Journal of Bodywork and Movement Therapies*, *4*, 31–38. doi: 10.1054/jbmt.1999.0129

Hernandez-Reif, M., Field, T., Largie, S., Cullen, C., Beutler, J., Sanders, C., ... Kuhn, C. (2002). Parkinson's disease symptoms are differentially affected by massage therapy versus progressive muscle relaxation: A pilot study. *Journal of Bodywork and Movement Therapies*, *6*, 177–182. doi: 10.1054/jbmt.2002.0282

Hesse, C. (2015). Porn and health: The mediating role of affection deprivation. Unpublished manuscript, Oregon State University.

Hesse, C., & Floyd, K. (2008). Affection experience mediates the effects of alexithymia on mental health and interpersonal relationships. *Journal of Social and Personal Relationships*, *25*, 793–810. doi: 10.1177/0265407508096696

(2011a). Affection mediates the impact of alexithymia on relationships. *Personality and Individual Differences*, *50*, 451–456. doi: 10.1016/j.paid.2010.11.004

(2011b). The influence of alexithymia on initial interactions. *Personal Relationships*, *18*, 453–570. doi: 10.1111/j.1475-6811.2010.01311.x

(2018). Pornography consumption as a coping mechanism for affection deprivation. Manuscript submitted for publication.

Hesse, C., Floyd, K., Boren, J. P., Lee, J. M., & Holland, C. F. (2018, February). Affectionate communication and testosterone. Paper presented at the annual conference of the Western States Communication Association, Santa Clara, CA.

Hesse, C., Floyd, K., Rauscher, E. A., Frye-Cox, N., Hegarty, J., & Peng, H. (2013). Alexithymia and impairment of decoding positive affect: An fMRI study. *Journal of Communication*, *63*, 786–806. doi: 10.1111/jcom.12039

Hesse, C., & Mikkelson, A. C. (2016). Affection deprivation in romantic relationships. *Communication Quarterly*, *65*, 20–38. doi: 10.1080/01463373.2016.1176942

Hesse, C., Mikkelson, A. C., & Saracco, S. (2018). Parent–child affection and helicopter parenting: Exploring the concept of excessive affection. *Western Journal of Communication*, *82*, 457–474. doi: 10.1080/10570314.2017.1362705

Hesse, C., Rauscher, E. A., Roberts, J. B., & Ortega, S. R. (2014). Investigating the role of hurtful family environment in the relationship between affectionate communication and family satisfaction. *Journal of Family Communication*, *14*, 112–128. doi: 10.1080/15267431.2013.866453

Hesse, C., & Trask, S. L. (2014). Trait affection and adult attachment styles: Analyzing relationship and group differences. *Communication Research Reports*, *31*, 53–61. doi: 10.1080/08824096.2013.844118

Hodges, S. D., Lewis, K. L., & Ickes, W. (2015). The matter of other minds: Empathic accuracy and the factors that influence it. In M. Mikulincer, P. R. Shaver, J. A. Simpson, & J. F. Dovidio (Eds.), *APA handbook of personality and social psychology*, Vol. 3: *Interpersonal relations* (pp. 319–348). Washington, DC: American Psychological Association. doi: 10.1037/14344-012

Hofstede, G., & Hofstede, G. J. (2010). *Cultures and organizations: Software of the mind* (3rd edn.). New York: McGraw-Hill.

Holt-Lunstad, J., Birmingham, W. A., & Light, K. C. (2008). Influence of a "warm touch" support enhancement intervention among married couples on ambulatory blood pressure, oxytocin, alpha amylase, and cortisol. *Psychosomatic Medicine*, *70*, 976–985. doi: 10.1097/PSY.0b013e318187aef7

Hopper, R., Knapp, M. L., & Scott, L. (1981). Couples' personal idioms: Exploring intimate talk. *Journal of Communication*, *31*, 23–33. doi: 10.1111/j.1460-2466.1981.tb01201.x

Horan, S. M. (2013a, November). Do message features help explain communicators' reactions to expressed deceptive affectionate messages? Paper presented at the annual meeting of the National Communication Association, Washington, DC.

(2013b, April). Further understanding affectionate communication as maintenance. Paper presented at the annual meeting of the Eastern Communication Association, Pittsburgh, PA.

Horan, S. M., & Booth-Butterfield, M. (2010). Investing in affection: An investigation of affection exchange theory and relational qualities. *Communication Quarterly*, *58*, 394–413. doi: 10.1080/01463373.2010.524876

(2011). Is it worth lying for? Physiological and emotional implications of recalling deceptive affection. *Human Communication Research*, *37*, 78–106. doi: 10.1111/j.1468-2958.2010.01394.x

(2013). Understanding the routine expression of deceptive affection in romantic relationships. *Communication Quarterly*, *61*, 195–216. doi: 10.1080/01463373.2012.751435

Horan, S. M., Parker-Raley, J., & Cafferty, L. A. (2015, November). Emotional dissonance: Withholding affectionate messages in emergency departments. Paper presented at the annual meeting of the National Communication Association, Las Vegas, NV.

House, J. S., Landis, K. R., & Umberson, D. (1988). Social relationships and health. *Science*, *241*, 540–545. doi: 10.1126/science.3399889

Howard, G. S., & Dailey, P. R. (1979). Response-shift bias: A source of contamination of self-report measures. *Journal of Applied Psychology*, *64*, 144–150. doi: 10.1037/0021-9010.64.2.144

Hróbjartsson, A., & Gøtzsche, P. C. (2001). Is the placebo powerless? An analysis of clinical trials comparing placebo with no treatment. *New England Journal of Medicine*, *344*, 1594–1602. doi: 10.1056/NEJM200105243442106

Hu, Y., & Goldman, N. (1990). Mortality differentials by marital status: An international comparison. *Demography*, *27*, 233–250. doi: 10.2307/2061451

Huang, S. C., Phelps, M. E., Hoffman, E. J., Sideris, K., Selin, C. J., & Kuhl, D. E. (1980). Noninvasive determination of local cerebral metabolic rate of glucose in man. *American Journal of Physiology*, *238*, E69–E82. doi: 10.1152/ajpendo.1980.238.1.E69

Huston, T. L., Caughlin, J. P., Houts, R. M., Smith, S. E., & George, L. J. (2001). The connubial crucible: Newlywed years as predictors of marital delight, distress, and divorce. *Journal of Personality and Social Psychology*, *80*, 237–252. doi: 10.1037/0022-3514.80.2.237

Huston, T. L., & Chorost, A. F. (1994). Behavioral buffers on the effect of negativity in marital satisfaction: A longitudinal study. *Personal Relationships*, *1*, 223–239. doi: 10.1111/j.1475-6811.1994.tb00063.x

Huston, T. L., & Vangelisti, A. L. (1991). Socioemotional behavior and satisfaction in marital relationships: A longitudinal study. *Journal of Social and Personal Relationships*, *61*, 721–733. doi: 10.1037/0022-3514.61.5.721

Hutcherson, C. A., Seppälä, E. M., & Gross, J. J. (2008). Loving-kindness meditation increases social connectedness. *Emotion*, *8*, 720–724. doi: 10.1037/a0013237

Izard, C. E. (1971). *The face of emotion*. New York: Appleton.

Jakubiak, B. K., & Feeney, B. C. (2017). Affectionate touch to promote relational, psychological, and physical well-being in adulthood: A theoretical model and review of the research. *Personality and Social Psychology Review*, *21*, 228–252. doi: 101177/1088868316650307

Jankowiak, W. R., Volsche, S. L., & Garcia, J. R. (2015). Is the romantic-sexual kiss a near human universal? *American Anthropologist*, *117*, 535–539. doi: 10.1111/aman.12286

Jaremka, L. M., Fagundes, C. P., Glaser, R., Bennett, J. M., Malarkey, W. B., & Kiecolt-Glaser, J. K. (2013). Loneliness predicts pain, depression, and fatigue: Understanding the role of immune dysregulation. *Psychoneuroendocrinology*, *38*, 1310–1317. doi: 10.1016/j.psyneuen.2012.11.016

Jaremka, L. M., Fagundes, C. P., Peng, J., Bennett, J. M., Glaser, R., Malarkey, W. B., & Kiecolt-Glaser, J. K. (2013). Loneliness promotes inflammation during acute stress. *Psychological Science*, *24*, 1089–1097. doi: 10.1177/0956797612464059

Jeffcoate, W. J., Lincoln, N. B., Selby, C., & Herbert, M. (1986). Correlation between anxiety and serum prolactin in humans. *Journal of Psychosomatic Research*, *30*, 217–222. doi: 10.1016/S0022-3999(86)90052-8

Jennings, J. R., Kamarck, T. W., Everson-Rose, S. A., Kaplan, G. A., Manuck, S. B., & Salonen, J. T. (2014). Exaggerated blood pressure responses during mental stress are prospectively related to enhanced carotid atherosclerosis in middle-aged Finnish men. *Circulation*, *110*, 2198–2203. doi: 10.1161/01.CIR.0000143840.77061.E9

Jiang, X. (2017). Tracking the sound of human affection: EEG signals reveal online decoding of socio-emotional expression in human speech and voice. In S. A. Hosseini (Ed.), *Emotion and attention recognition based on biological signals and images* (pp. 47–58). Rijeka: InTech.

Joiner, T. (2005). *Why people die by suicide*. Cambridge, MA: Harvard University Press.

Jones, E. E., & Wortman, C. (1973). *Ingratiation: An attributional approach*. Morristown, NJ: Learning Press.

Jorm, A. F., Dear, K. B. G., Rodgers, B., & Christensen, H. (2003). Interaction between mother's and father's affection as a risk factor for anxiety and depression symptoms: Evidence for increased risk in adults who rate their father as having been more affectionate than their mother. *Social Psychiatry and Psychiatric Epidemiology, 38*, 173–179. doi: 10.1007/s00127-003-0620-9

Jourard, S. M. (1966). An exploratory study of body-accessibility. *British Journal of Social and Clinical Psychology, 5*, 221–231. doi: 10.1111/j.2044-8260.1966.tb00978.x

Julius, H., Beetz, A., Kotrschal, K., Turner, D., & Uvnäs-Moberg, K. (2013). *Attachment to pets: An integrative view of human–animal relationships with implications for therapeutic practice*. Cambridge, MA: Hogrefe Publishing.

Juster, R.-P., Smith, N. G., Ouellet, É., Sindi, S., & Lupien, S. J. (2013). Sexual orientation and disclosure in relation to psychiatric symptoms, diurnal cortisol, and allostatic load. *Psychosomatic Medicine, 75*, 103–116. doi: 10.1097/PSY.0b013e3182826881

Kaba, F., Lewis, A., Glowa-Kollisch, S., Hadler, J., Lee, D., Alper, H., ... Venters, H. (2014). Solitary confinement and risk of self-harm among jail inmates. *American Journal of Public Health, 104*, 442–447. doi: 10.2105/AJPH.2013.301742

Kachel, S., Steffens, M. C., & Niedlich, C. (2016). Traditional masculinity and femininity: Validation of a new scale assessing gender roles. *Frontiers in Psychology, 7*, 956. doi: 10.3389/fpsyg.2016.00956

Kanazawa, S. (2001). Comment: Why we love our children. *American Journal of Sociology, 106*, 1761–1776. doi: 10.1086/321305

   (2004). Social sciences are branches of biology. *Socio-Economic Review, 2*, 371–390. doi: 10.1093/soceco/2.3.371

Kang, Y., Gray, J. R., & Dovidio, J. F. (2014). The nondiscriminating heart: Lovingkindness meditation training decreases implicit intergroup bias. *Journal of Experimental Psychology: General, 143*, 1306–1313. doi: 10.1037/a0034150

Karney, B. R., Bradbury, T. N., Fincham, F. D., & Sullivan, K. T. (1994). The role of negative affectivity in the association between attributions and marital satisfaction. *Journal of Personality and Social Psychology, 66*, 413–424. doi: 10.1037/0022-3514.66.2.413

Keefe, K., & Berndt, T. J. (1996). Relations of friendship quality to self-esteem in early adolescence. *Journal of Early Adolescence, 16*, 110–129. doi: 10.1177/0272431696016001007

Keller, H., Vöelker, S., & Yovsi, R. D. (2005). Conceptions of parenting in different cultural communities: The case of West African Nso and Northern German women. *Social Development, 14*, 158–180. doi: 10.1111/j.1467-9507.2005.00295.x

Kenny, D. A., & Nasby, W. (1980). Splitting the reciprocity correlation. *Journal of Personality and Social Psychology, 38*, 249–256. doi: 10.1037/0022-3514.38.2.249

Kenrick, D. T., Groth, G., Trost, M. R., & Sadalla, E. K. (1993). Integrating evolutionary and social exchange perspectives on relationships: Effects of gender, self-appraisal, and involvement level on mate selection. *Journal of Personality and Social Psychology*, *64*, 951–969. doi: 10.1037/0022-3514.64.1.951

Kenrick, D. T., Sadalla, E. K., Groth, G., & Trost, M. R. (1990). Evolution, traits, and the stages of human courtship: Qualifying the parental investment model. *Journal of Personality*, *58*, 97–116. doi: 10.1111/j.1467-6494.1990.tb00909.x

Kerver, M. J., van Son, M. J. M., & de Groot, P. A. (1992). Predicting symptoms of depression from reports of early parenting: A one-year prospective study in a community sample. *Acta Psychiatrica Scandanivica*, *86*, 267–272. doi: 10.1111/j.1600-0447.1992.tb03265.x

Kimata, H. (2003). Kissing reduces allergic skin wheal responses and plasma neurotrophin levels. *Physiology & Behavior*, *80*, 395–398. doi: 10.1016/j.physbeh.2003.09.004

(2006). Kissing selectively decreases allergen-specific IgE production in atopic patients. *Journal of Psychosomatic Research*, *60*, 545–547. doi: 10.1016/j.psychores.2005.09.007

King, C. E., & Christensen, A. (1983). The relationship events scale: A Guttman scaling of progress in courtship. *Journal of Marriage and the Family*, *45*, 671–678. doi: 10.2307/351672

Kirsch, I., & Sapirstein, G. (1998). Listening to Prozac but hearing placebo: A meta-analysis of antidepressant medication. *Prevention & Treatment*, *1*, article 2a. doi: 10.1037/1522-3736.1.1.12a

Kirschbaum, C., & Hellhammer, D. H. (1989). Salivary cortisol in psychobiological research: An overview. *Neuropsychobiology*, *22*, 150–169. doi: 10.1159/000118611

Kline, S. L., Horton, B., & Zhang, S. (2008). Communicating love: Comparisons between American and East Asian university students. *International Journal of Intercultural Relations*, *32*, 200–214. doi: 10.1016/j.ijintrel.2008.01.006

Kogan, A., Saslow, L. R., Impett, E. A., Oveis, C., Keltner, D., & Saturn, S. R. (2011). Thin-slicing study of the oxytocin receptor (*OXTR*) gene and the evaluation and expression of the prosocial disposition. *Proceedings of the National Academy of Sciences*, *108*, 19189–19192. doi: 10.1073/pnas.1112658108

Kondo, T., Zákány, J., Innis, J. W., & Duboule, D. (1997). Of fingers, toes and penises. *Nature*, *390*, 29. doi: 10.1038/36234

Koole, S. L., Sin, M. T. A., & Schneider, I. K. (2014). Embodied terror management: Interpersonal touch alleviates existential concerns among individuals with low self-esteem. *Psychological Science*, *25*, 30–37. doi: 10.1177/0956797613483478

Kort, R., Caspers, M., van de Graaf, A., van Egmond, W., Keijser, B., & Roeselers, G. (2014). Shaping the oral microbiota through intimate kissing. *Microbiome*, *2014*, 41. doi: 10.1186/2049-2618-2-41

Krueger, R. F., South, S., Johnson, W., & Iacono, W. (2008). The heritability of personality is not always 50 percent: Gene–environment interactions and correlations between personality and parenting. *Journal of Personality*, *76*, 1485–1552. doi: 10.1111/j.1467-6494.2008.00529.x

Kurina, L. M., Knutson, K. L., Hawkley, L. C., Cacioppo, J. T., Lauderdale, D. S., & Ober, C. (2011). Loneliness is associated with sleep fragmentation in a communal society. *Sleep*, *34*, 1519–1526. doi: 10.5665/sleep.1390

Kuwamura, K., Sakai, K., Minato, T., Nishio, S., & Ishiguro, H. (2014). Hugvie: Communication device for encouraging good relationship through the art of hugging. *Lovotics*, *1*, 10000104. doi: 10.4172/2090-9888.1000104

L'abate, L. (2008). Hugging, holding, huddling and cuddling (3HC): A task prescription in couple and family therapy. *Journal of Clinical Activities, Assignments & Handouts in Psychotherapy Practice*, *1*, 5–18. doi: 10.1300/j182v02n01_02

Lamb, M. E., Pleck, J., Charnov, E., & Levine, J. (1987). A biosocial perspective on paternal behavior and involvement. In J. Lancaster, J. Altmann, A. Rossi, & L. Sherrod (Eds.), *Parenting across the lifespan: Biosocial dimensions* (pp. 111–142). New York: Aldine de Gruyter.

Lamers, F., van Oppen, P., Comijs, H. C., Smit, J. H., Spinhoven, P., van Balkom, A. J., ... Penninx, B. W. (2011). Comorbidity patterns of anxiety and depressive disorders in a large cohort study: The Netherlands Study of Depression and Anxiety (NESDA). *Journal of Clinical Psychiatry*, *72*, 341–348. doi: 10.4088/JCP.10m06176blu

Landau, R. (1989). Affect and attachment: Kissing, hugging, and patting as attachment behaviors. *Infant Mental Health Journal*, *10*, 59–69. doi: 10.1002/1097-0355(198921)10:1<59::AID-IMHJ2280100106>3.0.CO;2-6

Lang, K. L., Livesley, W. J., & Vemon, P. A. (1996). Heritability of the big five personality dimensions and their facets: A twin study. *Journal of Personality*, *64*, 577–592. doi: 10.1111/j.1467-6494.1996.tb00522.x

Larsen, R., & Buss, D. M. (2017). *Personality psychology: Domains of knowledge about human nature* (6th edn.). New York: McGraw-Hill.

Laukka, P., Elfenbein, H. A., Söder, N., Nordström, H., Althoff, J., Chui, W., ... Thingujam, N. S. (2013). Cross-cultural decoding of positive and negative non-linguistic emotion vocalizations. *Frontiers in Psychology*, *4*, 353. doi: 10.3389/fpsyg.2013.00353

Laumann, E. O., Paik, A., Glasser, D. B., Kang, J.-H., Wang, T., Levinson, B., ... Gingell, C. (2006). A cross-national study of subjective sexual well-being among older women and men: Findings from the global study of sexual attitudes and behaviors. *Archives of Sexual Behavior*, *35*, 145–161. doi: 10.1007/s10508-005-9005-3

Lawson, A. (1988). *Adultery: An analysis of love and betrayal*. New York: Basic Books.

Lawton, L., Silverstein, M., & Bengtson, V. (1994). Affection, social contact, and geographic distance between adult children and their parents. *Journal of Marriage and the Family*, *56*, 57–68. doi: 10.2307/352701

Leary, M. R. (1990). Responses to social exclusion: Social anxiety, jealousy, loneliness, depression, and low self-esteem. *Journal of Social and Clinical Psychology*, *9*, 221–229. doi: 10.1521/jscp.1990.9.2.221

Leets, L., De Becker, G., & Giles, H. (1995). Fans: Exploring expressed motivations for contacting celebrities. *Journal of Language and Social Psychology*, *14*, 102–123. doi: 10.1177/0261927X95141006

Levesque, R. J. R. (2011). Parental responsibility laws. In R. J. R. Levesque (Ed.), *Encyclopedia of adolescence* (pp. 2012–2013). New York: Springer. doi: 10.1007/978-1-4419-1695-2_684

Levine, M. P. (2012). Loneliness and eating disorders. *Journal of Psychology*, *146*, 243–257. doi: 10.1080/00223980.2011.606435

Lewis, R. J., Heisel, A. D., Reinhart, A. M., & Tian, Y. (2011). Trait affection and asymmetry in the anterior brain. *Communication Research Reports*, *28*, 347–355. doi: 10.1080/08824096.2011.615960

Liccardi, G., Gilder, J., D'Amato, M., & D'Amato, G. (2002). Drug allergy transmitted by passionate kissing. *Lancet*, *359*, 1700. doi: 10.1016/S0140-6736(02)08580-X

Liccardi, G., Senna, G., Rotiroti, G., D'Amato, G., & Passalacqua, G. (2007). Intimate behavior and allergy: A narrative review. *Annals of Allergy, Asthma & Immunology*, *99*, 394–400. doi: 10.1016/S1081-1206(10) 60562-5

Light, K. C., Grewen, K. M., & Amico, J. A. (2005). More frequent partner hugs and higher oxytocin levels are linked to lower blood pressure and heart rate in premenopausal women. *Biological Psychiatry*, *69*, 5–21. doi: 10.1016/ j.biopsycho.2004.11.002

Lim, T. S., & Bowers, J. W. (1991). Facework: Solidarity, approbation, and tact. *Human Communication Research*, *17*, 415–449. doi: 10.1111/j/1468-2958.1991.tb00239.x

Lord, C., & Bishop, S. L. (2015). Recent advances in autism research as reflected in DSM-5 criteria for autism spectrum disorder. *Annual Review of Clinical Psychology*, *11*, 53–70. doi: 10.1146/annurev-clinpsy-032814-112745

Lovaas, O. I., Schaeffer, B., & Simmons, J. Q. (1965). Building social behavior in autistic children by use of electric shock. *Journal of Experimental Research in Personality*, *1*(2), 99–109.

Loving, T. J., Crockett, E. E., & Paxson, A. A. (2009). Passionate love and relationship thinkers: Experimental evidence for acute cortisol elevations in women. *Psychoneuroendocrinology*, *34*, 939–946. doi: 10.1016/ j.psyneuen.2009.01.010

Luecken, L. J., & Lemery, K. (2004). Early caregiving and adult physiological stress responses. *Clinical Psychology Review*, *24*, 171–191. doi: 10.1016/ j.cpr.2004.01.003

Lynum, L. I., Wilberg, T., & Karterud, S. (2008). Self-esteem in patients with borderline and avoidant personality disorders. *Scandinavian Journal of Psychology*, *49*, 469–477. doi: 10.1111/j.1467-9450.2008.00655.x

MacDonald, K. (1992). Warmth as a developmental construct: An evolutionary analysis. *Child Development*, *63*, 753–773. doi: 10.1111/j.1467-8624.1992 .tb01659.x

Malarkey, W. B., Kiecolt-Glaser, J. K., Pearl, D., & Glaser, R. (1994). Hostile behavior during marital conflict alters pituitary and adrenal hormones. *Psychosomatic Medicine*, *56*, 41–51. doi: 10.1097/00006842-199401000-00006

Maloney, J. M., Chapman, M. D., & Sicherer, S. H. (2006). Peanut allergen exposure through saliva: Assessment and interventions to reduce exposure. *Journal of Allergy and Clinical Immunology*, *118*, 719–724. doi: 10.1016/j.jaci.2006.05.017

Mancuso, G., & Berdondini, R. M. (2006). Kiss-induced allergy to amoxicillin. *Contact Dermatitis*, *54*, 226. doi: 10.1111/j.0105-1873.2006.0775I.x

Manning, J. T., Barley, L., Walton, J., Lewis-Jones, D. I., Trivers, R. L., Singh, D., . . . Szwed, A. (2000). The 2nd:4th digit ratio, sexual dimorphism, population differences, and reproductive success: Evidence for sexually antagonistic genes? *Evolution and Human Behavior*, *21*, 163–183. doi: 10.1016/S1090-5138(00)00029-5

Manning, J. T., Scutt, D., Wilson, J., & Lewis-Jones, D. I. (1998). The ratio of 2nd to 4th digit length: A predictor of sperm numbers and concentrations of testosterone, luteinizing hormone and oestrogen. *Human Reproduction*, *13*, 3000–3004. doi: 10.1092/humrep/13/11/3000

Mansson, D. H. (2013a). Affectionate communication and relational characteristics in the grandparent–grandchild relationship. *Communication Reports*, *26*, 47–60. doi: 10.1080/08934215.2013.798670

(2013b). College students' mental health and their received affection from their grandparents. *Communication Research Reports*, *30*, 157–168. doi: 10.1080/08824096.2012.763028

(2013c). Further validity tests of the Grandchildren's Received Affection Scale. *Communication Research Reports*, *30*, 201–210. doi: 10.1080/08824096.2013.806253

(2013d). Testing the Grandchildren's Received Affection Scale using affection exchange theory. *Psychological Reports*, *112*, 553–562. doi: 10.2466/10.07.PR0.112.2.553-562

(2013e). The Grandchildren Received Affection Scale: Examining affectual solidarity factors. *Southern Communication Journal*, *78*, 70–90. doi: 10.1080/1041794X.2012.729124

(2014a). Grandparents' expressed affection for their grandchildren: Examining the grandparents' own psychological health. *Communication Research Reports*, *31*, 329–338. doi: 10.1080/08824096.2014.963218

(2014b). Trust as a mediator between affection and relational maintenance in the grandparent–grandchild relationship. *Southern Communication Journal*, *79*, 180–200. doi: 10.1080/1041794.2014.894555

Mansson, D. H., & Booth-Butterfield, M. (2011). Grandparents' expressions of affection for their grandchildren: Examining grandchildren's relational attitudes and behaviors. *Southern Communication Journal*, *76*, 424–442. doi: 10.1080/1041794x.2010.508554

Mansson, D. H., Floyd, K., & Soliz, J. (2017). Affectionate communication is associated with emotional and relational resources in the grandparent–grandchild relationship. *Journal of Intergenerational Relationships*, *15*, 85–103. doi: 10.1080/15350770.2017.1294007

Mansson, D. H., Marko, F., Bachratá, K., Danišková, Z., Gajdošíková Zeleiová, J., Janiš, V., & Sharov, A. S. (2016). Young adults' trait affection given and received as functions of Hofstede's dimensions of cultures and national origin. *Journal of Intercultural Communication Research*, 45, 404–418. doi: 10.1080/17475759.2016.1213181

Mansson, D. H., & Myers, S. A. (2011). An initial examination of college students' expressions of affection through Facebook. *Southern Communication Journal*, 76, 155–168. doi: 10.1080/10417940903317710

Mansson, D. H., & Sigurðardóttir, A. G. (2017). Trait affection given and received: A test of Hofstede's theoretical framework. *Journal of Intercultural Communication Research*, 46, 161–172. doi: 10.1080/17475759.2015.1292994

(in press). A multinational comparison of grandchildren's received affection from their grandparents. *Journal of Intergenerational Relationships*.

Manusov, V. (1990). An application of attribution principles to nonverbal behavior in romantic dyads. *Communication Monographs*, 57, 104–118. doi: 10.1080/03637759009376189

Manusov, V., Floyd, K., & Kerssen-Griep, J. (1997). Yours, mine, and ours: Mutual attributions for nonverbal behaviors in couples' interactions. *Communication Research*, 24, 234–260. doi: 10.1177/009365097024003002

Marieb, E. N., & Hoehn, K. (2015). *Human anatomy and physiology* (10th edn.). Boston: Pearson.

Marinšek M., & Tušak M. (2007). *Ělovek–žival: zdrava naveza*. [Human–animal: Healthy relation]. Maribor: Založba Pivec.

Marlowe, F., & Wetsman, A. (2001). Preferred waist-to-hip ratio and ecology. *Personality and Individual Differences*, 30, 481–489. doi: 10.1016/S0191-8869(00)00039-8

Marston, W. M. (1924). A theory of emotions and affection based upon systolic blood pressure studies. *American Journal of Psychology*, 35, 469–506. doi: 10.2307/1414033

Maselko, J., Kubzansky, L., Lipsitt, L., & Buka, S. L. (2011). Mothers' affection at 8 months predicts emotional distress in adulthood. *Journal of Epidemiology & Community Health*, 65, 621–625. doi: 10.1136/jech.2009.0907873

Mashek, D. J., & Aron, A. (Eds.). (2004). *Handbook of closeness and intimacy*. Mahwah, NJ: Lawrence Erlbaum Associates.

Maslow, A. H. (1970). *Motivation and personality* (2nd edn.). New York: Harper & Row.

Master, S. L., Eisenberger, N. I., Taylor, S. E., Naliboff, B. D., Shirinyan, D., & Lieberman, M. D. (2009). A picture's worth: Partner photographs reduce experimentally induced pain. *Psychological Science*, 20, 1316–1318. doi: 10.1111/j.1467-9280.2009.02444.x

Matsunaga, M., Sato, S., Isowa, T., Tsuboi, H., Konagaya, T., Kaneko, H., & Ohira, H. (2009). Profiling of serum proteins influenced by warm partner contact in healthy couples. *Neuroendocrinology Letters*, 30(2), 227–236.

McCabe, M. P. (1987). Desired and experienced levels of premarital affection and sexual intercourse during dating. *Journal of Sex Research*, 23, 23–33. doi: 10.1080/00224498709551339

McCambridge, J., Witton, J., & Elbourne, D. R. (2014). Systematic review of the Hawthorne effect: New concepts are needed to study research participation effects. *Journal of Clinical Epidemiology*, *67*, 267–277. doi: 10.1016/jclinepi.2013.08.015

McCarthy, M. M., & Becker, J. B. (2002). Neuroendocrinology of sexual behavior in the female. In J. B. Becker, S. M. Breedlove, D. Crews, & M. M. McCarthy (Eds.), *Behavioral endocrinology* (2nd ed., pp. 117–151). Cambridge, MA: MIT Press.

McConnell, A. R., Brown, C. M., Shoda, T. M., Stayton, L. E., & Martin, C. E. (2011). Friends with benefits: On the positive consequences of pet ownership. *Journal of Personality and Social Psychology*, *101*, 1239–1252. doi: 10.1037/a0024506

McCroskey, J. C., & McCain, T. A. (1974). The measurement of interpersonal attraction. *Speech Monographs*, *41*, 261–266. doi: 10.1080/03637757409375845

McCroskey, J. C., & McCroskey, L. L. (1988). Self-report as an approach to measuring communication competence. *Communication Research Reports*, *5*, 108–113. doi: 10.1080/08824098809359810

McCroskey, J. C., & Young, T. J. (1981). Ethos and credibility: The construct and its measurement after three decades. *Central States Speech Journal*, *32*, 24–34. doi: 10.1080/10510978109368075

McDaniel, E., & Andersen, P. A. (1998). International patterns of interpersonal tactile communication: A field study. *Journal of Nonverbal Behavior*, *22*, 59–73. doi: 10.1023/A:1033952509743

McKinley, M. P., O'Loughlin, V. D., Pennefather-O'Brien, E. E., & Harris, R. T. (2015). *Human anatomy* (4th edn.). New York: McGraw-Hill.

McLeod, J. D., & Shanahan, M. J. (1993). Poverty, parenting, and children's mental health. *American Sociological Review*, *58*, 351–366. doi: 10.2307/2095905

McPhearson, M., Smith-Lovin, L., & Brashears, M. E. (2006). Social isolation in America: Changes in core discussion networks over two decades. *American Sociological Review*, *71*, 353–375. doi: 10.1177/000312240607100301

McQuade, A., & Gill, P. (2012). The role of loneliness and self-control in predicting problem gambling behaviour. *Gambling Research*, *24*(1), 18–30.

Mealy, L., Bridgestock, R., & Townsend, G. (1999). Symmetry and perceived facial attractiveness: A monozygotic twin comparison. *Journal of Personality and Social Psychology*, *76*, 151–158. doi: 10.1037/0022-3514.76.1.151

Mederos, M. (2015). Expressions of affection and tie signs in interracial and intraracial romantic relationships. (Master's thesis, San Diego State University.) Retrieved from https://search.proquest.com/openview/2aec0d9d6db f65aa2c4dbbcf78401c76/1?pq-origsite=gscholar&cbl=18750&diss=y.

Mendel, G. (1866). *Versuche über pflanzen-hybriden* [Experiments in plant hybridization]. (J. H. Bennett, trans.) Edinburgh: Oliver & Boyd.

Metts, S., & Planalp, S. (2011). Emotion experience and expression: Current trends and future directions in interpersonal relationship research. In M. L. Knapp & J. A. Daly (Eds.), *The Sage handbook of interpersonal communication* (pp. 283–316). Thousand Oaks, CA: Sage.

Mezulis, A. H., Abramson, L. Y., Hyde, J. S., & Hankin, B. L. (2004). Is there a universal positivity bias in attributions? A meta-analytic review of individual, developmental, and cultural differences in the self-serving attributional bias. *Psychological Bulletin, 130*, 711–747. doi: 10.1037/0033-2909.130.5.711

Michiels, D., Grietens, H., Onghena, P., & Kuppens, S. (2010). Perceptions of maternal and paternal attachment security in middle childhood: Links with positive parental affection and psychosocial adjustment. *Early Child Development and Care, 180*, 211–225. doi: 10.1080/03004430903415064

Migdat, T. A. (2016). The effect of marital therapy on physical affection. (Master's thesis, Brigham Young University.) Retrieved from http://scholarsarchive.byu.edu/etd/6418/.

Miller, S. C., Kennedy, C. C., DeVoe, D. C., Hickey, M., Nelson, T., & Kogan, L. (2009). An examination of changes in oxytocin levels in men and women before and after interaction with a bonded dog. *Anthrozoös, 22*, 31–42. doi: 10.2752/175303708X390455

Miller, W. B., Pasta, D. J., MacMurray, J., Chiu, C., Wu, S., & Comings, D. E. (1999). Genetic influences in childbearing motivation: A theoretical framework and some empirical evidence. In L. J. Severy & W. B. Miller (Eds.), *Advances in population: Psychosocial perspectives* (Vol. 3, pp. 53–102). London: Jessica Kingsley.

Miller, W. B., Pasta, D. J., MacMurray, J., Muhleman, D., & Comings, D. E. (2000). Genetic influences in childbearing motivation: Further testing a theoretical framework. In J. L. Rodgers, D. C. Rowe, & W. B. Miller (Eds.), *Genetic influences on human fertility and sexuality: Theoretical and empirical contributions from the biological and behavioral sciences* (pp. 33–66). Boston: Kluwer Academic Publishers.

Miller, W. B., & Rodgers, J. (2001). *The ontogeny of human bonding systems: Evolutionary origins, neural bases, and psychological manifestations*. New York: Springer Science.

Minde, K. K., Marton, P., Manning, D., & Hines, B. (1980). Some determinants of mother–infant interaction in the premature nursery. *Journal of the American Academy of Child Psychiatry, 19*, 1–21. doi: 10.1016/S0002-7138(09)60649-X

Minde, K., Trehub, S., Corter, C., Boukydis, C., Celhoffer, L., & Marton, P. (1978). Mother–infant relationships in the premature nursery: An observational study. *Pediatrics, 61*, 373–379. doi: 10.1542/peds.61.3.373

Minnix, J. A., & Kline, J. P. (2004). Neuroticism predicts resting frontal EEG asymmetry variability. *Personality and Individual Differences, 36*, 823–832.

Momtaz, Y. A., Hamid, T. A., Yusoff, S., Ibrahim, R., Chai, S. T., Yahaya, N., & Abdullah, S. S. (2012). Loneliness is a risk factor for hypertension in later life. *Journal of Aging and Health, 24*, 696–710. doi: 10.1177/0898264311431305

Mongeau, P. A., Knight, K., Williams, J., Eden, J., & Shaw, C. (2013). Identifying and explicating variation among friends with benefits relationships. *Journal of Sex Research, 50*, 37–47. doi: 10.1080/00224499.2011.623797

Moore, S. R., McEwan, L. M., Quirt, J., Morin, A., Mah, S. M., Barr, R. G., . . . Kobor, M. S. (2017). Epigenetic correlates of neonatal contact in humans.

Development and Psychopathology, 29, 1517–1538. doi: 10.1017/S0954579417001213

Morman, M. T., & Floyd, K. (1998). "I love you, man": Overt expressions of affection in male–male interaction. *Sex Roles, 38,* 871–881. doi: 10.1023/A:1018885417249

(1999). Affectionate communication between fathers and young adult sons: Individual- and relational-level correlates. *Communication Studies, 50,* 294–309. doi: 10.1080/10510979909388501

(2002). A "changing culture of fatherhood": Effects on closeness, affection, and satisfaction in men's relationships with their fathers and their sons. *Western Journal of Communication, 66,* 395–411. doi: 10.1080/10570310209374746

Morris, S. B. (2008). Estimating effect sizes from pretest-posttest-control group designs. *Organizational Research Methods, 11,* 364–386. doi: 10.1177/1094428106291059

Muise, A., Giang, E., & Impett, E. A. (2014). Post sex affectionate exchanges promote sexual and relationship satisfaction. *Archives of Sexual Behavior, 43,* 1391–1402. doi: 10/1007/s10508-014-0305-3

Müller, V., & Lindenberger, U. (2014). Hyper-brain networks support romantic kissing in humans. *PLoS ONE, 9*(11): e112080. doi: 10.1371/journal.pone.0112080

Murphy, M. R., Seckl, J. R., Burton, S., Checkley, S. A., & Lightman, S. L. (1990). Changes in oxytocin and vasopressin secretion during sexual activity in men. *Journal of Clinical Endocrinology and Metabolism, 65,* 738–741. doi: 10.1210/jcem-65-4-738

Myers, S. A., Byrnes, K. A., Frisby, B. N., & Mansson, D. H. (2011). Adult siblings' use of affectionate communication as a strategic and routine relational maintenance behavior. *Communication Research Reports, 28,* 151–158. doi: 10.1080/08824096.2011.565276

Nakanishi, J., Sumioka, H., Shioma, M., Nakamichi, D., Sakai, K., & Ishiguro, H. (2014, October 29–31). Huggable communication medium encourages listening to others. In *Proceedings of the Second International Conference on Human–Agent Interaction,* 249–252. doi: 10.1145/2658861.2658934

National Human Genome Research Institute. (2017). Genetic variation program. Retrieved from www.genome.gov/10001551/genetic-variation-program.

Neal, J. M. (2016). *How the endocrine system works* (2nd edn.). Chichester: John Wiley & Sons.

Nelson, R. J., & Kriegsfeld, L. J. (2016). *An introduction to behavioral endocrinology* (5th edn.). Sunderland, MA: Sinauer Associates/Oxford University Press.

Nemeroff, C. B. (2004). Neurobiological consequences of childhood trauma. *Journal of Clinical Psychiatry, 65*(Suppl. 1), 18–28.

Netterstrøm, B., Danborg, L., & Olesen, H. (1988). Glycated hemoglobin as a measure of physiological stress. *Behavioral Medicine, 14,* 13–16. doi: 10.1080/08964289.1988.9935118

Nettle, D. (2009). *Evolution and genetics for psychology.* Oxford: Oxford University Press.

Nicholson, B. (1984). Does kissing aid human bonding by semiochemical addiction? *British Journal of Dermatology*, *111*, 623–627. doi: 10.1111/j.1365-2133.1984.tb06635.x

Niedenthal, P. M., & Ric, F. (2017). *Psychology of emotion* (2nd edn.). New York: Routledge.

Noller, P. (1978). Sex differences in the socialization of affectionate expression. *Developmental Psychology*, *14*, 317–319. doi: 10.1037/0012-1649.14.3.317

Oaten, M., Stevenson, R. J., & Case, T. I. (2009). Disgust as a disease-avoidance mechanism. *Psychological Bulletin*, *135*, 303–321. doi: 10.1037/a0014823

Oaten, M., Williams, K. D., Jones, A., & Zadro, L. (2008). The effects of ostracism on self-regulation in the socially anxious. *Journal of Social & Clinical Psychology*, *27*, 471–504. doi: 10.1521/jscp.2008.27.5.471

Ockenfels, M. C., Porter, L., Smyth, J., Kirschbaum, C., Hellhammer, D. H., & Stone, A. A. (1995). Effect of chronic stress associated with unemployment on salivary cortisol: Overall cortisol levels, diurnal rhythm, and acute stress reactivity. *Psychosomatic Medicine*, *57*, 460–467. doi: 10.1097/00006842-199509000-00008

Ödegaard, K. (1967). Kissing as a mode of transmission of infectious mononucleosis. *Lancet*, *1*, 1052–1053. doi: 10.1016/S0140-6736(67)91559-0

Ohadi, J., Brown, B., Trub, L., & Rosenthal, L. (2018). I just text to say I love you: Partner similarity in texting and relationship satisfaction. *Computers in Human Behavior*, *78*, 126–132. doi: 10.1016/j.chb.2017.08.048

Öhman, A., & Mineka, S. (2001). Fears, phobias, and preparedness: Toward an evolved module of fear and fear learning. *Psychological Review*, *108*, 483–522. doi: 10/1037/0033-295X.108.3.483

Okura, Y., Urban, L. H., Mahoney, D. W., Jacobsen, S. J., & Rodeheffer, R. J. (2004). Agreement between self-report questionnaires and medical record data was substantial for diabetes, hypertension, myocardial infarction and stroke but not for heart failure. *Journal of Clinical Epidemiology*, *57*, 1096–1103. doi: 10.1016/j.clinepi.2004.04.005

Oring, E. (1984). Dyadic traditions. *Journal of Folklore Research*, *21*(1), 19–28.

Orth, U., & Robins, R. W. (2013). Understanding the link between low self-esteem and depression. *Current Directions in Psychological Science*, *22*, 455–460. doi: 10/1177/0963721413492763

O'Sullivan, L. F., Byers, E. S., & Finkelman, L. (1998). A comparison of male and female college students' experiences of sexual coercion. *Psychology of Women Quarterly*, *22*, 177–195. doi: 10.1111/j.1471-6402.1998.tb00149.x

Owen, W. F. (1987). The verbal expression of love by women and men as a critical communication event in personal relationships. *Women's Studies in Communication*, *10*, 15–24. doi: 10.1080/07491409.198711089701

Padilla-Walker, L. M., & Nelson, L. J. (2012). Black hawk down? Establishing helicopter parenting as a distinct construct from other forms of parental control during emerging adulthood. *Journal of Adolescence*, *35*, 1177–1190. doi: 10.1016/j.adolescence.2012.03.007

Palmer, M. T., & Simmons, K. B. (1995). Communicating intentions through nonverbal behaviors: Conscious and unconscious encoding of liking. *Human Communication Research*, *22*, 128–160. doi: 10.1111/j.1468-2958.1995.tb00364.x

Park, Y. S., Vo, L. P., & Tsong, Y. (2009). Family affection as a protective factor against the negative effects of perceived Asian values gap on the parent–child relationship for Asian American male and female college students. *Cultural Diversity and Ethnic Minority Psychology, 15*, 18–26. doi: 10.1037/a0013378

Parker-Raley, J., & Horan, S. M. (2014, November). How and why emergency department staff express inauthentic affectionate messages. Paper presented at the annual meeting of the National Communication Association, Chicago, IL.

Parks, M. R. (1995). Ideology in interpersonal communication: Beyond the couches, talkshows, and bunkers. In B. R. Burleson (Ed.), *Communication yearbook 18* (pp. 480–497). Newbury Park, CA: Sage.

Parks, M. R., & Floyd, K. (1996). Meanings for closeness and intimacy in friendship. *Journal of Social and Personal Relationships, 13*, 85–107. doi: 10.1177/0265407596131005

Parrott, T. M., & Bengtson, V. L. (1999). The effects of earlier intergenerational affection, normative expectations, and family conflict on contemporary exchanges of help and support. *Research on Aging, 21*, 73–105. doi: 10/1177/0164027599211004

Parsons, R. J., Cox, E. O., & Kimboko, P. J. (1989). Satisfaction, communication and affection in caregiving: A view from the elder's perspective. *Journal of Gerontological Social Work, 13*, 9–20. doi: 10.1300/J083V13N03_02

Pauley, P. M., Floyd, K., & Hesse, C. (2015). The stress-buffering effects of a brief dyadic interaction before an acute stressor. *Health Communication, 30*, 646–659. doi: 10.1080/10410236.2014.888385

Pauley, P. M., Hesse, C., & Mikkelson, A. C. (2014). Trait affection predicts married couples' use of relational maintenance behaviors. *Journal of Family Communication, 14*, 167–187. doi: 10.1080/15267431.2013.864292

Pendell, S. D. (2002). Affection in interpersonal relationships: Not just "a fond or tender feeling." In W. B. Gudykunst (Ed.), *Communication yearbook 26* (pp. 67–110). New York: Routledge. doi: 10.1080/23808985.2002.11679011

Pennebaker, J. W. (2017). Expressive writing in psychological science. *Perspectives on Psychological Science, 13*, 226–229. doi: 10.1177/1745691617707315

Pennebaker, J. W., & King, L. A. (1999). Linguistic styles: Language use as an individual difference. *Journal of Personality and Social Psychology, 77*, 1296–1312. doi: 10.1037/0022-3514.77.6.1296

Piazza, M., Chirianni, A., Picciotto, L., Guadagnino, V., Orlando, R., & Cataldo, P. T. (1989). Passionate kissing and microlesions of the oral mucosa: Possible role in AIDS transmission. *Journal of the American Medical Association, 261*, 244–245. doi: 10.1001/jama.1989.03420020096022

Podrazik, D., Shackford, S., Becker, L., & Heckert, T. (2000). The death of a pet: Implications for loss and bereavement across the lifespan. *Journal of Personal and Interpersonal Loss, 5*, 361–395. doi: 10/1080/10811440008407852

Polcari, A., Rabi, K., Bolger, E., & Teicher, M. H. (2014). Parental verbal affection and verbal aggression in childhood differentially influence psychiatric symptoms and wellbeing in young adulthood. *Child Abuse & Neglect, 39*, 91–102. doi: 10.1016/j.chiabu.2013.10.003

Polcari, A., & Teicher, M. H. (2007, October). Effects of parent verbal abuse and affection on psychiatric symptomatology. Abstract presented at the 54th annual meeting of the American Academy of Child and Adolescent Psychiatry, Boston, MA.

Prager, K. J., & Buhrmester, D. (1998). Intimacy and need fulfillment in couple relationships. *Journal of Social and Personal Relationships, 15*, 435–469. doi: 10.1177/0265407598154001

Prescott, J. W. (1970). Early somatosensory deprivation as an ontogenetic process in abnormal development of the brain and behavior. In I. E. Goldsmith & J. Morr-Jankowski (Eds.), *Medical primatology* (pp. 356–375). New York: S. Karger.

(1973). Commentary: Sexual behavior in the blind. In A. E. Gillman & A. R. Gordon (Eds.), *Medical aspects of human sexuality* (pp. 59–60). Baltimore, MD: Williams and Wilkins.

(1975). Body pleasure and the origins of violence. *Bulletin of the Atomic Scientists, 31*, 10–20. doi: 10.1080/00963402.1975.11458292

(1976a). Phylogenetic and ontogenetic aspects of human affectional development. In R. Gemme & C. C. Wheeler (Eds.), *Progress in sexology: Proceedings of the 1976 International Congress of Sexology* (pp. 431–457). New York: Plenum.

(1976b). Somatosensory deprivation and its relationship to the blind. In Z. S. Jastrzembska (Ed.), *The effects of blindness and other impairments on early development* (pp. 65–121). New York: American Foundation for the Blind.

(1979). Deprivation of physical affection as a primary process in the development of physical violence: A comparative and cross-cultural perspective. In D. G. Gil (Ed.), *Child abuse and violence* (pp. 66–137). New York: American Orthopsychiatric Association.

(1980). Somatosensory affectional deprivation (SAD) theory of drug and alcohol use. In D. J. Lettieri, M. Sayers, & H. W. Pearson (Eds.), *Theories on drug abuse: Selected contemporary perspectives* (pp. 286–302). Washington, DC: National Institute of Drug Abuse.

Prescott, J. W., & Wallace, D. (1978). Role of pain and pleasure in the development of destructive behaviors: A psychometric study of parenting, sexuality, substance abuse and criminality. In L. Otten (Ed.), *Colloquium on the Correlates of Crime and the Determinants of Criminal Behavior: Proceedings* (pp. 229–279). McLean, VA: Mitre Corporation.

Price, D. A., Close, G. C., & Fielding, B. A. (1983). Age of appearance in circadian rhythm of salivary cortisol values in infancy. *Archives of Disease in Childhood, 58*(6), 454–456.

Punyanunt-Carter, N. M. (2004). Reported affectionate communication and satisfaction in marital and dating relationships. *Psychological Reports, 95*, 1154–1160. doi: 10.2466/pr0.95.3f.1154-1160

Putnam, R. D. (2000). *Bowling alone: The collapse and revival of American community.* New York: Simon & Schuster.

Qualter, P., Quinton, S. J., Wagner, H., & Brown, S. (2009). Loneliness, interpersonal distrust, and alexithymia in university students. *Journal of Applied Social Psychology, 39*, 1461–1479. doi: 10.1111/j.1559-1816.2009.00491.x

Quinnett, P. G. (2009). *Counseling suicidal people: A therapy of hope* (3rd edn.). Spokane, WA: QPR Institute.

Rabinowitz, F. E. (1991). The male-to-male embrace: Breaking the touch taboo in a men's therapy group. *Journal of Counseling & Development, 69*, 574–576. doi: 10.1002/j.1556-6676.1991.tb02648.x

Radin, N. (1988). Primary caregiving fathers of long duration. In P. Bronstein & C. P. Cowan (Eds.), *Fatherhood today: Men's changing role in the family* (pp. 127–143). New York: Wiley.

Rajaram, S. S., Garrity, T. F., Stallones, L. F., & Marx, M. B. (1993). Bereavement: Loss of a pet and loss of a human. *Anthrozoös, 6*, 8–16. doi: 10.2752/089279393787002349

Rane, T. R., & Draper, T. W. (1995). Negative evaluations of men's nurturant touching of young children. *Psychological Reports, 76*, 811–818. doi: 10.2466/pr0.1995.76.3.811

Ray, G. B., & Floyd, K. (2006). Nonverbal expressions of liking and disliking in initial interaction: Encoding and decoding perspectives. *Southern Communication Journal, 71*, 45–65. doi: 10.1080/10417940500503506

Redlick, M. H., & Vangelisti, A. L. (in press). Affection, deception, and evolution: Deceptive affectionate messages as mate retention behaviors. *Evolutionary Psychology*. doi: 10.1177/1474704917753857

Regan, P. C., Jerry, D., Narvaez, M., & Johnson, D. (1999). Public displays of affection among Asian and Latino heterosexual couples. *Psychological Reports, 84*, 1201–1202. doi: 10.2466/pr0.1999.84.3c.1201

Regan, P. C., Kocan, E. R., & Whitlock, T. (1998). Ain't love grand! A prototype analysis of the concept of romantic love. *Journal of Social and Personal Relationships, 15*, 441–420. doi: 10.1177/0265407598153006

Reid, P. T., Tate, C. S., & Berman, P. W. (1989). Preschool children's self-presentation in situations with infants: Effects of sex and race. *Child Development, 60*, 710–714. doi: 10.2307/1130736

Richard, P., Moos, F., & Freund-Mercier, M. J. (1991). Central effects of oxytocin. *Physiological Review, 71*, 331–370. doi: 10.1152/physrev.1991.71.2.331

Richmond, V. P., & McCroskey, J. C. (1990). Reliability and separation of factors on the assertiveness–responsiveness measure. *Psychological Reports, 67*, 449–450. doi: 10.2466/PR0.67.6.449-450

Ridley, M. (2003). *Nature via nurture: Genes, experience, and what makes us human.* New York: HarperCollins.

Rinck, C. M., Willis, F. N., & Dean, L. M. (1980). Interpersonal touch among residents of homes for the elderly. *Journal of Communication, 30*, 44–47. doi: 10.1111/j.1460-2466.1980.tb01964.x

Rittenour, C. E., Myers, S. A., & Brann, M. (2007). Commitment and emotional closeness in the sibling relationship. *Southern Communication Journal, 72*, 169–183. doi: 10.1080/10417940701316682

Roberts, R. E. L., & Bengtson, V. L. (1993). Relationships with parents, self-esteem, and psychological well-being in young adulthood. *Social Psychology Quarterly, 56*, 263–277. doi: 10.2307/2786663

(1996). Affective ties to parents in early adulthood and self-esteem across 20 years. *Social Psychology Quarterly, 59*, 96–106. doi: 10.2307/2787121

Robey, K. L., Cohen, B. D., & Epstein, Y. M. (1988). The child's response to affection given to someone else: Effects of parental divorce, sex of child, and sibling position. *Journal of Clinical Child Psychology*, *17*, 2–7. doi: 10.1207/ s15374424jccp1701_1

Rodrigues, S. M., Saslow, L. R., Garcia, N., John, O. P., & Keltner, D. (2009). Oxytocin receptor genetic variation relates to empathy and stress reactivity in humans. *Proceedings of the National Academy of Sciences*, *106*, 21437–21441. doi: 10.1073/pnas.0909579106

Rosenberg, M. (1965). *Society and the adolescent self-image*. Princeton, NJ: Princeton University Press.

Ross, L. (1977). The intuitive psychologist and his shortcomings: Distortions in the attribution process. In L. Berkowitz (Ed.), *Advances in experimental social psychology* (Vol. 10, pp. 173–220). New York: Academic Press.

Routledge, C., Ostafin, B., Juhl, J., Sedikides, C., Cathey, C., & Liao, J. Q. (2010). Adjusting to death: The effects of mortality salience and self-esteem on psychological well-being, growth motivation, and maladaptive behavior. *Journal of Personality and Social Psychology*, *99*, 897–916. doi: 10.1037/ a0021431

Rubin, R. B., Perse, E. M., & Barbato, C. A. (1988). Conceptualization and measurement of interpersonal communication motives. *Human Communication Research*, *14*, 602–628. doi: 10.1111/j.1468-2958.1988.tb00169.x

Rubin, Z. (1969). The social psychology of romantic love. (Paper, University of Michigan.) University Microfilms No. 70-4179.

   (1970). Measurement of romantic love. *Journal of Personality and Social Psychology*, *16*, 265–273. doi: 10.1037/h0029841

Rushton, J. P., Fulker, D. W., Neale, M. C., Nias, D. K., & Eysenck, H. J. (1986). Altruism and aggression: The heritability of individual differences. *Journal of Personality and Social Psychology*, *50*, 1192–1198. doi: 10.1037/ 0022-3514.50.6.1192

Russell, A. (1997). Individual and family factors contributing to mothers' and fathers' positive parenting. *International Journal of Behavioral Development*, *21*, 111–132. doi: 10.1080/016502597385018

Russell, D. (1996). UCLA loneliness scale (version 3): Reliability, validity, and factor structure. *Journal of Personality Assessment*, *66*, 20–40. doi: 10.1207/ s15327752jps6601_2

Sabatelli, R. M., & Cecil-Pigo, E. F. (1985). Relational interdependence and commitment in marriage. *Journal of Marriage and Family*, *47*, 931–937. doi: 10.2307/352336

Salt, R. E. (1991). Affectionate touch between fathers and preadolescent sons. *Journal of Marriage and Family*, *53*, 545–554. doi: 10.2307/352731

Sanchez-Anguiano, A. (1999). Psychological effects of captivity among United States Navy aviators, Vietnam: A longitudinal study, 1974–1997. (Doctoral dissertation, University of South Florida.) *Dissertation Abstracts International*, *60* (3-B), 1046.

Sapolsky, R. M. (2002). Endocrinology of the stress response. In J. B. Becker, S. M. Breedlove, D. Crews, & M. M. McCarthy (Eds.), *Behavioral endocrinology* (2nd ed., pp. 409–450). Cambridge, MA: MIT Press.

Saxbe, D. E., Repetti, R. L., & Nishina, A. (2008). Marital satisfaction, recovery from work, and diurnal cortisol among men and women. *Health Psychology*, *27*, 15–25. doi: 10.1037/0278-6133.27.1.15

Scarr, S., Webber, P. L., Weinberg, R. A., & Wittig, M. A. (1981). Personality resemblance among adolescents and their parents in biologically related and adoptive families. *Journal of Personality and Social Psychology*, *40*, 885–898. doi: 10.1037/0022-3514.40.5.885

Schachner, L., Field, T., Hernandez-Reif, M., Duarte, A., & Krasnegor, J. (1998). Atopic dermatitis symptoms decrease in children following massage therapy. *Pediatric Dermatology*, *15*, 380–395. doi: 10.1046/j.1525-1470.1998.1998015390.x

Schiffrin, H. H., Liss, M., Miles-McLean, H., Geary, K. A., Erchull, M. J., & Tashner, T. (2014). Helping or hovering? The effects of helicopter parenting on college students' well-being. *Journal of Child and Family Studies*, *23*, 548–557. doi: 10.1007/s10826-013-9716-3

Schmidt, C., & SeiffgeKrenke, I. (1996). Perceptions of friendships and family relations in chronically ill and healthy adolescents: Quality of relationships and change over time. *Psychologie in Erziehung und Unterricht*, *43*(2), 155–168.

Schneiderman, I., Kanat-Maymon, Y., Ebstein, R. P., & Feldman, R. (2013). Cumulative risk on the oxytocin receptor gene (*OXTR*) underpins empathic communication difficulties at the first stages of romantic love. *Social Cognitive and Affective Neuroscience*, *9*, 1–6. doi: 10.1093/scan/nst142

Schnur, J. (2005). Asperger syndrome in children. *Journal of the American Association of Nurse Practitioners*, *17*, 203–208. doi: 10.1111/j.1745-7599.2005.0053.x

Schoch-Spana, M. (2000). Implications of pandemic influenza for bioterrorism response. *Clinical Infectious Diseases*, *31*, 1409–1413. doi: 10.1086/317493

Schrodt, P., Ledbetter, A. M., & Ohrt, J. K. (2007). Parental confirmation and affection as mediators of family communication patterns and children's mental well-being. *Journal of Family Communication*, *7*, 23–46. doi: 10.1080/15267430709336667

Schuck, P. (1998). Glycated hemoglobin as a physiological measure of stress and its relations to some psychological stress indicators. *Behavioral Medicine*, *24*, 89–94. doi: 10.1080/08964289809596386

Schultz, N. C., & Schultz, C. L. (1987). Affection and intimacy as a special strength of couples in blended families. *Australian Journal of Sex, Marriage & Family*, *8*(2), 66–72.

Schuster, M. A., Beckett, M. K., Corona, R., & Zhou, A. J. (2005). Hugs and kisses: HIV-infected parents' fears about contagion and the effects on parent–child interaction in a nationally representative sample. *Archives of Pediatric and Adolescent Medicine*, *159*, 173–179. doi: 10.1001/archpedi.159.2.173

Schwartz, G. E., & Russek, L. G. (1998). Family love and lifelong health? A challenge for clinical psychology. In D. K. Routh & R. J. DeRubeis (Eds.), *The science of clinical psychology: Accomplishments and future directions* (pp. 121–146). Washington, DC: American Psychological Association.

Scott, W. A., Scott, R., & McCabe, M. (1991). Family relationships and children's personality: A cross-cultural, cross-source comparison. *British Journal of Social Psychology, 30,* 1–20. doi: 10.1111/2044-8309.1991.tb00919.x

Segrin, C., Givertz, M., Swiatkowski, P., & Montgomery, N. (2015). Overparenting is associated with child problems and a critical family environment. *Journal of Child and Family Studies, 24,* 470–479. doi: 10.1007/S10826-013-9858-3

Segrin, C., Woszidlo, A., Givertz, M., Bauer, A., & Taylor Murphy, M. (2012). The association between overparenting, parent–child communication, and entitlement and adaptive traits in adult children. *Family Relations, 61,* 237–252. doi: 10.1111/j.1741-3729.2011.00689.x

Selye, H. (1936). Thymus and adrenals in the response of the organism to injuries and intoxications. *British Journal of Experimental Pathology, 17*(3), 234–248.

(1956). *The stress of life.* New York: McGraw-Hill.

Shankar, A., McMunn, A., Banks, J., & Steptoe, A. (2011). Loneliness, social isolation, and behavioral and biological health indicators in older adults. *Health Psychology, 30,* 377–385. doi: 10.1037/a0022826

Shaver, P., Hazan, C., & Bradshaw, D. (1988). Love as attachment: The integration of three behavioral systems. In R. J. Sternberg & M. L. Barnes (Eds.), *The psychology of love* (pp. 68–99). New Haven, CT: Yale University Press.

Shaw-Zirt, B., Popali-Lehane, L., Chaplin, W., & Bergman, A. (2005). Adjustment, social skills, and self-esteem in college students with symptoms of ADHD. *Journal of Attention Disorders, 8,* 109–120. doi: 10.1177/1087054705277775

Shepperd, J., Malone, W., & Sweeney, K. (2008). Exploring causes of the self-serving bias. *Social and Personality Psychology Compass, 2,* 895–908. doi: 10.1111/j.1751-9004.2008.00078.x

Shier, D., Butler, J., & Lewis, R. (2015). *Hole's human anatomy and physiology* (14th edn.). New York: McGraw-Hill.

Shiovitz-Ezra, S., & Ayalon, L. (2010). Situational versus chronic loneliness as risk factors for all-cause mortality. *International Psychogeriatrics, 22,* 455–462. doi: 10.1017/S1041610209991426

Shuntich, R. J., Loh, D., & Katz, D. (1998). Some relationships among affection, aggression and alcohol abuse in the family setting. *Perceptual and Motor Skills, 86,* 1051–1060. doi: 10.2466/pms.1998.86.3.1051

Shuntich, R. J., & Shapiro, R. M. (1991). Explorations of verbal affection and aggression. *Journal of Social Behavior & Personality, 6*(2), 283–300.

Sifneos, P. E. (1973). The prevalence of "alexithymic" characteristics in psychosomatic patients. *Psychotherapy and Psychosomatics, 22,* 255–262. doi: 10.1159/000286529

Silverstone, P. H. (1991). Low self-esteem in different psychiatric conditions. *British Journal of Clinical Psychology, 30,* 185–188. doi: 10.1111/j.2004-8260.1991.tb00936.x

Skuse, D. H., Lori, A., Cubells, J. F., Lee, I., Conneely, K. N., Puura, K., … Young, L. J. (2014). Common polymorphism in the oxytocin receptor gene (*OXTR*) is associated with human social recognition skills. *Proceedings of the National Academy of Sciences, 111,* 1987–1992. doi: 10.1073/pnas.1302985111

Smart Richman, L., & Leary, M. R. (2009). Rejections to discrimination, stigmatization, ostracism, and other forms of interpersonal rejection: A multimotive model. *Psychological Review*, *116*, 365–383. doi: 10.1037/a0015250

Smiler, A. P. (2011). Sexual strategies theory: Built for the short term or the long term? *Sex Roles*, *64*, 603–612. doi: 10.1007/s11199-010-9817-z

Smith, D. E., Willis, F. N., & Gier, J. A. (1980). Success and interpersonal touch in a competitive setting. *Journal of Nonverbal Behavior*, *5*, 26–34. doi: 10.1007/BF00987052

Smith, K. E., Porges, E. C., Norman, G. J., Connelly, J. J., & Decety, J. (2014). Oxytocin receptor gene variation predicts empathic concern and autonomic arousal while perceiving harm to others. *Social Neuroscience*, *9*, 1–9. doi: 10.1080/17470919.2013.863223

Smith, P. S. (2006). The effects of solitary confinement on prison inmates: A brief history and review of the literature. *Crime and Justice*, *34*, 441–528. doi: 10.1086/500626

Smolkovic, I., Fajfar, M., & Mlinaric, V. (2012). Attachment to pets and interpersonal relationships: Can a four-legged friend replace a two-legged one? *Journal of European Psychology Students*, *3*, 15–23. doi: 10.5334/jeps.ao

Sofronoff, K., Eloff, J., Sheffield, J., & Attwood, T. (2011). Increasing the understanding and demonstration of appropriate affection in children with Asperger syndrome: A pilot trial. *Autism Research and Treatment*, 214317. doi: 10.1155/2011/214317

Sofronoff, K., Lee, J., Sheffield, J., & Attwood, T. (2014). The construction and evaluation of three measures of affectionate behaviour for children with Asperger's syndrome. *Autism*, *18*, 903–913. doi: 10.1177/1362361313496336

Soler, C., Núñez, M., Gutiérrez, R., Núñez, J., Medina, P., Sancho, M., ... Núñez, A. (2003). Facial attractiveness in men provides clues to semen quality. *Evolution and Human Behavior*, *24*, 199–207. doi: 10.1016/S1090-5138(03)00013-8

Sompayrac, L. (2016). *How the immune system works* (5th edn.). Chichester: John Wiley & Sons.

Sorokowski, P., Sorokowska, A., Butovskaya, M., Karwowski, M., Groyecka, A., Wojciszke, B., & Pawlowski, B. (2017). Love influences reproductive success in humans. *Frontiers in Psychology*, *8*, 1922. doi: 10.3389/fpsyg.2017.01922

Sowislo, J. F., & Orth, U. (2012). Does low self-esteem predict depression and anxiety: A meta-analysis of longitudinal studies. *Psychological Bulletin*, *139*, 213–240. doi: 10.1037/a0028931

Spanier, G. (1976). Measuring dyadic adjustment: New scales for measuring the quality of marriage and similar dyads. *Journal of Marriage and the Family*, *38*, 15–28. doi: 10.2307/350547

Stafford, L. (2010). Measuring relationship maintenance behaviors: Critique and development of the revised relationship maintenance behavior scale. *Journal of Social and Personal Relationships*, *28*, 278–303. doi: 10.1177/0265407510378125

Stanton, S. C. E., Campbell, L., & Loving, T. J. (2014). Energized by love: Thinking about romantic relationships increases positive affect and blood glucose levels. *Psychophysiology*, *51*, 990–995. doi: 10.1111/psyp.12249

Steel, Z., Marnane, C., Iranpour, C., Chey, T., Jackson, J. W., Patel, V., & Silove, D. (2014). The global prevalence of common mental disorders: A systematic review and meta-analysis 1980–2013. *International Journal of Epidemiology*, *43*, 476–493. doi: 10.1093/ije/dyu038

Stephan, C. W., Stephan, W. G., Saito, I., & Barnett, S. M. (1998). Emotional expression in Japan and the United States: The nonmonolithic nature of individualism and collectivism. *Journal of Cross-Cultural Psychology*, *29*, 728–748. doi: 10.1177/0022022198296004

Stephan, W. G., Stephan, C. W., & de Vargas, M. C. (1996). Emotional expression in Costa Rica and the United States. *Journal of Cross-Cultural Psychology*, *27*, 147–160. doi: 10.1177/0022022196272001

Sternberg, R. J. (1986). A triangular theory of love. *Psychological Review*, *93*, 119–135. doi: 10.1037/0033-295X.93.2.119

   (1997). Construct validation of a triangular love scale. *European Journal of Social Psychology*, *27*, 313–335. doi: 10.1002/(SICI)1099-0992(199705) 27:3<313::AID-EJSP824>3.0.CO;2-4

Stoney, C. M. (2008). Lipid, lipoprotein, and inflammatory markers of atherosclerosis. In L. J. Leucken & L. C. Gallo (Eds.), *Handbook of physiological research methods in health psychology* (pp. 323–339). Los Angeles, CA: Sage.

Stoney, C. M., Niaura, R., Bausserman, L., & Metacin, M. (1999). Lipid reactivity to stress: I. Comparison of chronic and acute stress responses in middle-aged airline pilots. *Health Psychology*, *18*, 241–250. doi: 10.1037/ 0278-6133.18.3.241

Storey, A. E., Walsh, C. J., Quinton, R. L., & Wynne-Edwards, K. E. (2000). Hormonal correlates of paternal responsiveness in new and expectant fathers. *Evolution and Human Behavior*, *21*, 79–95. doi: 10.1016/S1090-5138(99)00042-2

Stravynski, A., & Boyer, R. (2001). Loneliness in relation to suicide ideation and parasuicide: A population-wide study. *Suicide & Life-Threatening Behavior*, *31*, 32–40. doi: 10.1521/suli.31.1.32.21312

Subar, A. F., Freedman, L. S., Tooze, J. A., Kirkpatrick, S. I., Boushey, C., Neuhouser, M. L., ... Krebs-Smith, S. M. (2015). Addressing current criticism regarding the value of self-report dietary data. *Journal of Nutrition*, *145*, 2639–2645. doi: 10.3945/jn.115.219634

Sumioka, H., Nakae, A., Kanai, R., & Ishiguru, H. (2013, October 23). Huggable communication medium decreases cortisol levels. *Scientific Reports*, *3*, 1–6. doi: 10.1038/srep03034

Swain, S. (1989). Covert intimacy: Closeness in men's friendships. In B. Risman & P. Schwartz (Eds.), *Gender in intimate relationships: A microstructural approach* (pp. 71–86). Belmont, CA: Wadsworth.

Takahashi, H., Ban, M., Osawa, H., Nakanishi, J., Sumioka, H., & Ishiguro, H. (2017). Huggable communication medium maintains levels of trust during conversation game. *Frontiers in Psychology*, *8*, article 1862. doi: 10.3389/ fpsyg.2017.01862

Tausczik, Y. R., & Pennebaker, J. W. (2009). The psychological meaning of words: LIWC and computerized text analysis methods. *Journal of Language and Social Psychology, 29*, 24–54. doi: 10.1177/0261927X09351676

Taylor, G. J., Bagby, R. M., & Parker, J. D. A. (1997). *Disorders of affect regulation: Alexithymia in medical and psychiatric illness.* New York: Cambridge University Press.

Taylor, S. E., Klein, L. C., Lewis, B. P., Gruenewald, T. L., Gurung, R. A. R., & Updegraff, J. A. (2000). Biobehavioral responses to stress in females: Tend-and-befriend, not fight-or-flight. *Psychological Review, 107*, 411–429. doi: 10.1037/0033-295X.107.3.411

Teh, J. K. S., Cheok, A. D., Peiris, R. L., Choi, Y., Thuong, V., & Lai, S. (2008, June). Huggy Pajama: A mobile parent and child hugging communication system. In *Proceedings of the Seventh International Conference on Interaction Design and Children*, 250–257. doi: 10.1145/1463689.1463763

Teh, J. K. S., Tsai, A., Koh, J. T. K. V., & Cheok, A. D. (2012, March). Mobile implementation and user evaluation of the Huggy Pajama system. Paper presented at the annual IEEE Haptics Symposium, Vancouver, BC.

Thibaut, J., & Kelley, H. (1959). *The social psychology of groups.* New York: Wiley.

Thornhill, R., & Gangestad, S. W. (1994). Human fluctuating asymmetry and sexual behavior. *Psychological Science, 5*, 297–302. doi: 10.1111/j.1467-9280.1994.tb00629.x

Tichenor, V., McQuillan, J., Greil, A. L., Contreras, R., & Shreffler, K. M. (2011). The importance of fatherhood to U.S. married and cohabiting men. *Fathering: A Journal of Theory, Research, and Practice about Men as Fathers, 9*, 232–251. doi: 10.3149.fth.0903.232

Tinsley, H. E., & Weiss, D. J. (1975). Interrater reliability and agreement of subjective judgments. *Journal of Counseling Psychology, 22*, 358–376. doi: 10.1037/h0076640

Toda, S., Fogel, A., & Kawai, M. (1990). Maternal speech to three-month-old infants in the United States and Japan. *Journal of Child Language, 17*, 279–294. doi: 10.1017/S0305000900013775

Tost, H., Kolachana, B., Hakimi, S., Lemaitre, H., Verchinski, B. A., Mattay, V. S., ... Meyer-Lindenberg, A. (2010). A common allele in the oxytocin receptor gene (*OXTR*) impacts prosocial temperament and human hypothalamic-limbic structure and function. *Proceedings of the National Academy of Sciences, 103*, 13936–13941. doi: 10.1073/pnas.1003296107

Toth, K., & King, B. H. (2008). Asperger's syndrome: Diagnosis and treatment. *American Journal of Psychiatry, 165*, 958–963. doi: 10.1176/appi.ajp.2008.08020272

Trask, S. L., Horstman, H. K., & Hesse, C. (2016, November). Deceptive affection across relational contexts: A group comparison of romantic relationships, cross-sex friendships, and friends with benefits relationships. Paper presented at the annual meeting of the National Communication Association, Philadelphia, PA.

Trickett, P. K., Noll, J. G., Susman, E. J., Shenk, C. E., & Putnam, F. W. (2010). Attenuation of cortisol across development for victims of sexual abuse. *Development and Psychopathology, 22*, 165–175. doi: 10.1017/S0954579409990332

Trivers, R. L. (1971). The evolution of reciprocal altruism. *Quarterly Review of Biology*, *46*, 35–57. doi: 10.1086/406755

(1972). Parental investment and sexual selection. In B. Campbell (Ed.), *Sexual selection and the descent of man 1871–1971* (pp. 136–1790). Chicago, IL: Aldine.

Troll, L. E., Neugarten, B. L., & Kraines, R. J. (1969). Similarities in values and other personality characteristics in college students and their parents. *Merrill-Palmer Quarterly*, *15*(4), 323–336.

Trzaskowski, M., Yang, J., Visscher, P. M., & Plomin, R. (2014). DNA evidence for strong genetic stability and increasing heritability of intelligence from age 7 to 12. *Molecular Psychiatry*, *19*, 380–384. doi: 10.1038/mp.2012.191

Trzesniewski, K. H., Donnellan, M. G., Robins, R. W., Moffitt, T. E., & Caspi, A. (2002, February). Do juvenile delinquents have high or low self-esteem? Paper presented at the annual meeting of the Society for Personality and Social Psychology, Savannah, GA.

Tully, J., Viner, R. M., Coen, P. G., Stuart, J. M., Zambon, M., Peckham, C., . . . Booy, R. (2006). Risk and protective factors for meningococcal disease in adolescents: Matched cohort study. *British Medical Journal*, *332*, 445–450. doi: 10.1136/bmj.38725.728472.BE

Turkle, S. (2017). *Alone together: Why we expect more from technology and less from each other*. New York: Basic Books.

Turner, R. A., Altemus, M., Enos, T., Cooper, B., & McGuinness, T. (1999). Preliminary research on plasma oxytocin in normal cycling women: Investigating emotion and interpersonal distress. *Psychiatry*, *62*, 97–113. doi: 10.1080/00332747.1999.11024859

Twardosz, S., Botkin, D., Cunningham, J. L., Weddle, K., Sollie, D., & Schreve, C. (1987). Expression of affection in day care. *Child Study Journal*, *17*(2), 133–151.

Twardosz, S., & Jozwiak, W. (1981). The expression of affection: Suggestion for research with developmentally disabled children. *Analysis and Intervention in Developmental Disabilities*, *1*, 217–238. doi: 10.1016/0270-4684(81)90033-1

Twardosz, S., Schwartz, S., Fox, J., & Cunningham, J. L. (1979). Development and evaluation of a system to measure affectionate behavior. *Behavioral Assessment*, *1*, 177–190.

Tyler, J. M., Kearns, P. O., & McIntyre, M. M. (2016). Effects of self-monitoring on processing of self-presentation information. *Social Psychology*, *47*, 174–178. doi: 10.1027/1864-9335/a000265

Umberson, D. (1992). Relationships between adult children and their parents: Psychological consequences for both generations. *Journal of Marriage and the Family*, *54*, 664–674. doi: 10.2307/353252

Umberson, D., & Montez, J. K. (2010). Social relationships and health: A flashpoint for health policy. *Journal of Health and Social Behavior*, *51*, S54-S66. doi: 10.1177/0022146510383501

US Department of Agriculture. (2017, January 13). The cost of raising a child. USDA. Retrieved August 11, 2017, from www.usda.gov/media/blog/2017/01/13/cost-raising-child.

Uvnäs-Moberg, K. (1998). Oxytocin may mediate the benefits of positive social interaction and emotions. *Psychoneuroendocrinology*, *23*, 819–835. doi: 10.1016/S0306-4503(98)00056-0

(2003). *The oxytocin factor: Tapping the hormone of calm, love, and healing.* Cambridge, MA: Perseus.

Uvnäs-Moberg, K., Arn, I., & Magnusson, D. (2005). The psychobiology of emotion: The role of the oxytocinergic system. *International Journal of Behavioral Medicine*, *12*, 59–65. doi: 10.1207/s15327558ijbm1202_3

van de Mortel, T. F. (2008). Faking it: Social desirability response bias in self-report research. *Australian Journal of Advanced Nursing*, *25*(4), 40–48.

Van der Graaff, J., Branje, S., De Wied, M., Hawk, S., Van Lier, P., & Meeus, W. (2014). Perspective taking and empathic concern in adolescence: Gender differences in developmental changes. *Developmental Psychology*, *50*, 881–888. doi: 10.1037/a0034325

Van Orden, K. A., Witte, T. K., Cukrowicz, K. C., Braithwaite, S., Selby, E. A., & Joiner, T. E. (2010). The interpersonal theory of suicide. *Psychological Review*, *117*, 575–600. doi: 10.1037/a0018697

van Raalte, L. J. (2017). The influence of cuddling on relational health for cohabiting couples. (Doctoral dissertation, Arizona State University.) Retrieved from https://repository.asu.edu/items/44251.

van Raalte, L. J., Kloeber, D., Veluscek, A., & Floyd, K. (2016, November). Exploring the association between unwanted affection and mood, anxiety, stress, and relational satisfaction. Paper presented at the annual meeting of the National Communication Association, Philadelphia, PA.

van Zoonen, K., Kleiboer, A., Beekman, A. T. F., Smit, J. H., Boerema, A. M., & Cuijpers, P. (2015). Reasons and determinants of help-seeking in people with a subclinical depression. *Journal of Affective Disorders*, *173*, 105–112. doi: 10.1016/j.jad.2014.10.062

Vaquera, E., & Kao, G. (2005). Private and public displays of affection among interracial and intra-racial adolescent couples. *Social Science Quarterly*, *86*, 484–508. doi: 10.1111/j.0038-4941.2005.00314.x

Vespa, J., Lewis, J. M., & Kreider, R. M. (2013, August). *America's families and living arrangements: 2012.* Washington, DC: United States Census Bureau.

Victor, C. R., & Yang, K. (2012). The prevalence of loneliness among adults: A case study of the United Kingdom. *Journal of Psychology*, *146*, 85–104. doi: 10.1080/00223980.2011.613875

Vilagut, G., Forero, C. G., Barbaglia, G., & Alonso, J. (2016). Screening for depression in the general population with the Center for Epidemiologic Studies Depression (CES-D): A systematic review with meta-analysis. *PLoS ONE*, *11*(5): e0155431. doi: 10.1371/journal.pone.0155431

von Sadovszky, V., Keller, M. L., & McKinney, K. (2002). College students' perceptions and practices of sexual activities in sexual encounters. *Journal of Nursing Scholarship*, *34*, 133–138. doi: 10.1111/j.1547-5069.2002.00133.x

Vukasović, T., & Bratko, D. (2015). Heritability of personality: A meta-analysis of behavior genetic studies. *Psychological Bulletin*, *141*, 769–785. doi: 10.1037/bul0000017

Waite, L. J., & Lehrer, E. L. (2003). The benefits from marriage and religion in the United States: A comparative analysis. *Population and Development Review, 29*, 255–275. doi: 10.1111/j.1728-4457.2003.00255.x

Wallace, D. H. (1981). Affectional climate in the family of origin and the experience of subsequent sexual-affectional behaviors. *Journal of Sex and Marital Therapy, 7*, 296–306. doi: 10.1080/00926238108405431

Walter, M., Bureau, J.-F., Holmes, B. M., Bertha, E. A., Hollander, M., Wheelis, J., ... Lyons-Ruth, K. (2008). Cortisol response to interpersonal stress in young adults with borderline personality disorder: A pilot study. *European Psychiatry, 23*, 201–204. doi: 10.1016/j.eurpsy.2007.12.003

Waring, E. M., McElrath, D., Lefcoe, D., & Weisz, G. (1981). Dimensions of intimacy in marriage. *Psychiatry, 44*, 169–175. doi: 10.1080/00332747.1981.11024102

Watzlawick, P., Beavin, J. H., & Jackson, D. D. (1967). *Pragmatics of human communication: A study of interactional patterns, pathologies, and paradoxes.* New York: Norton.

Weekes, D. P., Kagan, S. H., James, K., & Seboni, N. (1993). The phenomenon of hand holding as a coping strategy in adolescents experiencing treatment-related pain. *Journal of Pediatric Oncology Nursing, 10*, 19–25. doi: 10.1177/104345429301000105

Weiner, B. (1985). "Spontaneous" causal thinking. *Psychological Bulletin, 97*, 74–84. doi: 10.1037/0033-2909.97.1.74

Weisman, O., Pelphrey, K. A., Leckman, J. F., Feldman, R., Lu, Y., Chong, A., ... Ebstein, R. P. (2015). The association between 2D:4D ratio and cognitive empathy is contingent on a common polymorphism in the oxytocin receptor gene (*OXTR* rs53576). *Psychoneuroendocrinology, 58*, 23–32. doi: 10.1016/j.psyneuen.2015.04.007

Welsh, D. P., Haugen, P. T., Widman, L., Darling, N., & Grello, C. M. (2005). Kissing is good: A developmental investigation of sexuality in adolescent romantic couples. *Sexuality Research & Social Policy, 2*, 32–41. doi: 10.1525/srsp.2005.2.4.32

Werker, J. F., & McLeod, P. J. (1989). Infant preference for both male and female infant-directed talk: A developmental study of attentional and affective responses. *Canadian Journal of Psychology, 43*, 230–246. doi: 10.1037/h0084224

Westermarck, E. (1891). *The history of human marriage.* London: Macmillan.

White, L. (1999). Contagion in family affection: Mothers, fathers, and young adult children. *Journal of Marriage and Family, 61*, 284–294. doi: 10.2307/353748

Wiedermana, M. W., & Kendalla, E. (1999). Evolution, sex, and jealousy: Investigation with a sample from Sweden. *Evolution and Human Behavior, 20*, 121–128. doi: 10.1016/S1090-5138(98)00046-4

Wilkinson, C. A., & Grill, L. H. (2000). Expressing affection: A vocabulary of loving messages. In K. M. Galvin & P. J. Cooper (Eds.), *Making connections: Readings in relational communication* (2nd ed., pp. 160–167). Los Angeles, CA: Roxbury.

Williams, S. J., & Willis, F. N. (1978). Interpersonal touch among preschool children at play. *Psychological Record, 28*, 501–508. doi: 10.1007/BF03394565

Willis, F. N., & Hoffman, G. E. (1975). Development of tactile patterns in relation to age, sex, and race. *Developmental Psychology, 11*, 866–867. doi: 10.1037/0012-1649.11.6.866

Willis, F. N., & Reeves, D. L. (1976). Touch interactions in junior high students in relation to sex and race. *Developmental Psychology, 12*, 91–92. doi: 10.1037/0012–1649.12.1.91

Willis, F. N., Reeves, D. L., & Buchanan, D. R. (1976). Interpersonal touch in high school relative to sex and race. *Perceptual and Motor Skills, 43*, 843–847. doi: 10.2466/pms.1976.43.3.843

Willis, F. N., Rinck, C. M., & Dean, L. M. (1978). Interpersonal touch among adults in cafeteria lines. *Perceptual and Motor Skills, 47*, 1147–1152. doi: 10.2466/pms.1978.47.3f.1147

Wlodarski, R., & Dunbar, R. I. M. (2004). What's in a kiss? The effect of romantic kissing on mate desirability. *Evolutionary Psychology, 12*, 178–199. doi: 10/1177/147470491401200114

(2013). Examining the possible functions of kissing in romantic relationships. *Archives of Sexual Behavior, 42*, 1415–1423. doi: 10.1007/s10508-013-0190-1

Women's Health. (2016, June 16). Here's what actually happens at "cuddle parties." *New York Post.* Retrieved from https://nypost.com/2016/06/16/heres-what-actually-happens-at-cuddle-parties/.

Wood, J. T., & Inman, C. C. (1993). In a different mode: Masculine styles of communicating closeness. *Journal of Applied Communication Research, 21*, 279–295. doi: 10.1080/00909889309365372

Workman, L., & Reader, W. (2014). *Evolutionary psychology* (3rd edn.). Cambridge: Cambridge University Press.

Wu, M. S., Zhou, C., Floyd, K., Dong, S., Wang, L., Liu, J., . . . Han, B. (2014, February). Self and relational benefits of affectionate communication: Evidence from a "no-contact" culture. Paper presented at the annual meeting of the Western States Communication Association, Anaheim, CA.

Wu, N., Li, Z., & Su, Y. (2012). The association between oxytocin receptor gene polymorphism (*OXTR*) and trait empathy. *Journal of Affective Disorders, 138*, 468–472. doi: 10.1016/j.jad.2012.01.009

Yamazaki, R., Christensen, L., Skov, K., Chang, C.-C., Damholdt, M. F., Sumioka, H., . . . Ishiguro, H. (2016). Intimacy in phone conversations: Anxiety reduction for Danish seniors with Hugvie. *Frontiers in Psychology, 7*, article 537. doi: 10.3389/fpsyg.2016.00537

Young, L. J., & Wang, Z. (2004). The neurobiology of pair bonding. *Nature Neuroscience, 7*, 1048–1054. doi: 10.1038/nn1327

Zanolli, K., Saudargas, R., & Twardosz, S. (1990). Two-year-olds' responses to affectionate and caregiving teacher behavior. *Child Study Journal, 20*(1), 35–54.

Zasloff, R. L. (1996). Measuring attachment to companion animals: A dog is not a cat is not a bird. *Applied Animal Behaviour Science, 27*, 43–48. doi: 10.1016/0168-1591(95)01009-2

Zebrowitz, L. A., Brownlow, S., & Olson, K. (1992). Baby talk to the babyfaced. *Journal of Nonverbal Behavior, 16*, 143–158. doi: 10.1007/BF00988031

Zhang, E. Y., & Cheok, A. D. (2016, October). Forming intimate human–robot relationships through a kissing machine. In *Proceedings of the Fourth International Conference on Human–Agent Interaction*, 233–234. doi: 10.1145/2974804.2980513

Zhang, Q., & Wills, M. (2016). A U.S.-Chinese comparison of affectionate communication in parent–child relationships. *Communication Research Reports, 33*, 317–323. doi: 10.1080/08824096.2016.1224166

Zhong, L., & Dailey, R. (2017, November). Expression of deceptive affection in dating and marital relationships: Investigating personal and relational attributes. Paper presented at the annual meeting of the National Communication Association, Dallas, TX.

Zinger, I. (1999). The psychological effects of 60 days in administrative segregation. (Doctoral dissertation, Carleton University.) *Dissertation Abstracts International, 60* (6-B), 2932.

Index

Printed in Great Britain
by Amazon

23829407R00165